A Memoir of
Friendship

Also by Blanche Howard

Novels

Penelope's Way

A Celibate Season
(with Carol Shields)

The Immortal Soul of Edwin
Carlysle

Pretty Lady

The Manipulator

Plays

A Celibate Season

Also by Carol Shields

Poetry

Others

Intersect

Coming to Canada

Novels

Unless

Larry's Party

The Stone Diaries

The Republic of Love

A Celibate Season
(with Blanche Howard)

Swann

A Fairly Conventional Woman

Happenstance

The Box Garden

Small Ceremonies

Story Collections

Dressing Up for the Carnival

The Orange Fish

Various Miracles

Plays

Departures and Arrivals

Thirteen Hands

Fashion, Power, Guilt,
and the Charity of Families
(with Catherine Shields)

Anniversary: A Comedy
(with David Williamson)

Criticism

Susanna Moodie: Voice and Vision

Anthology

Dropped Threads:
What We Aren't Told
(edited with Marjorie Anderson)

Dropped Threads:
More of What We Aren't Told
(edited with Marjorie Anderson)

Biography

Jane Austen: A Life

A Memoir of Friendship

The Letters between

Carol Shields
Blanche & Howard

Edited by Blanche Howard &
Allison Howard

Foreword by Anne Giardini

VIKING
CANADA

VIKING CANADA
Published by the Penguin Group
Penguin Group (Canada), 90 Eglinton Avenue East, Suite 700, Toronto, Ontario, Canada M4P 2Y3
(a division of Pearson Canada Inc.)

Penguin Group (USA) Inc., 375 Hudson Street, New York, New York 10014, U.S.A.
Penguin Books Ltd, 80 Strand, London WC2R 0RL, England
Penguin Ireland, 25 St Stephen's Green, Dublin 2, Ireland (a division of Penguin Books Ltd)
Penguin Group (Australia), 250 Camberwell Road, Camberwell, Victoria 3124, Australia
(a division of Pearson Australia Group Pty Ltd)
Penguin Books India Pvt Ltd, 11 Community Centre, Panchsheel Park, New Delhi – 110 017, India
Penguin Group (NZ), cnr Airborne and Rosedale Roads, Albany, Auckland 1310, New Zealand
(a division of Pearson New Zealand Ltd)
Penguin Books (South Africa) (Pty) Ltd, 24 Sturdee Avenue, Rosebank, Johannesburg 2196, South Africa

Penguin Books Ltd, Registered Offices: 80 Strand, London WC2R 0RL, England

First published 2007

1 2 3 4 5 6 7 8 9 10 (RRD)

General introduction, section introductions, letters of Blanche Howard
and selection copyright © Blanche Howard, 2007
Letters of Carol Shields, copyright © Carol Shields Literary Trust, 2007
Foreword © Anne Giardini, 2007

The Publisher gratefully acknowledges the support of the Carol Shields Literary Trust

Manufactured in the U.S.A.

LIBRARY AND ARCHIVES CANADA CATALOGUING IN PUBLICATION

Shields, Carol, 1935–2003

A memoir of friendship : the letters between Carol Shields and
Blanche Howard / edited by Blanche Howard & Allison Howard.

ISBN-13: 978-0-670-06613-1
ISBN-10: 0-670-06613-3

1. Shields, Carol, 1935–2003—Correspondence. 2. Howard, Blanche, 1923– —Correspondence.
I. Howard, Blanche, 1923– II. Howard, Allison III. Title.

PS8587.H46Z488 2007   C813'.54   C2006-906816-X

Visit the Penguin Group (Canada) website at **www.penguin.ca**

Special and corporate bulk purchase rates available; please see
www.penguin.ca/corporatesales or call 1-800-810-3104, ext. 477 or 474

For our daughters and sons,
and theirs

Carol Shields's Family

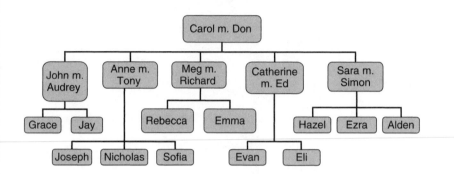

Blanche Howard's Family

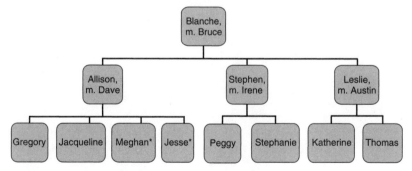

* Jesse and Meghan are Allison's stepchildren (Dave's children)

Contents

Foreword   xi

Introduction   xv

1   *Two Women 1975–1978*   1

2   *Two Writers 1980–1983*   28

3   *Ambition 1983–1984*   53

4   *Obsession 1985*   86

5   *Rejection 1985–1987*   106

6   *Work and Play 1987–1988*   152

7   *Joy 1989–1990*   182

8   *Fragility 1990–1992*   212

9   *The Meaning of Life 1992–1994*   261

10   *Turning Point 1995–1996*   315

11   *Trust 1997–1998*   346

12   *Journeys 1998–1999*   407

13   *Dark Night of the Soul 2000–2001*   457

14   *A Differently Ordered Universe 2001–2003*   514

15   *Flightless Birds 2003*   544

Acknowledgments   551

Foreword

Letters—real letters—have been eclipsed at a steadily accelerating rate by the telephone, telegraph, teletype and telex, by e-mail and voicemail, by text messaging, video-conferencing, net-meeting, facsimile and skype (so new a medium it hasn't yet earned a place in the dictionary). In comparison with all of these, however, letters entrain an extended history, and long-accepted conventions impose on letters constraints that, although subtle, cause them to have an agreeable arc and form. Letters have resonance for both the sender and the receiver. The writer brings to a letter some measure of purpose and of craft, and the reader brings, in turn, a set of hopeful expectations. Old-fashioned letters, on paper, vellum or card, have, in addition, an inherent potential for permanence.

The virtues of the many newer forms of conveying ideas, news, advice, thanks and sentiment—their ease and swiftness of transmission—are also their failings. Buttons and screens don't provide the rich, tactile pleasure that the sender of an old-fashioned letter gets when writing, sealing and posting it, and can't match the receiver's delight in holding and opening a stamped, addressed envelope—the only one of its kind—and devouring the enclosed pages. Files and bytes can't easily be secreted in a cigar box or drawer to be unfolded and re-savoured at will so that over time a unique geography of creases and limp margins become a part of the letter's gestalt.

The anticipation of receiving an insubstantial stream of electronic data by phone line, cable or ether cannot match the gratifying pleasure of waiting for the letter carrier to come into view with his or her bulging shoulder-slung sack of mail. One of the oddest accounts of the sheer sensory bliss of mail is John Updike's recollection in his book of memoirs, *Self-consciousness*, of when, as a young boy, he would see through the window the postman approaching and would lie down inside the front door so that he could experience the "clicking shower of mail" cascading on top of him. In this collection, Blanche Howard recalls that my mother, Carol Shields, during a stay in France "swooped down on the mailbox as if it might contain the meaning of life, and perhaps it does."

Aside from the universal appeal of those missives that begin "Please find enclosed a cheque in the amount of $ . . . ." or "We are delighted to accept your novel for publication," it is impossible to define what makes a "good" letter. However, one that starts with the words or thought "Dear Friend" is almost always guaranteed to be welcome. Over thousands of years, letters have been the means by which friendships have been created and sustained, notwithstanding distance, whether measured in kilometres or even over time— Updike's *Self-consciousness*, for example, contains a letter to his grandsons clearly intended to span the years that it will take them to grow old enough to read and appreciate it.

This book, *A Memoir of Friendship*, contains the very best kinds of letters—letters between two friends, both of them women of letters, both of them also, among other things, mothers, wives, workers and thinkers. These letters comprise, from start to finish, the ingredients of friendship and indeed of life itself—books, ideas, compulsions, politics, moves, illness, loss, celebrations. In my mother's first letter to Blanche Howard, on August 6, 1975, she asks Blanche—older by a dozen years, already a published author and a woman familiar with the ins and outs of business—for advice on her first publishing contract. Within months, a gleeful, conspiratorial tone has been set that will last through to 2003, the year in which, late on a beautiful summer day, my mother died a few weeks after her 68th birthday.

Both writers took enormous pleasure in each other's long-distance company. Their letters are energetic, supportive, enquiring and filled with a spirit of openness and adventure. They reflect the changing times and their writers' full lives. These letters are engaged from start to finish in creating, observing and commenting. Blanche and Carol became braver over the years. They were always wise.

Blanche, September 27, 1986: "Perhaps as various philosophers tell us, it's the becoming that counts." Carol, May 18, 1999: "I've discovered biography does not have nearly the truth of fiction, but does have other rewards." Just before Christmas 1988, at age 53, Carol began a list of the possible advantages of growing older. Her list included not worrying about going to parties and running out of conversation, and the relief of giving up all pretense of being a well-rounded person. Blanche, age 65, added: becoming calmer, a lessening of the urge to smarten up the world, and the satisfactions of children, grandchildren, retirement and pensions, and freedom.

The letters between Carol and Blanche extend from the seventies into the new millennium and evolve from typewriter to word processor to computer to e-mail. Both of them were tentative and doubtful about e-mail at first, but they grew to love it, recognizing that because of its speed, it allowed for a more conversation-like dialogue.

These letters chart a friendship that begins with a spark—a request for advice—that was kindled over time into a love that was always steadfast, enduring and sustaining.

Anne Giardini

Introduction

When my daughter Allison first put to me the idea of editing and publishing the collection of thirty years of correspondence between Carol Shields and me, I balked. I was busily immersed in other writing projects and wasn't sure if I had either the physical or emotional energy to tackle what promised to be a huge and challenging task. Some time later, however, when Anne Giardini, Carol's eldest daughter, approached me with an enthusiastic endorsement of the project, I reconsidered. Encouraged by Allison's offer to be a full partner in co-editing the book, I saw the opportunity to realize what had, in fact, been a dream that Carol and I had toyed with over the years, teasing each other with the suggestion that we would appear on *Oprah* and reassuring ourselves that we had written nothing too private to appear in print.

Carol and I first met in 1971. My husband had been elected to Parliament during the Trudeaumania wave of 1968 and we were living in Ottawa with our youngest daughter. Carol's husband, Don, was a professor at the University of Ottawa. Perhaps because my first novel, *The Manipulator*, had been accepted by McClelland & Stewart, and Carol's poetry collection, *Others*, had also been accepted, a mutual friend, Madeleine [Basford] Nelson, asked me if I would like to accompany her to a University Women's Club meeting at Carol's home.

"When I lived in Ottawa I used to participate in a group that was called Canadiana," Madeleine recalls. "We discussed current events, art, literature—really anything that was of interest and importance in our country's life—past or present. Sometimes we met at Carol's home on The Driveway. I am not sure why I think of that house so often, but I do. I remember the natural hardwood floors, the piney smell and Carol's unfailing warm welcome and calm demeanour."

On this occasion, Madeleine introduced me to our hostess, a diminutive, young-looking blond woman who, I was surprised to learn, had five children between the ages of three and twelve. At that time, I was caught up in the chancy world of politics and my first novel was being edited, while Carol, with five children to nurture, was engaged in making a momentous decision on whether to proceed with a Ph.D. program or to embark on writing a first novel. I remember at that time being heavily influenced by Joseph Campbell and his advice to "Follow your bliss!", and so I counselled her to set aside the Ph.D. for the time being. (I don't take entire credit for having saved a remarkable talent for the world; others waded in with similar advice.)

When my husband and I left Ottawa for North Vancouver two years later, Carol and I wrote at first with the diffidence of good acquaintances who share a specialty, sliding from talk of the books of others to the temerity we felt in daring to launch our own first efforts. Friends and family began to creep in from the wings—the children's achievements and setbacks, our husbands' struggles and triumphs. And finally, that most implacable of distractions, encroaching mortality.

Communication by letter is such an ephemeral thing on which to graft a friendship, the way it contrives to be simultaneously revealing and concealing. Revealing, in that sometimes the writer herself is surprised by what she has penned; concealing, in that the subtle shadings of personality—the impatient shrug, the toss of the head, the dismissive wave of the hand, the sliding lilt of laughter—are missing. Disillusion may be lurking; even betrayal.

Carol and I were fortunate in that our friendship was bolstered by frequent reality checks, although each reunion brought its own subtle realignment. We lived in the same city for two years in the late seventies; my husband and I joined Carol and Don in France for two holidays. There were countless flying visits as one or the other of us paused en route to another destination. And, in what could have undone the most solid link, we co-authored a novel.

Allison and I gathered together a thousand pages of correspondence, which had to be whittled down to what you see before you; decisions about what to cut were often difficult. Without Allison, I couldn't have done it. Health problems prevented her from sitting for long hours at a computer, so much of the editing was done the old-fashioned way, with pencil and paper. Back and forth went envelopes crammed with sections of marked-up manuscript, this process interspersed with frequent phone consultations, e-mails and visits that closed the 400 kilometres between our homes in Penticton and North Vancouver, B.C.

When one or the other of us visited, we worked side by side at the kitchen table, mirroring in many ways the process Carol and I had taken when we co-edited A *Celibate Season*, and in so doing an unexpected benediction came our way: we shared a closeness that would have eluded us in a solely computer-generated enterprise. We marvelled repeatedly at how simpatico we were in deciding which passage to exclude or keep. In a way, Carol had prepared me for this; she too had co-authored works with one or another of her daughters, and in letters she mentions frequently with what delight and with what a sense of blessing she shared that time with them.

In the end, Allison and I believe that we have done a credible and respectful job not only of conveying to the reader the intimacy of a deeply felt friendship, but also of having placed that friendship within the social, political and cultural context of the period during which the letters were written.

The paper chains held for nearly thirty years, until Carol's death in 2003. We wrote about our hopes, our successes, our failures, our children and daily routines, and the realities of cultural politics. We began to go over each other's manuscripts and eventually we co-wrote a novel, A *Celibate Season*, by letter and occasionally in serendipitous meetings. In time, the letters succumbed to the electronic age and e-mails flashed back and forth through space until finally, in March of 2003, she wrote,

> Blanche. What is the meaning of life? It is known to "everything except language" and the "ignorant freedom of my talking mind" (Les Murray). That is, I think, we all know and recognize it, but have no words for it.

> She died in July.

Blanche Howard

1

Two Women
1975–1978

Carol Shields and I became friends in 1971 in spite of what seemed to us at the time a significant age difference (I was forty-seven and she was thirty-five). Happily, a mutual passion for reading easily transcended this trivial social constraint and we began to seek each other out; our rapt and absorbing discussions would probably have gone on indefinitely had not the pressing needs to cook dinner and tend our families pulled us back from our beguiling, fictitious worlds. However, in 1972, in the same month as my first novel, *The Manipulator*, was published, my husband lost his bid for re-election to Parliament and in 1973 we moved back to British Columbia and settled in North Vancouver.

Perhaps it is fitting that Carol's first letter to me was written from France, since France was where they vacationed, and where over the years Don used his sabbaticals to work and teach in his field. I remember being overawed that Carol and Don should be spending almost a whole year in Brittany. International travel then wasn't as common as it is today, and in my admiration it didn't occur to me that it could be a lonely life, especially for a person like Carol, whose great interest was in words and language—*English* words and language. I think now that she must have found even a self-imposed exile occasionally daunting. Don, out all day at a French university or working with French colleagues, soon mastered the language; Carol was busy mastering the intricacies of English as she worked on a second novel, and of course five small children in a foreign environment would require an enormous amount of watchfulness. Yet in all her letters she never once alluded to being lonely; it wasn't in her nature to be other than grateful for the opportunity to savour new experiences.

For all of that, it isn't surprising that she longed to hear about the milieu she had left. "I have an overwhelming wish just to talk to someone about the whole subject of writing," Carol wrote in her next letter, and I, from the mountainous seclusion of our North Vancouver home, felt the same need.

I sometimes wonder at the serendipity of that first letter. If Carol had not sold her first novel to McGraw-Hill and written to me as someone she knew who had at least a limited experience with publishers' contracts, would any of these memories of a time past be mine? And I muse especially about how much emptier our lives, or at least my life, would have been. For these letters go beyond words on paper, at least for me; they bring into evidence those mysterious and subterranean cords that bind two people in friendship. Friendship—how would we live without it?

> *August 6, 1975*
> *Saint-Quay-Portrieux, France*

Dear Blanche,

I am writing to you for some advice; I've finally finished the novel I was writing, and finally (after being turned down three times) found a publisher for it. The contract arrived yesterday and, although everything looks fine, we haven't the least idea about such things. Don had the happy idea of writing to you—which pleased me since I've been wanting to write to you anyway—and seeing what you think. I know you aren't a lawyer, but you have been through this and may have some ideas. If you do I would love to hear from you.

Just a word about why I'm writing from such an exotic address; Don's sabbatical has rolled around at last, and France seemed a good idea for a number of reasons, most importantly the exposure to French. I think we thought it would sink into our consciousness effortlessly, but after two months here we are rather discouraged— it looks like a long road to bilingualism. Ah well, perhaps another two or three months . . . Aside from the language problems we are having a tremendous time. The weather has been the best in years, we are told, and the scenery in Brittany alternates from the rugged to the very soft, almost English type of landscape.

I'd love to hear if you are doing any writing. When I saw you in Ottawa just before you moved you were reading Russian writers for a sense of atmosphere and setting. I've been reading Jane Austen all summer, partly as a cushion against cultural shock, but partly out of curiosity. In the introduction to one of the books the editor admits that she writes about extraordinarily dull affairs but nevertheless the reader feels compelled to keep turning the page. I am on the sixth and last book now and I still haven't quite managed to figure out what magic she has.

Even if you've no advice re contracts and such problems, please do drop me a line and let me know what you are doing these days.

All best wishes,
Carol Shields

ᴐI replied that the contract was very similar to mine and that I thought it was no doubt standard for that publishing house and was probably adequate. Carol acknowledged my response with a postcard:

Many, many thanks for welcome letter. And congratulations! I'll look forward to *Pretty Lady* & will send detailed report. Have you another *en train*?

Best,
Carol Shields

5 fevrier 1976
Saint-Quay-Portrieux, France

Dear Blanche,

I have an overwhelming wish just to talk to someone about the whole subject of writing.

My book—*Small Ceremonies*—will be out this month and I am experiencing a number of strange sensations, mostly negative, and I'm curious to know whether you have felt the same. First of all, a novel is such a "public" thing, very much more than a little book of poetry.

Actually I read in *The Canadian Forum* last night that only 4% of Canadians ever enter bookshops (hard to believe) so I don't suppose it is all that public—still it seems to conflict somehow with privacy. Although why bother to write books if they're not going to be published? You can see my thoughts are going in circles—perhaps this is nothing more than a species of stage fright.

Next subject—reviews. Do you have some sort of philosophy about reviews? That is, can you read them with the necessary detachment and equanimity? I haven't thought much about this until last night when I read two "cruelies" in *The Sunday Times*, one of them a real butchery, an attack on the author rather than what he'd written. Perhaps people are less sensitive than I think. Otherwise they'd all have leaped over the cliff long ago. I find I'm writing denser all the time which worries me as I am an admirer of clean clear prose. I've just finished the novel I've been working on all winter; have enjoyed writing it but when I read it all over the other day, I thought, what a lot of rubbish this is. Do you ever feel that way—that there's nothing at the centre?

I'm afraid all these remarks seem very pessimistic, a very false message since we've had an extraordinarily good year.

Don has written a book with two Frenchmen—you will be amused to know that they had signed a contract with a publisher before they had written one word! I am quite proud of my children, who are fairly fluent by now and who have survived remarkably well in a fairly rigorous school system. They are convinced that Canada is the best of all possible countries and are counting the days before we go home.

Have you read Mavis Gallant? Penelope Mortimer? I would love to hear from you if you can spare the time.

Best,
Carol Shields

❧Carol's daughter Anne saw the French experience from a somewhat different perspective:

The fact is that we all, except for Sara, hated the school system there, which we found to be tyrannical and repressive. Only Sara, the youngest, was so engaging and energetic that she was able to charm the school system. She had, and has, my mother's ability to enjoy and be interested in wherever she found herself. That year in Brittany was harder for my mother than comes across in this note. Here is an extract from an essay I wrote about my mother, published in *Prairie Fire* in 2002:

My mother got her master's a few years later, in 1975. That was a sabbatical year for my father, and we were spending it in Brittany. We lived for the first two months in an airy, broad-beamed house set on a large lot between a bend in the road that led away from the village, Saint-Quay-Portrieux, and the sea. When the owners of this house returned, the seven of us moved into a small, ugly house close by the road, and nearer to the village. The owner, an old man who smelled of many baths forgone, lived in the basement. We were two to a bedroom, and my older brother, John, who elected to go to boarding school in a nearby town, Guingamp, stayed in a box room under the rafters when he came home on weekends.

My mother was writing a book, *The Box Garden*, and, lovely though it must have been to have us out of the house at school all day so she could work, her French was rudimentary and she was lonely, which I sensed even through the fog of my self-absorption. She had left her enormous electric typewriter at home in Ottawa, and was using a clumsy manual machine.

When I asked her about that year recently, she told me that she felt that *The Box Garden* suffered from having been written on that typewriter, which discouraged revisions and the process of adding layers, or "thickening," that she loves to do (she compares it to making a stew) and that has become so effortless in the era of computers and word processors.

When my three sisters and I got out of school, we watched bad French TV, justified on the basis that it would improve our vocabularies (we could all croon the latest pop tunes), and read from the stock of books we had brought with us. Before long, we had exhausted our supply. My engineer father, to whom every problem has one or more logical solutions, arranged for Foyles, a bookstore in England, to ship us boxes of books. Each parcel was greeted with the joy of the shipwrecked. Books were fought over, shared, even torn in half or thirds to meet competing demands. The organizing principles behind the orders that were placed were, as far as I recall, that the books we ordered had to be paperback (to reduce price and shipping costs) and should appeal to anyone between the ages of seven and forty. It was also preferable if they were long and densely printed. I remember reading *The Black Prince* by Iris Murdoch, all of the short stories of Somerset Maugham, Hardy's *Far from the Madding Crowd*, *Working* by Studs Terkel, Mary Stewart's King Arthur books *The Crystal Cave* and *The Hollow Hills*, and *Watership Down,* by Richard Adams.

—Anne Giardini

❧Two or three of my early letters are missing, but in this response Carol's mention of Margaret Laurence refers to my having met her at a Writers' Union meeting in Toronto in 1976, which in writerly circles of the day was akin to meeting the Queen. I had been feeling very discouraged after a meeting with Anna Porter at McClelland & Stewart about my new novel, *The Immortal Soul of Edwin Carlysle*. Even though they had accepted it, Anna seemed unhappy and at once I thought the novel worthless (such is the ego of the beginning writer). Later, at the annual general meeting, Christie Harris introduced me to

Margaret Laurence, who took my hand and said she had read both my novels and indicated that she actually liked them. My doldrums vanished before this unexpected benediction.

June 20, 1976
582 Driveway, Ottawa

Dear Blanche,

I'm getting to Vancouver next Sunday. John is graduating from grade 13 Tuesday night. McGraw-Hill loosened up for the trip and also the hotel. I was delighted to hear about your conversation with Margaret Laurence—it exactly fulfills my expectation of what she'd be like. In Toronto last week (for the Book Fair) I had lunch with McGraw-Hill's promotion manager Chris Watson, who told me she had had *Pretty Lady* [Blanche's second novel] out of the library twice and found it fascinating.

Best,
Carol

October 14, 1976
North Vancouver

Dear Carol,

It was fun having a good talk with you on Tuesday and I keep thinking of dozens of things we didn't get around to discussing. The most important thing I didn't ask you—you said that your editor loved your manuscript. Does that mean that it is definitely accepted by McGraw-Hill, or do others have to pass on it first? I would think that means it is accepted, but the ways of publishers are still mysterious. (Not as mysterious as the ways of Canada Council.)

I'm still wondering if the person at the Canada Council knew what she (he?) was talking about when she said that you required such well-known sponsors. Surely Margaret Laurence can't be called on by all and sundry, do you think?

I will be very anxious to hear about your progress both with the novel and with the documentary you are doing. I was telling my son about the latter—he has evolved a theory that survival depends on heightened social consciousness among corporations as well as among individuals, and I was telling him about the citizens' action group with which you've been involved. We were trying to evolve an idea of how much awareness could come about without actual government regulations, which always lead to top-heavy bureaucracy, and came to the conclusion that enlightened citizens' groups have to be the answer.

Sincerely,
Blanche

October 20, 1976

Dear Blanche,

I thoroughly enjoyed our afternoon and I too thought of many topics we missed. Ah, well, next time. (Please excuse this typing; the letter *A* is broken and must be shifted manually.) I really do think you'll enjoy Sara Jeannette Duncan's *The Imperialist.* The candidate in the book wins the election but loses his seat. What destroys him in the end is his zeal, his passion, a quality which Canadians seem to view with alarm. I am doing a seminar on her next week and enjoying the research.

Yes, McGraw-Hill have taken the novel, although I believe they want a few changes. They have given me $2,500 for an advance this time, more money than I've ever made in my life, but as my son pointed out, it just means fewer royalties in the future.

Thanks again for a really good afternoon.

Carol
P.S. Now I can picture you in your study.

January 13, 1977
3866 Regent Avenue
North Vancouver

Dear Carol,

I'm sitting staring out my study window at a typical "winter" day—cloudy, threat of imminent rain. However for once we can't complain as the winter has been remarkable, more days of sun than

I'm sure Vancouver has ever experienced, starting back last September, and nothing more than a brief skiff of snow one night that disappeared before noon the following day. I know this first paragraph is designed to drive you quite mad, but I have fallen into the West Coast habit of feeling superior on account of the weather. Maybe it's because out here we seldom feel too superior over anything else— never mind, forests are beautiful but man cannot live by trees alone.

The projected novel on politics is going extremely well. I must say I've been pleased with myself at the progress I've made so far—if it doesn't all fall together now, I haven't even decided who will win the election, although naturally I'm leaning toward the Liberal candidate. By the way I loved *The Imperialist*, was continually amazed at how nothing changes. She wrote extremely well, didn't she? And the insights into English–U.S. characteristics are still so very valid. Doesn't it annoy you though, in retrospect, that women still didn't have the vote at a time when they were as politically astute as Duncan?

I very much enjoyed the article your sister sent, especially the remark about ideas being infinite in number, for instance. Is that what the dreaded writer's block is, when they cease being infinite? Also the remark that it's a job where the actual doing matters more than the results. I suppose, though, that that could be said of most jobs.

All the best,
Blanche

March 3, 1977
Ottawa

Dear Blanche,

My writing class had a reading last night. I'm enjoying it a lot, and two or three show some promise. But the teaching of writing?—I still have grave doubts if it does much. There's a certain discipline to writing on a weekly basis, but in some ways I feel they take these courses to put off the day they will really get down to writing. Which goes to prove, I suppose, that in the end writing is only done in isolation. Sad thought.

Only a month or so before the Canada Council grants are announced, and I grow daily less hopeful about my chances.

I have just finished the American novel by Judith Guest— *Ordinary People*—after having heard from everyone the astonishing story of its success. I do think there are some real flaws in it but— I shed real tears, a number of times in fact. And I can't remember when I last cried over a book. She really managed to get inside that teenage boy and the relationship between the parents. I'd be interested in knowing what you think of it. Now I'm looking forward to some free time so I can read Clark Blaise's new book *Days and Nights in Calcutta*. Written with his wife. Our accountant friend and neighbour has recently told me that I can write off any and all books I buy—but why am I telling *you* this. Another book I read recently—because I had to give a seminar on it—was Sheila Watson's *The Double Hook*. Just dreadful imitation Faulkner (as someone in our class put it) and yet she had rave reviews in Canada just fifteen years ago.

About writing, Blanche, I find it has become a compulsion. I hadn't intended to do much this winter, but when a day goes by without at least a page written, the day seems useless. Is that a sort of puritan urge?—to fill the day with accomplishments? It is a little frightening to be overpowered that way.

All good wishes,
Carol

ᔊ Carol's skepticism about the teaching of writing was turned on its head when Wayson Choy, in an interview in the magazine *Read* in 2004, had this to say:

[In 1977] Humber College, where I taught English, allowed me a sabbatical to be with my father and to enrol again in the UBC Creative Writing Program. As luck would have it, Carol Shields was the no-nonsense short story instructor. She believed that if you were going to be a writer, you should be able to create a story from any source. For one assignment, she tore up pieces of paper, each marked with a colour, and set the rule: whichever colour you picked up, that colour had to become a major part of your next short story assignment. I got pink.

Unknown to me then, my chance selection of pink proved to be a sign. Let me explain about "signs." My immigrant grandparents were working all hours during my childhood in the 1940s, so I was partly raised by some of the last surviving pioneers of Vancouver's Chinatown, the elders who originally sojourned from Old China villages. They imbued in me the folk wisdom of paying attention to signs; that is, to note events and coincidences that would prove meaningful to my fate. For example, I didn't know what picking up "pink" might mean. I sensed the colour had some significance, but I was stuck. It wasn't until a few days before the assignment was due that I walked into the kitchen and my two aunts and my father were mulling over my mother's pieces of jade. I overheard one of my aunts mention that as well as the usual green jade, there existed a pink jade. I left the kitchen. After about an hour, I walked back in and they were talking about the peony bush blooming in my aunt's garden. For some reason, the phrase "jade peony" gripped me, and I immediately saw in my mind's eye an elderly hand shakily pressing a piece of pink jade into a small boy's open palm. The first sentence came to me. That night, I typed out . . . "When Grandmama died at the age of 83, our family held its breath." That story, "The Jade Peony," was one of two selected by Carol and my classmates to be submitted to UBC's *The Alumni Chronicle* writing contest. It won, and the story was published a year later. I thought that would be the end of things, but the story appeared at a time when multicultural voices were gaining attention. "The Jade Peony" became a favourite of anthologies, and then, in 1992, . . . Douglas & McIntyre offered me a contract to write a book. Three years later, the novel, *The Jade Peony*, was published. I'm amazed to think where my writing life would be today if, more than 25 years ago, Carol Shields hadn't challenged her students by tearing up those pieces of paper. Her no-nonsense ghost must be smiling.

—Wayson Choy

May 19, 1977
Winnipeg

Dear Blanche,

I wanted to tell you that I enjoyed your book, *The Immortal Soul of Edwin Carlysle*, very much. I've lent it to a physicist friend who is at Queen's and I'm anxious to hear what he thinks. Don and I are old *Double Helix* [James Watson] fans—we took turns reading it aloud to each other one hot summer week years ago. I've made a couple notes of things I liked. I liked where you described Anastasia's feelings about her house. And I like the whole analysis of the "in love" psychology—it is what I hope to do in my next novel. I especially like to read about it as a middle life happening. (Projection?) I saw your TV interview in Ottawa and feel that what you've got is an ability to establish a "Relationship" with the interviewer which makes it more of a conversation than an interview. Far warmer and less artificial. I hope I've learned something. I'll be anxious to hear from you regarding the rest of your tour and the Writers' Union meeting. There was a fair amount on it in *The Globe* which you've probably seen. What amazed me was the increase in membership. Also the injustice to writers who have double North American contracts. My big news is that I may be coming to Vancouver June 27th. I'm not supposed to tell anyone this but I've won the CAA fiction prize (they are planning a press release) and they will present it in Vancouver. At any rate the prize will pay for a big part of the Japan trip so it is like found money.

All best,
Carol

July 3, 1977
Winnipeg

Dear Blanche,

It was wonderful having dinner with you and Bruce—peaceful, delicious, relaxing. And I do enjoy a chance to talk books and writing—only hope Bruce wasn't bored to death. It really is a world to itself I'm finding.

The dinner at UBC was lovely, thanks to the taxpayers of B.C. The sun came out just as we were gathering and that made it perfect. I sat with the prize-winning poet Sid Stephen and his wife, both charming. (They are on a camping trip and had their two daughters outside in a van.) I had a nice long chat with Fred Kerner (editor of Harlequin). He is a dear man and not in the least apologetic about his company. He feels they are reaching a previously unreading public and leading them into the pleasures of reading. He backs this up by all kinds of market research, really impressive. The median income is $18,000, women with secondary plus education, etc. They are trying to reach the secondary minus group, not by lowering standards but by promotion in that area. I asked him if a Canadian setting presented a problem and he said absolutely not; they have used four or five Canadian settings and are on the lookout for more . . . He was familiar with all your books, by the way, Blanche, and has read *The Manipulator.* I didn't have the nerve to ask what they paid for manuscripts.

Carol

October 11, 1977
North Vancouver

Dear Carol,

At long last *The Box Garden* made it to Vancouver and I read it immediately, and I'll try to sort out my impressions.

[The suspense] was extremely well-handled, and in this I am totally at odds with *The Vancouver Sun* review, which I enclose.

I loved the mother and her sayings, was disappointed that there weren't more of them actually, since you have such a good ear it was a pleasure to read them (again think *The Sun* reviewer is nuts).

I find it hard to judge a novel by someone I know. People have always told *me* that, but I didn't realize the truth of it since I didn't formerly know any novelists, besides myself. Anyway, the upshot of it all is that I think Barbara Amiel's review was stupid—I have been suspicious for some time that the fluidity of her writing might actually hide a certain emptiness, in fact the thought first crossed my mind when I read her review of *Bear*. I reread it and could find no judgment of any sort, just a careful fence-straddling for fear she might be proven wrong. I think she has learned to write elegantly and wittily, but that her judgment isn't good.

I'm beginning to wonder if you can write a novel that doesn't have a central person, but explores the development of several people—I keep thinking of *War and Peace*, although what's-his-name (I can't remember, the one who toyed with the Masons) was probably the central character. Perhaps only if you are writing the massive type of novel, like Michener's.

I seem to be feeling optimistic—which I think goes to show that inner feelings don't have a great deal to do with outer events. . . . So as you see my good cheer is unjustified, possibly the first sign of an unbalanced mind. This isn't to say that I haven't gone through great periods of discouragement. In mentioning it once to a friend who has tried to do some writing, she said, "For heaven's sake, you don't realize what you've got. Already published three times, and learning your craft—many people spend years before even one novel sees the light of day, and your very first one was accepted!" Her remarks did help me see my career in some sort of context, and I pass them on to you for whatever they're worth.

I have been doing a bit of accounting on the side—obviously novels will never make us rich, or even above the poverty level.*

---

*Professionally I am a chartered accountant, and had worked in an accounting practice for ten years before we went to Ottawa.

It cuts into the writing time, but gives me some needed self-esteem.

The next Writers' Union conference will be in Ottawa in May, so I'll look forward to a good visit with you. In the meantime, don't be discouraged, you have a tremendous amount of talent and Barbara Amiel will never write anything more uplifting than the Demeter murder story.

All the best, and thanks again for the comments and for the Canada Council thing. Excuse the terrible typing—why are your letters so error-free? All best,

Blanche

~ The reference to the Canada Council dates back to a time when they required three sponsors with an application. This always led to a great deal of soul-searching and probably nuisance for those writers who were approached. Since Margaret Laurence had offered, when I met her, to sponsor me, I did write to her and had this reply.

> *October 14, 1977*
> *8 Regent Street*
> *Lakefield, Ontario*

Dear Blanche:

I've sent off the references to the Canada Council, and I do hope you get the grant.

I think M&S should have pushed *Edwin Carlysle* as science fiction, of which there is all too little in this country. I found it fascinating and thought-provoking, and have said so to the C. Council.

Please excuse short letter. I have to go to Toronto tomorrow for a week, and have a million things to do before then.

All best wishes,
[signed Margaret]
Margaret Laurence

25 October, 1977
Winnipeg

Dear Blanche,

I was in Saskatoon two weeks ago with Don, and when I asked for [*The Box Garden*] in their biggest bookshop they escorted me over to the gardening section. Ah well . . .

Your remarks on the book were very greatly appreciated. I had a long talk yesterday with Beth Harvor,* an Ottawa writer (very good), about whether or not writers should expect some editorial help. We both think it's necessary. What after all is an editor for? But getting *good* help is the problem. She has been trying to get a story in *The New Yorker* and has almost succeeded a couple of times, but she has had valuable editorial advice from one of the fiction people there, advice which really turned her around. Anyway, as a result of this conversation we have agreed to try editing each other's work.

I'm feeling better about *The Box Garden*—there have been quite a few good reviews and an excellent one by Harry Boyle in the *Ottawa Citizen*—to me a good local review was more important than anything; not sure what that means. I do think it's a badly flawed book and I think part of it was because I listened to the critics last time round—all that talk about nothing happening. I won't make that mistake again. Also I think you've got to take a few knocks and I guess I've just never had to take any. I very much liked your remark about inner feelings not having a great deal to do with exterior events—it's an idea I'd like to expand on in a novel study.

And now—I want to thank you for *Writers at Work*. I can't tell you how much I have appreciated reading this book. The series was unknown to me, by the way. I read one interview every night before I went to sleep; it reminded me of reaching for a chocolate from a bonbon box. My favourite was the interview with Updike. I am and always have been an admirer of his, but I was exceptionally struck with some of his comments. Most particularly I was interested in his ideas of the way in which a novelist transforms reality and how

---

*Elisabeth Harvor.

reality can intrude. I also like—and thought you must have—his remarks about giving his characters a professional background (other than an academic background). The Anthony Burgess interview interested me too—especially his comments on how language can be enriched by experimenting with syntax—this is what I'm wound up in at the moment. Blanche, the whole book was fascinating and helpful and even inspiring. I've already lent it to Beth.

I don't think I'll ever make much money at writing, and the only reason I would want to would be to relieve Don a little of the running of this ship. It certainly would give us more alternative than we have at the moment. I suppose there is always the fear of taking a wrong turning—but then, is any turning "wrong"?

I've just sent off my application for the Writers' Union AGM. I was a little dashed to hear it was going to be in Ottawa this year—darn. Anyway, you certainly are welcome to stay with us. I'm hoping my friend Joan Clark will come too from Alberta.

All is well here although one of my children, Margaret, has mono and must spend a few weeks at home. It's been a busy fall and I'm looking forward to a nice dull winter.

All best wishes,
Carol

December 9, 1977
North Vancouver

Dear Carol,

I've had an unbelievably busy fall, friends who haven't visited in years, some freelance accounting jobs, and other distractions too numerous to mention. I sometimes wonder where the pastoral existence of yesteryear in North Van has fled, but I'm sure I have no one to blame but myself.

Thank you for two things: the Canada Council application, and the copy of *The Box Garden*. Yes, Margaret Laurence did sponsor me, and actually found time to write me a little note saying that she found *Edwin Carlysle* "fascinating and thought-provoking" (I have it memorized and sometimes say the words in my sleep). Imagine the time she must take over CanLit! I met Pauline Jewett at a party (torn between calling her Pauline in social occasion or Dr. Jewett as befits a university president, settled for uh), and she told me she'd been talking to Margaret L. that day, and that M.L. is reading *all* Canadian fiction published this year, I think as one of the judges for Gov Gen's award. Something like 150 books. Must be tough on even a speed reader. Anyway, Margaret L. also said in her note that M&S should have promoted *Edwin Carlysle* as science fiction, and I think she is right.

Back to *The Box Garden*. I'm delighted that you are getting so much good publicity. I hope you saw Arnold Edinborough in *The Financial Post*. He gave you a nice little review among his books that he recommends for Christmas. Have also seen numerous other respectful mentions, including the excellent one in *Saturday Night*. That must have given you quite a shot in the arm! You really do seem to have made the breakthrough with your two novels—deserved, and I offer you my heartiest congratulations.

I tried *Saturday Night* with an excerpt from the political novel that I felt very good about, and they sent me one of their encouraging rejection slips saying they'd like to hear from me again (they seem to have two kinds, I've had the other which just says bluntly no), but no comment of any sort, so that I'm left to wonder whether maybe they've merely changed rejection slips.

Have you read *Spit Delaney's Island*? I think when you do you will be impressed with Jack Hodgins. He is writer-in-residence this year at SFU and is the most likeable person you'd ever want to meet. Perhaps he'll be at the Writers' Union conference—so glad you joined, and I agree that it's too bad it's Ottawa from your viewpoint.

We are going to Hawaii for a couple of weeks in February, then back to face the fray, maybe. The spring is shaping up to be hectic, and Allison is expecting again in June.

I must dash. It is actually snowing this morning, an event that sends all Vancouverites into deep trauma, since they never put on snow tires and promptly skid all over the roads and prevent more responsible citizens from moving about. But I have to shop—Bruce has invited the entire staff to a wine and cheese here tomorrow night and so far I've done nothing about it. If I skid all over our mountain I will be getting my just desserts.

I hope you and yours have a wonderful Christmas, and that the daughter with mono is making a good recovery. I spent an Ottawa winter with Leslie in its throws (or is it throes? Yes, it is) so know that it isn't that pleasant.

Oh, one other thing, I was asked to join a most fascinating study group. A German immigrant, young, M.A., is an expert on Thomas Mann, and as she is taking a break from studying is conducting a very serious little group in an in-depth study of his novels. So far we've done *Death in Venice*, and I was fascinated by the layers of imagery, most of which had escaped me in first reading (I have no background in literature study, a thing that has always made me feel a lack). We are doing *Doctor Faustus* next. I read the novel years ago when it first came out, and was deeply impressed—wonder how I'll feel about it now on second reading.

Merry Christmas!

Blanche

January 2, 1978
Winnipeg

Dear Blanche,

You aren't going to be able to believe this! We are moving to Vancouver. I still can't believe it myself, that is I can't believe that our Ottawa life is going to come to an end. Briefly, Don has been restless at the university since our return from France and has been looking about for something else. He will be joining R.M. Hardy as chief engineer and partner beginning July 1st. Though he was reluctant to leave the university life (at least the romantic idea of the university life) he does feel this is a good move. Also the idea of Vancouver as viewed from our ice-bound nest in the east was attractive.

I am becoming more positive by the day. As you know I love this house and can't believe I'll ever find one I like as well again. And after ten years here we have many good friends. I'm enormously comforted by the fact that I do know a few people in Vancouver, and once we have found a roof to put over our heads it will be better. It is wonderful to have a portable profession—I discovered that in France. Like money in a Swiss bank. We may have only three children living with us; John hopes to study in Europe next year and Anne plans to come with us but live in residence. Our daughter Cathy will be going into grade 12 so it will hit her hardest, but she was overjoyed to find there was no grade 13 in B.C. We will be out in March or April to house hunt. We already have heard the bad news; that houses are much more expensive than in Ottawa. We think it might be interesting to live in a modern house for a change. I am hoping to get one course to teach, possibly at UBC, and must begin to write some letters about that.

We are all well. Margaret is almost over her mono infection. It is really a question of sitting on her now and seeing she doesn't get too tired. It was a busy Christmas season and I'm only twenty pages into my new Christmas book, by Peter DeVries. (He is an acquired taste but addictive.) I also blew an enormous amount of money on what is supposed to be the book of the year, Marilyn French's *The Women's Room*, but haven't read it yet. I read in the Writers' Union newsletter that you were looking into doing a CanLit program on a Washington station—all that sounds wonderful. I met a bookstore operator—also at the New Year's party—and asked him how he'd rate the various publishers. He thinks General Publishing is the best organized of all and gives their authors the tenderest care. McGraw-Hill is hopeless, he said, "no business sense." He sniffs at McClelland & Stewart and had some funny stories to tell about the Pierre Berton machine. Do you know anything about Lester & Orpen? Apparently they are very receptive to novels in outline form. The worst thing about writing, I have decided, is the tremendous amount of self-motivation it demands—I can't think of another profession which is as unsupported from the outside.

This is a most rambly and incoherent letter—too many thoughts and no organizing structure, as some young slip of an editor might say. But I was anxious to share our news with you. And look forward to hearing from you. All best wishes for a successful and happy new year.

Carol

> *January 31, 1978*
> *North Vancouver*

Dear Carol,

At last a breathing space and time to answer your letter. January has been a very hectic month—I took on an accounting year-end which turned out to be more complicated that expected. Then we had two sets of house guests. Also have been asked to speak twice on my writing—I think the aspiring really believe we have a magic formula that we're being too miserable to impart. Thank heavens on the 13th we leave for two beautiful (I hope) weeks in Hawaii. Bruce is greatly in need of rest too, having organized his unity group into a great seminar at UBC so that he would have material for a brief to the Pepin–Robarts task force [on Canadian unity] next week.

Anyway, I'm so pleased about the forthcoming move to Vancouver! It will be great for me to have a fellow writer to talk to about my problems.

We've had a mild winter here, a statement guaranteed I'm told to send easterners into a mild frenzy. I gather it's been a disaster year there.

All the best,
Blanche

> *February 27, 1978*
> *Ottawa*

Dear Blanche,

We will arrive on April 5th (bringing our daughter Cathy) and will have a little over a week to look and buy. It is going to be a very crowded week; I just hope we find the perfect house within

24 hours so we can then relax and enjoy ourselves. Our house is still for sale. We've had three offers but not the right one yet. As you can imagine, there are a great many buyers from Montreal these days, also from the Quebec side here.* My friend Margaret Dymond who lives in Vancouver writes that the French language situation is not something one discusses in Vancouver!! Thanks heavens, for us, that you're there.

I've been reading some strange novels lately by an Englishwoman named Fay Weldon. She has a strange narrative style and the books read rather like plays. Interesting though. Rather radicalized on the subject of feminism as is another book I read recently, *The Women's Room*, by Marilyn French. (This book has been called the book of the year in some American reviews.)

We still have heaps of snow here, very dirty and crusted, but the skating has never been better. I'm going today for one last skate since they are talking of closing the canal on March 1st. We keep referring nostalgically to the last time we do this in Ottawa or the last time we see that—nevertheless we're getting rather excited about the move.

All best,
Carol

➤Carol was living in Vancouver by the time I received the Canada Council grant. The Shields family settled here in the spring of 1978 in a roomy two-storey house in the Kerrisdale district, on Churchill Avenue.

They were a happy two years. Carol and I not only enjoyed each other's company, we were relieved that our husbands liked one another. It sometimes happens that the significant other in a relationship is bored by or can't stand the sight of his/her counterpart, but our husbands hit it off from the first. We had a small sailboat and I remember them sailing with us, and the four of us dining and dancing at the UBC Faculty Club.

---

*The threat of separation was pushing many people to leave Quebec.

I had two very dear friends who were as fond of reading as Carol and I were, Katinka Clarke and Marilyn Flitton, and there were vigorous and exuberant dinner parties where the talk of books was as ubiquitous as the talk of the weird world of B.C. politics.

When Carol first arrived, I had a luncheon for her on the cedar deck of our house in the rain forest of North Vancouver. I remember that she arrived flustered, a few minutes late, as she had been determined to use public transit. She didn't realize how leisurely the system operated in our newly developed area on the lower slopes of Fromme Mountain. It was a beautiful day, I remember, with perhaps a dozen guests. One of my friends who had been in Ottawa when we were, Barbara Perrault, wrote me afterwards of her impressions of Carol:

Dear Blanche:

Thank you for including me among your luncheon guests last Thursday. It was great fun putting faces to the names of people I've heard you mention so often. I was especially pleased to meet Carol Shields. She is so warm and very natural. She told me she has had two novels published and I look forward to reading them.

Blanche, your gardens looked lovely—don't ever tell me again that you don't have a green thumb! The impatiens and hostas appear to be thriving around that wonderful new cedar deck Bruce built. When I told Ray about the deck he looked a little wistful. Since his appointment to Cabinet he has had little or no time at all to be a handyman.

I am so glad you live close enough to be a neighbour. Carol asked me if I was happy to be back on the Coast and naturally I told her how much I love it here, although I also found myself telling her that I have been experiencing culture shock since returning to B.C. She agreed with me that life seems to move at a different pace and people here are more casual in dress and temperament. She is such an attentive listener and seemed very interested in my perspective about life during the Trudeau era on the Hill in Ottawa—it was fun, wasn't it, meeting political luminaries, dining at embassies and watching the perils of Pierre!

I hadn't known until she told me that you had won the Canadian Booksellers award for *The Manipulator.* You certainly managed to make the best use of your time in Ottawa, learning French and becoming a published author.

Again thanks for a wonderful afternoon. I enjoyed all of your friends, particularly Carol who was both charming and delightful.

Kindest regards,
Barbara Walker Perrault

∿ Carol and I became active participants in the still fledgling B.C. chapter of the Writers' Union of Canada. The meetings were informal and we were frequently entertained by the music of Keith Maillard and his guitar or by somewhat unrestrained partying, often at the beautiful home of Jan Drabek and his tolerant wife Joan.

The ethos of the sixties was still shaping, in the seventies, the attitudes of those who were young, or lately young. Carol and I felt that this great social upheaval had somehow eluded us. We discussed at some length the necessity of buying clothes that would allow us to fit in with the super-casual jeans-clad members of the Writers' Union instead of the garb befitting wives of professors and politicians. I still remember Carol phoning one day and announcing triumphantly that she had solved the dilemma: she had bought a denim skirt.

In fact, clothes did interest us, or rather our inability to afford to buy the ones we would have liked interested us. We confided to one another that we sometimes dreamed of being let loose in a dress shop and told to just choose what we wanted. Both of us had sewing machines and had made some of our own clothes when the children were young. Now I longed for a really good outfit. One day I found the perfect black wool suit in Chapman's, an expensive store that sells the kind of well-cut clothes that never wear out. The price tag was prohibitive and after a lot of hesitation I phoned Carol, who lived fairly close, and asked if she would have time to come over and help me decide. She did, and together we agonized over the price, and finally she said, in effect, go for it. And I did, and since it was a classic design I wore the suit until, many years later, it finally began to show shiny patches of wear.

Carol became a very good friend of another of the Writers' Union members, Sandy Frances Duncan (known to us simply as Sandy). In an excerpt of a piece entitled "Open Letter" and published in the magazine *Room of One's Own*, Sandy wrote of those days.

July 1988
Gabriola Island, B.C.

Dear Carol,

I don't remember when you and I met. Probably at a Writers' Union meeting, around Christmas '78? Later, when we talked about meeting we agreed we felt like kindred spirits reconnecting, although I think we used Anne of Green Gables' term—or my variation on it, bosom buddies.

So there you were with all your clocks in that square house at Churchill and 49th, not feeling at home in Vancouver. A cold unfriendly city in spite of all its beauty. I remember saying out of a childhood memory trace, "People wait to be formally introduced here," and, "in my experience it always takes a year to feel at home." In a gently acerbic tone, you pointed out that it had been a year. But you never did feel Vancouver was your city, did you? I can understand that, as I've said, and also why you felt so immediately at home in Winnipeg—both you and Don grew up in the centre of the continent, with sky not ocean to map the wildness. I do think where we're placed the first few years of life profoundly shapes our geographic comfort zones. Though—maybe if you'd stayed—?

What I remember best about your time in Vancouver is talking. We ate lunch and talked, we walked and talked, we talked on the phone. We talked about: has any woman writer of stature sustained a life-long love relationship; and conversely: has any woman who sustains a long-term relationship achieved greatness? Well, Gertrude Stein, we agreed, and Virginia Woolf, George Eliot, but two were socially marginalized, and look at the cost to Woolf. "She might have walked into the river sooner without Len," I said. "Is it possible?" you asked. "Yes, it has to be," I replied firmly, my marriage then still intact. "But at what cost?" we deliberated, and sometimes finished, "Every writer needs a wife," that chestnut not so hard and wrinkled ten years ago.

You fumed about reviews by men which stated or implied that you should work a "bigger canvas," ones which referred to your children ("how do you find time to write?"), your dresses ("Ports International," which you denied), and you said you would never let an interviewer into your house again.

We talked about whether it was possible, really possible, for a man to write a woman's point of view (did Flaubert?) or a woman to write a convincing man. You were working on *Happenstance*— "but does Jack sound like a man?" We talked about how men swear and how women swear—I was writing *Finding Home*.

Always we talked about our children—or, to be precise, about ourselves as mothers. But we didn't talk much about husbands, did we—ourselves as wives? When one of your children asked why you never wrote about anyone in her twenties, we laughed. Those years a blur of housewifely-ness (your word), pregnancies, colic, and diapers. How could one write? Moreover, what was there to write about? (Oh cringe, were we that arrogant?)

Remember your umbrage at someone telling you she'd "read your book last night"? "If I spent a year writing it, she could at least have taken two nights to read it!"

We laughed, but always with a touch of awe, at bits of life that we could use in fiction—the woman who matched the colour of her negligees and candles, the anonymous voice in the fitting room next to yours who said, apparently of her corset or bra: "Is this uplifting enough?"

I do remember when you told me you were leaving Vancouver—March 1980. A balmy day, the flowering plums along Marine Drive profusely pink. We walked down all the steps to Wreck Beach, along the log-strewn, swampy trail to Tower Beach and up again. I fought bereftness, filed it to examine later.

Love,
Sandy

2

Two Writers

1980–1983

On July 10, 1980, I wrote in my journal, "Carol and Don Shields moved here for two wonderful years, and have just left for Winnipeg. How I'll miss Carol! We would talk books and writing by the hour, and she is one of the world's truly nice people."

And in fact, Carol's equable nature became legendary among her friends, although in an essay I wrote for *Prairie Fire*, she herself offered a possible explanation. "Carol told me once that if she didn't write she would become neurotic. I think this is true of most writers; Freud may have merely put a new spin on an old truth. Certainly writing is a search that may, like psychoanalysis, lead us into secret labyrinths where thoughts we have never suspected are discovered, where ancient and forgotten fears thrust themselves, like stalagmites, into consciousness, where we catch glimpses of desires so evanescent that they scatter like cockroaches before the light. And always, the compulsion, the need, to know more."

This talk must have taken place in July of 1980. "It seems to me that the act of creation keeps me stable," I wrote in my journal. "Carol says the same thing. We both agree that those who don't write must have trouble coping with their neuroses." Yet in the following letter, written in September, I told her I had decided to take a break from writing.

September 22, 1980

Dear Carol,

It seems ages since you left and I wonder how things are going. I can imagine you've been up to your ears getting settled, and with the new book coming out this fall (I can hardly wait to see it).

First and foremost, Bruce has changed his job. He has been appointed to the Immigration Appeal Board (here in Vancouver) a very decided step up for him. Needless to say, he was thrilled about it—as you know, he had been getting very twitchy in the Citizenship Court, and this offers a great new challenge and has erased all thoughts of retirement from his head. Allison and Leslie threw a surprise party for him to celebrate the appointment, and invited all our friends (we'll dine out all winter on their hard work). We did wish the Shieldses had been among them.

I am embarked on rather a strange new career, for me. As you know, I had decided to take the year off from writing—getting discouraged, and feel it is time to reassess the situation. So at an opportune moment (for me) I got a phone call from the head of the business management section at Capilano College, asking me if I would teach a course in second-year finance—four hours of lecture a week, daytime, and Cap College is only five minutes from here. I decided to try it, although with great misgivings about my rustiness in the field—and find to my intense amazement that I'm really enjoying it! Also (and also to my amazement) that I know more than they do! Ah wonders. Anyway, it is a far cry from writing and perhaps good to clear my mind. So there it is, everything changes. We had our four sets of eastern company, one after another, all summer, but survived—actually we enjoyed them all, it's just a bit much in the same summer. The Writers' Union had their great

river-rafting adventure and it was great fun, although strenuous.
I would have felt far more courageous if Christie [Harris] and Tom,
ages 75 and 81 respectively, hadn't sat upright in the face of the
dangerous rapids saying things like, "Isn't this fun?" and "Oh,
I think Tom needs a bit of challenge now and then." (This from
Christie, sitting between terrified Leslie and me.) The first day was
cold and rainy, but the second sunny. Unfortunately, most of the
group were not prepared for the soaking everyone got, except us,
because Leslie's office crowd had gone before and said to be sure to
wear rubber boots and rain gear, so we alone stayed dry and warm.

Write soon and tell me all. Bruce sends greetings to you both.

Blanche

P.S. Oh yes, one of the reasons for the letter. My Vanier Institute meeting has been put off until December 4th and 5th in
Winnipeg.* Hope you'll be around that weekend.

∼Carol was acquiring new friends, among them Maggie Dwyer, who, in
a piece entitled "My Friend Carol," wrote of their first encounter, published
in *Carol Shields, The Arts of a Writing Life* (edited by Neil Besner):

Carol has a gift for friendship. Everyone who knows her agrees
on that. Ours began in the summer of 1980 when she and Don
moved into the house next door to mine on Harvard Avenue in
Winnipeg. When I knocked on their door, my welcoming gift
of freshly baked muffins in hand, I was greeted warmly, as if the
appearance of a friendly neighbour was the next small turn in
the plot of the novel she was writing. The Shieldses had arrived
before their furniture, and Carol and Don and their children
were ensconced in their lawn chairs. I do not recall our conversation. Only our laughter . . .

---

*I had been appointed by the Prime Minister's Office to sit on the board of the
Vanier Institute of the Family and the meetings took place at various places
across Canada.

Friends often ask favours of each other, and Carol is generous to her friends. When I found myself in the early, bedazzled stage of my whirlwind romance with my husband John, I asked a group of friends including Carol and Don to meet him. I was in starry-eyed love, floating high over the full moon; I needed to see the reactions of good friends to give me some sense of perspective. Is he as wonderful as I think he is, I asked, the veritable man of my dreams? Or am I infatuated? Am I merely in a swoon? Delusional? Strictly gone? So eager to dwell in The Republic of Love that I could not say? . . .

She took my dear unsuspecting John aside at the party and said, "Now tell me about yourself." Although he continues to refer to this episode as "the night she grilled me," I know that Carol meant her words to be taken as an invitation rather than an interrogation. He tells me that for close to an hour she questioned him closely about childhood and family, his education and previous marital history and his children. His intentions, his character and his prospects were deemed satisfactory, and so, with my friend's blessing, though obviously not entirely on the strength of her approval, I married him.

—Maggie Dwyer

October 6, 1980
191 Harvard Avenue
Winnipeg, Manitoba

Dear Blanche,

I can't begin to tell you how welcome your letter was, not only the letter, but all the good news within. We were both delighted to hear about the two new jobs in the family. What a surprise, though now that I stop to think of it, I always did think you would be a good teacher. Four hours a week lecturing sounds like a lot to begin with—is it? Bruce's job sounds ideal, a departure, but not a total departure.

I'll be interested to hear if you *really* can give [writing] up completely, or if you will be slipping off to the typewriter with an idea

occasionally. You may find that the year's teaching will refuel your
writing ideas. I am wondering what kind of students you have, what
age and interest. Lately I've been reading Virginia Woolf's diaries and
letters, and am interested to see that between novels she spent a year or
so doing essays and reviews, establishing a kind of rhythm that (more
or less) sustained her. It has also been interesting reading her diaries at
this time if only to discover how enormously sensitive she was to
reviews. She dreaded them. When her friends wrote with comments,
she read the letters for every nuance. She was in a constant state of
insecurity about the worth of her own writing—all of which seems
extraordinary and wasteful somehow. Since *Happenstance* is now out,
I find all these reflections interesting. I've had three reviews so far that
I know of—a very nice one from Bill French (he thinks, tho, that I
should find a "larger canvas" next time), a short notice from that awful
Burt Heward on the *Ottawa Citizen* who thinks it would be nice if
I were more vivid, like Richler for instance, and a rave on Saturday
from the *Winnipeg Free Press*. I find this a period of great anxiety, and
hate myself for feeling this way. However, the good news is that
Penguin is making a "substantial bid" on November 1st. I told Don
that if it works out I'll never ask for another thing. "Ha," he says. The
new novel is moving along; I worry that there doesn't seem much
plot to it. It is really, I'm afraid, going to be one of those "growth-of-
awareness" things. ("And then I realized . . . ") But I'm loving writing
about this woman and it just seems to unroll itself . . . *Happenstance*
comes out in the States next week.

Winnipeg has been good to us so far. We all love the house,
though Don and I had a set-to last night about the dining room
wallpaper which he likes and I would like to get rid of. It feels like
a real house, and I love to just walk around in it.

The garden needs doing—as do all Winnipeg gardens—and
I am looking forward to that next spring. We live on a most
pleasant street, and I've already met more people in the
neighbourhood than I met in two years on Churchill. The local
bookstore, a minute away, gave a tea party for *Happenstance* on

Friday, and I met packs more. Everyone asks if I find life slow here, and I'm at a loss about that since my life is always rather slow wherever we've been. I've only been to a few university "functions" and found them exactly like the U of Ottawa ones, everyone discussing the quality of their rhubarb instead of anything intellectually sparkling, ah well . . . I miss you and Sandy [Frances Duncan] terribly. Don is not teaching the first term and can concentrate on the many personnel problems that have been accumulating over the years. (There are twenty-three in the department and at the moment three of them are undergoing nervous breakdowns—do you think this is more than the national average?) I am teaching a little too—two afternoons at the U of M's inner-city campus and one evening with their extension department. It does take time and energy, but I feel I've got to get out of this little room and be sociable from time to time. I like the teaching and the contact, but what I hate is reading the stuff they write. It is utterly discouraging almost all of the time.

The children are all fine. John got into McGill law school. Anne and Cath in Vancouver, and Marg and Sara are adjusting here fairly well—though we all look forward to mail.

Love to you both,
Carol

P.S. I heard on the radio this morning that Alice's [Munro] book has been shortlisted for the Booker Prize in Britain!

May 19, 1981
North Vancouver

Dear Carol,

At last I seem to be crawling out from under the quantity of work I took on in April and for which I should have had my head read. I did end up very fatigued, proving, I suppose, that I'm not as young as I used to be, if such proof were necessary.

We had a little Writers' Union meeting at Keith's house last night, to honour Bob Harlow who is marrying a nice person named Ruth Clarke, who was associated with the National Book Festival. It was a quite good party, although [one of the women] was very loud and giggly. I thought she was tight, but that shows my naïveté, according to Bruce, who says a fair amount of puffing was going on in the kitchen. Christie [Harris] was there, glowing from her many triumphs, with great tales of the presentation by the GG of the medal (Order of Canada), plus the receiving of the $5,000 Canada Council children's book award. (She was astonished that everyone in the small village in Quebec, where for reasons obscure probably even to themselves Tim Porteous [director] of the Canada Council handled the presentations, spoke only French. There is such a long gap in that sentence between the subject and predicate that you're going to have to read it again.) What else? Jan Drabek is making money from the Open Learning Institute but not doing much writing, Keith's film option has lapsed which means he can sell it again, and that's about it.

Marilyn phoned me after reading *Happenstance* and had really enjoyed it. She is interested in history and found that she related tremendously to your main character. Also a friend of hers (who left a remote Canadian farm and a dreadful marriage, went to university and got a scholarship to get her PhD at Yale—in middle age) has now read all your novels and thinks you are a wonderful writer. She loves your use of the language, and the way you are able to evoke the exact feelings of events. She also likes the fact that you write of ordinary people and situations and somehow make them important (transcendence?).

I must go and cease this rambling. My short return into the world of careers convinced me that it isn't for me any more, although I must admit to having enjoyed the stimulation of being out there in the interaction of the real world once again. But one can't do everything, with which profound philosophical remark I'll sign off for now.

Love,
Blanche

June 7, 1981
Winnipeg

Dear Blanche,

I haven't heard from Sandy since seeing her at the AGM, but am planning to write to her this week. You would have enjoyed the meeting I think; it was relatively quiet this year, and everyone seemed anxious to avoid anything the least contentious. The real talkers were absent. My roommate turned out to be Eleanor Wright Pelrine who writes on political subjects. I liked her enormously. [H] angered quite a lot of people by being more authoritarian than ever—if you can believe it—but ran a fairly smooth meeting. The B.C. group was large, vocal, united and awe-inspiring (so I was told). I had an interesting week in Toronto seeing three publishers, Lester & Orpen Dennys, Macmillan, and Clarke Irwin. I also met with the Penguin people. They all seemed interested in seeing the new manuscript, even Penguin who have in mind a paperback original. I was most impressed with Lester & Orpen Dennys and will probably go that way. It was a rather peculiar exercise in a sense, since I don't have a finished manuscript at the moment, but did want to get a feel for various editors and I think I have. I hope you will do what you did last time, read it for me and make some suggestions. I was so grateful and thought you had hit on the missing spots so well, particularly in the development of the son's character.

We have four children home, and Anne will be arriving in a couple weeks. I am most grateful to both you and Sandy for advice and encouragement all winter. No one ever told me parenting was so long and so hard. Is there such a thing as parent burnout?

In July we are going with Marg and Sara to a Manitoba horse farm for a week, and then in August we go to Hungary. A busy summer. Nevertheless I am finding odd hours for writing, and, of course, I am at the final quarter of the book and it is going easily. I am still a little worried that not much is going on in this book but . . . I did meet Adrian Lang* not long ago. An afternoon parlour reading was given in their house for about fifty-five women, all to raise money for the Manitoba Workshop Theatre. We had an afternoon of readings from Irish literature given by two excellent actors from London, Ontario. It was like an event from the 19th century, wonderful!

What are you reading at the moment? I'm reading Bernard Malamud, *Dubin's Lives* (in paperback now), and finding it sad but quite wonderful. You'd be interested, I think, in his ideas about biography vs. fiction—the main character is a biographer. I think I told you about Edmund Gosse's little book *Father and Son*—the best thing I've read for ages. Again it deals with retrieval from the past and an honest presentation of the past. One of my neighbours was horrified that I'd never read Proust, so perhaps I will start. Have you ever read anything of his?

Thank you both for taking me in last April—it was wonderful.

Love,
Carol

September 10, 1981
North Vancouver

Dear Carol,

What a long time since I wrote! At first my excuse was the postal strike, then your trip to Hungary, and just talked to Sandy and hear you're off to Africa. You certainly are well travelled these days.

The reason I was talking to Sandy is that she asked me to do a small audit for the newly formed Federation of BC Writers, and so I asked her to come up today and have lunch with me. We had a wonderful talk—wishing you were with us—sitting outside, with lunch and a bottle of red wine.

---

*Adrian is a friend I had known in Ottawa and who also sat on the board of the Vanier Institute of the Family.

I'm pleased that you are thinking so positively of Lester & Orpen Dennys—did you decide on them? Everyone speaks very highly of them. Anne Macaulay that you met at Macmillan was the one who edited *Pretty Lady*—she worked for General Publishing then. She was a good editor, I thought, and we had a very good relationship. I would love to look at your manuscript when you finish it, and am glad that the suggestions last time helped.

Leslie is going with me to Ottawa and Montreal in a couple of weeks' time, when I go for Vanier Institute meetings.

We went to Smithers the first week in June, to visit Stephen and of course Katinka and Bill.* I had just finished reading *The Portable Jung*, and was very fired up about an inspired essay in it called "Answer to Job." To my surprise, Katinka had also been reading the same thing, but had progressed from Jung's ideas re the relationship of eastern and western modes of thought to a study of books on eastern philosophy and Zen. Katinka's father (who was an early Canadian poet, Carroll Aikins, from a Winnipeg family) in his last years was very much into eastern philosophy, and in fact donated his very large collection of books on the subject to UBC where it has, I'm told, formed the basis for their department on such things. Life forms strange patterns sometimes. Anyway, I'm still on my Jung kick, but if I ever feel I've completely understood him I'll dip into some of the eastern books she recommended. Oh yes, there is another essay in *The Portable Jung* about the creative process and its relation to the unconscious—remember when we discussed that? If you see the book around (pocketbook) you might find that an absorbing essay.

While there, Katinka gave me a novel to read that I found over-whelming—Penelope Mortimer's *The Home*. Do try and get it from the library. She writes a lot like Margaret Drabble, but the depth of feeling that she finally evokes in this seemingly simple and usually humorous book quite staggered me. I'd be interested in what you

---

*Smithers, B.C., is about 700 miles northwest of Vancouver. Katinka and Bill Clarke had spent a year in Vancouver when the Shieldses were there, and had now returned to their home in Smithers.

think. Besides that I've read Jack Hodgins' *Resurrection of Joseph Bourne*, and can see why it won the GG's award. It wouldn't be everybody's cup of tea though, not the kind of book I normally care that much for. On the other hand, it is brilliantly conceived, the characters are strong and wonderfully well drawn, the scenery is evoked with almost overwhelming clarity—scenery isn't the right word, more the sense of the place, the brooding and crazy spirit of it. At first I didn't care much for it and thought the beginning a bit amateurish, but after I got into it I got quite caught up in the odd characters, and the final bit of the book is very gripping, ending with a climactic dance scene that is masterful. After all this, have you read it? And if so, do you agree with any of the above? What else—oh yes, Doris Lessing's second sci-fi book, a reread of Henry James' *The Ambassadors* for my reading club, and now we're looking at Ibsen's *A Doll's House*. You asked if I'd read any Proust—yes, most of *Remembrance of Things Past* (in English, not French. I'm told that it is much more captivating in French, but I wouldn't be up to that. It's tough enough in English.) Actually, I enjoyed it greatly, but it certainly isn't in the modern idiom (any more than Henry James). You have to like 19th-century literature, I think, to enjoy either of them.

How I miss our talks on the phone! There isn't anyone else who is that interested in my career (or lack of it, in recent years). Also I miss our book discussions terribly. Do hope you'll be this way before too long.

All the best to Don.

Love,
Blanche

October 20, 1981

Dear Blanche,

I was so happy to get your letter, though I nearly cried when I realized that I'd miss you by just a week. I had already planned my trip to Vancouver—a mother-hen trip to check up on daughters—and didn't feel I could change it. My hope is that you will get to Winnipeg on one of your many trips across the country.

I do miss someone to talk books with; I've met people here, of course, but you and I always seem to have the same references. Penelope Mortimer's book *The Home* is wonderful!! I read it the year we were in France and can remember the sensations at the end—I sat at the kitchen table unable to move. The grief of it was simply transferred. I've looked at it since, just the ending, and nothing happened, so I can only think it is some wonderful kind of cumulative thing she did. Her (the character's) circle of human contact just grew smaller and smaller until it all but disappeared—and this seemed caused by random accident more than anything else. A book which gave me something of the same feeling is one by Hilma Wolitzer called *Ending*. Beth calls her the Jewish Alice Munro. By the way, I'm always impressed with the scope of what you read—the Jung study sounds like ambitious reading. Maybe reading novels all the time does soften the brain slightly.

I was pleased to hear your manuscript is out again—and in New York too—and hope that one morning the mailman comes up with some good and positive news. You didn't mention what you were working on at the moment—I'd love to hear. I am having a month off between novels and am loving it—am doing painting and pickling and all such domestic things. *Broad Daylight* (provisional title) [it became *A Fairly Conventional Woman*] went to Penguin last week. If they decide against it, I'll send it to Lester & Orpen Dennys. I know it needs editing and so—I hope it's still okay— I am mailing a copy off to you today. I would be interested in your suggestions. One paragraph is for Bruce—it is a kind of justification for novels which deal only *indirectly* with serious moral issues. Serious—now what does that mean?

All is well here. Margaret Atwood read from her new book last night and I had the job of introducing her. (I hope I didn't grovel too much.) It was a warm and witty reading, and I don't know when I've been to a reading that brought out 300 people. I was so impressed with the way she conducted the question and answer session. And in her velvet dress with embroidered yoke she seemed the kind of presence people delight in; she made it an occasion.

I haven't even mentioned the trip to Africa or the family, but must get to the paint store before the sale ends at noon. Shall save other news for next time. Please write.

Love,
Carol

November 11, 1981

Dear Carol,

It's been a couple of weeks since I finished your book but life has been rather hectic lately, so this is the first opportunity I've had to write. Just as well—I wanted to see if my first impressions held up, and give it time to filter down through the old psyche. First impressions have held up—it's a wonderful book, by far the best you've done, funny and warm, and I identify with the heroine and care about her. I loved it! In fact, I burst out laughing in several spots, but at the same time was touched where I should have been, and so on. Brenda is very believable and full of human foibles and just right.

I've been thinking a bit about the business of novels. It seems to me that novels have a dimension that one doesn't hear talked about a great deal (I suppose if I knew anything about the formal analysis of literature I'd find it full of this)—namely a cohesion outside the life of the actual writing and people and events. Sort of like crystal, a true novel should have a structure that is independent of the way the substance forms its molecules. Many fine writers don't quite do this—Alice Munro for instance, who writes so wonderfully and whose individual stories are masterpieces, doesn't write novels with this separate structure. To some extent I think that's the failing of *Joshua Then and Now*. Richler has tried to execute that structure independently of the individual parts but it hasn't quite come off because it's a bit too artificial. In this novel I think you've achieved that—given the story as a whole a cohesive existence outside the lives of the protagonists. I think *Box Garden* and *Happenstance* managed it, but to a lesser degree than this one does, although I can't quite put my finger on why.

[The thing] that bothered me about the scene [in which Brenda sleeps chastely with Barry] was the failure of consciousness on the part of Brenda. In my recent spate of psychology readings I've come across a definition of consciousness which is a bit different than the one we usually think of. Various philosophers and psychologists—Hannah Arendt, Jung, Rollo May—define consciousness as that ability peculiar to humans of standing outside themselves and contemplating their own selves as a differentiated being—e.g., the knowledge of one's own death, place in time, and so on. The old duality of man. So that, when a person behaves without reflection, they are acting unconsciously, as Brenda does in the scene with Barry. Margaret Atwood's heroine in *The Edible Woman* did a number of things that surprised her—she didn't know she would do them, she wasn't conscious, by this definition. I think that's what bothers me about Brenda in this case—up until now she has been a tremendously conscious person. In this one instance, however, she doesn't speculate—it seems to me that if she registered some element of surprise, for instance, as she speculates about her homecoming, would she think that there would have to be a time when she came to terms with her own actions? Or thinking it, would she register some surprise that it didn't (or did?) bother her in any way, that that seemed inconsistent with the kind of person she really was? She is a person who is aware of and interested in appearances, would she think to herself that the appearance of unfaithfulness was against her?

I'm not urging this, I'm merely mentioning the possibility. I'm not even sure that it's a good idea, all I know is that something tugged at me over that small scene, as though in some way it was unfinished.*

I was at a reception recently at UBC and met the dean of Arts and Science who said to me, "I never read novels, I'm afraid." (What else is new?) He enlarged to say he was a historian, and he thought that novels could tell him nothing that he couldn't find out better by reading the facts. I said, "Surely *War and Peace* would

---

*Three pages of detailed suggestions have been omitted.

give you some insights into the events surrounding the Russian invasion? Or at least the theories that Tolstoy advanced." He muttered something about there being some exceptions, but said that he thought fiction did little to enlarge the scope of the mind, that his wife disagreed with him and was a novel-reader. I remarked that it was a bit hard on the likes of Shakespeare who stuck to fiction, and his response was, "Ah, but my wife doesn't read Shakespeare, I'm afraid."

I must close. I do love this novel, and hope you get lots of positive response and enthusiasm from publishers.

All the best to Don.

Love,
Blanche
P.S. We have the boat (and a huge loan). Name *The Golden Bough*. (*Mandala* was taken.) Having an "Open Boat" on Saturday—wish you were here.*

March 1, 1982

Dear Carol,

It was lovely to come home from a fast cold trip to Ottawa and find your nice letter [to do with the suggestions for the novel], and ignore the guilt that I probably owed you one, but never mind, here I am. Your reason [for not going to the Writers' Union AGM] is so much more glamorous than mine!—and I think a 25th wedding anniversary really is a milestone of some sort—not quite sure what. In any case, I remember ours very clearly. It was while we were in Ottawa, and we went to Toronto to see *Hair*, which I disliked and Bruce liked. But we

---

*The boat was a 34-foot motor-sailor and the Open Boat was a near disaster when a record-breaking wind came howling in from the northeast. The boat—attached to an unstable mooring—rocked so violently that it was amazing there was only one bad case of seasickness, although there was one semi-serious accident that resulted in a broken nose. The food was heated and drinks poured under conditions that would have led lesser souls to abandon the whole thing and head for the nearest dry land.

had a wonderful time nevertheless, got together with old friends and drank far too much and somehow sort of confirmed that we'd go on together forever, at least it seemed like a sort of confirmation. (And here we still are, of course. Not cause and effect, I don't think.)

I enjoyed your article from Marian Engel and immediately felt better about the old and very deplorable jeans I wear. The two *Atlantic Monthly* reviews, [enclosed] I thought were very interesting, especially the analysis re whether John Irving is really writing literature or not. I haven't had the courage to read the *Hotel New Hampshire*, have you? Have just read a strange but brilliant French novel, *The Ogre*, by Michel Tournier, and am into Hugh MacLennan's *Voices in Time*. Am enjoying it greatly.

I'm pleased that Macmillan has taken your novel. I think they do a good job with serious writers, and certainly Louise Dennys' desire for subplot was a signal that you should be wary. Odd that editors can't accept that novels have an individual style, and that yours succeed precisely because of that individuality. I sometimes think people learn in university that novels have plots and subplots, and so they are thrown if that isn't the case.

Our lives go along much as usual, although the boat has represented a much greater drain on our resources—due to falling stock market and rising interest rates—than we ever anticipated, and this is the reason I've taken a two-month job doing income tax.

Am glad to hear you are reading Paul Scott [The Raj Quartet]— I thought he was wonderful, fusing really good writing with solid history.

I don't miss teaching this year, and have had a very busy year although I'm hard pressed to say what it is I've been doing. Rewriting the two novels, of course, babysitting a bit [for Allison], still on the Vanier Institute board and the Liberal Riding Association, and much more involved with the Unitarian Church than before.

Have a lovely time in France. I envy you a trip like that. Don't know how you keep up with everything, writing, teaching, family, the whole bit. My energy quotient isn't what it used to be, I'm afraid.

All best and love to you both,
Blanche

August 20, 1982

Dear Blanche,

Almost every morning there is a story in *The Globe* about B.C. politics—first the cabinet scandals and now this peculiar switching of parties. I wonder what you and Bruce make of it all. At least things are lively. I suppose they are here under the surface but we would never know about it.

I saw Adrian Lang not too long ago and she had the idea that you might be getting to Winnipeg in the not-too-distant future. Which is why I am writing: to persuade you, to offer you a room (we now have our first guest room ever), and to let you know I could do with your company should you get this way. It seems a long time since I've heard your news, and I'd love to know if you're writing at the moment or what? I'll be in Vancouver for the promotion in October and certainly hope to see you then. I am facing the publication with the usual trepidation. Actually, that's not quite true, thanks to a fairly hectic schedule and the fact that I'm well into a new novel which is proving a pleasure to work on and which, I like to think, is something of a departure. About writing, I'm feeling somewhat freed up at this time—not in terms of content but in terms of style and direction and shape. I've been reading the American writer William H. Gass and the British Henry Green, both of whom have given me confidence in a writer's ability to move more independently. I've always thought it was important to find one's own voice—and now it seems as important to find one's shape. A book I'm reading now, and one which I think you'd like, is *The Writer on Her Work*, a Norton paperback. I was particularly interested in Joan Didion's remark that she writes to find out what she's thinking. The essays are enormously varied in intent, some of them how-to's, some of them meditations or diaries. Wonderful.

Another book I've loved reading is Eileen Simpson's *Poets in Their Youth*. Wonderfully graceful. Heavens, this is a rambling paragraph.

Don and I had five weeks in France in the spring in celebration of our 25th anniversary. We also had Sara and Marg along. [After Paris we] went to Montpellier and settled down in a holiday flat on the beach owned by a friend of a friend. I wrote every morning on the sunny balcony and Don cultivated the fine art of doing nothing, finally, at age 47, kicking the work ethic. Or so he claimed. I think he was getting edgy toward the end. We've had three children here for the summer, but John goes back to McGill soon and Margaret is going off to York, leaving only Sara, poor child, at home. Strange new set of adjustments to make. But then, you know all about that.

Love,
Carol

August 25, 1982
Dear Carol,

I am going to be in Ottawa for about three weeks in November—wish you were still there—because I want to take advantage of a Vanier Institute trip to go to the Liberal convention, and they are inconveniently rather far apart. My friends are going to have their caring strained to the utmost by the time I wander around begging accommodation. But thank heavens I'm not going anywhere in October, and look forward immensely to a visit. Do try to stay here if you have time. Lucky you, with your book coming out—although as you say it's an emotional time, and while it sounds wonderful I remember that those were some of the worst times about writing a novel. (What are the good times? The writing of it, I guess—which makes for an argument—one which I can't quite buy—that one should write for the pure pleasure of it, and not for an audience.)

My life has been considerably hampered by the fact that I've now taken a job. I think I told you in the spring that I was going to go in and do tax returns. While there, they asked me if I would stay on part-time and go to work on their bookkeeping, which had been allowed to fall into disrepair. It was a tremendous challenge—straightening out and digging through systems is something I quite enjoy. However I can't do any writing—unfortunately, I don't seem to have the energy to do both, one of the hazards of aging I suppose.

You mention B.C. politics, and I must say they are rather despairing now. Bennett's answer to recession is to cut social services and challenge the unions. God knows how it will turn out. In the meantime, B.C. has been hit the most severely and suddenly of any province in the last while—we seemed recession-proof for so long that when it hit, the economy zoomed down. Unemployment is unbelievable, with tales of layoffs almost every week, not to mention bankruptcies, forced house sales, and so on. It doesn't look as though things may be bottoming out—interest rates hold the key of course, and one of the reasons I decided I must work was because we didn't want to take a beating on our stocks, but after buying the boat couldn't meet the interest on the loan without either selling them or bringing in additional income.* At first I thought this recession was unique in that the middle class were the ones hurting here, those who had borrowed to invest, but now with the closure of forest mills and mines it is hurting everyone.

I'm excited to hear that you are moving in new directions in your writing. I was listening to John Barth on CBC the other day and he ridiculed those writers (me) who say characters take over, but I think, as you say, a writer has to move independently, and what works for John Barth doesn't work for everyone. I think you have a great opportunity to develop, since your base is now strong enough to move in other directions. By the way, did you hear Margaret Atwood on the same program? She thinks the material of everyday life isn't sufficiently interesting to use for a novel. I think she's very wrong—not only are your novels a good example, but many of the greats—Tolstoy, Proust, to name a couple—D.H. Lawrence, *Sons*

---

*Interest rates went as high as 25%.

and Lovers—built their masterpieces precisely on the daily interaction of people in the ordinary society of their day.

Have you read *The White Hotel*? I loved it. Am now reading Anne Tyler—so far I like her very much. Joan Didion's remark, that you quoted—she writes to find out what she's thinking—is tremendously interesting. I sometimes think I talk to find out what I'm thinking—am often surprised at viewpoints I put into words that I didn't know I thought.

We had a memorable two-week cruise on the boat this summer with old friends from Toronto that we hadn't seen that much of in the last thirty years. That is one way to discover levels about yourself and others that you didn't know existed, and would perhaps not wish to know. Wonderful stuff for a novel, if you didn't care to keep your friends. One rather surprising thing—we didn't have a mirror on board, and though at first Ruth [Beatty] and I missed it greatly, we forgot about it and forgot what age we were supposed to be, and ended up behaving almost like adolescents, at least with an uproariness neither of us had remembered we possessed. Are reflections the true cause of behaviour changes as years go by?

All well here. Leslie has been dating a lawyer who is the son of Katinka. Katinka and I are delighted, and hope it leads to marriage.

I'm babysitting today, and like the mothers will be glad when school starts.

Best to Don and much love,
Blanche

December 1982

Dear Blanche,

Merry Christmas from Winnipeg. Isn't this an insane and hectic time of year—I both love and resent it, but I do love getting off a few letters—as well as getting some back.

All the children are coming home for Christmas. As you know, I think, we have only Sara with us this year. Rather odd. Don rather likes it, but I am still adjusting, and I don't think this is an easy

period for many people. I remember often what you once said
about getting out of the habit of wanting, of not even thinking
about it, and then suddenly finding it's too late. (I am filled with
gloomy thoughts this morning; perhaps I should go out for a brisk
walk. If only the wind-chill factor weren't 2000.)

I'm already looking forward to coming to Vancouver in early July
for the Women and Words conference at UBC. I am sure you must
be planning to attend. It will be a truly exciting affair, I think, a
landmark in a way. We're scrambling around here for travel funds
from the province—and feeling a little guilty in these tough
economic times to be asking for this kind of money.

Alice's [Munro] new book is full of wonderful things. I've heard it
described as "uneven" but I think this points to a new sense of experi-
mentation in some of her stories. She is certainly moving from rural to
urban and the "talk" in the stories reflects this to a great extent. I've
been reading Muriel Spark lately; her last book is such a delight, so
"jaunty." And I loved Updike's latest, as I think any writer would.
There's a wonderful chapter when the great writer comes to Toronto.

I'm working on some short fiction and plays this winter, setting
the novel aside. Writing plays is more fun than any writing I've ever
done and most of the ideas I get these days come to me in dramatic
form. I wish we had more of a theatre scene here, though we're
better off than many cities.

Don sends good wishes along to you both.

With love,
Carol

April 6, 1983

Dear Carol,

A person is definitely too busy when they haven't time to write
when a dear friend has a story published in *Saturday Night.*
Congratulations! And apologies for being this slow—I've become so
trapped in the rat race of my job that I have difficulty remembering
all my lectures against being trapped in rat races. The story was
really fine, and amusing too. It was a lovely sensitive story, my only

difficulty being that I had trouble with the male voice of the protagonist. Allison found the same thing, and we weren't sure whether it
was because we know you and at once translated the words into your
voice, or whether the characterization had a feminine slant. Has
anyone else mentioned this to you? The dialogue was very good and
the story moved along in a completely satisfying way.

I'm back in the business world with rather a vengeance. I've ended
up more or less running the place, at least the financial end of the
several associated companies we have in the group, and it isn't quite
what I want to do. (How would I know? I never seem to be doing
quite what I want to do, have come to the conclusion that I want to
do so many things that there will never be one right thing.) In any
case I've served fair warning that I'm winding down after the end of
our busy season. Not much writing getting done, although I did "sell"
(read give, or have accepted) one short story to *Cross-Canada Writers'
Quarterly.*

Your Christmas letter says you'll be out in early July, and I'm
looking forward to seeing you. Leslie and Austin (you may remember
Katinka's son, lawyer, known since childhood, one of the world's nice
people) are getting married July 2nd, and Aunt Blanche (now 80) is
coming out for the wedding and will stay with me a couple of weeks.
I haven't seen much of the writers' group because of my heavy work
involvement and my diminishing energy. Also with the dearth of
published material I was beginning to wonder if I should keep on
being a member.

Adrian mentioned that she'd talked to you. We had a strange time
at the last meeting of the Vanier Institute, as we decided to challenge
the executive director. The ensuing board meeting was straight from
the courtroom scene of *The Caine Mutiny,* do you remember when
Captain Queeg took the stand and blew under cross-questioning?
Our man revealed himself to be as paranoiac as Richard Nixon and
about as devious, but too many of the board members waffled and
we still have him. I'll tell you all about it sometime.

My reading is so far behind—you mention Updike and Muriel
Spark and I haven't even read either—so frustrating. I'm reminded of

you bursting into tears in London.* I think I told you how impressed
I was with D.M. Thomas' *The White Hotel*, although I have friends
who didn't like it at all. I am reading, but with no sense of direction.
Recently read a good new one of Walker Percy's, *The Second Coming*.
His stories are wonderful, but he repeats the same theme over and
over so that the novels all run together in my mind. (Who said, "I
love his novel. I always read it whenever he writes one"?)

In between all this, we do get out on the boat quite often,
went cross-country skiing a couple of times this winter, and Sunday
celebrated our 38th wedding anniversary, which seems impossible. In
May we are going to California, since in all the years we've lived in
B.C. we're never been there. Among the things we are going to do is
take a short five-day cruise from L.A., stopping in San Diego and in
Mexico for a day. I'm looking forward to the sheer indolence of it.

Must run. Give all my best to Don and the young.

Blanche

April 13, 1983

Dear Blanche,

First, my good wishes to Leslie. How wonderful, and how
strangely things work out. To think that you and Katinka are about
to become mothers-in-law to each other's children. I haven't met
Austin but perhaps I will in July.

I will be in Vancouver April 21–24, staying with either Anne or
Catherine before going up north for Book Week. I would have
written all this sooner but we have been through a rather difficult
time. Don has been ill since February and was finally operated on
a week ago Monday for an intestinal tumour. We think he's
making a good recovery and may even be home within the next

---

*This refers to a story Carol told about being in London many years earlier
when Don was finishing his studies and she read somewhere that Updike was
rated as being the finest writer in the United States. Carol at that time hadn't
even heard of him and burst into tears when she realized how far removed she
had become from the world of literature.

few days. He will have to take it easy for a few weeks, working only half days, etc.

Thank you for your kind words about the *Saturday Night* story. A funny aside is that I wrote and submitted it to last year's *Chatelaine* contest (under a male pseudonym) and got it back almost instantly. It was Bella Pomer [Carol's agent] who asked me if I had any stories around and she who submitted it to *Saturday Night*. Yes, someone else did mention that the narrative voice seemed more female than male. This is something I'll have to look at more closely, since I do like writing in the male voice occasionally. (Do you think there might be something wrong with me?) The other person who mentioned it also knows me, so that muddies things a bit; one of the reasons I wanted to write it under a male name.

I do have so many things to talk to you about: rat race, Adrian, writing, getting older, being selfish, Sandy, books, ups and downs, children and, of course, life, but will wait until next week when I very much hope you will have a couple of hours, more if possible.

Love,
Carol

August 23, 1983
North Vancouver

Dear Carol,

As I gather you've heard, I'll be in Winnipeg September 8th, and I gather we've all been invited to Adrian's for dinner on the night of the 7th.

I'm feeling a bit twitchy about the [Vanier Institute] meeting at that time as I'm having a big party to celebrate Leslie's marriage to Austin on the night of the 10th, but I'm telling myself that since it's being catered I have nothing to worry about. A new exercise in calmness?

Am dying to hear what you are up to. I'm finished my job except for a continuing consultation basis—about twice a month—and can hardly wait to get back to this typewriter.

All the best—looking forward greatly to seeing you.

Blanche

❧ This visit with Carol turned out to be fortuitous, since it was then that Carol suggested we co-author a novel. They lived in one of the lovely old houses in Winnipeg with wood paneling and a wide staircase from a large centre hall. Carol motioned to me to watch her cleaning lady do the dusting—one slow inch of the banister followed by another inch, done so painstakingly that we found ourselves holding our breaths and bursting with pent-up laughter when we went outdoors.

Carol remembered us as having made the decision to write the novel as we sat on the swing outside. "A novel of letters," we exclaimed, although at that time the epistolary novel was a form that was being shunned. Carol was the one who had noticed that as women were being liberated by the feminist revolution, couples were bound to come up against career conflicts, and so we decided to have our husband and wife faced with separation. Beyond that we didn't plan, which is the way I operate but was unusual for Carol. Usually she knew where she was going with her novels and was able to write three polished pages a day.

As I wrote in an essay in *Prairie Fire,*

Separation has never happened to either of us in real life. Unlike our protagonists, Carol and I have settled quite happily wherever our husbands have taken us. This may be due in part to the social strictures of the times that shaped us; I was a young wife and mother in the early fifties while Carol was still an adolescent (by the end of the decade she was married with two small children). At a time when housework and husband-support was raised to what Galbraith dubbed a "convenient social virtue," it seemed a natural thing to do and be. Indeed to yearn otherwise carried social disapprobation. When entering a hospital in labour, Erma Bombeck attempted to have "writer" entered under vocation, but a no-nonsense nurse scratched it out and put in "*housewife.*"

3

Ambition

1983–1984

And so began Carol's and my ambitious project to co-author a novel. Other than having in mind the rough outline of separation brought on by our fictional husband's and wife's conflicting careers, we had no idea about where we were going or how to get there. Carol had expressed a wish to write the part of the man and early in the game she came up with the title, *A Celibate Season*, which was our one plot determinant. We hadn't even thought about what our protagonists would be called, and as I went through a list of possibilities I remembered a friend named Jocelyn upon whom the nickname "Jock" had descended. (One reviewer thought this was a deliberate attempt to give Jock a name that would nudge the reader into an awareness of role reversal.)

Because Vancouver was suffering from a recession at the time and architects were scrambling for work, Chas became an architect, thus giving the couple a good reason for Jock to accept the position of legal counsel for a Royal Commission on the Feminization of Poverty. I started the ball rolling by sending off a letter from Jock when she first arrives in Ottawa, ensconced and lonely in the faded luxury of the Château Laurier. Carol's return letter from Chas introduced new characters and situations to which I now had to adjust, thus establishing a pattern that took on an enigmatic life of its own, and one that gave us an enormous amount of fun as we lobbed curves at one another and slid around them with the next instalment.

Co-authoring an artistic endeavour of any sort is fraught with the potential for damage to the relationship. Gilbert and Sullivan, for instance, were renowned nearly as much for the depth and ferocity of their animosity as for their witty lyrics, and at the annual writers' festival in Sechelt one of the audience asked Carol if she and her collaborator were still on speaking terms. We were; on the occasions when Carol and I were able to go over the manuscript together we were diligent and focused, and demurrals were more often than not over the placement of commas or the occasional upstart semicolon. If anything, far from driving us apart, the writing of the novel cemented our friendship.

September 13, 1983

Dear Carol,

That was a terribly unsatisfactory phone call from the airport—up until just before I phoned there had hardly been a soul in the whole building, and no sooner did I get you than they must have unloaded a 747. Hope I didn't sound too vague—only heard about every second word. (I suppose I'm getting to the "Speak up don't mumble" stage.)

Anyway, I loved having a visit with you, and am thinking about our great project [the novel we had decided to write together]. I'm sure it was you who urged me to read *Between Friends*, by Gillian Hanscombe, wasn't it? In any case, I'm just starting it, and as you no doubt know it is in the same format as we've discussed, letters between two friends. Allison said she absolutely loved it—the best book she'd read in years, so I'm looking forward to it.

The party Saturday night was very successful, I think.* Sixty-five people in this house is a mite crowded, but no one seemed to

---

*A party to celebrate Leslie and Austin's wedding.

mind, and my caterers did a superb job. I was, needless to say, quite weary afterwards but am recovered now and on my way to Ottawa tomorrow, then to Toronto and Calgary with Bruce. Sometimes Iwonder if the jet is an unmixed blessing—think howmuch simpler it must have been for Jane Austen to schedule her time.

John Aikins (Austin's uncle and head of the Law Reform Commission) remembers [Carol's daughter] Anne* very well, and said that she is a very bright young person and that he thought highly of her. He was quite enthusiastic in his response.

Must run. *Many* thanks for your great hospitality.

Love to Don too.
Blanche

October 16, 1983
North Vancouver

Dear Carol,

Well, here's chapter one, and I can't tell you how much more fun it is to write something for someone else's eyes than just to write for the faceless mass who may or may not read it. I kept thinking, Will Carol like this? And she'll laugh at that, and so on. I think it's a great idea and can hardly wait to hear what response the husband gives.

I'm not sure if I remembered the names we decided on correctly, and whether you will like the nicknames I gave them.

I think this will work very well, as the two styles will be dissimilar. I think it will also have the advantage of having three different story lines, the development of what happens to her in Ottawa, to him in Vancouver, and to their relationship. If we can bring all that off!

Well, must run and photocopy. If you get a chance to scribble a note, I'll be anxious to hear if you like the start.

Love,
Blanche

---

*Carol's daughter Anne worked there during the summer while studying law.

October 21, 1983

Dear Blanche,

Chapter one arrived today and I love it, all of it—and my only-worry is trying to respond with the same vigour. First, here are the general things I liked: the sense of voice, her voice, which you seem to have established in the first paragraph. It seems to me a likeable voice but with enough edges to keep her interesting and enough open curiosity (almost innocence) to make her the reader's eye into the Ottawa world. Next, I like the lively surface texture. As they say in show biz, it moves right along. Next, I like the tone, the honesty of a delicate vulgarity but the essential decency. And then I like the fact that you've established what I presume are to be the main characters in the first few pages.

Your reference to "feminists" gave me pause, but then I realized you were setting her up for her conversion. I very much like the fact that you've established that they *do* have a robust sex life. The rotten teenagers [remark] had the kind of truth about it that makes her seem utterly perceptive and unique. I also liked the fact that you didn't let the letter writing mode keep you from dialogue—and all the dialogue was delightful.

We didn't talk about the time of the story, whether it's this year or what. But this year might be perfect, at least from the point of view of Chas in Vancouver suffering under the Bennett regime. (I don't think there's any point in hiding our politics, do you?) All is well, fall is here, Ian (my pseudonym) has had 2 acceptances!* Now *he* is a serious writer!

Love,
Carol

November 1983

Dear Blanche,

Here at long last is Chas's letter. One problem was that it was harder than I thought it would be. I think I thought it would be as

---

*Carol, testing what she thought might be gender-related discrimination, had begun sending out her poetry under a pseudonym.

simple as rattling off a letter. In fact, it was as hard as a, well, a novel. All the "seeding" done. My feeling is that it will get easier. I also found it hard to measure up to the lively adventurous tone of Jock's letter. I'm still not entirely happy with Chas. I don't think he's quite likeable enough, but I suppose I can touch him up later.

My other reason for being slow is that I got into one or two other writing projects. One was a series of short stories I wrote—all rather short and weird and unlike anything I've done before. It was one of the best creative periods I've had in some time and I was reluctant to stop. (I hope Bella [Carol's agent] can place some of these stories—she is very pleased with them.)

And now here is my good news. I've won the CBC Literary Award for Drama for this year—for a little play I entered in their competition last summer and then forgot all about [*Women Waiting*]!* They are bringing me to Toronto next week for what they call a mini–academy award night. This is all very exciting and exactly what I needed at this time—I love to write plays! I will have a chance to sit down and talk to Bella, and am wondering if I should mention our project to her. Perhaps it would be better to wait a bit. I do feel it will go. My one worry is the timing. By the time we finish and it gets between covers, some of the Bennett–B.C. stuff may seem stale. (But the Ottawa material will not. By the way, did you read about Heather Menzies' comments on women being thrown out of work by technology?—I thought she was very brave and intended to write to her but . . .)

Anne took advantage of the seat sale and spent a week here in Winnipeg with us—she was here when the strike was settled in B.C. She got me caught up on the state of affairs there and the very high level of emotional feeling. (She was very nearly run down by a professor's car when she was on the picket line out at UBC.) Catherine had to cross the picket line at Simon Fraser U in order to hand in a paper and it was a wrenching experience for her,

---

*Carol's radio drama *Women Waiting* won first prize in the CBC annual literary competition.

especially when she saw friends in the line. I can see how personally affected thousands of people were. What is your feeling about
the settlement—and about the future of the Bennett regime?
Anne felt *The Globe and Mail* has not given the B.C. situation
the coverage it should have, and so I imagine we have a very
incomplete picture. (As for the Winnipeg paper, it is very local,
and our plebiscite is what has captured attention all fall.)

Our first snow arrived last night, lovely.

All best,
Carol
P.S. Let me know what you think about Chas. He is a bit crude and
pompous but I hope life will knock some of the rough edges off
him later.

November 24, 1983

Dear Carol,

Am thrilled with Chas, in spite of your reservations! I love the fact
that his voice is so entirely different from Jock's, and I think that's
why this novel should be unique. I write in rather a breezy open style
so that Jock's character comes over that way, as you mentioned, and
you write with more observation and a sort of interior questioning,
which makes Chas come to life as perhaps somewhat more intro-
verted and thoughtful, a wonderful counterpoise to Jock—and it's
easy to see why they would be happily married and why he would
be the type of man who is able to accept the unconventional arrangement that their lives have forced on them. And there was so much
quiet humour in Chas's letter—I found myself chuckling aloud
repeatedly, and again your humour is more subtle than my brand,
so that again we have a nice balance. Oh I think this is going to work
so well—except now it's my turn to be nervous about whether I can
maintain the standard you've set.

But before I get into specifics, I'm so excited about you winning
the CBC drama award! Really, you are having a wonderful creative
spell, what with the two acceptances that "Ian" has had and the plays

that are going forth. I'd love to take a turn at writing a play sometime—people have often told me I should, since dialogue is fairly easy
for me—and maybe if this comes off we might try one together. Since
the Vanier Institute thing, I keep thinking of one called *Member of the
Board*, and maybe will find time one day. Time is my enemy right
now—as usual, even though I've quit work, I've gotten myself too
involved with numerous things that erode the writing time, but I
might as well face the fact that I'm an extroverted person and so will
probably always do this to myself. Having my 60th birthday did not
help, even though Allison and Leslie threw the most wonderful party
for me, 14 people for a sit-down dinner and a complete surprise. I got
so angry about the B.C. political situation that I fired off many letters
to the editor, all of which were published—one way to get published,
I suppose, although not what I'd hoped for.

By the way, it wouldn't hurt to mention our project to Bella. I had
a thought which is probably wildly optimistic, but here it is. You
remember in the late 19th century that it was the custom for magazines to publish novels in instalments—Dostoevsky published *Crime
and Punishment* that way, and *The Brothers Karamazov*. I got thinking
that with our format, it would be an interesting thing if a magazine
could be found that would be willing to revive the idea—I suppose
there isn't a Canadian one that would consider it, although it's just
possible (remotely) that *Saturday Night* might like the experimental,
or traditional (take your pick) aspect of it. What do you think?

Do try to have a day available [in Vancouver] when just you and
I can talk and work this over. I want to get you and Don of course
over for dinner, naturally, and so we'll mull all of that over when
you get here.

By the way, do you have any copies of your poetry book
Others that you would like to sell? If so, Allison would very much
like to buy one. Also, would you mind bringing a copy of your
Susanna Moodie thesis? Allison has been taking a course at
Capilano College and has done (or is doing) a paper on pioneer
novels, and would love to read it if you don't mind loaning it for
a few days.

I loved [your chapter] and can hardly wait to answer, yet have this nervousness about making it come off. Looking forward immensely to your visit!

Love,
Blanche

January 8, 1984

Dear Blanche,

I was so glad to get Jock's letter (as well as yours and Allison's) and, no, I don't think the description of the apartment is too long. I love it, and think I read between the lines her joy in having, for a change, a place which is entirely her own.

I agree, too, that temporary separations for reasons of work are more commonly accepted than Bruce or Don think,* and that we needn't make a big thing about rationalizing it.

Please tell Allison that I've ordered the copy of *Others* and will send it along next time. I am awfully flattered that she enjoyed it— it seems such a long time ago now.

I'm returning *Between Friends* which I read with a great deal of interest—and I liked the idea of a round robin of letters. I was disturbed though by the intensity of the relationships between the women and what looked often like a wish to control each other. It also introduced feminist ideas which were new to me and which some-times seemed paranoid—the non-penetration stricture, for instance.

It was so good of you and Bruce to invite us on Christmas Day and then again for dinner. I think it's important to let our letters [between Chas and Jock] generate their own themes.

This is so much fun!

Love,
C

---

*It seems that Don and Bruce had been emphatic about the impossibility of sustaining a marriage that involved a lengthy separation.

January 14, 1984

Dear Carol,

Chas's new letter is superb—I found him wonderfully warm (remember, you worried that he didn't come through that way the first time? He does now), and I also got the strong feeling of masculine disorder (the beds, etc.), or just plain masculinity, the different viewpoint from a woman's, and in fact I'm very excited about it. Now I'm wondering if I can keep up the standard, but I think it's so good to have two such different voices and viewpoints. As you say, this is the most fun I've had in years, writing.

I just finished [Ellen Godfrey's] excellent book on the Belshaw case, *By Reason of Doubt*. Do read it if you get the chance, it's in paperback. Now I have a number of accounting jobs and a lot of Liberal jobs, so I'm glad I got a bit ahead on letter material as I'm anxious for us to maintain the momentum now, aren't you?

Great seeing you, my best to Don.

Blanche

February 3, 1984

Dear Blanche,

I've just finished a most wonderful book which both you and Allison would like. It's an early feminist novel called *The Odd Women* written by someone called George Gissing in 1897. I liked the feminist views and, of course, it was a delight to be imbedded in a Victorian novel again, all those tea parties and letters and calling cards and suppers and walks in gardens and misunderstandings, the richness of it all. He talks rather a lot about "ladies" and lower-class women, and I couldn't help thinking that things haven't changed so much, though I suppose society is much more fluid now.

I am worried about profanity. In my zeal to effect masculinity, have I got too many "hells" and "goddamns"? I don't want him to sound "loud." He is not the sort of man to wear a plaid suit but sometimes I feel he sounds like it. Am also hoping I have the chronology of [political] events in Vancouver more or less right. I've a few old *Maclean's* articles and am leaning on those. You may have an anecdote or two to toss in.

California was hot and sunny, and we stayed in a part of San Diego which was a little like Kits,* a trifle ragged about the edges but with a wonderful beach. We had many walks along the sand, ate wonderful California food, saw a couple plays, bought old Canadian books in a little second-hand bookstore, slept late, etc. We are restored! And I came home to the good news that my stage play will be produced by one of the small theatres here in Winnipeg next fall. For some reason this has given me a sense of a new beginning, just what I need halfway through my 48th year.

Allison's five-dollar cheque was too large and so I've sent *Intersect* along. It is so badly bound that it will disintegrate on the second reading.** Shame!

Love,
C

                                                    February 17, 1984
Dear Carol,

Re your question about whether you are using too much profanity—no, I don't get Chas coming over "loud," in fact I find him wonderfully masculine in the best sense. There was only one thing that bothered me, and I had rationalized it away until Allison read it and was struck by it, and that was the statement that Sue's sexual abuse team sounded "hare-brained and far-fetched." Remember when I said I reacted with anger and then dismissed it? Well, Allison found it too strong too—she thinks he should show the usual masculine lack of awareness of such problems, but not be quite so denunciatory—perhaps some comment

---

*Short for Kitsilano, a district in Vancouver.

**The fly-leaf of the small book reads, "For Allison, our resident critic. With thanks, Carol Shields."

that, for a problem that must be so rare, it seems like a fair financial commitment. She also pointed out that in my letter when
I say Gil must be lonely (or queer), nobody uses "queer" any
more and it should be "gay."

I'm enclosing copies of the letters (all published) that I sent to
various newspapers during the [B.C.] strike, hoping that they
may help you with the atmosphere and also might give you something to quote from. When the teachers went out, tension was
very high, and people began stopping by picket lines to either
revile or nourish the strikers. Some teachers contemplated signs
("Don't feed me any more") and so on. In some schools where
the ideology was badly split, there is still bitterness between those
who crossed the lines and those who didn't. I think that is why,
ever since the strike ended (sometime in November, I don't have
the date unfortunately), there hasn't been a word from anyone.
I think the level of anger actually frightened people—so
un-Canadian. [Further comments on the B.C. political situation
omitted.]

Must go. I'm excited about our work and just wish I hadn't
got myself so involved in Liberal Party politics this year, but that's
the way it goes.

Love to all,
Blanche

March 10, 1984

Dear Carol,

[I] thought you recreated the B.C. situation wonderfully.
Especially liked Davina—applying butter like a professional
plasterer. Allison has "Good" written all over it, but to my
surprise commented that it hadn't gripped her quite as much as
previous letters, and I wondered if we need to feed in a bit of a
hook—don't know what to suggest, especially since all individual
scenes are wonderful. We can maybe ponder that when we get
together.

Your life sounds wonderful and hectic like mine—Liberal involvement very great but exciting, and I will be a delegate to the leadership. We are working in a week in Bermuda just before Easter, because we both have trips east just before. Hope to do writing then. Am gradually working my way through accounting commitments, and hope to keep up the current pace with our letters. This one is a bit on the short side, but will make up for it next time.

Love,
Blanche

March 29, 1984
bright, sunny, springlike

Dear Blanche,

I'm somewhat uneasy about this chapter—about the direction and tone of it—but am anxious to send it off because I'm entering one of those frighteningly busy periods.

Blanche, I think it's wonderful that you're going to the leadership convention. Can we, do you think, use (borrow) some of the tension of the leadership race in our novel?

The big news is my play which—I probably told you this—will be workshopped in a public performance in mid-April. We "go into rehearsals" Monday and stick at it for two weeks. All most exciting for me, but playwriting has its negative side—you can't just mail it off to a publisher but, in fact, have to see it through, and this means you can't start on anything new. I do get paid for this which is nice, and I'm sure I'll learn a great deal. What is the news of your novel? I don't know how you can do this plus your Liberal Party work. Our friend Charles Huband (former Liberal leader here) is sure it will be [John] Turner. Don and I think Turner has changed in the last ten years, or maybe we have. Did he always speak in the jerky and artificial manner or is that a Bay Street mannerism?

Had better dash. I do appreciate Allison acting as sounding board.

Carol

April 5, 1984

Dear Carol,

[This chapter] is more than somewhat rough, but I thought to keep up the impetus I'd get it off before we go. We both have meetings in the east next week and found that we could go on to Bermuda for very little extra, so are spending ten days there.

A thought about the Christmas vacation disaster [in our novel]. What if Chas decides to surprise her and begin those changes he was talking about to the house before she comes home? Christmas would be terribly cold in the house—he might have opened some of it up to the air and covered it with plastic. She of course would be mad as the devil about changes without her consultation. (Know of a woman that happened to—it may finish the marriage yet.)

My political involvement has been frenetic. As a riding president my phone rings all the time, [and] today I was interviewed (by phone) by *The Globe and Mail*, *Maclean's*, and CBC Radio. Have had prior interviews with *The Toronto Star* and Southam—our own papers are on strike. Not the personal type of interview, but these people are doing a general overview of what presidents think. Also having my vote solicited (personal meetings with Mark McGuigan and John Turner at the weekend B.C. convention) and in addition on Saturday are having the first delegates selection meeting in Canada, I think. We leave Sunday and I haven't yet even checked through my failing wardrobe. I've never heard a thing from Ellen Godfrey [of Porcupine Press]— obviously my novel didn't set them on fire. Just as well, as I've been too busy to do anything about it. I've had a lot of well-paid accounting to do this year and like you, feel I should earn something occasionally instead of spending it running around the country to interesting things.

All best, and to Don,
Blanche

᳁Carol and I went to the Writers' Union AGM in Ottawa, where we slipped out of workshops and meetings to sit in the sun on any handy bench and work on the novel.

May 22, 1984

Dear Blanche,

You'll find this [chapter] short and rather rough—I was anxious to get it off so we could get into our post-Christmas correspondence or, more accurately, into the fray.

I've just got back from my travels, and nothing could possibly dislodge me from the hearth—or the porch rather. How distracting it all has been with only a tiny percentage of pleasure attached to it. I want to do a number of projects, some of them, oddly enough, of a domestic nature. I am dying to get some bedding plants in and clean out some drawers. Is this just conditioning, do you suppose? What we are accustomed to do in the spring of the year? It's lovely here. Last night the lilacs came into bloom, wonderful. I am reading a book which Don bought in the States. It is Simone de Beauvoir's final interview and essay with Sartre. Rather sad reading and curious, though I don't know why, to find that the famous are as wracked with petty physical ailments and ridiculous grudges as the rest of us. I'm also reading Virginia Woolf's letters, the third volume which somehow I missed. Have you delved into all that? Sometimes the voice is wonderfully fresh and other times a kind of petition or cry to be noticed.

I can't tell you how much I loved our long talks in Ottawa.

Love,

C

May 23, 1984

Dear Carol,

Wasn't it great to be able to get together in Ottawa? When I got home I reread the entire manuscript to date and found that it hangs together very very well—in fact, I think many of our doubts about lack of description and so on are groundless, since it speeds right along when you go through it, and of course we'd been concentrating on each small part and had lost the vision of the whole. I loved the way it hung together after a thorough read.

Allison told me she thought that if either partner fell by the wayside we should re-think the title *A Celibate Season*—although I've always loved that. She thinks that no matter what happens it either gives the story away or gives false expectations—what do you think?

I am also enclosing the story of mine that appeared in *Cross-Canada Writers' Quarterly*—it's been so long since anything was published that I thought you might like to see it.

I came home from the W.U. conference with rather a bad taste in my mouth, as we discussed—I think it had to do with the surroundings as much as anything, and the unpleasant cafeteria for the big night. No place to escape the noise. Also the B.C. Boys were a pain in the butt, to paraphrase Jessica [a character in the novel].*

Now for the hard part—getting that post-Christmas letter together. My best to Don.

Love,
Blanche

June 4, 1984

Dear Carol,
[Details of the plot of *A Celibate Season* omitted.]
Don't forget to send your address in France: I'm off next week to the great leadership convention—like you, I'm tired of travelling,

---

*For some reason, the somewhat macho atmosphere of this particular AGM had upset us both. I remember Carol being quite indignant after the banquet because she had been seated beside a man who talked the entire time about his projects and never once asked her what she was writing. Carol and I also lamented that those who were dancing were hanging onto all the old conventions—women lined up on chairs waiting to be asked. I stayed in a rather rundown residence at the University of Ottawa, with four bedrooms opening onto a common room. The B.C. contingent had decided to whoop it up until all hours, and finally, thinking that in all the ruckus no one would recognize my voice, I shouted from my cell-like room to tone it down. Not only was I recognized but I had to put up with shouts of "Come on, Blanche, come out and join the party!"

but this should be fun. Wish I could pick up the phone and talk to you as of yore.* Am finally getting things back together, overdid it hacking the blackberry and alder and putting out bedding plants and pulling up small trees—which grow around here like weeds. Terrible cold rainy May, June ditto so far.

Love,
Blanche

June 5, 1984

Dear Blanche,

How extraordinary it was to be watching the news the other night and suddenly see you in the middle of the screen, rising to your feet to applaud Don Johnston. Amazing.**

I am so glad you felt, in rereading, that the book is standing up and that the pace seemed about right. I don't think we can slow down this type of book too much if we want the breezy feel of letters. I will sit down and do this as soon as I have a chance. At the moment I'm on a committee planning a Women and the Arts Festival for two years down the line and also reading a first novel for a writer friend here and also [there] will be a short story in next month's *Canadian Forum*. Yours in *WQ* was a most complex story and I liked the complex way you unfurled it—taking your time, setting it up, etc.

Winnipeg looks lovely despite the canker worms which are everywhere, falling on our heads and squishing underfoot. I can never believe that all this green can come back after a Manitoba winter—but it does! Onward. You to Ottawa—have a tremendous time and take notes.

Love to Bruce as well as you,
Carol

---

*At that time long distance rates were very high, so Carol and I seldom indulged.

**This was the Liberal leadership convention at which John Turner was elected.

June 18, 1984

Dear Blanche,

I kept looking for you on TV last week and though I didn't see you, I imagined you were having a magnificent time. The number of women there was impressive, though some of those interviewed were not. I am afraid I am not convinced that John Turner is uniquely gifted to govern our country. He has a fine head of silver hair, and I fear that image was all in this race. It was all exciting drama and there were many grand moments. If you have time, I'd love a personal view.

This chapter was written in great haste, I'm afraid. (I hope it will further fan your fury.) As you can imagine we're upside down getting ready to go away. The house is rented and that means I've had to clean cupboards, etc. that I haven't touched for four years. (I've found this oddly satisfying.) We are very much looking forward to it. Don and I are watching the French news and trying to get our ears attuned. Onward!

Love,
C

July 1, 1984

Dear Carol,

Dominion Day—sorry, Canada Day—is soggy and cold—ten degrees, which has been the unremitting temperature since May 1st. I hope France is better—lucky you!

The convention was wonderful and noisy and exhausting and fun. I came home and promptly went to bed for two days with the flu. My 81-year-old aunt visits me every summer and is here now for two weeks, so I try to work in the afternoons when she has her nap but it isn't easy. In addition, it now looks as though Iona [Campagnolo] will run in our riding, and [John] Turner today committed himself to run in B.C., so if they call the election sooner rather than later I will be hurling myself into the fray. Let's face it, politics is an adrenaline-producing high for me defying all rationality.

Well, must go and try to get started on typing up this letter, before Aunt Blanche wakes up.

Au revoir and love to both,
Blanche

July 11, 1984

Dear Carol,

Scribbling this hurriedly in the middle of great election fever. In case you haven't heard in the depths of France, the election call is for September 4th and Iona is running in our riding. I am co-chairman of the election campaign. So much for the summer.

Being chairman of the campaign means that I'm not involved in the day-to-day operation of the thing, but as a trouble-shooter and the one who sort of keeps things on the line in both the North Van and Burnaby offices. So I'll still have time to work steadily on the novel in between meetings. The only question is will Bruce survive my continual absence?

Hope you're having a productive and relaxed summer. My best to Don.

Cheers,
Blanche

August 1, 1984
Tours, France

Dear Blanche,

We arrived yesterday and all three of your letters were here, two of them mysteriously forwarded from Bouaye. You've given me much to work with, and I am once again enjoying getting down into my other persona. I thought your description of the erotic atmosphere on the plane absolutely first rate, a difficult and nebulous sensation to wrap words around and I do feel you've done it. We will, of course, have to do some mending and polishing—and other bits of altering at the end.

Well, Blanche, yes we did know about the election—it was in the English papers, first page news in some, and we are sorry to be missing the excitement but very glad we're getting home two days before the actual election. I can't imagine how all this will turn out—no doubt you have your predictions. We have had a very chopped-up first month, some time in Wales, Brittany, Paris and very little actual time in Bouaye. Now we're settled into a lovely modern apartment just around the corner from the French course and nothing will budge us for a month. Don and I, shaking like a pair of fools, took the placement test this morning and Sara was appalled at the sight of her parents being cowed by such a thing. Results tomorrow.

Just before leaving I was notified of a small Manitoba arts grant and immediately ran out and bought this smashing little typewriter that does everything. (I was a little ashamed of my electric greed when I visited Jane Austen's house two weeks ago—her writing table was 18 inches across in the corner of the family parlour and had her quill and pot of ink, etc.)

Good heavens, I'm running on and on and not saying anything. France is wonderful, beautiful, *il fait beau*, etc. Give my love to Bruce and tell him to hang in there, you'll return!

Onward Liberals!

Love,
C

August 1984
[France]

Dear Blanche,

It's pouring rain, *comme les chiens* as they say here, but Don's promised to take this to the post office if I hurry.

We're now into our French classes, after the humiliation of the test. I am not quite at the bottom this time; Don is at the top but is exhausted after a morning of trying to keep up. We ask ourselves now and then why we're putting ourselves through all this. My class, though, is a wonderful assortment of people, a Baptist U.S. minister, a nun from Colombia, an Italian businessman, numerous beautiful Scandinavian girls, a Korean art historian, a Syrian doctor, and a Canadian track star—so he told us anyway.

Hope all is well. Anne arrived last night and brought us up to date on the election.

Love,
C

August 15, 1984
[France]

Dear Blanche,

This is rather a rough copy. I am on my last typewriter ribbon and not sure I can buy another in Tours, and so am trying to make it last.

Today is a national religious holiday with everything shut up tightly. Anne and Sara are off on a cycle trip along the Loire and so it is very quiet in our apartment, just my typing and the sound of Don groaning over his French homework—he is taking his studies more seriously than I am and is, of course, profiting (as the French love to say). We love Tours and are feeling at home here after just two weeks. The days go by so quickly with our course, our touring around (though we are châteaux-saturated) and our other work. I spend most afternoons writing, working on my short stories which are coming quickly—but is this good or bad? I've just finished my first science fiction piece. Anne says it is not really science fiction. Whatever it is it is a departure and fairly exhilarating. I'd like to do two more stories before we leave Tours [at the end of the month].

We are off to our favourite café for our late afternoon coffee. What I like about France, and miss so in Winnipeg, is the street life, the musicians, the people out for a walk, all of it.

Love to Bruce and to you too,
Carol

August 30, 1984

Dear Carol,

Your summer in France sounds wonderful and I wish ours had been as good. The weather here was great and we had one wonderful week on the boat with the cousins from Boston, but otherwise the campaign has been hard slugging and discouraging. At this point it doesn't look too hopeful that Iona will win. The campaign was complicated by having one shitty little man . . . and he has caused untold grief. He indulges in back-biting and accusations, bad-mouthing and well-covered woman-hating. (Do you get the impression that I'm not crazy over him?) He is a carbon copy of the guy that I shaped the Manipulator* after, so perhaps I'm overreacting. Anyway, it hasn't made for a great spirit. On top of that Bruce had to have a small operation and was in hospital ten days. His brother John had to have heart surgery and hovered in intensive care for five days.

Everyone is well again now, or at least John is mending slowly and now the only thing I'm waiting for is for Leslie to have her baby which was due on the 22nd. She is so tired of waiting and having people phone every day to see if she's still with us.

Am delighted to hear of your short story collection and arts grant. We had thought we might finish [the novel] in September but that looks a bit optimistic. What I would like you to consider, though, is when you would like to see me in Winnipeg (assuming you aren't coming to Vancouver).

This will be my last Vanier Institute meeting unfortunately as my six years are up.

Welcome back to Canada, and the best to Don.

Love,
Blanche

The Manipulator won the Canadian Booksellers Association Award for outstanding first novel.

August 1984
[Winnipeg]

Dear Blanche,

Bella insists I have my whole short story collection typed and ready by the third week of September—when I go to Toronto. Otherwise she doesn't see a spring publication which is what she's hoping for. (You can see I have let her take over my life.) I am a slow and plodding typist and still have revising to do on two stories, and so I am settled in for a solid two weeks— yet I can't bear to hire a typist since it is too expensive and prevents me from my last-minute attempts to touch things. By the way, we loved your comment "I'll be doing quite a bit of grandmother stuff with the new baby." Hope all goes well with Leslie—probably already has, also hope Bruce is recuperating and that your political lacerations are not causing you any difficulty.

I must go to bed. Teaching, typing and just settling back in has been exhausting. But, oh, it's lovely to be home. My children accuse me of kneeling down and kissing the front lawn—which I don't—but I can understand the impulse. Do you have a date for November—can you let me know as soon as possible?

Love to all,
Carol

September 17, 1984

Dear Carol,

Leslie's baby is a girl (Katherine after Katinka). All is well but a bad labour. Election was awful—much gossip when I see you. I'm managing to write ahead a bit so will whip the next one off when I get your note.

Love,
Blanche

September 28, 1984

Dear Carol,

You'll be surprised to get these very rough drafts of future letters, but I have had a bit of free time lately so decided to work ahead a bit in order to get my own plot figured out in my mind, and it occurred to me that they might be of help to you in working through what Chas is saying.

All is well here. We've had a beautiful summer and fall, every day great sunshine so that we've all been lulled into thinking it hardly ever rains in Vancouver. I didn't end up doing as much grand-mother stuff as I expected, as Leslie and Austin had themselves well organized—there is something to be said for this business of being older when beginning parenting.

Your life sounds hectic these days, and I hope the trip to Toronto at least resolves one of the pushes. As for me, I'm trying not to be quite so involved in outside activities, and hope not to work too much [at accounting] this winter. It's not that I'm slowing down (perish the thought) but I find it very hard to work and do anything creative. It's all I can do to get in some writing when not working.

Love,
Blanche

September 28, 1984

Dear Blanche,

I am feeling very bad about being so slow. There has never been a month like this and I hope there never will be again. I like my time leisurely and unscheduled, and very much hope that sanity will come back. I am, however, making two trips this month, one to New Brunswick and one to Toronto, but feel that I can keep up our writing schedule in between.

Like you, I sat down and read through the whole book and am pleased at the solid way it seems to hang together. My only concern is with your last chapter. However, as I said, I don't know where it's going. What does Allison say or has she read it? I think she might have some thoughts. I know you have a purpose, which is why I am hesitant to say too much.

Love to you and Bruce—in haste,
Carol

October 8, 1984
Dear Carol,

I just finished making my plane reservations, and hope I'm not spending more time in Winnipeg than you can afford. I'm delighted that the play will be on the weekend and really want to see it—if you and Don don't want to go again, I have no problem about going alone.

Your life sounds hectic these days, like mine was last winter and this summer. Finally things seem to have settled a bit and I'm enjoying having time to read a bit again—perhaps will actually get down to more writing, who knows? I'm hoping not to work at accounting this winter, but things usually seem to come up. Mary Mahoney and son Michael (at UBC law school, second year) were up for Thanksgiving dinner last night, along with family and grandchildren—the baby fussed throughout, Leslie and Austin leaped up at each sound—and we had a great visit.

Love,
Blanche

November 1, 1984
Dear Blanche,

I'm anxious to get a chapter off to you, even though I feel I'm rushing and not doing a good job.

Life continues to be frantic, but at least there are no more trips. My course is gobbling up the time, and so are two boards that I now sit on. I'm not sure this is how I want my life to go. Hope we get time to talk about some of this when you're here. Don asked

me to ask you if there was any chance of Bruce's being here when
you are. We would, of course, love to have both of you. I'm glad
you liked the play. I have never had so many letters and phone calls,
and can only determine that the whole world listens to *Morningside*.
I'm off to the post office before it closes.

C

November 1, 1984

Dear Carol,

Loved your last chapter as always, and laughed out loud at "fuck the
purple boots." The only suggestion I would make is that you enlarge a
bit on [Chas's] lonely evenings in Winnipeg, since I think the local
colour would add to the book. I guess what I'm thinking about is
along the lines of that scene you did in *Happenstance* where he walks to
work in Chicago, only not as detailed of course. What do you think?

Allison sat down and read it all to date and said she loved it.
She said she can hardly wait to read the end and thinks we both
have hit just the right note. She says it hangs together wonderfully,
so perhaps your feeling that it doesn't is because of the hectic time
you've been through which—as I know—lends a fractured feeling
to all facets of life. Allison does want me to clean up a couple of
scenes which tend to be a bit boring—the dinner at Van's, the
story of Verna—but had no criticism of any of yours.

All best,
Blanche
P.S. Have you read Alice Adams' *Listening to Billie*? You'd like it.

November 5, 1984

Dear Blanche,

I am going to get the follow-up letter to you in a couple days.
Should be there in time before you leave. I think we'll get through
the book and get our ends tied up nicely. Isn't it nice patting this
thick and still growing manuscript.

Please thank Allison for all her looking over our shoulders. You are right—this is a fragmented time for me. But working on this gives me a through-line—as they say in showbiz, and so I appreciate it. I have a feeling of coming to a conclusion now, but confess I am less sure than you are what it is to be at my end.

I'm off to the Xerox machine and then to the post office.

Love,

C

❧ Looking back over the twenty-odd years since that time, Allison remembers her involvement as ex-officio editor:

"Editing" for Mom and Carol was always a lot of fun. Looking back, it is both flattering and surprising to me to realize how seriously they took my comments and suggestions, considering my lack of experience as either an editor or a writer. What they particularly appreciated was the cultural perspective of my generation, so frequently I made suggestions regarding current trends, expressions, musical references, and "political correctness." What was amusing was that two such talented, intelligent, and otherwise worldly writers were frequently oblivious to contemporary cultural landmarks. (They would poke fun at themselves about this, telling each other humorous stories about their attempts to "get with it.")

One example that stands out in my mind occurred while I was reading *A Celibate Season*. Mom and Carol were using the word "queer" to describe a gay character in the book. Both were surprised to learn from me that the use of the descriptive "queer" would be considered offensive, but took my word for it and changed it.

Over the years I continued to edit for Mom. Carol and I had contact through visits, letters, messages via Mom, and the colourful postcards Carol liked to send. I often sent her entertaining "news stories" from our local rag, from which she got a good laugh. As anyone who knew Carol will recall, she had the uncanny knack of making one feel as though he or she were the most interesting person she could be spending her time with. She often referred to me in her notes and conversations as her "almost daughter" and I happily adopted her lead and referred to her as my "almost Mom."

The task of editing the letters between Mom and Carol for this book was an emotional one. Memories of Carol, of the loss of my father, and of my own past absorbed me throughout. While my early relationship with Carol was vicariously earned, it grew genuinely through her writing partnership with Mom, and through my role in reading, editing and critiquing their various works. A true friendship was nurtured as I warmed to Carol's legendary curiosity, sincerity and generosity. While editing their letters I laughed and cried—and wished the end was not what it was. – Allison Howard

November 22, 1984

Dear Carol,

Many many thanks for your warm hospitality and for the good social events, especially your very-successful dinner party. I enjoyed myself greatly and think we made wonderful progress—I only hope you weren't overtired. Sorry to hear of your rotten kidney problem and urge you to take care not to overdo the stresses. As for me, I had quite a sore throat after returning.

Allison laughed when I told her all about your play [*Departures and Arrivals*]. She said she used to sit out at the airport when she was meeting people and that idea went through her head that it would be a great play setting.* Many of the numbers in it were terrific—hope there is some success with it down the road.

Must run. Best to Don and Sara, and thanks again.

Blanche

P.S. Do you get *City Woman*? Write-up in it on Leslie (among others).

---

*The play is a series of short vignettes that take place in an airport concourse.

❧In the piece "Collaborating with Carol" that I wrote for *Prairie Fire*, I recalled that visit in some detail:

I stayed in the Shields family's lovely Victorian home, the kind with oak paneling and big halls and a wide, sweeping staircase. On a bitterly cold and slippery night (me smug in the superiority of Vancouver rain), we went to the university to see Carol's delightful little play, *Departures and Arrivals*, and the next day we worked diligently all day at the dining room table, each reading aloud our own letters and interrupting one another with corrections, cutting, adding, changing, arguing over commas. At five o'clock Carol announced that eight people were coming to dinner so we had to clear the table.

I remember that the evening was merry and that we involved the guests in a vigorous discussion of whether or not *A Celibate Season* was a good title. Some said yes, some said no, but nobody (including the authors) knew of a possible derivation that was pointed out later by an astute reviewer [Meg Stainsby]. St. Paul, in a letter to the Corinthians, asserted that celibacy is desirable within a marriage, but only for a "season." As far as we knew the title was entirely original, but we may have been deceived; the brain has its hidden ways, it can explore forgotten recesses and toss used tidbits up like newly-minted gems.

November 23, 1984

Dear Blanche,

I loved having you here, not just because we got so much work done, but because you always do so much for me—cheering me on and dispensing wisdom and trading ideas, etc., etc. Hope these two chapters are okay. We're ticking right along. The play seems to be going very well. The phone's been ringing all day—people who've seen it. No newspaper critique. Seems there was an agreement not to review the university plays—since Chris Johnson who runs the department reviews for *Stereo Morning* on CBC. All that worry for nothing. How fragile we writers are.

Love,
Carol

December 5, 1984

Dear Blanche,

Once again I'm running like mad before the post office closes. I've got my "big" chapter to start tomorrow. (Lucky you, you've done yours.) Many thanks for your excellent suggestions which I've made. I'm feeling good about it.

Also feeling good about Bella for the moment. She negotiated a contract with General Publishing last week for my book of short stories and my next novel (not ours). I got everything I wanted. Macmillan came up in the end with almost everything, but not a paperback format which I wanted for the stories—surely paperback is the future. It comes out in the spring, called *Various Miracles*, their title but I like it. Paperjacks is part of General Publishing and that is where it seems to me our book may fit.

Be sure to listen to CBC's *Sunday Morning* on December 16th. They're having a special on Jane Austen and will be recording a Jane Austen–birthday tea party which will be held at our house this Friday afternoon. A sort of staged media event but lots of fun and I've been able to invite loads of my bookish friends. We have another condo offer in. A book for Allison is on its way—and I am loving the Sylvia Plath.

Hope all is well. So amazed and glad to hear about Katinka.

Love,
C

December 1984

Blanche,

Do let me know if this [Carol's big chapter of *A Celibate Season*] is unacceptably kinky. What does Allison think? The typing is going well. In fact, I'm enjoying it. I do bits between insane bouts of Christmas shopping and am up to April.

Cheers!

C

~In that chapter, Chas finds himself in bed with two women. Much later, when I was promoting *A Celibate Season*, I went to an evening book club where the women were a little taken aback at this somewhat unorthodox scene. On the way home, the woman who had picked me up cleared her throat and blurted out, "Tell me something. How did they do it? The three of them, I mean."

I thought for a second and then said, "Carol wrote that scene, I guess you'll have to ask her."

December 17, 1984

Dear Carol,

I love your "big" letter and found it wonderful, pathetic and touching. It reveals so much about Charles' essential decency and is not in the least unacceptably kinky. (Haven't been able to ask Allison as she is rushing around madly in her new job and trying to get ready for Christmas.)

And that's the last one. Leaves me with a peculiar feeling of mixed happiness and regret. It's been a lot of fun writing these, and waiting for the response.

Christmas is going to be sparse this year as all children are going to be somewhere else. Stephen was home last week but left for Smithers yesterday, and Leslie and Austin are going there for Christmas.

Much Christmas love to all,

Blanche

P.S. *Loved* your comments on the Jane Austen birthday party—you were lucid and articulate and enormously interesting. Wish they'd stuck with interviewing you more than the other person.

December 19, 1984

Dear Blanche,

I wish I had my final chapter to send you. I've begun it, but then the children began to arrive . . . but hope to get it to you by New Year's. I did want to get my comments off to you, though, since you're busily typing your way to the end. I like everything you've sent, think it hums along nicely, so these comments are only suggestions.

Hope you can make sense of all this. I am dashing off to finish the Christmas shopping with Catherine. It is a joy to have her. She keeps me laughing.

I've had almost too much good news lately. Have won second prize in the CBC Literary Awards short story competition. Bob Weaver phoned, and a few minutes later Bella did too. I reminded her that [our] novel would be arriving very soon, and for the first time she sounded interested. She did say that she thought a made-up single name was a good idea since she felt it would sell better. I'm not at all sure and asked her to wait until she sees it. I think she's expecting a different kind of book. (I think I thought it would be a different kind of book and perhaps conveyed that to her earlier on.)

And now I must get off. Again a happy Christmas.

Love,

C

December 20, 1984

Dear Carol,

We are snowed in today, it is like working in the middle of a Christmas card here, with the snow settling on the branches of the Douglas firs and the little lake partly frozen. Allison was thrilled with the book and says she knows she's going to love it.

Have a lovely Christmas, all of you.

Blanche

December 26, 1984

Dear Carol,

CONGRATULATIONS! On the CBC competition. This *has* been your year, hasn't it? I hope it bodes well for this novel—anyway, wonderful news, please alert me when it will be read.

I had a bit of pause over the small publisher idea after reading in *The G and M* that Audrey Thomas, in leaving Talon, had been able to leave also the $500 advance in favour of a $10,000 one. Not that I'm suggesting we could hope for the latter with a small book like this, but it gives one, as I say, some pause.

Thank you for all your suggestions, all of which were good and which I've used. (How could I misspell Don Johnston after working for him?) The [phrase] "A person spends half their time . . ." was maddening, since I was anxious to use the more idiomatic and old-fashioned "a person" but could find no way around "their" (did you read that amusing article in *The Atlantic Monthly* about a year ago on this problem?). Got bogged down then in *Fowler's* and read this excellent advice: "The wise man, in writing, evades these problems by rejecting all the alternatives—any of which may set up friction between him & his reader—& putting the thing in some other shape; & in speaking, which does not allow time for paraphrase, he takes risks with equanimity & says what instinct dictates." Wonderful. Anyway I didn't like your suggestion "People" because of above, so changed it (rather obviously) to "A person spends half *the* time."

You mentioned that you were allergic to Wite-Out. Do you ever use this correcting tape (sample enclosed)?

Christmas was fine—did a lot of meal preparing but enjoyed it. The first (soggy) white Christmas in 15 years here. I have a lot of turkey left over, since there were only four of us—[including] sister-in-law and a friend. Had Allison and the children over for brunch of pancakes because Terry had to work during the day. I made some really good mince pie (seldom do such noble things so have to brag about it) and ate far too much. Bruce has capped off the Christmas season by being in bed today with a severe cold.

Love to all and am overjoyed with all your good fortune.

Love,
Blanche

December 1984

Dear Blanche,

We've had a wonderful and hectic Christmas, all our children and various assorted relatives, one immense party—last one in this house (which is now sold to a lovely family of lawyers). The children are now departing, one by one, and I've had a chance to get this final letter done. It seems a little flat to me for some reason—please offer criticism if you're moved to.

We move to our apartment (we can't bear the word "condo") on March 1st.

Wonderful to hear you've had a white Christmas.

Love,
C

4

Obsession

1985

When a writer finishes a novel, there is often a period of feeling let-down—at least there is for me, and I know other writers who have expressed a similar sense of abandonment. The fictional people who have populated your mind for months and whose every thought is known and whose hopes and aspirations are clearer to you than your own are frozen in time. Life does not go on, at least for them. It was always a one-sided love affair anyway; since you were their creator, they didn't know you. Creators are, by definition, unknowable.

In my case there were other and more obscure reasons for my sense of loss. I came to writing late in life; other than being a voracious reader, my education and profession had not fitted me for it. At university I studied the hard sciences, mathematics and physics, and in my profession worked as a chartered accountant. Collaborating with Carol taught me subtle things that I had missed: the power of the thing that isn't said, the anathema visited upon the bedraggled cliché, the over-riding need for tight structure, and above all, the importance of words. It was her brilliant playfulness with the English language that was bringing Carol to the attention of the tight little world of CanLit, while, in spite of my three published novels and many short stories, the near misses (I was frequently shortlisted for prizes) and outright rejections were eroding my self-confidence.

Carol's wish to work with me gave me, as Chas said when he published a small poem, the feeling that I was legitimate. At the time, I worried that her motive might be purely one of kindness, but I no longer think this. I brought skills to the table, I see this now. I was the one who thought of relieving the tedium of letters with a direct rendering of conversations, and I remember her surprise that we could do this. Both of us loved humour and both of us had an ear for dialogue, and we felt we were hitting our respective strides in our fictional letters when we could make the other laugh. During the editing process we were both able to block out the intrusive world and concentrate solely on the task at hand. In earlier years, she had looked to me as a mentor and perhaps she still did; but in my eyes she had become the mentor.

Now the time had come to introduce Chas and Jock to the world. The world, as it turned out, wasn't holding its breath.

January 7, 1985

Dear Carol,

Well, here it is in all its typed glory—can hardly believe I'm actually mailing it off. By the way, I love your final letter and think it strikes just the right note—mature, older and wiser, and a touch of humility. A very good ending, in other words. Now that I have your final letter, Allison is reading the remainder.

Love,
Blanche
P.S. Pleased about your apt. purchase—tell me what it's like when you have time. Hope life is a bit less hectic now.

January 14, 1985

Dear Blanche,

Well, I mailed off our opus this morning to Bella, registered mail, and am now sending you the Xeroxed letters from Chas.

The Xeroxing this morning was something of a musical comedy. The machine broke down three times and when I asked the secretary in the Economics Department to help me out, she fixed me with a look and said, "You from the English Department?" I said yes and she said, "That figures." I had to stop several times to let other people go through, got totally muddled, etc. Machinery is not my forte. Never mind! It's off! Three weeks, I wrote Bella.

In a moment of greed I said I would judge the Alberta Culture short story competition—and they have just arrived: 100 stories to read. I'm taking them to Florida with me on Saturday—not for sun and fun but to visit my ailing father. From now on I am saying no to such things and making a greater effort to protect my time. (I've said this before.) I want so much to be working on this novel which is so wonderfully satisfying for some reason.

Mainly we're all well and happy. We've been selling odds and ends and clearing out the basement—both cleansing and painful. The new era starts March 1st. Unbelievable. Hope all is well. Let me know if Allison approves of our complete ms. And I'll write or phone when I hear from Bella. What are you going to do next?

Love,
C

> *January 23, 1985*
> *North Vancouver*

Dear Carol,

Allison read the rest of the book and is wildly enthusiastic about it. She loved both of our "big" scenes, thought yours was exactly right and that it worked wonderfully, also liked mine very much. She thought we were absolutely brilliant to have hit on the unsent letters (after the soul-searching we did). She says it is a bit like an added bonus, getting a chance to peek inside them when they are not presenting themselves to someone else. She did have a few criticisms—perhaps if Bella doesn't want it, we can work it over a bit before sending it somewhere else.

Minor points, but I'll set them out so we don't forget them—[among others] I shouldn't have used "seat" in the April 17th letter, where Mia says he pats her on the seat—gather the word isn't used at all any more and I should have said "bum."

I have some rather disquieting news about Allison—she and Terry have separated. It's been pretty upsetting—naturally I worry about the effect on the kids—but there doesn't seem to be anything I can do about it. By the way, she is loving the book you sent and it has inspired her to start keeping a journal, and she must be a true journal-keeping type as she can hardly wait to write in it. (I've started several but never remember to keep them up.)

Let's keep writing whenever we have time, since I miss the contact after all our involvement over the year.
Love to all, and greetings to Don,

Blanche
P.S. I am more than a little bemused by the envelope in which you sent the ms, which is adorned with a sheet of fifty 3-cent stamps. Have you been hoarding 3-cent stamps? I sincerely hope you didn't have to lick them.

February 4, 1985
Dear Blanche,

I can't imagine how we're going to get packed up by February 26th. Luckily life has been too busy for me to worry about my sentimental attachment to this house, and I can see, though I'm reluctant to admit it yet, that condo-life may trim life down to manageable size. Well, we shall see.

I am so very sorry to hear about Allison, for her, for him, for the children, and for you and Bruce. I suppose it is possible that the spark will return. Love has many lapses, as we all know. The steady flame, just a myth probably. Perhaps journal keeping will help her sort things out. (I've just read a little gem of an article by Joan Didion on journal keeping. She says a number of valuable things—such as that a journal is the only way of keeping in touch with our former selves, something she sees as psychologically healthy. My daughter Cath recently told me she burnt her diary of her 16th year because she couldn't abide that silly self—a pity, I think.)

Bella has given our ms to General Publishing—she felt she had to do this. She is not enthusiastic, feeling it is not mass market and not quite anything else either, that parts of it are creaky, etc. At any rate, she thinks it has excellent film possibilities, something I didn't think of but which you mentioned.

My reading these days is composed of over a hundred short stories for a competition sponsored by Alberta Culture and six new novels for the Books in Canada First Novel Award. So far the novels are no more than competent. One of them is so weighted down by symbolism that it gives me hives. It is not a very patriotic thing to say, but the minute I finish this bland bunch, I'm getting back to some of the new British novels. I want something that bites and feeds.

Do thank Allison for her kind words, tell her I too have started a journal, partly out of panic caused by time zipping past me, partly because I wanted to write one golden sentence a day—but have not done this, I'm afraid. Mostly whining and cavilling. What does this mean?

[Handwritten]
It's freezing here—34°.

Love,
Carol

February 18, 1985

Dear Carol,

It was nice to hear from you and I was greatly interested in Bella's reaction, also reassured by your assessment of her literary judgment. She may be right, that it isn't mass market, but I think it is probably in the usual category of novel and as such would have a good chance somewhere. Let's hope General Publishing sees it our way. Since Bella thinks it would have good film possibilities, I hope she is doing something about that—it seems to me that, with the CBC suddenly filming plays like mad, they would be a natural to approach. Ah well, patience.

I was greatly saddened this weekend to hear of Marian Engel's death.* Poor woman—it seemed as though she was just hitting her stride, and then to be cut down at so young an age. And she never did see her great interest—public lending rights—come to fruition. (I wonder if any of us will?)

I am going to make a determined effort to simplify my life, and in fact have already announced that I won't be running this year for the executive of the B.C. Liberal Party. The Vanier Institute is finished, as you know, and with the easing out of the Liberals I am left with only one big job on my plate still, the business of being church treasurer. The other thing I realized I wasn't getting enough time for is reading. Poor you, being stuck with a bunch of amateur novels! I don't blame you for wanting to get into something British. By the way, I absolutely loved *Touchstones: Letters Between Two Women* [Patricia Frazer Lamb and Kathryn Joyce Hohlwein]. What resonant chords—in that era I too was devouring *The Mandarins*, *The Outsider*, and most of the others they mentioned. I was struck by one curious omission, considering their hemmed-in lifestyles—neither of them seemed to have come across Simone de Beauvoir's *Le Deuxième Sexe*, which, considering their bilingualism and their plights, would have seemed a natural. I read it in the fifties, shouting an inward, "yes, yes, me too," and wonder what kind of insights it might have brought to bear for them. Otherwise my reading has been *The Globe and Mail*, old magazines, and the strange semi-autobiographical and ancient

---

*Noted Canadian author Marian Engel died of cancer on February 16, 1985, at age 51.

The Story of San Michele by Axel Munthe. Deplore it, but it left an impression.

Sorry you've had such a rotten winter. Ours has been colder but sunnier than usual, and last week I had a couple of glorious days over on the Island, as Bruce's board had their semi-annual soul search (actually reviewing decisions) over there in a luxury resort and I tagged along for two days, and actually wrote!

Poor you, moving—a hateful duty—but I do hope you will love being in an apartment and I will be most interested to hear your initial reactions. The best to Don.

Blanche

March 19, 1985

Dear Carol,

I suppose no news is good news—how long do you think they'll take to do a "quick" appraisal? Anyway, fingers crossed.

Am reading Alice Adams' *Superior Women* and have quite mixed feelings about it. It is good reading as always, but the characters do not develop and some of the lesser ones are quite stereotyped and never come alive. Still, I'm finding it well worthwhile, in the entertainment department.

I note that *The G and M* mentioned your spring collection of short stories and I'm looking forward to them. Let me know when they will be published.

Oh yes, I read Matt Cohen's *Flowers of Darkness* and was moderately impressed. It started off rather floridly but developed quite remarkably by the end of the book. The main character who seemed very stereotyped at first turned out to be surprisingly human. Have you read any of his stuff?

I hope your life has calmed down after your hectic (though wonderfully successful) year. Drop a line when you crawl out from under—I miss our frequent communication.

Love to all,
Blanche

March 25, 1985

Dear Blanche,

Don and I are off to San Francisco tomorrow for a week (and Sara to Toronto to look over York U and the U of Toronto for next year) but I will get your letter of appraisal off before we go. I love your idea [for a new novel]. And I think books about older people are about to boom what with the geriatric bulge. I'm very interested in your idea of using your interest in psychological things.

I must tell you, Blanche, that we have settled very quickly into our new high-rise life and I am finding the transition much easier than I'd imagined, surprisingly so. I love being able to look out at the river—which is now breaking up and therefore particularly interesting—and I already see that I am going to have more time. When rereading my journal recently, begun Christmas Day, I noticed that my recurring theme is the need for more time. Perhaps this move has accomplished that. I thought I'd be bothered by the lack of a separate dining room, but it bothers me not at all. And I love my nifty new kitchen. Underground parking is wonderful in this climate too. And, inside, it feels like *a house.* I am not admitting any of this to Don, of course. I am wondering, too, if just taking a flyer on something new hasn't made a difference.

All best,
Carol

April 13, 1985

Dear Blanche,

I had a letter from Bella yesterday, not good news I'm afraid, and want to let you know right away so we can get busy on our own. Too bad about the time lost. This is what she says: "General has decided to pass on *A Celibate Season.* The consensus was that the characters were rather slight and not well developed, that the novel isn't strong enough for a literary trade paperback but is too 'smart' and not gutsy enough for mass-market. Since my own response to the novel is pretty lukewarm, I've come to the conclusion that it would be foolish for me to take it on. It's difficult enough these days to place work you're really excited about; it's disastrous to try to sell anything less than wholeheartedly."

This is awfully rushed. Don and I are off this bright afternoon to see *A Passage to India* and he's calling for me now. Will write a proper letter next time.

Love,
Carol

April 15, 1985

Dear Carol,

I am completely ashamed of myself in having taken so long to write to thank you for the wonderful book *Touchstones: Letters Between Two Women*. It has taken a place in my "top ten" favourite books. I loved it. I found I had to keep re-checking the dates, as much of it was so contemporary to me that it seemed impossible that it was written 30 years ago. I have since lent it to Mom and a good friend, which has prompted great discussions. It also made me wish for a friend who was as interested in corresponding as I. I really regret the fact that so few people are letter writers any more and certainly none of my friends are. It seems incredible when I look at the piles of letters from old boyfriends, etc., that we really did write that much.

I am mostly well, coping anywhere from excellently to not so— with single parenthood. The kids have been terrific.

I think your and Mom's book deserves every kind of success, I just hope our Canadian editors have enough brains to see that. I agree that it would make an excellent movie (could get quite excited about this!) In fact I can see it *all* in my head!

All my best regards to you and thank you again for the great book.

Love,
Allison

April 16, 1985

Dear Carol,

Your letter came today and of course I was disappointed about General Publishing. (In any case, I wrote off the covering letter to Deneau Publishers.)

Right now until the end of April, I am going flat-out, working more than full time, but once tax season blessedly finishes I'll be quite free and will have some time to devote to working on sending out *A Celibate Season.*

Yes, I think it would be good to contact publishers when you are in Toronto in mid-May. Thrilled about your new book coming out. Also about the nomination for the National Magazine Award.

Must go. Maybe after you've had a chance to get this letter I'll phone you and see what you think. Hope you liked *A Passage to India*—we enjoyed it thoroughly, in fact I think I'll reread the novel. Read a decidedly lukewarm but lengthy review of it by John Updike in *The New Yorker.* Did you read Alice Munro's short story [from *The Progress of Love*] in the July *New Yorker?* Wonderful.

Much love,
Blanche

April 21, 1985

Dear Blanche,

I have a few things to report. I was overtaken by a fit of bravery when in T.O. and contacted three publishers. I had heard through a friend that Methuen Publishing was looking for offbeat fiction and so I had breakfast with their fiction editor, who did indeed seem interested. I have arranged for Bella to send Methuen the copy she has. Next I had a meeting with Denis Deneau of Deneau Publishers, now in Toronto. (I had met him in Ottawa years ago working on the NDP team.) He too sounded interested, though warned me they don't do a lot of fiction. Next I met with a woman from Avon Books. She is *very* interested, her only concern being

that it might be a bit short for a mass-market paperback. Would
you send a Xerox copy to Denis Deneau (I told him your letter
would be coming) and I will Xerox one for Avon. All these people
promised to report to me by May 16th. (All these people also
bought me breakfast, lunch, etc., very pleasant and nice to be on
that sought-after end for a change.) By the way, I still don't know if
Arts Manitoba has enough money to send me [to Vancouver] in
May, should know in a few days. My book [*Various Miracles*] is not
coming out until the end of May and this is why I decided we
should get moving on this. I can also contact McClelland & Stewart
then if I go. I know you're very busy, but what do you think of
giving Douglas & McIntyre in Vancouver a call? I understand that
they are going into fiction and have an editor named Denise
Bukowski who was my editor on *Happenstance*. I didn't discuss the
book with Ed Carson at General Publishing. I think he is skittish
about anything with a domestic tone. I know he thought *A Fairly
Conventional Woman* was too housewifey. (Who does he think reads
novels? I wonder.)

It looks as though Don and I will be going to France for six
months, July to December, on an exchange. Exciting for Don,
and for me it promises that lump of uncluttered time which I so
badly need. My half-century mark is coming up in June, and I am
astonished to report that life has never looked so full of promise;
strange and wonderful and surprising.

Love,
Carol
P.S. Had a lovely letter from Allison.

April 25, 1985

Dear Carol,
Got your very upbeat letters—Canada Post is really speeding up.
I guess I'd better send [the manuscript] special delivery, although it will
cost us a lot, but what the hell. We'll each keep track of our costs and
settle after the glorious day when we get a marvellous advance.

Anyway, thank you thank you for doing all that promoting in Toronto. I feel ever so much more hopeful now—mustn't get too hopeful about Avon, I suppose, but they could really give us a big market.

Glad that you are feeling so positive with the half-century mark coming up—I remember clearly when mine happened, it was just after we moved back here and were living temporarily in a little townhouse, and life looked a bit bleak at that time. I'm not feeling as positive as you about my life right now, but nothing serious, I don't think, just the grind of work and the continuing depressed B.C. economy, which has got to the point that we can't rent a small condo we invested in and are subsidizing the mortgage.

Must get to bed. If anything positive happens, phone. Much love to all, and am looking forward to your new book and to the reviews. (Does that thought still turn your stomach to water?)

Love,
Blanche

April 29, 1985 [after two phone calls]

Dear Carol,

It was good to talk to you this morning (I rented the condo yesterday so am not feeling too gloomy about money, therefore decided to blow it). I felt I needed to hear from you directly. Maybe if things get to a point where we have to discuss a decision I can arrange to go down to Bruce's office and phone on the government line. (Don't tell the Tories.)

Anyway, the enthusiastic response from Douglas & McIntyre helped.

My spirits greatly improved with the end of a very grinding tax season—have shed the conviction that nothing is ahead but physical and probably mental deterioration and returned to hearty optimism. Very pleased to hear of your plans for next Christmas—we have a spare room if there is need. Stephen is getting married in October, so will be having a jaunt to Smithers [B.C.] then.

Love,
Blanche

May 10, 1985
Dear Carol,

Another quick note to respond to the Methuen comments, which just arrived. Oddly enough, I feel better now that I've read them because I think on most counts she is wrong, especially regarding the use of reported dialogue. Her thought that no one would report dialogue in that way indicates her unwillingness to credit the reader with a small necessary suspension of belief, as you say, and certainly Allison had no problem with that and didn't even mention it in fact. Also I can't agree that we have included too much of issues—in Chas's case, B.C. politics had deprived him of a job and there was enormous emotion about the subject, and I would suspect his letter would have been much fuller on the subject in real life. The other reason I take exception to that is that women's fiction (whatever the hell that is) is often criticized for failure to deal with anything in the outside world, and I found this to be the failure of Alice Adams' *Superior Women*. Tanya Long [the editor who responded] asks if a loving man and wife separated for the first time in twenty years would really spend time on [politics]. They might do more delving into motivations and so on—but we hadn't envisioned that type of novel.

Oh yes, odd that she found the two voices alike, don't you think? I think they are quite different—but then, reading *Touchstones: Letters Between Two Women*, I was surprised that their two voices were so alike.

It is a mite discouraging, isn't it? Insofar as our strategy is concerned, I don't have a great deal of faith in myself but have a great deal in you, since you have been much more successful than I. I have always been very lousy at promoting myself—probably a female thing, I noted that you said you had an attack of courage in Toronto when you contacted the publishers, and it would have taken an attack on my part to do the same. A man probably wouldn't have had the slightest compunction about walking in and pushing himself—I'm going through a negative feeling about the progress women have made, especially after reading the analysis in the Writers' Union newsletter about women's progress in the writing world.

All is well here. (Very green this morning—raining.*) I am immensely happier now that I'm back and writing in the mornings again. It may be bad for my pocketbook but seems to be good for my psyche—as we've discussed before. You'll be amused at one of the things I'm doing now—have always thought I'd like to try a play, as you did, and since our readers (including Bella) think *A Celibate Season* would make a great movie, I am practising by writing it as a stage script. If it turns out to be at all interesting, will send it when I finish. Also am working on a short story which I think is quite good, but who am to know?

Well, must close. Had only intended to write a note, but was psyched up by Methuen's letter. Glad to hear you're enjoying apartment living—hope we can market this before you start for France. The time goes so quickly, doesn't it?

Love,
Blanche
P.S. Just read Patrick White's *Voss*. It is a work of genius—I was enormously impressed.

May 23, 1985

Dear Blanche,

Many thanks for your notes and letters and warm words of congratulations.** It was a delightful surprise—Robert Enright

---

*In *A Celibate Season*, Chas writes, "Do you think it's healthy breathing green air?
**Carol won the Canadian National Magazine Award for her short story "Mrs. Turner Cutting the Grass."

phoned Don with the news and Don phoned me out of a library
board meeting—lovely. (I think life would be sweet if we could win
something every day.)

I immediately sat down and wrote the two pubs [publishers] in
Toronto and hope to hear from them soon. I too hope we can get
A Celibate Season sailing soon, a matter of finding the right publishers. Your idea of a play sounds intriguing and I am very anxious to
know how you're structuring it. I saw a play last winter called *Sea
Marks* [Gardner McKay] which is partly composed of exchanged
letters; the stage was divided in two, and one side was lit while the
other was in darkness, the actors striding about the room, composing the letters in their heads.

The new book will be out in a week [*Various Miracles*, a collection of short stories]. Curiously, it looks as though it will be
published on June 2nd, my 50th birthday. Naturally I see this as
an omen. (*Small Ceremonies* was accepted for publication on my
40th birthday.) Doubt if there'll be much promotion (an interview on *Stereo Morning*, already recorded). And a good thing too
since we leave for France on June 27th. We'll never be ready!
Please write often and I promise to do the same. We can strate-
gize?? I'm very pleased that you are truly back to writing again
after still another interruption. Once you have a routine established you'll be off.

Blanche, you must read *Parallel Lives: Five Victorian Marriages* by
Phyllis Rose, the marriages all literary ones. A gossipy delight. But
also scholarly and sound with many ideas about marriage and
power—something I'm afraid I haven't thought much about but
find interesting. I wish you were closer so we could discuss
such things—you always seem to have thought about just about
everything. I'll write or phone if there's any news.

Love,

C

May 30, 1985

Carol,

I guarantee to keep writing while you are in France. As a matter of fact, I finished the first act (very roughly) of the play and am astonished at how visual it is. I found myself actually laughing this morning, after a break from it of a couple of weeks, at the scene in Davina's first class, and Gil and Chas at Thanksgiving dinner.

Hope you have a wonderful birthday. I am having Leslie and Austin and baby, and Allison and children for dinner for Leslie's birthday same day, so we will toast you as well.

(The period has stopped working on my typewriter and I have to get a new one, but dread not only the cost but the decisions.) Will order *Parallel Lives: Five Victorian Marriages* from the library immediately.

Love,
Blanche

May 1985

Dear Blanche,

We're up to our neck in the frenzies here, but wanted to let you know that Deneau phoned this afternoon (when I was out) and said that they had decided, after much thought, not to take the novel. You should be getting the ms, plus letter of explanation and so on. I confess I was disappointed. Ah well.

I'm sending the letter from Shaun Oakey [of Douglas & McIntyre]—upon whom I am now pinning hopes. Would you mind phoning him and telling them your address and tell him that I am out of the country.

We have a hundred things to do. Many many thanks for your congratulatory call. I got the *Ottawa Citizen* review today which was lovely. A great surprise since the interview—remember, . . . the cretin—went disturbingly, he asking such things as Don's age and how my health was (after noting I held one shoulder stiffly).

Sorry to be so brief and disjointed. Am so glad the play is buzzing along and am anxious to see a glimpse of it.

Love,
Carol

❧This is written into a birthday card for Carol's 50th, June 2, 1985, the same date as my daughter Leslie's birthday:

Dear Carol,

No, I'm not one of those superwomen who write down all their friends' birthdays and never fail to send a card, but I did remember that it was the same day as Leslie's. And this being a landmark one, I'm anxious to add my blessings.

On my 50th I remember Pat Mahoney* was in town and said about 50 that it was the old age of youth and the youth of old age. I was struck by it at the time but don't now find that it was as depressing as it sounds. In fact, life improved quite noticeably thereafter.

All very well here. I am buoyant again (Why? No reason) and realized once more that the annual dislocation of working intensely and then stopping abruptly invariably throws me for a while.

Had a wonderful weekend on the boat—visited [friends] Marilyn and Norm at their summer cottage on Gambier Island.

A very happy fiftieth!
Blanche and Bruce

❧This is the first letter written on Blanche's new computer, a 64K IBM, which operated on DOS and whose software, WordStar, was on 5 ¼–inch floppy disks:

---

*Former cabinet minister in the Trudeau government.

July 23, 1985

Dear Carol,

Don't get hopeful as I have nothing to report. Shortly after you left I phoned Shaun Oakey (sounds like a made-up name), but all I got was a reaffirmation that they were very interested and that it wouldn't be too long until they let us know.

By the way, I had an interesting talk with Alan Twigg, who is a book reviewer among other things (I'm not sure what the other things are, professor I think, in any case well known in B.C.). He had sent me a circular letter as he had once reviewed and liked *Pretty Lady* [my second published novel] and was doing some writing on historical landmarks for a Centennial edition. In response to his question about what I was working on, I'd told him about *A Celibate Season*, so he asked me about it, and before I had much chance to explain about lack of interest by Toronto publishers (having mentioned its involvement with B.C. politics), he said we'd never interest a Toronto publisher because they thought nobody was interested in what took place out here, and that there was a crying need for more publishers outside of Toronto. He was so definite and impassioned about it that it set me wondering whether perhaps that had more to do with the rejections than we thought.

Now, on a more upbeat note (no place else to be after all that gloom). We've had a wonderful summer, many many days without rain and with solid sunshine. However, the forests have been burning up—the way of the world, nothing can be revelled in without an apology to the environmentalists or small-*l* liberals or whatever. We are going out on our boat this weekend for about a week, just the two of us, so hope the weather holds. I've just had my 82-year-old aunt on her annual visit—she is a very nice person, all her upstairs intact, but the pace varies between slow and stop. She enjoys $1.49 day at Woodward's, so I wait every year to stock up on things like tea towels and napkins and all the little things one normally never gets around to buying, but I must admit to a certain twitchiness sometimes. All of which sounds rather miserable, considering that I enjoy her company greatly. In any case, I've been doing some interesting reading, and am now ensconced in *Parallel Lives: Five Victorian Marriages* which I'm finding absolutely fascinating. How I wish we could discuss some of the implications of it. Also have read *Beautiful Women, Ugly Scenes* (C.D.B. Bryan), because of an enthusiastic review in *The Atlantic Monthly*, but have very mixed feelings about it. It is the story of a marriage from the viewpoint of a man's feelings, and well written, but I felt by the time I was finished that it was somewhat self-serving, a position that the author would agree with, since there is much *mea culpa*–ing in it which rings a bit false. Also read Alison Lurie's *Foreign Affairs*— did you recommend it, or was it a review in *The G and M*? In any case, it was most enjoyable and I heartily recommend it—in the genre of those well-told English women authors, except that she is American writing of England, more or less à la Henry James.

Later. A pause of several hours while I went over to the church to try to get a computer program running on a computer that was donated to us, as it turns out, for good reason. The make of computer—Franklin—is now obsolete, so much running to and fro to computer stores, where a whole new subculture is now in progress. Did you know that there are computer groupies? These seem to be pretty well exclusively youngish men, often bearded, probably unemployed, and they hang around computer stores exchanging strange jargon with the store manager—also usually young and possibly bearded. The advent of middle-aged women generates a lot of looking askance—computer groupiness is a macho-dominated subculture, whose elitism would be forever destroyed by the feminine. If you think I'm exaggerating, go into one when you come back—or perhaps the disease has spread to France. I'm not the only female who has noticed the lethargy with which women are served, and the feeling is definitely one of invading the pool hall in the old days. If by chance one is fortunate enough to get the attention of the manager, the advice is usually expanded upon by one or more groupies.

As soon as it is in any sort of form at all, I'll send you a copy [of the play]—a thing very easy to do now, with the great computer. Actually, I'm loving it, but do hope the novel sells so that I'll have a tiny bit of justification of the expense.

Much planning for Stephen's wedding in early October. Leslie's baby continues to be the entire focus of attention of her parents. Allison is managing all right on her own, but of course I worry about the hazards of single parentship.

I do hope your writing is coming well, and that you are loving the peacefulness. I'm delighted of course that you will be here for Christmas.

I must turn on the printer and type all of this out—that's the luxurious part—plus the ability to go back and correct typing errors. So far I haven't done much composing right onto the screen, but think I will adjust to it well.

Écrivez bientôt!

Love,
Blanche

5

Rejection

1985–1987

~In the book *Thinking, Willing and Judging*, the philosopher Hannah Arendt muses on the business of solitude. Thinking, she says, is the human situation in which one keeps oneself company; a solitary but not a lonely affair. Only when the world intrudes does thinking split in two, forsaking solitude and sometimes sliding into loneliness.

Carol never admitted to loneliness, although she did mention the peculiar friendlessness they were faced with in France and the amount of time she had for introspection. And she practically begged for letters. Our letters, filled as letters must be with news, did not sound lonely, but in fact they plastered over the many hours of solitude when she was bent over her typewriter and I over my word processor. When we rose for air we waited for life to pour in and fill the vacuum, for the return of husbands from their workplaces or friends who might come by for coffee.

For my life, too, was afflicted from time to time with loneliness. We lived on the lower slopes of a mountain in the middle of a rain forest. Winters in North Vancouver are dark without snow to reflect the light. Grey clouds clinging to the mountaintops dump rain at twice the rate for Vancouver itself. Our modest cedar home was set on a good-sized lot on which an enlightened developer had saved the trees, but these trees, cedar, Douglas fir, western hemlock, expanded in girth and shot up to twenty, thirty, fifty feet. From my den, all I could see was a brave patch of soggy lawn among the trees and a pond in the near distance where only ducks and geese touched down.

I welcomed Carol's letters with the same enthusiasm with which she seemed to welcome mine. In them we felt free to moan about the unenlightened publishers who were rejecting *A Celibate Season*— shared moaning is somehow not as ego-deflating as solitary moaning. And so when tidbits in the form of letters from the outside came sliding through the mail slot they boosted our sagging spirits with the reminder that soon, very soon, the world would again intrude in all its joyous, boisterous, reckless and sometimes unwelcome diversity.

August 20, 1985
Bouaye, France

Dear Blanche,

Your long newsy letter was wonderfully welcome. I suppose it is a measure of our sense of dislocation that letters are doubly, or more, valued. I lunge at *le mandat*, poor lad. I'll be most interested, of course, to hear if you've had further news from Shaun Oakey. I absolutely approve of the other things you've done, and am glad to have the benefit of your business sense. A thought occurred to me: if all present publishers turn us down, perhaps we should consider Pulp Press in Vancouver. Or Talon Books. Both these presses have spread their wings in the last two years, doing commercial things but taking risks on those kinds of books that are not easily classifiable—which, it seems, ours is.

Thanks for alerting me to the fact that my book doesn't seem to be in Vancouver. Indeed it is frustrating. The whole writing métier is heartbreaking at times. I am so sorry about your grant application and know how you feel. (I didn't apply this year because I just didn't feel I could set myself up for that kind of rejection again for a while.) I had, last week, a most wonderful writing day. Everything seemed to go along and I felt as though I were flying—a day like that does in a sense make up for all the draggy, dispiriting days when you feel it's hardly worth it. I am sure you know about the New Play Centre* on Granville Island where all B.C. residents can get free advice on their plays or even, I believe, parts of plays. If they like something they will organize a reading with actors, which is wonderfully helpful and also a lot of fun.

Re Alan Twigg's theory about regional presses, I certainly agree. The most interesting books I've read this year were done by regional presses. By the way, you would like *A Nest of Singing Birds* by Susan Haley, recently published by NuWest Press in Edmonton, [about] the ins and outs of a philosophy department in a Canadian university.

I'm glad you like *Parallel Lives* [Phyllis Rose]. I made so many check marks in the introduction that I surprised myself. It was rather hotly debated in my book club—we always get off the subject—that is, the power politics of marriage. Everyone in the group had done a great deal of thinking about this, and I had never even given it a thought. Where have I been? But I've honestly never experienced marriage as a power struggle. I was furious reading *Beautiful Women, Ugly Scenes*. Don had laid out over $20 for the hardcover, knowing how much I had loved *Friendly Fire*, also by C.D.B. Bryan. I thought it one of the cheapest and most carelessly edited books I'd ever seen. I did like Alison Lurie's *Foreign Affairs*, that is I enjoyed being inside it, but nothing much has lingered. But should it? Out of a sort of duty I have read Proust's *Remembrance of Things Past*—Vol. 1, anyway, wondering at times if it was ever going to come to anything. It never quite does, but is so full of lovely things and the most complicated psychological insights made perfectly simple by that supple prose. Also read Gail Godwin's *Mr. Bedford and the Muses*, a quite enthralling novella and some stories that never quite achieve the kind of rondure I love. Just

---

*Now the Playwrights' Theatre Centre.

finished Anita Brookner's *Look at Me*, which I adored but can well imagine everyone wouldn't. She is a slightly more contemporary [Barbara] Pym. You might like *Judgment Day* by Penelope Lively— in fact, I'm sure you would. I've brought heaps of second-hand paperbacks over, stuff I can leave behind. One is an anthology of women's writing put together in 1975, a mere ten years ago, and I am amazed how "quaint" much of it seems, predictable, adhering to those consigned corners of femininity, which includes most family relationships.

Don and I are both working quite hard at the moment, I on my novel and on a film script I've been asked to try my hand at, and Don at the research station, hurling clumps of earth around in a giant centrifuge—this duplicates the effect of gravity, thus allowing them to test models of earth structures with greater accuracy. We give each other many treats to spell ourselves from all the hard work, lovely meals out, weekends at the seaside, etc. Our model for the year has become Deny Thyself Nothing. WELL, almost nothing. We are well settled, living in a flat, rather uninteresting suburb ten miles from Nantes. The most peculiar thing is having absolutely no friends. Don sees people at the lab, of course, but most of them are on vacation. In August, as you will remember, France barely limps along. Between this peculiar friendlessness, cultural shock and empty nest, I am astonished at how tranquil and sane we're remaining, easing into little routines and making small daily discoveries. One does get introspective though, and because of that I am thankful to be a writer and have a place for all that introspection to go.

There is an amazing TV program each Friday evening during prime time. Six or seven writers sit around on little chairs and discuss *literature*. The French regard for writers is very great, as you know, probably out of proportion to the worth of most of them, but how nice it is here to say, if anyone should ask, that you write books.

The David Watmough piece was a joy to read. I could hear him puffing between the lines. I hadn't even realized he'd published a book this year, much less been passed over for a Gov Gen's Award.

Sara is in Tours at the moment taking a French course, and goes back to Winnipeg in September to start university, sharing a little apartment with two other girls. So we are truly on our own. Everyone else is fine. I'd like to scold them into writing more frequently, but so far have resisted. Letter writing does not seem a part of their culture, and looks more or less doomed—what a pity, thinks me.

All good wishes to Bruce. Hope you'll have time—please!—to write before the wedding.

Love,

C

September 6, 1985

Dear Carol,

I finally got *Various Miracles* (mid-August). When Bruce picked it up at Duthie's he asked them if they had any other copies, and they said they'd brought in five but they were all gone, and they had ordered more. A mixture of encouraging and discouraging, *n'est-ce pas*? When we were in Victoria on our summer boat trip I went into Munro's Books—it is great, has everything, I would say one of the best in Canada—and the girl in charge was surprised to hear about [*Various Miracles*], and took the name from me.

Oh yes, I loved it. I think "Accidents" remained my favourite— I'd read it before—but I also love "Mrs. Turner Cutting the Grass," and thought some of the little asides delicious, such as the remarks about the cellulite in her legs and the adolescents' reaction to it. Also loved the glimpses of her life and thought them wonderfully authentic. I think my next runner-up was the one about the writer whose wife was dying. Also I was dazzled by "The Metaphor Is Dead—Pass It On." I can see a great improvement in style between your earlier pieces and the later ones. I do think short stories is a genre that you have mastered.

I suppose you've heard the news of Tim Porteous's leaving the Canada Council. However, they've made an appointment that seems to have met with general approval, a person named Roberts who was in a diplomatic post in Moscow, and who is very knowledgeable about the arts and has already said he is committed to the arm's-length relationship. In addition, he was one of Trudeau's boys and has been quite enthusiastically endorsed by Maureen Forrester, who was consulted this time. Porteous did the arts world quite a favour, it seems, in his blast against the Mulroney government, since they knocked themselves out this time to do the seemly thing.*

As you will see, I have finished the first draft of the play. The first draft was great but would have taken seven nights to perform, and I seem to remember that even G.B.S.** didn't get away with that in *Back to Methuselah*. I have done some editing on Act 1. I'm hoping you will find time to do some suggesting and some slashing.

I was interested in your remarks about power struggles and marriage. Oddly enough, in retrospect I see that our marriage has had a lot of them, but I didn't recognize them as such until about five years ago when Leslie made some remark about the two of us being engaged in occasional power struggles. It was never something I was conscious of at the time, but now that I've been made aware of it I do see that it used to happen. (I don't think it does any more, except in tennis, which we've recently taken up.) We are both highly competitive people, but I don't think I've ever been much into power—certainly not with my children, since my own mother made me aware of those pitfalls. In any case, it would be an interesting thing to discuss some time, and certainly *Parallel Lives* gave delicious examples of it. Allison loved the book and joins me in thanking you for mentioning it. I've signed up for a course at Cap College† this fall on Women's History—very interesting professor, very bright and challenging—so maybe I'll have more insights when I'm finished.

---

*Instead of just naming the new executive director, they actually consulted with the (unpaid) head of the Canada Council.

**George Bernard Shaw.

†Capilano College.

Not too long ago I too reread Proust—forced the poor reading club to do it—and found it much easier going than the first time, and like you, wonderful with its insights. Right now am reading Annie Dillard's quite remarkable *Living by Fiction*, which is smallish and which I will send on to you if you haven't already read it. Also read a funny and touching novel by Nora Ephron, *Heartburn*—a strange thing, in its way, full of the wryest of Jewish humour and, oddly enough, recipes. The protagonist is a middlebrow Julia Childs, as apparently she is in real life also, and the work is a true story. In spite of the slapstick humour it was quite touching.

Your life sounds at once ideal and frightening; frightening to be, as you say, absolutely away from friends—I'm so extroverted I think I'd find that very hard, but ideal in the way that you can shed all the little duties and meetings and the host of things that always add up to a hectic life for one whole year, and get lots of wonderful work done. I'm making quite an effort to stay less fractured. I'll be finished as church treasurer in the spring, and am lying low with Liberal politics.

Our ten days on the boat was excellent—we realize we've made a mistake in the past in not going out by ourselves and just bumming from port to port. The wedding plans are going apace, and I found a great dress at Chapman's summer sale—remember when you helped me buy the dress for [a previous] wedding? Katherine [my granddaughter] just had her first birthday party, which besides relatives included a group of about four yuppie couples, all thirtyish young professionals whose undivided attention is focused on their one-year-olds. Said one-year-olds, by the way, were the best-behaved group of that age I've ever seen—a result, perhaps, of the undivided attention?

Do write soon.

Love,
Blanche

P.S. Was surprised, on reading Adele Wiseman's *Crackpot*, to find such an accomplished (and neglected) novel. Have you read it?

September 13, 1985

Dear Carol,

Well, here's Act 2, hot on the heels of Act 1, which I trust you've already received.

Nothing at all new to report. I signed up for a course at Cap College, rather to my own surprise, but am enjoying it tremendously. It is on the history (or non-history) of women insofar as it can be pieced together from historical records and anthropological sources, and has an excellent instructor. Barbara Perrault phoned me and told me how interesting it was, and (believe it or not) that they needed more bodies, a familiar theme I couldn't resist.* In any case, for some reason I've been wanting to take a course for years but have had some sort of block that's prevented me—probably fear that if I ever got back into the halls of academe I wouldn't be pryable loose. (Loved university when I went.)

Must run.

Much love,
Blanche

September 19, 1985

Dear Carol,

[I'm sending] the rest [of the play] for which I'm sure you've been waiting with barely controlled impatience. Instead of doing the cutting before you saw it, I'd like it if you would give me your thoughts.

We leave on the 28th for a week in Smithers—Stephen's wedding is on October 5th. The whole family is going and it should be fun. When we get back, if I haven't heard from anyone [re the manuscript], I will phone and try to be pushy.

---

*This was a theme in *A Celibate Season*.

How I envy those who can be! I remember listening in admiration as Jan Drabek recounted phoning General Publishing or somebody and giving them hell for taking so long to make a decision. Alas, either I'm too socially conditioned to be nice or I'm just nice by disposition but I don't have that kind of courage. It seems incredible that [Denis] Deneau couldn't at least respond and let me know what they've done with the other ms, which I would send to someone else.

I was at a Liberal meeting the other night and got talking to a couple of lawyer friends, and found that one of them, Mark Moseley, has been working closely on a case with your John. Mark was most interested to hear about you—I gather John has never mentioned your career as a novelist. The young! Also this issue of *City Woman* has a small article on harassment in the marketplace and quotes Anne on the subject of patronizing remarks (patted on the head and told she is cute. God that used to happen to me! Whatever happened to cute?).

I watched *Death of a Salesman* on TV, and as the review said, though Dustin Hoffman and Kate Reid were wonderful, the pathos somehow didn't work. Dated.

Must run (to class). Loving the course I'm taking.

Much love, and to Don,
Blanche

September 1985
[France]

Dear Blanche,

We are leaving for a week in England in just a few minutes, but I want to get a brief note off to you, and then will send a detailed one when we get back—I presume it is fine if I scribble on your beautiful word-processed sheets. (By the way, Don and I stayed up to watch interviews with 4 French writers last night, and the most spectacular point that came across to me was that they *all* wrote with pens! Remember pens?!)

I was so very pleased—you know I value your judgment—that you like *Various Miracles.* You have by now heard from Doubleday, I'm sure. They wrote asking where to send the ms. I was pleased she liked it, even though she didn't want to publish it. I think we certainly should keep trying. There's always Borealis in Ottawa, the little outfit that did my poetry books. They have done a couple of novels.

I loved Dillard's *Living by Fiction.* I saw it reviewed in *The Globe* and ordered it immediately, the sort of thing I don't usually do. My copy is underlined from start to finish. Our book group did *Heartburn* and was divided about it; some saw it as a very serious book whose author had failed to recognize its seriousness. Some thought—this is a feminist group—that she should *not* have given him the recipe for the salad dressing in the end—exactly the forgiving, reconciliating touch I liked. The woman who chose the book is a professional marriage counsellor. You must read, if you haven't, a book called *Ending* by Hilma Wolitzer.

And now the play. I think you've done a *remarkable* job of compressing, transposing, etc., really treating it like a new vehicle, which it is. And you've "snapped up" the dialogue, which I think you have to do for the stage.

I have to get to the bank and post office before we leave so must leave it at that, but will send scribbled-upon script back next week. We are all fine, busy, sometimes homesick and looking forward to a good soak in the English language.

I love your letters.

Love,
Carol

October 15, 1985
[France]

Dear Blanche,

First I must tell you how much I enjoyed reading [the play].
I laughed out loud, just as I did when your chapters came in the

mail back in Winnipeg. I think you have a nice comic touch—I
love your earthy bits. And I think you've done an amazing job of
taking one form, giving it a stir, and coming out with another.
Davina is better in the play than in our book, funnier and fuller,
also more likeable. I am a little afraid that my comments will not be
very reliable because of having been aware of the story in its other
form, and for this reason I would encourage you to go the New Play
Centre route to see what they say or perhaps get someone else—do
you know any playwrights out there?—to give you an assessment.
My feel for pacing, especially at the end of the play may well be tied
up with my previous involvement with the story and you may need
someone better able to take a fresh approach. Does this make sense?
I'm thinking while typing, not always a good thing. [A detailed
examination of Carol's take on the play preceded this and is
omitted.]

Don had a call from UNESCO last week, a very poor connection,
asking if he would like to go to mumble mumble for the first two
weeks in December. He said yes, and then worried what he said yes
to. But it is Albania! Of all the exotic places! Naturally I'm going too.
We'll just get back to France in time to pack up and leave on the
19th of December.

Our week in London was excellent, an R-and-R trip, Don
called it. We saw six plays in five days, and what struck me,
I must say, was how few good plays there are. I mean, compared
to how many good novels there are around. Even Chekhov's
The Seagull is pretty unshapely to the modern ear. We saw one
piece of experimental theatre in a pub about Tom Paine which
was really the best thing we saw. Don is now reading his
Rights of Man, which was written in the same pub where the
theatre was.

Am glad the word processor is proving a success.

I *love* your letters. I've enjoyed this thoroughly.

Love,
Carol

October 24, 1985

Dear Carol,

Your two letters and the ms arrived from France. On the same day I finally got the ms back from Deneau with nothing but a note saying sorry for the inconvenience.

Thank you so much for all your work on the play ms. I like all your suggestions, and they gave me some good ideas and a framework to make changes on. I wish I knew a playwright—for some reason, I've backed away from the writing community here, never go to meetings or keep up contacts, and I don't know why I've done this, but I suspect it is because I've not felt like a bona fide writer, having published so little for so long.

How long will you be in Vancouver? I'm hoping that you might all come over Christmas after dinner—this year all the family will be here—now that the grandchildren are older, they aren't quite such a hazard to conversation, and the baby is as good as can be. I would also like to have a dinner party for you and Don. If you have any thoughts on times available and what you might like to do, please let me know. Tempus is fugiting with its usual recklessness.

I was most interested in your comments on plays in England, because I shared with you your disappointment re the theatre. I am wondering now if this is an increase in sophistication, or what. All my life I adored the theatre and one of the main purposes of our last trip to London was to see the plays, and yet I came away disappointed. I seemed to note the failures more than the successes, and had difficulty getting caught up as I used to. I don't know where the fault lies, but it did strike me that your comments mirrored my own feelings to a great extent.

I'm going to work on it [the play] right away. The week in Smithers was great, although I have never been wined and dined so often and so thoroughly. Three of Irene's [daughter-in-law] German relatives came over, not speaking a word of English (or French) and so they insisted on sitting in the kitchen and baking non-stop. Also, in a small town everyone has to have a whack at entertainment, so I felt quite bloated by the end of the visit. The wedding was lovely, and Stephen and Irene are starting married life with more than we've acquired in forty years.

Mostly my time has been taken up with the courses I'm taking. The instructor, Marlene Legates, is wonderful, a young woman who has a lot of scholarship (a thing I feared I might not get in a first-year university course at Capilano College), a PhD from Yale and publications on her period of expertise (Middle Ages). I'm finding it enormously stimulating, partly because my formal academic background was all science or accounting and I haven't done much history. Anyway, am in the throes of an essay, for which I'm finding the word processor invaluable. (Yes, I do love it, although was shaken to hear that the French literati use pens.) It's because of the ease of using it that you are subjected to these long letters—perhaps it'll start a rebirth of correspondence among individuals, what do you think?

Albania! Your life is exciting these days, isn't it? Glad to hear you're getting much writing done. I have been working on a couple of short stories, besides our play, and feel that I'm making progress, but also feel that with my 62nd birthday coming up I'd better damn well be making progress.

I enjoy getting your letters greatly, often passing them on to Allison for the comments on books we've been reading. Also I save them—someday when you're famous I'll pass them back and you can reap the reward from the archives.

Love,
Blanche

7 novembre 1985
[France]

Dear Blanche,

I am writing this in rather a rush since we are leaving, yet again, for England, but I wanted to tell you our Christmas plans. We have rented accommodation for the whole week—December 22–28—at Penny's Cottages [Galiano Island]. Our children will come and go.

Don suggested some time ago that I write asking you and Bruce to come over for a night. I wish I'd written earlier because they may be fully booked now. Does this sound like a good plan? We think it would be tremendous. I will have a kitchen and so on, and can put another leaf in the table.

About your play: if I were you I wouldn't hesitate giving it to Pam Hawthorne at the New Play Centre. They don't consider solicitations a bother—that is what they are there for (almost the only B.C. cultural grant I think for writing) and they welcome manuscripts.

Blanche, you've always written wonderful letters, but I do think— can't explain—that more of your VOICE comes through since you got your word processor. I save your letters too, particularly those which have dealt with our book, because if it is ever published, our letters might be of interest—Lord knows to whom. By the way, thank you so much for the Irving Layton review, which I thought was delicious. I miss that sort of news from the writing world quite a lot.

Your course sounds wonderful and I will have all sorts of questions to ask you when (I hope) I see you. Such as: Is it really a history or is there some consciousness raising as well? Who else is in your class? What ages, I mean. And mainly, who are you reading? I have got on to a stunning feminist writer from England called Marina Warner. She is brilliant, committed, prolific and also, I believe, beautiful. She writes some fiction, but mainly books which deal with how women have been perceived in art/literature/philosophy. (She leaps with ease from one to another.) One book was on the Virgin Mary, how she was viewed in different ages. Warner's latest, just out, deals with women turned into allegory; liberty, justice, truth, etc. She hints that male gallantry bestowed these qualities on women as compensation for exclusion and subjugation. I think Allison would like her too. I hope in some way we're related—I was a Warner before I became a Shields.

I'm struggling with the final section of my novel. I wish I could remember who it was that said a writer writes two books simultaneously, the one that comes out of the pen (or word processor) and the golden book in the head. I think of this frequently, because

I know what I want to do and am trying to do it, but somehow not succeeding. My hope is that, sitting in a café in Albania—if they have cafés—I'll be able to pull it all together.

We're meeting lots of people and I've had to retract my idea of their chilly inhospitality. I sometimes wish, though, that they understood the virtues of SIMPLE entertaining. I always feel they've bankrupted themselves for a mere dinner. Oh, we are getting fat; eating is our hobby here. Don and I go once a week (sometimes twice, often twice) to a little place in the country full of ambience, imaginative food and low prices.

Shall have to run if I'm going to make the post office before five. Do please try to come to see us in Penny's Cottages. We can walk and talk and get ourselves properly caught up.

Love,
Carol

❧Bruce and I did catch the necessary ferries on December 27th to go to Galiano Island to see the Shieldses. Carol said she would love to meet [author] Jane Rule who lives on the island, so she phoned, and Jane and her lovely partner Mary invited us (with husbands) over for tea. I had been suffering from what seemed to be food poisoning. We had eaten at a restaurant the evening before and I woke up feeling distinctly woozy but so determined to see Carol that we took the trip anyway. I felt wretched all day, but Carol made me lie down for a while, and later I felt better, especially when we were welcomed at Jane Rule's home. Their place was warm and cozy and Christmasy, and the hot tea and pleasant talk revived me.

January 4, 1986

Dear Carol,

It was splendid seeing you and yours on the 27th, in spite of my propensity to throw up. As I said on the phone, your young are a wonderful lot, and I feel I've gotten to know them a bit now.

Here as you see are the assessments on the play, and the play itself.* (Perhaps you should read the play first, then the assessments?) Elizabeth Dancoes, as you will see, is far more positive than Claire Brown. Do you know either of them?

I wonder what you think of Margaret Atwood's new book [*The Handmaid's Tale*]. Allison absolutely loved it and agreed with Jane Rule, that the drawing back in the last part that bothered me was just right (although I question Jane's belief that it was a matter of integrity—on the other hand Allison thought so too). I also wonder if its appreciation depends on a more jaundiced view of the male half of society than I happen to have. Do give me your thoughts.

I'm reading Isak Dinesen's *Out of Africa* right now, and find the writing most interesting, as well as her insights. I can't for the life of me figure out how they would have made a movie out of it (although I gather there is some doubt that they have).

Must close, and sorry this is short. By the way, I did have a card from Adrian [Lang], lovely picture of the family. Did you see it? Best to Don.

Love,
Blanche

February 10 1986
[Winnipeg]

Dear Blanche,

Please forgive this rather long silence. As you can imagine, dropping back into life here has been a little overwhelming after our long leisure-filled months in France. Teaching, for one thing—mainly trying to stay one lecture ahead of the class. And finishing the novel [*Swann*], which was promised for January 1st

---

*I had followed Carol's suggestion and sent my play based on *A Celibate Season* to the New Play Centre for comments.

and now absolutely must be delivered on February 15th—when Don and I go to Toronto for a few days. They have the first 4/5ths, but await the "resolution" which I intend to finish today, around midnight probably. If only I knew what the resolution is! All this frantic scrambling is about to end (tho there will be a little rewriting, not much apparently) and, yes, I would like to work a bit on the play and would like to keep your script.

Now for some comments. I think both the critiques are positive and probably right, particularly about the need to simplify. More and more, seeing plays, I feel they lack the kind of density of thought that one can bring to a novel. Not that this makes them less pleasurable or imbued with possibility; just that one must think in terms of making a single point, not five or six. I'll certainly be coming for the [Writers' Union] AGM, and by that time, if we've both got some ideas and scenes written down, maybe we could have a brainstorming. By the way, I think—though I'm not sure you agree—that these two responses were exceedingly positive.

You asked about the Margaret Atwood book, but, of course, I've hardly read anything. Except for Lucy Maud Montgomery's journals, which I got for Christmas and absolutely loved. I felt I was inside that woman's head, wonderful. Also sad.

Love,
Carol

February 19, 1986

Dear Carol,

A quick note in response to yours. We're going through a rather trying time right now, because a couple of weeks ago Bruce was diagnosed as having prostate cancer. He was in Toronto at the time and had phoned back to get the test results from the doctor, so he came home that weekend. The doctor hit us with rather bad news, that although such cancers have a very high cure rate [Bruce's] was of a type that had a 30% chance of having spread, and so before operating they would do a bone scan, which they did on Monday. We had a harrowing day yesterday until we got the wonderful news that the scan was negative, indicating it probably hadn't spread and they could operate. That was supposed to happen tomorrow, but as we got ready to go to the hospital today we were told that there were no beds (at the General), a result of the Socred's restraint. (As if I wasn't already mad enough at them!) So the operation will be postponed until next week, probably Monday.

I've thought of you often during this, because of the hard time you went through when Don had his trouble. Both of us are having pretty wild mood swings, plunged into despair at the first news, then optimistic because of the good cure rate, then despairing after the consultation with the doctor, then euphoric after the bone scan, and so on, and now hunkering down for more waiting. However, we both feel optimistic now, and expect the worst to be over soon. The surgery is major and there is quite a long recovery period, but it will be a great relief to have it behind us. The family have been wonderfully supportive—I feel for those who, when the evil days come, have no children.

Very little word on *A Celibate Season*. I've phoned John Juliani twice at the CBC. The first time he said he was definitely interested but that the CBC was involved in deciding whether to continue with the novel-reading. The second time they had just been hit with the new budgetary restrictions and he said everything was up in the air and as soon as anything had been decided he would let me know. I don't know if no news is good news or not. As for Douglas & McIntyre, incredibly, nothing. I will phone them as soon as my head is together again. I'm so glad you would like to work on the play a bit. Initially I was disappointed at what I took to be a lack of enthusiasm by the two critics, but after calming down I felt as you do, that they were positive and probably right. I am interested in our idea of the one-act play and would like to work on it, except that I'm not sure if I'll find the time. Besides the medical worries, I have a few clients whose

accounting I do—this year I'm not going in to work full time—
and so will be busy off and on at that.

Delighted to hear your novel is nearly done—by now it must be
done—and wish you great good fortune with it.

I [had] a great talk with Christie Harris [children's author] who
is better than ever after having her hip joints replaced and is active in
writing and promoting a book with someone helping her in
California. May the Lord grant that we will be that blessed in the
years ahead! (Hope I'm not sounding gloomy. Reminders of mortality
take some digesting.)

Must run, and I'll drop a note when Bruce has had the operation.
My best to Don and any of the young who are around.

Love,
Blanche

March 11, 1986

Dear Carol,

A quick note to tell you that I finally talked to Shaun Oakey today
after leaving two messages. He began by telling me how embarrassed
he is over the length of time they've kept our ms, and explained that
the western editors had all read it (including Scott McIntyre himself),
and they had then sent it on to the eastern editor, who had got
behind due to having a baby and other unnatural phenomena. The
western editors had been enthusiastic but because of the holdup had
been unable to make the decision. He hopes to have the answer by
the end of the month.

I, lying only slightly—in spirit if not in letter, responded that
Morningside had the ms and would be interested (anxious, I
implied) to hear what Douglas & McIntyre intended to do with it.
I also hoped that the eastern editor wouldn't be influenced by the
kind of parochialism that sometimes grips those in Toronto when a
story is set with a western background, pointing out that a story
worth telling should be tellable regardless of background, a point
with which he heartily agreed. (He has an English accent.)

Noncommittal, however. I expanded on the CBC budget cuts as the reason for the present delay, but shook nothing more from him but more abject apologies and the promise that they "hoped" to have the answer by the end of the month. I don't intend to phone CBC until then, because if the answer is positive it might give more leverage.

Bruce got home from the hospital last Wednesday, still bearing two drains and a catheter. A home nurse comes in twice a day and changes the dressings, and I run up and down stairs and in my lady's chamber as well as my lord's, doing a thousand and one other things. None of them are writing, or even the accounting jobs that sit accusingly in my den. I'm frustrated that there seems to be no possibility of my working on that one-act play idea you mentioned, although things may get easier. Bruce is a good patient, but the surgery was major enough that recovery will be a long slow process. However, I swore that if he was going to be well I'd have my tongue torn out by the roots before I ever complained again. (So there I'll be, tongueless.)

Must close. Can't tell you how much I'm looking forward to seeing you in May, along with the stimulation of getting out and seeing people at the convention. Allison stayed with Bruce Saturday night while I went to the Liberal convention dinner, and I sat beside a very nice young man who turned out to be an articled student at Bull, Housser & Tupper, so I asked if he knew Anne, and he said he did and that she was very well liked by everyone there, and that she was very competent.

Many thanks for the phone call the other night. It is amazing how comforting it is to know one has friends at such a time. Hope you have crawled out from under the various deadlines—if so, Allison highly recommends a book *In The Clear Light* by Fiona Kidman. Haven't read it yet myself.

Love,
Blanche

Mar 24, 1986

Dear Carol,

Can you believe this, after last week's conversation? [Douglas & McIntyre had rejected *A Celibate Season*] Either it was killed in the east or they were hanging on to see if something more exciting came in before deadline day. A pox on them & their ilk!

Many thanks for your thoughtful gift to Bruce, who is looking forward to reading it when he can sit up again. Poor guy had a setback last week—a testicular infection (from the catheter probably), so had to stay in bed with an ice pack and massive doses of antibiotic. It's a month today since the operation & still on his back! Poor soul. Good thing the doctor told him to book off 3 months.

I'm scared now to phone our last bastion, the CBC.

Love,
Blanche

April 1986 – cold and windy

Dear Blanche,

It was wonderful hearing from you and finding Bruce is up and around and that the prognosis is so good! What a relief this must be to you, and what a good feeling finding life slipping back to normal once again. (We never appreciate normal when we have it . . .)

You will be interested to hear I met your friend Jo [Hutchinson] in Ottawa. She introduced herself after a panel discussion at the national library—Robert Weaver, John Metcalf and Norman Levine and me, subject: the short story in Canada. I was, of course, asked to speak on women writers in Canada. Hmmmm. This was for the National Book Festival last week. We had a few minutes to talk and get acquainted.

I also ran into Adrian Lang the other day. She's looking glamorous as ever and is now working for a consulting firm—some sort of liaison between government and business, I think. A lobby group? Probably. Not sure though, and of course one doesn't ask.

We are leaving tomorrow for a three-week trip to Texas. We'll be driving, attending two conferences, and coming slowly home up the Mississippi. All new territory for both of us, and we're quite pleased to have carved this little trip out.

I plan to spend an hour or two writing each morning in "The Coffee Shops of America."

It will be wonderful seeing both of you. This will surely be the biggest AGM in years. I think Don may want to come to the open events, certainly the reception. Do you think Bruce will feel up to it? Give him our best.

Love,
Carol

➶ Carol's remark that the Writers' Union convention would be the biggest in years was based on the fact that Vancouver was hosting Expo '86, and we supposed—correctly, as it turned out—that many writers would take advantage of the opportunity to attend Expo.

May 20, 1986

Dear Carol,

I'm wondering if we might snare you for June 3rd [for dinner]— I thought of June 2nd, but remembered it's your birthday and presume family would like to do something. There is an AGM reception on the evening of the 29th, M. Atwood apparently giving readings, so maybe the four of us could go.

Had a note today from Caroline Heath (Fifth House Publishers), who says on the basis of the excerpt I sent she would like to see the ms. Perhaps I'll wait to send it until we've talked and decided what tack [regarding the rationale re timeliness] to take.

Also had a phone call from John Juliani (CBC), who says there is a whole new crowd at the CBC and he is holding off presenting anything until he gets the feel of what they want. He says *Morningside* will still be using drama, but for the time being he is feeling his way. I asked him if there was anything we could do to facilitate the presentation, and he said, yes, a synopsis suggesting that it could be broken down into, say, ten 15-minute episodes with an example of an episode would be a big help. So I thought I could perhaps work on that.

Bruce is getting better all the time and all is well. Must run, but am looking forward greatly to seeing you both.

Love,
Blanche

❧ The weather for the May Writers' Union AGM was unusually hot and sunny, and Carol and I sneaked away from many of the workshops to sit outside and go over our work on *A Celibate Season*. Shaun Oakey, who by then had assumed a villainous stature in our minds, was present and I suggested we confront him. I tried to be aggressive in pointing out that he had led us down the garden path, and while the poor man sputtered and looked distinctly uncomfortable, Carol (sensibly) slipped away. At our dinner later I gave her a bad time about it. (The poor man was no doubt merely following orders.)

June 4, 1986

Dear Blanche,

I didn't manage to get hold of you yesterday and finally decided you had gone off sailing. But we both wanted to tell you how thoroughly we enjoyed the evening—from sitting out in the garden through that delicious meal and into the night. It is always a treat to see Marilyn [Flitton] and good to see Sandra [Djwa] and Bill, and, of course, Allison—wish we'd had more time. And of course I loved having some time with you and am now hoping that you'll really come to Paris and Bruce can travel the cathedrals and test his forest-clearing theory which I think has great possibilities and originality. Many thanks to you both for such a memorable evening.

I wrote to Caroline Heath this morning and am now having a good hard look at our September letters. I hope to have the ten, perhaps twelve, pages off to you by the weekend. Imagining a radio broadcast has made me imagine real voices for the first time. A man

named Fred Diehl was the director of my *Women Waiting* play, and
he asked me to send him something else. I am wondering—when
we get our trial script together—if we might send one [to] him as
well as your CBC connection.

I think they will have to back down on this somehow. Surely
we're not going to stand for this. Are we?

Love,
Carol

June 10, 1986

Dear Carol,

Sorry I missed your phone call. So glad you enjoyed the dinner—
wasn't it grand and noisy and like a party out of *A Celibate Season*?
I seem to remember my contribution as consisting largely of shouting at Marilyn to shut up, something I don't remember ever actually
doing before. Something in the air perhaps? Rhododendron fever, or
the miracle of sitting out in North Vancouver in *June*? (The weather
has now backed off, no longer hot but very pleasant.) My only
regret is the usual one, that we had too little time to talk. This has
been a most social week. Saturday night another dinner party for
the Buchanans [Judd and Kay, old friends from Ottawa], this time
equally unrestrained but unreservedly political. As our contribution
to Canada this time we worked on the Japanese-Canadian question
and the faults in the Liberal party.

Other things. Your invitation to visit you in Paris is receiving pretty
serious consideration in the Howard household, but are you sure you
want house guests for a week? It is such a beguiling opportunity that
we are toying with the idea of a couple of weeks in May, one with you
and one touring about the French countryside and staying at little
inns. But I know that with children coming and going you may find
your schedule more hectic than you expect, so please think carefully
about whether or not you want to cope with Howards, and whether
or not late May sounds like a good possibility.

Love to all,
Blanche

June 16, 1986

Dear Blanche,

A quickie. [A discussion of the radio plays we were attempting to write from *A Celibate Season* for the CBC is omitted.] I sort of like the reference to Stanfield—"is he still alive?"—and chuckled. Why not leave it in, and if CBC thinks it's cruel, they can take it out. I sent it off quickly. I often wish I had an at-home copy machine, but I suppose Pierre Berton has that kind of luxury. And, yes, I think you should send to both Fred Diehl and [John] Juliani, but perhaps you should say to Juliani that you've done so, explaining that Fred Diehl had directed *Women Waiting* and asked me to submit other ideas. (Always risky this, politics everywhere, maybe better to leave off mention.)

All well here. Cool and sunny, but after the blustery Newfoundland climate, this seems balmy. I had a wonderful time. Met some women writers there, wonderful women, and also Mary Pratt, who is a delight. One of the women I met told me a hilarious story about how she'd gone to a Toronto literary party and been introduced six times in one evening to Pierre Berton—and he never noticed. I think I'll write a story about this.

Love,
C

June 19, 1986

Dear Carol,

Glad you had such fun in Newfoundland. The Pratts are good friends of mutual friends of ours who live half the year here and half in N.S., so we've heard much about what great people they are.

Just forced myself through Rudy Wiebe's *The Scorched-Wood People* for my reading club. It was hard going at first but quite exciting toward the end, but don't break your neck getting it.

Love,
Blanche

June 19, 1986

Dear Blanche,

A couple of comments about the summary. I found when going over the first episode that I was cutting, cutting, cutting. Of course, if we concentrate on the theme of separation, that will automatically exclude a lot of the political comment. My other concern is how much they will want to read, but feel they would appreciate brevity.

The other problem is the prudishness of the CBC. For this reason I've struck out the menstruation story, and know we'll have to go very delicately over the affairs in the unsent letters. Tightrope walking.

About coming to Paris, we do hope to have lots of visitors. I intend to give them a key and a Metro map and let them do their own touring about and regard us as a particularly friendly inn where they may pitch in in the kitchen if they wish. So you see, I am not worrying about getting boxed in. Do let us know, as soon as possible though, your dates, because we have room for only two others and I will have to start a schedule of some sort.

Sorry this is so awfully rushed. Best to Bruce.

C

June 23, 1986

Dear Blanche,

Just a note to say, yes, I think it is an excellent idea to cut letters down. They sound more letterish for one thing. I've also been told that people like books with short chapters. (Of course it's only a step to short sentences and short words . . .) I think the story will "set up" better, faster and more dramatically.

We've had beautiful weather, hot and sunny, but I've been indoors, bent like a monk over my desk, trying to get the changes in the novel [*Swann*] done before I go east on July 4th. Also have to write a lecture. They want me to speak on "the writer's secrets." If only I knew some.

About Rudy Wiebe, I am so fond of him but have only ever managed to finish one [book]. At the moment I am reading almost nothing and suffering from malnutrition. But am keeping a list of books that I plan to read when things let up a bit. Suggestions are welcome.

Love,
C

Dear Carol,
    You said that it is surprisingly easy to change timeliness, and you are absolutely right. We really do repeat near-term history all the time, and problems tend to be more or less universal. I changed the specifics in B.C. to simple labour unrest (we've seen plenty of that on TV lately, and it's always the case pretty well) and had a big teachers' strike. Anyone out of B.C. won't question that at some point there was a teachers' strike—hasn't every province had one or more?—and only B.C.ers will relate it to a specific event, which is okay.
    Bruce is getting stronger all the time and I hope that nasty little stretch is finished with. Certainly has focused me on mortality and aging and other usually ignored topics. Today is the anniversary of Bruce's election to Parliament—1968, 18 years, hard to believe. Also that the one event changed our lives so profoundly.

Love,
Blanche

June 1986
Dear Blanche,
    I'm still fretting and picking over the novel [which would become *Swann*], which is now essentially done and in my editor's hands. I'll be spending all of Saturday with her making minor adjustments—hope we don't discover anything major to do, because I believe I've put enough energy into this book and that you can always do too much, over-tinker, and it shows. I've just reread, in order to get some ideas for the lecture I'm giving next week, Flaubert's letters—in English naturally, which are so delightful and say so many wise and useful things about writing. What are you going to do when you finish these

revisions? I expect you have a plan. Have you ever thought of doing an intellectual police story? I've recently met Eric Wright who writes one a year and thinks it's the last stand for the traditional (i.e., plotted) novel. He is such a nice man that I even read one of his books, *The Night the Gods Smiled*, and was surprised (what a snob!) to find it so well written. I even thought that someday, down the road, I might have a try . . . but for now am anxious to work on some stories.

Have also reread *Transatlantic Blues* by Wilfrid Sheed, nice jaunty style, a little tiresome but here and there it sings. Dribbles off in the end though, which I fear my book does. My new title idea [for what was to be *Swann*] is *The Rivers of This Country*. Now I have to try to fit it in somehow, some internal reference.

It was tremendous to hear that Bruce is back at work and feeling so well.

Love,
Carol

July 9, 1986

Dear Carol,

[Discussion about the comments received from editors who had seen *A Celibate Season* has been omitted.]

Was interested in your remarks about mystery stories. Some of the genre writing these days is excellent, and like you I was astounded to find some excellent stuff in *Tesseracts*, the sci-fi anthology that Judith Merrill edited. Guess we don't know what's going on in other fields. I told you they asked for a rewrite on a sci-fi story I'd submitted, didn't I?

Was also interested in your thought that you might have a try at mysteries down the road, and had an amusing idea that we could perhaps write one together while you're in France, handing each other new clues and problems as we wrote alternate chapters. There would have to be certain ground rules, such as no clues that the person putting them in can't see her way to resolving, and it would probably be more along a fun type of puzzle to do than something publishable. Does the idea grab you at all?

Have read two wonderful novels: Fiona Kidman, *In the Clear Light.* New Zealand writer, very unusual. And Anita Brookner, *Hotel du Lac,* truly wonderful. You've probably read it. She is so subtle and manages a Faustus-like character tempting the spinster-writer-heroine, and I didn't even notice the Goethe atmosphere until mulling it over afterwards. Must run. All best.

Love,
Blanche

July 15, 1986

Dear Blanche,

Enclosed, alas, is the bad-news note from Fred Diehl; no doubt you have received something similar from John Juliani by now [the CBC contacts]. Well, how were we to know they'd done something similar . . . and so on. Onward—

Let's hope Caroline [Heath, of Fifth House Publishers] will take a chance on this. Another possibility is a Saskatchewan press called Coteau Books. The fact that they are in Medicine Hat (or is it Moose Jaw?) may be worrying, but they have the right idea about publishing, that is they are putting out books in the mass-market format and selling them for under $5. (They are doing an anthology of love stories to come out in the fall, which is how I discovered them.) I do feel that eventually we'll place it. I had some good luck this week which makes me feel optimistic—years ago David Williamson and I wrote a play together. Recently we cut it down to a one-act piece, and it will be done in Toronto at Solar Stage (a lunchtime theatre) next October. We're delighted, especially since we began to think this would never float.

I'm most interested in your mystery novel proposal—though next year won't work for me since I've already committed myself to 16 stories (about aging and dislocation). But the next year . . . What we need is a superb idea. Let's keep a list of ideas. Do you think we can write one which doesn't require police or detectives—a sort of amateur sleuth? With an odd setting—like a hospital? Or a Writers' Union meeting? Hmmm.

Don is calling—we're off to do some errands. All best.

Love,
Carol

July 22, 1986

Dear Carol,

Here it is, all the rest of it [the revised *A Celibate Season*]! Sent guests off sailing with Bruce on Saturday and had a whole day's go at it because I was determined to get it off before I leave on my strange holiday to the Lloydminster H.S. Reunion this weekend with a woman I haven't seen since Grade 12 (1940) when I was 16. (Will soon know whether or not you can go home again.) Don't know why I feel impelled to do this but I suppose it will be *un aventure*. I'll be spending a few days in Calgary while I'm at it—too bad we are missing one another there.

Must run and get this mailed, and then am meeting the friend with whom I'm driving to Calgary for lunch. Something eerie about trying to find the person you once knew as a teenager beneath the grey hair and wrinkles of a woman in her sixties. Why am I doing this?

Hope your time works out okay on this [editing the book]. As long as you can indicate all your changes before you go in August, I'll have no difficulty getting it off before the end of September.

Love,
Blanche

August 8, 1986

Dear Carol,

I'm hurrying to get this off before house guests return from Expo and we take off on the boat tomorrow for four days. Got home from the reunion Tuesday to find a corporate client of mine had been reassessed $12,000 in tax and was having a nervous breakdown, in which I joined her. Got it more or less

straightened out (I hope, tax dept. error I sincerely pray), then
Bruce's Boston cousin and husband arrived last night and [I] am
whirling around like mad. (Where are the quiet times of yester-
month?) The reunion was a lot of fun, all us old dolls and guys
in our sixties suddenly becoming kittenish and animated
and quite different and I loved the whole thing. The woman
I travelled with was very nice—more so than I remember—and
we exchanged stories throughout the thousand-odd miles there
and back.

Please do anything you think will work [this follows several
paragraphs of suggestions on *A Celibate Season,* omitted]—I have
more faith in your judgment re structure than in mine. I do hope
you get yourself packed and ready on time—your summer has been
wild, hasn't it?—but once there, you can rest in language anonymity
for a while. I hope. I will write at more length re my own doings
when things quiet down (one more batch of house guests and one
more Expo dinner party).

All the best to you, and Don too.
Blanche

8 septembre 1986
12/14 rue Xaintrailles, Paris

Dear Blanche,

A very short note to tell you we are settled at last—after 2 weeks
of wandering—and I should have the last pages off to you within
a week. Today's our first "normal" day, that is Don has gone off
to work and I'm settled at the typewriter. Funny how anxious we
both were to get back into a rut, any rut. Hope you haven't given
up on me.

Warm and sunny here, the sky, unlike Winnipeg, always a bit hazy.
Yesterday, Sunday, Don and I strolled boul. St-Germain, bought
a *Sunday Times* and sat in the front row of a café—heaven. Our apt.
is Spartan, but we're looking around for plants and posters. We're in
a neighbourhood described by our landlord as petit bourgeois. Lower

middle-class, I think this means. Our landlord will appear in a story one day, you can be sure. He is a world authority on the 16th century, a prof at the Sorbonne, and a sharpie businessman. Our apt., we gather, is a sophisticated form of tax evasion.

Love,

C

September 27, 1986

Dear Carol,

The final draft reached me on Thursday, and today I had a quiet day (Saturday, Bruce working on boat) so was able to finish it off and get it in the mail to Caroline Heath.

I was very lucky to pick up your CBC talk on writing *Various Miracles*. I thought it was excellent, extremely literate and articulate, and that you read wonderfully well on the radio.

My life plugs along relatively unchanged, which as one ages is perhaps a triumph in itself. I'm taking an excellent history course— Reformation to the French revolution—at Cap College, same prof as last year, and enjoying it thoroughly. Also, and I think this bespeaks madness, have started another novel—hope springs infernal, but what else do I do with my life? It's odd that in spite of my lack of success I don't feel happy unless I'm working away, so perhaps as various philosophers tell us, it's the becoming that counts.

Our reading group did *Pride and Prejudice*, and it was such a relaxing treat to read it again. Also read an interesting bio of Jane Austen by Lord David Cecil—no doubt you've read it, but if not you'd enjoy it. Next we are doing V. Woolf, *The Waves*, and I'm reading an interesting analysis of her that claims that her "Madness" was spelled out in her various novels for all to see, and that it probably wasn't madness but justifiable neurosis. Author's name Roger Poole [*The Unknown Virginia Woolf*]. Haven't got far enough to decide if he's going to make a case or not. I think I told you how much I've been enjoying Anita Brookner.

Interesting that Robertson Davies [*What's Bred in the Bone*] and
Atwood [*The Handmaid's Tale*] are both on the short list for the
Booker Prize, isn't it? My own opinion is that Davies' is the better
novel, although Atwood's is far more flamboyant and memorable
(like *The World According to Garp*). The trouble with Atwood's, I've
finally decided, is that there is no relief from the misogyny. By that
I mean that there is no redemption, or transcendence, or other
aspect of humankind rising above, which was not true with the
novel with which it is most often compared, *1984*. In that novel the
love between the man and woman pitted itself against the brutality
of the state, but in Atwood's there is never a gleam of something
better than the lowest common denominator. Have you read it
yet, and if so, do you think that may be it? Or perhaps redemption
isn't the missing thing—thinking of *Madame Bovary*—as long as the
protagonist is fulfilling the destiny implicit in the undeveloped
character.

I decided this year to go back to the Writers' Union, which I have
neglected terribly for some years (partly because I wondered if I
could describe myself as one any more, but on second thought, or
third or fourth, decided I could do so as much as most of them).
Many of the old crowd there, including Sandy [Duncan] who is
looking wonderful. Christie [Harris] was there, exclaiming about
how wonderful it is to be able to walk again after her hip operations
and looking as lovely as always. A very nice young woman named
Jan Hudson is chairman this year, and very good at it she is. George
Payerle as bumptious as always, Jan Drabek a bit more subdued.
Very good turnout, about 15.

Oh this will amuse you—I went to a Liberal thing one night
and the man who is running the Liberal campaign provincially (yes,
Vander Zalm has called the election) is named Rick Antonson. He
was being very charming to me, told me he was a vice-president at
Douglas & McIntyre. Well! I think I have untapped rivers of
vengeance flowing in my veins, because I immediately took the
opportunity to tell him our sad story re Shaun Oakey, and got several
apologies and assurances that that sort of thing shouldn't happen.

Ha! Oh, by the way, went to a bash for [John] Turner the other night (poor guy, Keith Davey's new book, excerpted in *Saturday Night*, is giving him a very bad time.) Anyway, your John [Carol's son] came up and we had a nice visit. He tells me you are successfully dodging bombs.* I do hope all this isn't ruining your stay.

Another by the way—I never did hear from John Juliani. Not even to return the script. I suppose you know that the task force the Tories commissioned to look into the CBC came back with a strong recommendation to throw some more money into it, and it looks as though this may happen. So I won't bother him about it until we've heard from Caroline Heath.

Expo is almost over, and with luck the awful traffic will decrease. It has been enormously successful, and against everyone's expectation the crowds have escalated since the end of summer instead of the other way. Bruce and I saw quite a bit of it, although we have missed a few things we'd like to see.

This is turning into quite a chronicle with rather a lot of prattling on. I do hope you are enjoying *le nouveau experience*, and have found new friends or at least become reaquainted with old.

Bruce is feeling wonderful now, and sends his greetings. Our very best to Don. Write soon and tell all.

Blanche

31 octobre 1986
[France]

Dear Blanche,

Your lovely long letter, written a month ago, was a treat. Aren't we marvellous to get the novel off when we said we were going to! Thanks to you, let me add—all that typing and "piecing." You must feel like a quilter. It will be interesting to hear how she responds. Being a pessimist, I'm already thinking of plan B, and have recently been marginally involved, via an anthology they produced, with

---

*This refers to a spate of terrorist bombings that occurred in Paris.

Coteau Books. Part of something called Thunder Creek Publishing Co-operative. They are growing rapidly and have a belief in good commercial publishing at reasonable prices. You may have gathered other ideas by now too.

I loved your remark "Happiness is Becoming" and have typed it out and put it over my desk along with my other old favourite "Happiness is Capability." I don't think it is in the least absurd for you to be starting a new book, and am curious to know what it is, what genre I mean, but probably it isn't a good idea to talk about it at this stage. I will get the book you suggest, Lord David Cecil's on Austen. We've joined the British Council Library here, a wonderful little haven next door to the Canadian Cultural Centre where I also like to drop in and catch up a bit on gloomy afternoons. I have been doing some Bloomsbury reading too, and last week Don and I did five days in London, the highlight of which was a day trip to Charleston,* Vanessa Bell's country house, just recently opened to the public and written up in *The New Yorker*. You would have loved it, with your belief in houses as our second body. It is a lovely 17th-century farmhouse, exceedingly crude in construction but made livable by her painted designs and flowers which are everywhere, on the door panels, walls, tables, chairs, cupboards—sounds like a mad Turkish jumble, but it is lovely and soft, one of the most comfortable houses I've ever seen. From there we took a taxi over the downs, five miles away, to Virginia's Monks House, simpler and a little less hospitable, but again the sense of a house truly belonging to someone. A marvellous day full of unexpected adventures and encounters and conversations.

I read Robertson Davies' book just before coming away and Atwood's just after arriving. I thought the first was heartless and off balance somehow by the time structure, something he usually handles with such skill. I really just skimmed Atwood's. Don't know why it failed to take me in, but I expect it had something to do with the confusion of settling in here, so perhaps I should try it

---

*Charleston near Firle in Sussex.

again now that we're so much more settled. And we are. Did I tell you Adrienne Clarkson's lovely metaphor, that living in France was like wearing a beautiful shoe with a stone in it. I think I was highly conscious of the stone for the first few weeks, but now the shoe fits well, the little string of new habits has been memorized, and time is going by too quickly. Do you have your dates yet? I'm so glad Bruce is feeling his old self. Oh, we'll have so much to talk about! There have been no bombs for ages and our shopping bags are no longer searched at the post office and department stores. Bella Pomer, who was planning to come this month, wrote me a note and said she had cancelled "under the circumstances." It took us a few minutes to figure out what she meant, since in a city this size it all seems a little abstract.

Catherine is here with us, doing a three-month apprenticeship with UNESCO in their bureau that looks after the protection of historical sites—she loves it and is blooming, and we adore having her. And I am writing, but never as much as I would like and never as well. I think short stories don't give me quite as much carrying-over satisfaction as novels, and my few stories written here are so far a trifle dry and academic. Next week I am going to Germany to give a reading at the University of Trier where they have a Canadian Studies program—and I am absolutely delighted. This is part of a four-day conference, and I plan to attend every session.

Am off now to stand in line and buy our November bus passes. Today is All Saints' Day here, a gloomy occasion with much visiting of graves and so on.

Much love to you and Bruce,
Carol

November 18, 1986

Dear Carol,

For the first time in history I am totally unable to concentrate on writing this morning, since I'm anxious to spread the news and celebrate—so will spread the news to Paris and tell you that Leslie just had her baby—a boy this time, and the labour only three hours long. I feel absolutely jubilant (naturally). Will be going up this afternoon after my history class, and can hardly wait to see the new little life. When Austin phoned this morning the baby was crying lustily (Leslie is in one of those maternity hospitals where the baby is with the mother from the start), so he must be healthy.

It was great to get your letter, and note that you sound very "up" this time, so I gather you are now accustomed enough to France not to go through withdrawal for the first while. [I] was delighted also that Catherine is able to be with you for three months—I always found, during our Ottawa life, that the worst part was separation from family. When I saw John, he mentioned that he'll be going for a month at Christmas, so it sounds as though your life is far from lonely this year.

Enclosing the rather strange response from Juliani—"claustrophobic" is not one of the complaints we've had before and I'm not sure what the hell it means, if anything, are you?

Another reason I have been anxious to get a letter off to you is to make sure that you know that you have to apply for your Public Lending Rights [PLR] for this fiscal year before December 15th. Surprisingly, they did get a budget allocation which has to be used before March 31st, so they sent out forms to everyone—no doubt yours has come, but I don't know what arrangements you made for the transfer of mail. The payments are to be based on library holdings.

We are still hoping to come to Paris towards the end of May, but can't firm up our dates just yet as there is a chance that we may go on to Russia. Bruce is a member of Veterans Against Nuclear Arms, and they are organizing a May trip, so we thought we might tie it all in together. We are planning on a week maximum in Paris, and I am looking forward to seeing you and having some great conversation.

No word from Fifth House—does anyone ever do anything fast in this business? I have been writing up a storm—don't know what's got into me, but am at the last chapter of the first draft of a novel. It just seemed to flow out, don't know if it's any good at all.

I learned a great deal from you while doing *A Celibate Season*, about being novelistic, about indirect quotes and a lot of other things, and feel that technically I've done a lot better. This novel is written very much in a vernacular, breezy style and I hope [with] a certain amount of humour, and I copied your technique of compressing it into a small time frame—two weeks from the day the female computer programmer quits her job until the denouement—and as I say, [it] went together so fast that I wrote a number of chapters in three hours each, which is fast for me. Mind you, it is very rough, needs a lot of fleshing out and so on, but it has kept me excited and non-neurotic all fall. In addition, am enjoying the history course and as I am managing about the only A's in the (freshman) class of 35, feel that so far my brain is continuing to work. (Important reassurance when you've just had your 63rd birthday.)

Was interested in your comments about Robertson Davies' and Atwood's books, and am wondering if you have read Anita Brookner yet. I have just finished a quite astonishing book, *The Bone People* by a New Zealand Maori woman named Keri Hulme. It is absolutely unusual, a combination of literary and suspense-gripper and psychological study and mythological tract and anything else you might want to add. A big thick book that sweeps you along in places and in other places makes you mad—I don't know where to put it in my catalogue of what books are. She couldn't get it published at first and finally the New Zealand Women's Collective printed it. Then the U of Louisiana, which has a prize (Pegasus) for out-of-country books, printed it, and lo and behold, it is now a best-seller, out in paperback.

Must go, as Jacqueline [granddaughter] is with me this morning (bad cold, and she's propped in front of the TV—some grandmother!) and is mentioning the idea of lunch. Give my best to Don and Catherine, and write soon.

Love,
Blanche

December 10, 1986

Dear Blanche,

This brief note is really to wish you and Bruce a merry Christmas, also to send congratulations to Leslie—clever girl—and also to say how thrilled I am that you've actually come to the end of the first draft of a new novel. I am amazed and delighted (being such a slow old plodder) how quickly it has happened. You seem slightly worried yourself that it went so quickly, but surely this is the best sign. You say tantalizingly little about its content except for the clue: "female computer programmer quits job." I loved your remark about the writing keeping you non-neurotic; have you ever wondered how other people, non-writers, keep their neuroses at bay? What on earth do they *plunge* into? I suppose it's partly the pleasure of being submerged, but also the intricate pleasure of *making*. Uprooted here in Paris and having lost my tongue, I feel gratitude that I'm able to bring along my little sewing kit (as it were). Having said that, I wish my writing were going better. I keep writing what seem to be exercises, but have just given myself a double dose of Iris Murdoch, hoping to take on some of her largeness and colour. We shall see.

Thank you so much, Blanche, for alerting me to the PLR date. Luckily had got memos from the union and also through Bella, and managed to get things off in time—I suppose we'll all get a cheque for $10 or so, enough to cover postage on our applications. Still, the principle will have been served, and established.

John arrives this morning, Sara tomorrow and Meg the day after. Anne and her Tony come on the 23rd. We have the loan of two auxiliary apartments and so should manage. It looks very much as though we'll be returning to Albania for two weeks in February, another UNESCO contract for Don. I'm thrilled, he's a little less so. (He is trying to talk me into a week in Istanbul—what a romantic!) But I feel quite happy staying here for some reason. I guess I'm really feeling at home now, know my way around to a certain extent, and see more here than we'll ever be able to take in. We did have an overnight in the country recently, an *auberge* that was really a 12th-century mill, surrounded on three sides by water—ducks, swans, geese. After the solid cement of the 13th *arrondissment*, this was pure heaven. And amazingly, it was only 30 minutes by train from home. We plan to go again when all the children are here.

I've just written a sort of fan letter to a man called Reynolds Price who wrote an article in *The New York Times Book Review* (Nov. 9) called "Men, Creating Women." It is a plea really for men to write about women and vice versa, exceedingly sensitive and humane, also written with wit and humility. He says so exactly what I didn't quite know I believed. His belief is that we're born with a full range of sympathies, but that these become narrowed and throttled by gender and that this is currently poisoning our fiction.

As you can see, I'm still struggling with this typewriter, which has an odd little hesitation before each stroke. Perhaps this will complete my conversion to word processor, though I doubt it.

Love,
Carol

February 14, 1987

Dear Carol,
Some Valentine's Day special!
Not sure what we should do next. What do you think?

Blanche

FIFTH HOUSE LTD. PUBLISHERS
February 2, 1987

Blanche Howard,
After all this time, I'm afraid I have to say that I cannot offer to publish *A Celibate Season*. I apologize for the long delay. Because I liked certain aspects of the novel, but had serious reservations about it, I gave it to a second reader, whose observations echoed my own.

February 17, 1987
[France]

Dear Blanche,

I've already put mid-May in my calendar, and we'll be looking forward to it. It'll be wonderful poking around Paris in the warmth. It's been a fairly chilly and snowy winter here—everyone complains, even we complain, though when we return to Winnipeg, [Paris] will seem pretty palmy.

I gather you haven't heard from Carolyn [Heath] about the novel—or perhaps you have and are saving the bad news for a bit. I've had a few draggy weeks of writing—finding myself being overly critical and stiff—but seem to have worked out of it now and have two or three things bubbling about. I tried, when the children were here, to do a little work, but in the end gave it up and concentrated on being a mother. I did love having them (the silence after they left was nice too, I confess). Perhaps you know that Anne is now engaged to her Tony and will be married next December in Vancouver (the 19th, at a church not yet decided upon and a reception out at UBC—put it on your calendar). We are truly fond of Tony. I believe I told you that Anne's only reservation was that he didn't read novels. I think he will learn. Flexibility is his most noticeable quality, and a good thing too, since their first year of married life will be rather eccentric with Anne studying in England and Tony working in Florence.

Don and I have just come back from a week in Albania—yes, again—where we had further adventures. I'm more convinced than ever that this is one of the oddest and, for me, beguiling places in the world. I've been reading a little history of it, which confirms my impression of a relatively thin layer of civilization atop a barbaric past. The strangest experience of the week was attending an English lit class at the university and seeing how Marxist rhetoric can make a clone out of G.B. Shaw. Hilarious and frightening. I told my guide that it "blew my mind" and she immediately wrote it down in her list of idioms. (She is a linguist, currently writing a thesis comparing the Albanian and English languages.) More travels ahead. My research on mermaids continues.* Please let me know if you come across any while you and Bruce are out in the boat. (Actually, there are some West Coast Indian legends about mermaids which closely accord with the Nordic tales, amazing.)

Hope all is well with you both, with your novel and your student life and grandmothering.

Love,
C

20 fevrier 1987
[France]

Dear Blanche,

Your letter was here when I got back from Strasbourg yesterday, having crossed with mine. I'm writing a quickie, so you can organize your plans for May. And please don't think a week is too long—it isn't. We're looking forward to it!

By the way, Strasbourg is a marvellous medieval city. I only had glimpses in my two-day stay, but hope to get back there. What parts of France are you thinking of visiting? I know you're already familiar with Burgundy from your séjour à Dijon.

I stayed with Simone Vauthier in Strasbourg, in a most delightful apartment on a tiny street off the main square. She has made herself into *the* French expert on the Canadian short story. I spoke for two hours to her Canadian lit class and found them very open and enthusiastic. Afterwards five of us went out for a wonderful dinner with much discussion about life and literature, the sort of evening I miss here in Paris. Hope all goes well with Bruce's checkup.

About Ann Beattie, you must be referring to her new(ish) book—about a writer of an advice column? I haven't read it, but read her short stories in *The New Yorker* and once read an odd book called *Chilly Scenes of Winter.* She is unique.

Love,
C

---

*Carol used the mermaid theme in her next novel, *Republic of Love.*

March 6, 1987

Dear Carol,

Lovely to get your two nice long letters, although I gather you hadn't had the note about the reject from Fifth House yet.

Bruce and I are delighted that our plans in May will work out all right for you. We haven't made any plans yet about the other two weeks, but since we didn't manage to see the south of France on any of our other trips, we might give that a whirl. I must say I'm looking forward to it tremendously, particularly the opportunity to see both of you and have some good talks. Interesting that you say you miss talks about life and literature in France, because I find I miss them *here*. My life doesn't seem to be peopled with friends who are interested in literature these days, I think partly because the city is too big and so I don't see a lot of Marilyn and Sandra [Djwa] and such-like more kindred spirits. So here I am travelling all the way to Europe in anticipation of such treats.

Your life sounds very interesting, especially the trips to Albania and Strasbourg. Great that you are being asked to conferences on the short story, etc. Speaking of the short story, no doubt you have read *The Progress of Love* [Alice Munro]. I'd love to hear what you think of it.

I can understand why you didn't get any work done over Christmas, and think you were wise to give up and concentrate on being a mother. I'm finding I'm spending quite a bit of time grandmothering, and like all things in a writer's life that present any distraction, have times of ambivalence about it. On the one hand, it is wonderful to watch them growing and to feel close, but on the other, time runs by so quickly and writing is such a slow discipline, isn't it?

We're delighted to hear of Anne's wedding plans, and I am putting December 19th on the calendar.

We were in Victoria for a rather curious reason. Bruce had a friend in high school and in the air force named Michael Gelber (old Toronto family, brother Arthur) who now lives in New York

and was going to San Francisco for a speech and so detoured up
to see us and wanted to see the Island. He is an interesting man,
doctorates in literature and recently (although he is a senior citizen)
in psychology. He writes strange things, such as liturgical chants for
the synagogue, a play on Job, and a book of prayers. Some of these
he brought along for us to read, and he even took up an evening
chanting some of the chants (an entertainment not highly
recommended). Also he is one of those highly articulate, gregarious
people, fun in small doses—for instance, Bruce reminded him that
they'd done *The Pirates of Penzance* in high school, so he promptly
sang the entire score, all parts, on the trip into Victoria from the
ferry. Large doses would have exhausted me, but it was an
interesting weekend.

The Ann Beattie book I told you about was *Love Always,* but
in the end I wasn't as enthusiastic about it as I had expected to
be. The protagonist writes a parody of an Anne Landers–type
column, *very* witty, but the book is so negative about all the
males that it leaves you wondering if perhaps women writers
are overdoing it. All the males are either wimpy or hollow men,
and I wonder if perhaps there isn't a dangerous tendency here to
one-sidedness that is a bit alienating. (One of the things I like
about your novels—the men are whole, as well as being quite
often nice.) I've also read John Mortimer's book *Paradise
Postponed,* which is witty but exactly like watching a TV play,
which I gather it has been. The language is rather old-fashioned
and it is a very visual book, neatly done, almost complete with
scene changes.

You haven't told me at what stage your novel is. Will it be in
the spring list? And how is your current novel going? When I
come I'll bring some excerpts of my current one so you can get
an idea of it.

What other news? The Tories are enormously unpopular, about
24% in the polls, thanks to a few scandalous affairs. Leslie's baby is
round and cute, and the two-year-old is regressing to bottles and

baby-talk. Stephen and Irene's new baby is apparently coming
along well. Gregory (oldest grandchild) is now five foot five and
beginning some of the more unattractive aspects of puberty, a state
that I have difficulty sympathizing with Allison over since she was
our most rebellious and put us through hoops that Gregory will
never even think of.

Must quit rambling and do something about dinner.

Love to both,
Blanche

April 18, 1987

Dear Carol,

Bruce mentioned one day that he thought it would be nice if
you and I had some time together just to talk—rather sweet of him,
I thought—and so arranged to do some immigration things in
Paris. I do hope you will feel that you can take a day, or at least a
part of one, off, and that we can do that catching up that we always
complain never happens.

All was well with Bruce's checkup, as we had thought it would
be. Another hurdle.

To my utter astonishment PLR landed $720 in my lap.
Remember when we both thought it would be lucky if we got
enough for postage? I was more than agreeably astonished that my
books are still that alive and well and living in Canada. If I did that
well, you must have done very well. Also I see by the Writers' Union
latest [newsletter] that you got a Canada Council grant, and I am
delighted! About time, among other things.

By the way, you asked me about mermaid references. Have you
found T.S. Eliot's in *The Love Song of J. Alfred Prufrock?*:

Shall I part my hair behind? Do I dare to eat a peach?
I shall wear white trousers, and walk upon the beach.
I have heard the mermaids singing, each to each.
I do not think that they will sing to me.

I have seen them riding seaward on the waves
Combing the white hair of the waves blown back
When the wind blows the water white and black.

We have lingered in the chambers of the sea
By sea-girls wreathed with seaweed red and brown
Till human voices wake us, and we drown.

A nice poet named Jean Mallinson spoke at our church and
said how much she admired your short stories, and thought
"The Metaphor Is Dead—Pass It On" absolutely brilliant. Also saw
the paperback of *A Fairly Conventional Woman* in a bookstore in
West Vancouver.

We arrive at Charles de Gaulle airport on the morning of
May 3rd, and have arranged for a car to rent.

Looking forward enormously.

Love,
Blanche

> *22 avril 1987*
> *12/14 rue Xaintrailles*

Dear Blanche,

Forgive this brief scribble—I am without a typewriter for a few
days, like having my best friend in hospital.

I am sending a cheque in the hope that you will do a bit of shopping for me. I need:

1) 1 large Ban roll-on deodorant (non-perfume)

2) pantyhose, one-size-for-all or medium (I buy the ordinary
ones from the supermarket usually), sandal foot, in beige and in the
light grey colour. About 6 pair should see me through. French
pantyhose *sag* and hurt at the toes and last only 10 minutes.

What mundane needs. *Bon voyage. À bientôt.*

Love,
Carol

6

Work and Play
1987–1988

∿ We spent a lovely week in Paris with Carol and Don. They lived in an apartment, somewhat sparse but adequate, on either the 7th or the 11th floor, I can't remember which. I do remember that periodically the elevator broke down and we had to climb all those stairs.

The weather wasn't what one would expect of Paris in May, but we had already had two weeks of sun in France, some of it near Cannes on the Riviera. Don had to spend a few days in Normandy and I think Carol was relieved to have someone share the apartment, and perhaps she had found Paris a bit lonely with Don off at the university during the day. In spite of her promise to just turn her guests loose, she ended up taking us to many of the major sights. Between bouts of sightseeing, and even during them, we talked non-stop about books and the cultural scene in Canada. And it was then, laughing at its naïveté, that we began kicking around our thoughts on "the meaning of life," our tone dismissive yet with that undercurrent of wistfulness that is evoked by insoluble mystery.

One day, as we were about to cross the Champs-Elysées, Carol had one foot on the pavement when a car ran a red light. She was saved by Bruce flinging out his arm to stop her. Another day, when we were in the Louvre, Carol stood transfixed before a Rousseau painting of a doll, La Poupée, and we lingered in front of it for a long time. When we headed downstairs to the washroom, we were faced with the formidable woman who, for a franc or two, dispensed toilet paper to those in need, and after we had handed our francs into her disapproving and ungrateful hands, she returned to fierce concentration on her knitting. "Madame Dufarge," Carol whispered to me, and we giggled uncontrollably as we equated this woman with the one, in Dickens *A Tale of Two Cities,* who during the French Revolution purled a stitch for each head that rolled into the executioner's basket.

We met some of the friends Don had made at work and one day went on a picnic with them, and I remember a terror-filled ride in an ancient car at high speed, so crowded in the back seat that Carol had to sit on someone's knee.

She lived for the daily mail, or twice daily as it was then in France. She swooped down on the mailbox as if it might contain the meaning of life, and perhaps it does.

The galley proofs for Carol's novel *Swann* had just arrived and between outings I read them, managing, much to Carol's surprise, to finish it all, for it is a long book. I saw at once that this was a breakthrough in her writing. She had abandoned the domestic milieu of her other novels and ventured into the mystery genre, except that *Swann* is not merely a mystery, it is also a stunning work of literary fiction. Yet when I finished it I wasn't quite sure who had "done it," and Carol seized on my slight bewilderment to change the ending slightly at that late date. The novel went on to great acclaim.

May 26, 1987
North Vancouver

Dear Carol and Don,

We made it, partly because of my single-minded attention to every small change in the sounds of the motors and plane direction.

We can't thank you enough for your enormously warm hospitality. We both feel that it was the best holiday we've ever had, and most of the credit for that goes to the great finale in Paris. We have regaled our (probably bored) daughters with blow-by-blows re the Orsay, the Louvre, the Champs-Élysées—and that's a lot of blow-by-blows. I keep thinking of that haunting doll by Rousseau and wondering why I've never seen it before.

Of course the weather here was perfect the whole time we were away, and I must say the green cleanliness of Vancouver hits one with new sharpness after the grime of Paris—but as Bruce points out, rhododendrons are fine in their place but they aren't the Orsay. Leslie and Allison were at the plane to meet us, and we were surprised, as one always is, that nothing much seemed to have happened while we were away.

Allison says that it is a measure of the excitement of their lives that on Saturday night she and Leslie hoped the plane would be late so they could hang around the airport and watch the people.

You'll be interested, Carol, in the enclosed rejection of my story. I appreciated Wayne Hughes' [editor-in-chief of *Prism International*, UBC's literary magazine] thoughtful analysis and think he is right in most respects, although I was disappointed that he found the narrator's voice irritating, as this flippant glib voice is the voice of the novel. However, I'm hoping that the voice is right for a commercial-type novel and can see why it isn't for a literary mag. I think his reservations were some of the same that you had, and it has taught me the difficulty of trying to extract a short story from a novel-in-progress.

Love from both,
Blanche

June 5, 1987

Dear Carol,

I hope you did want this, Alice Munro's latest [*The Progress of Love*]. Anyway, a very small gift in return for the holiday, although

I am sorry [the book] isn't something that Don will enjoy to the same extent. He was very much part of and reason for the good time we had.

I didn't win the Distinguished Woman Award in my category [the annual YWCA awards] but console myself that I was in good non-winning company with Jane Mortifee, Sandy Wilson, Grace McCarthy, and about 60 others. Some of the winners were Doris Shadbolt, Rosemary Brown and Kay Alsop. In any case, we had fun as [film director] Sandy Wilson* came and sat with us and we were able to catch up with her life, and my daughters caught up on mutual friends.

I keep thinking about your novel and am more than ever convinced that it's a winner. Certainly it's the most complex and sophisticated thing you've done, and I'm dying to see what the William Frenches of the world think.

I toasted you on your birthday—did you feel it from afar? We had a family dinner here on yours and Leslie's birthday—ten to sit around the table now. When little Tommy gets big enough to sit, I'll need a new dining room. By the way, on the age thing, there's a great full-page *G and M* story on June Callwood and her 63rd birthday coming up. She is one great achiever!—I felt as though I'd been sitting around all these years.

Must run. I hope you enjoy this, and much love to you both.

Blanche

July 1, 1987 – Paris – hot, humid, blue sky

Dear Blanche,

WE loved having the two of you here. (The wonderful chocolates lingered for a whole week, reminding us of your visit.) I do appreciate your wise counsel, Blanche, and more than I can say your patient reading of my galleys with all the comments and suggestions. I am

---

*The award-winning film writer and director of several movies, including *My American Cousin*, had been a family friend in Penticton.

nervous about the book, know there are odd holes in it, but I guess I have to let it go and say it was the best I could do at this time.

Until three days ago we've had foul weather. Sixty sunless days, all of May and June. Suddenly we're baking, or rather broiling. Tonight we are invited to the Canadian Embassy for a garden party, which should be interesting. Our days are going so quickly. I'm working on my stories—number 15 at the moment—and worry that I'm not "using" Paris enough. I love the street life right now in the city, tables everywhere, flowers, exceedingly odd clothing or rather non-clothing.

I've just finished an odd and funny (sort of) book that I think you might like. *White Noise* by Don Delillo, paperback by Penguin. A comic novel but with a sort of background of scientific peril. It is so much a book of our times that I am feeling my own work falls into some reactionary mode. I've also finished Patrick White's *Voss* (overwritten but magnificent) and am reading his autobiography, which is delicious especially his early youth.

Will this find its way through the conduits—or sit at the bottom of a mail sack?

So much news but how to disseminate it without mail! Curses!

Carol

July 24, 1987 [Postcard]
Paris

We leave very soon for our Portugal idyll, then home 3 September. *The Progress of Love* arrived yesterday. Blanche, I am thrilled. I'm forcing myself to save it for next week. Wonderful cover! Other news: my U of Manitoba appointment came through, just as I'd adjusted to the idea of unemployment. Don't know how I feel about this—a little relieved, I think. The 16 stories are done but I want to do a couple more. Don and I have just celebrated our 30th anniversary. Amazing!

I dreamed about Leslie last night??

August 24, 1987

Dear Carol,

Welcome back! Wonder how you feel, setting foot on Canadian soil after such a long time. Some trepidation, I expect, with the novel coming out—mentioned, by the way, in William French's column on new fiction for the fall. I think of the novel often, and the character that sticks in my mind and with whom I feel continuing affinity is Dr. Cruzzi (sp?). He seems to have hit some sort of chord—I think he came alive wonderfully. Rose, too, is well rounded and thoroughly believable. I still think it's a winner.

Enjoyed your letter and was very glad to get the postcard also, and know you got the book before leaving Paris. Hope the Portugal idyll was everything you hoped for. We are off to Smithers on Friday for ten days. I'm looking forward to it—we are driving this time, and the trip through the Caribou should be nice at this time of year.

Am reading—very slowly—Northrop Frye's *The Great Code.* Fascinating and amazingly erudite. Also have picked up on Antonia White—have you read her? A writer from the twenties, really interesting.

Blanche

September 26, 1987
North Vancouver

The Editor, *The Globe and Mail*

Dear Sir,

For those of us who are *aficionados* of the work of Carol Shields, it was heartening to read the excellent review of her new novel *Swann,* in your Murder and Mayhem section, carried on the right-hand page of the Saturday, September 26th issue.

Shields' first four novels were also well-reviewed in *The Globe and Mail,* but in the category that was presented Saturday on the left-hand page. Therefore, when your reviewer states that "*Swann: A Mystery* is a first novel by Winnipeg short-story author Carol

Shields," one can only assume that *The Globe and Mail*'s right hand knoweth not what the left hand doeth.

Yours truly,
Blanche Howard

October 14, 1987

Dear Carol,

I have just finished *Swann* and have decided that the occasion demands the sacrifice of a long-held practice of not writing letters that are not actually essential to avoid bankruptcy or jail.

Loved *Swann*. The mystery is delicious. The outcome surprising. I liked the characters, who although doing many ordinary and not-so-ordinary things always manage to do them in an interesting and erudite way. Every line seems to be a supermarket of words and ideas tumbling out one after the other in an endless cornucopia of patterns on the brain.

What about Mary Swann? You left the reader to figure out the source of her genius. Was she an idiot savant? Would the poems have been as outstanding without the forced editing result-ing from wrapping fish? Is "fish" a mystic symbol? Was Mary Swann a mystic who received the poems from the collective unconscious? Was she a trance medium who received the poems from another entity? I don't expect you to spoil all the fun by telling.

At any rate *Swann* has to be the first volume of a trilogy. If Robertson can do it, can Carol be far behind? I think R.D.* had better look to his laurels. Congratulations.

Now the wedding. We are both looking forward to it with great anticipation and hope that you and Don will stay here with us. I imagine that other family accommodation will be fully taxed, so why not plan to make this your headquarters. We'll expect you.

---

*Robertson Davies.

Our regards to Don and once more congratulations. We look forward to seeing you soon.

Love,
Bruce

October 15, 1987
[Winnipeg]

Dear Blanche,

The Calgary episode [book tour] was an exercise in humiliation since I was competing with Rick Hansen no less, touring on the same day. One of the bookstores I visited (and where I signed 6 copies) had 400 copies of his book and was working out crowd-control strategies for his arrival. Toronto was interesting in a sense too; I was taken to three bookstores that sell nothing but mysteries. Can you believe this? And was interviewed on a radio show that discusses nothing but mysteries. There's a whole enormous audience that I never knew about.

Ottawa was wonderful except for an interview with Burt Heward (literary (!) editor of the [*Ottawa*] *Citizen*) who kept asking me how much I earned. And he didn't exactly ask if I was contemplating divorce but wanted to know if there were any great ruptures in my life. (I was polite, but will never do another round with that man.) The reviews have been just wonderful, and I'm starting to relax. I'm sure there will be some baddies coming up, but I've had enough to balance them. (Thank you again, Blanche, for devoting your week in Paris to editing for me.)

Well, it is wonderful to be home, though Don misses his Paris cafés and his *Le Monde* and his cronies. Winnipeg looks wonderful and feels like home—what more can I say. I grumble about the teaching, but am compensated by having the most beautiful office, the best I've ever had—with a phone, window, shelves—all those grown-up things. And Don and I've been hauling plants, pictures, posters, a rug even, full coffee and tea service, etc. I am really digging in here because I'd like to keep this [office at the university] forever. I hope I can work here (tho all I've done so far is type up the stories I wrote in Paris).

I'd be happy to read it [the novel Blanche was working on] for you. I've just read Updike's *Roger's Version*, out in paper now, and found the computer parts difficult. Obviously other readers didn't, since it was a great success.

Far better than Updike was *The Progress of Love* [Alice Munro] that I read in Portugal. I loved it! Everything else I brought along to read seemed pedestrian after it. Do you remember a wonderful and haunting story called "The Queer Streak"? I thought I had read most of the stories in *The New Yorker*, but in fact, more than half the book was new to me—and all worth rereading anyway. There is one story called "Fits" that truly puzzles me though. Tell me what you think it means. Is Peg implicated in the murder-suicide? I've read it over two or three times and am still mystified. I love it though, the part about her husband walking on top of the snow, wonderful. I do thank you, Blanche, for the pleasure of this book. Heavens, I'm glad she's one of ours.

No, I haven't read Antonia White but other people have mentioned her to me. And Northrop Frye?—no, not yet. (One of the things I miss most about Paris is having time to read.)

The sun is shining—I'm going out for a walk. Shall write again as soon as I've reread *C.S.* [*A Celibate Season*].

Love,
Carol

October 25, 1987

Dear Carol,

By now you must have Bruce's letter, and as you can see he loved the book. I had bought a copy to have you autograph when you come, for Allison for Christmas. As you can gather, Bruce was enormously impressed and entertained—so you have a whole new type of audience, obviously. I'm delighted but not surprised at the good reviews you are getting.

As for my novel, I keep getting raves with the rejects. Bantam wrote a glowing letter in which she said it was "a wonderful example of intelligent, amusing, entertaining prose at work," and went on to say that the readers had been enthusiastic. However, she said they usually only did reprints and she thought it should go to a hardback publisher.

We had a sad event on Thanksgiving weekend—[my friend] Katinka's death on the Friday, and the funeral on Monday. At the funeral they worked the eulogy around her poetry.

I was interested in your reaction to the story called "Fits" in *Progress of Love*. At our book club we had a long discussion on it. At first I thought that Peg had gone right into the bedroom to look at both of them—something she needn't have done. (She said she saw a leg in the hall, but the constable had said his head was there and she would have had to step over it to go in.) The question is, why would she do that? I don't think she was implicated in the deaths—remember the snowplow established that they had not been out the day before—but it seems that she climbed right over his horribly mangled body and into the bedroom, and got blood all over her coat.

However, one of the women in the group pointed out that in the description on page 114 of what she did at first, she turned around to go to the bedroom, and saw only that the door of the room was open. So neither leg nor head was in the hall. The only explanation I can think of is that she moved his body there—that was why the blood was on her coat and her shoes. Why would she do it?*

We are looking forward enormously to your visit in December. Bruce is very well now, although they have never been able to knock out the infection entirely. He feels fine as long as he stays on an antibiotic, which wouldn't be too bad except that it is the kind that he can't have any alcohol at all with. So I am forced to drink all wine for both of us. (Such self-sacrifice.)

Must run. I think it's true that computers lead to long-windedness because they are so fast and easily correctable.

Love to Don and from Bruce,
Blanche

---

*There follows a rather intricate examination of the story and a possible explanation.

30 octobre 1987 [Postcard]

Infinite thanks, my dear Bruce, for your letter—which you may be sure will be saved and often reread. What a delight! We're looking forward to seeing you both in December. At the moment we seem to have a place to stay (John's apartment on 12th Avenue) but we do thank you for your offer. I wish I knew more about weddings, doing the right thing, all that sort of stuff. I expect we'll just enjoy it all when the time comes.

All best,
Carol

❧ In December 1987, Anne and Tony Giardini were married in Vancouver. Somehow, in the midst of much activity, Carol and Anne were able to plan a large sit-down dinner. Sandy Duncan and I were seated at the table with Carol and Don, and Carol's siblings and their spouses.

January 1, 1988

Dear Carol,

1988! It seems no time since we were writing 1984(!) in *A Celibate Season.*

Enclosed are the critiques of the play [*A Celibate Season*, from the New Play Centre].

It was lovely but all too short having a visit with you & Don, and thank you for including us in the wedding party at your table.

We had a couple of days at Whistler with the whole family, including 2 babies. As you said about your Paris Christmas, Bruce & I found it a bit overwhelming. The Christmas dinner (15) was, however, a great success, and I seem to have survived all the activity very well.

Read Sylvia Fraser's book [*My Father's House: A Memoir of Incest and Healing*]—somewhat lurid, *very* disturbing

About your February visit [to give a lecture at Douglas College in New Westminster]—I would *love* to go if it is a public thing. If not, stay with me anyway & I'll get you there and back. I WANT TO DO THIS!

Love to both from both here,
Blanche

January 13, 1988

Dear Blanche,

A quick note at the end of a long day. The critiques from the New Play Centre are excellent!* Thoughtful, positive, encouraging. Aren't you delighted? I'm hoping that after the next read-through (a whole $5 knocked off) they'll offer to do a workshop reading, which would be helpful to you and might lead to a production by them.

I asked Dale Zieroth [at Douglas College]—and what a lovely man he is—what I'll be doing. It is a sort of in-college week, but visitors are certainly welcome, he says, and he's doing lots of promotion. For a poet to be so well organized! I'll be talking to the class about Susanna Moodie, will visit a couple of creative writing classes, a Can lit class, give a reading or two, and look at student manuscripts. I hope we'll have lots of time to discuss your novel, which I'm now reading and enjoying and marking with exclamation points and bursts of "ha." You have found a good sharp, amusing voice to tell this.

We're fine, though Don broke his arm cross-country skiing last week and is suffering from the inconvenience of it. It's an odd thing to tie a grown man's shoes. Five more weeks of this. I'm still playing the wedding day over in my head, a golden day. And we loved seeing you and Bruce and sitting under that enormous Christmas tree.

I started the new novel yesterday, two terribly tentative pages, thrusting about for the voice and not quite finding it.

---

*I had reworked *A Celibate Season,* the play, and the New Play Centre had sent me two glowing assessments and an offer of $5 off if I wanted to rework it once more for them.

You're in Mexico now—hope it's been wonderful for all three of you, sunshine and interesting things to look at.

Love to you both,
Carol

❧Bruce and I went with Allison and her two children, Gregory and Jacqueline, to Mexico for a week, a holiday prompted by the fact that Allison was due to have serious back surgery on her return. Then Carol came to Vancouver for her lecture at Douglas College in New Westminster. She gave an excellent talk—I remember her discussing the difficulties involved when one gender tried to write the other, and cited an example where a male author had his female protagonist putting on her slip then pulling on her jeans.

February 13, 1988

Dear Carol,

A quick note to tell you how sorry I am you didn't win the GG's award. I think it was your bad luck to hit a year when the competition was evidently fierce—although I haven't read M.T. Kelly. Nevertheless it was an honour to be shortlisted.

Many thanks for the lovely dinner at John's*—such a treat to see Don too. Hope his arm is better. Bruce enjoyed himself thoroughly, and we both like Dale [Zeiroth] and his wife. He really is a nice man, isn't he?

The day at Douglas College was a highlight. I loved your lecture and have thought much about it since. I do think those engagements must be strenuous, particularly as you had to battle our big snowstorm.

Your comments on my novel are *enormously* appreciated, and I'll be anxious to see how you like the ending.

Love,
Blanche

---

*Carol had whipped up a dinner for us and her Douglas College host, poet Dale Zieroth and his wife.

❧Allison was due to undergo surgery for a severe congenital spinal condition very soon, which involved two operations, and I phoned Carol to tell her about it. I also told her about our planned trip to Boston when the surgery was over to visit the cousins with whom we often sailed, and then to tour the Maritimes.

14 avril 1988

Dear Blanche,

I've been thinking of you all day, also of Allison, the ordeal of all this, and the worry—Lord! It is so terribly draining, yet has to be got through—and will, of course. I'm glad you have this trip to look forward to—it does sound interesting—new territory, which is always wonderful, especially *that* territory, so full of history. We don't know it at all, unless you count four days in Boston back in the sixties.

I've spent the day writing a manifesto (3 pages) to present in Weyburn, Saskatchewan—that is what we were asked to do. Subject: What makes modern fiction modern? I had some fun with this and did a little thinking, mostly in the middle of the night, I'm afraid, which is when I'm finding myself waking up. What would you say about this subject? Hate to get saddled with a theory since I always seem to be changing my mind.

Later: we've just finished dinner and are off to a reading at a bookstore downtown, an English writer called Graham Swift, rather marvellous, though his last book has had poor reviews—I'll try to sneak out without buying it. But I've liked his others. Am thinking about Allison—when she is able to read again—has she read *The Accidental Tourist*? An odd and charming book by Anne Tyler (though Beth Harvor thinks it's shallow and perhaps it is).

I'll phone next week to see how it went.

Love,
Carol
Love to Bruce XXX

❧Allison's operation was traumatic, with complications that even at this late date I find I can't talk about. Carol and I phoned on a fairly regular basis during the six weeks that Allison was in hospital.

April 29, 1988

Dear Carol,

Many thanks for the phone call the other night. Stephen [son] arrived yesterday—another morale booster—although there was a downer at the hospital with the suspicion that there has been some leg nerve damage (weakness, [problems with] motor coordination). However, later the doctor assured her that all will recover with physio. She's in the body cast now and taking tentative steps, with the support of parallel bars and 3 staff. I had a downer all evening, then an upper after doctor's assessment. What a roller coaster!

Just read an Alice Munro story in a *New Yorker*. Great!

Love,
Blanche

May 26, 1988

Dear Blanche,

This is the briefest of notes. What a lot you have been through—all of you—but I was relieved that all is in place now, including the body cast which must be quite something to get used to. I believe I understand your torment having just been through a bit of trauma here. Anne was hit by a truck in Cambridge (she was on her bike) just four weeks ago. There have been many phone calls and letters and a fair bit of imagining other possibly worse scenarios—she has a concussion, broken wrist and fractured knee but is mending. John was in Europe on a case and was able to spend a day with her. And we'll see her in just three weeks. Is there anything more overwhelming than one's child in danger? (Actually Anne's chief concern was her exams, but the university is apparently going to give her a pass and forget the exams.) Every day she says she is better and better.

I've had a funny day of errands, letters, cleaning cupboards, ironing, trying to alternate mental with physical tasks. [I] wanted to send a note saying how positive Elizabeth Dancoes* sounds and how exciting all this is getting to be.

I've just read *The Radiant Way* (Margaret Drabble) and confess I'm disappointed, but am nevertheless sending it along to Allison since it is long, long long. I thought [the author] was into some odd stylistic tics, and brought some funny plot stuff in at the end. (Ah, but she can still charm in places.)

My love to you and Bruce,
C

May 28, 1988

Dear Carol,

Sometimes I think Happy Birthday is a contradiction in terms, but happy happy anyway.

Things are improving here, but slowly. Allison couldn't walk, as we feared, after the operation and had total numbness from the knees down and some between hips and knees. She started physio in hospital, the doctors expressing confidence that all functions would return. She came home from hospital 2 weeks ago in a body cast and able to get around a bit with a walker, but soon graduated to canes. Two days ago they removed the body cast and put her in a back brace. She is in bed about 90% of the time but the legs are definitely strengthening and she thinks the numbness is slightly improved. So I think we will see total recovery. Apparently spinal cord injuries usually do recover and nerves regenerate themselves.

She qualifies for a homemaker and her friends have organized themselves into shifts so that many dinners are covered. So it hasn't been as rough on my time since she got out of hospital and I've

---

*The playwright who was working with me on *A Celibate Season* at the New Play Centre.

actually pretty well got the play changes made. Her 39th birthday was Wednesday.

Scary, but thank God it seems to be almost over. I'm actually too superstitious to say that and am touching wood. *Bon voyage!*

Blanche

July 19, 1988

Dear Carol,

I wish I could say that there was something interesting to report, but as usual everything is in limbo. If limbo should indeed turn out to be a place to go after death, writers will have no difficulty with it.

I do hope this works out, as I think after this spring's trauma I need to have something involving in my life that doesn't include offspring. Allison is making excellent progress, although the walking isn't quite right yet and she still has no sensation below the knees. However, nerves regenerate at one millimetre a day and so they say they are confident it will return in time. (Who trusts *them* any more?) But otherwise her health is returning and her back is much better, although not perfect.

What of Anne? I do hope all went well and am so glad she didn't lose her year. But it is worrying. Do pass along my best wishes to her.

We had a wonderful trip, very relaxed. Spent time with Bruce's cousin Mary and her husband Al in Boston—Concord, actually— and had a wonderful time exploring old Unitarian churches, touring Harvard Yard, learning all the history of the area, and taking side trips to Cape Cod, Nantucket and Martha's Vineyard. They live in a solar house which Al has engineered until it needs papers to run, and which amused me enough that I can see it as the focus for another play, should this one encourage me (or us?) to be so rash again. The reunion, prior to that in Ottawa, was fun too. Toured the new art gallery and saw the excellent Degas exhibition they had mounted as an opener. After Boston, drove north to Bar Harbor and took the five-hour ferry trip over to Yarmouth, N.S., then drove along through charming, impoverished little fishing villages (are impoverished people

nourished by charming?) Lunenburg, Peggy's Cove, and on to Halifax.
Then spent a day with friends [June and Ted Pulford] outside of
Sackville, N.B.—he had been an art professor at Mount Allison U and
now paints full time, excellent watercolours. Then drove back through
New Brunswick and Quebec to Ottawa, then home. A relaxed and
pleasant holiday and good weather.

I did a lot of reading and seemed to luck into nothing but good
novels—what a nice change! By the way, many thanks for sending
The Radiant Way to Allison—she enjoyed it, but I think she felt
about it the way you did. One of her friends gave her a novel,
Disturbances in the Field by Lynne Sharon Schwartz, which
impressed me enormously. Also read *The Tiger in the Tiger Pit*, by
Janette Turner Hospital, and liked it also enormously. She does a
wonderful job with her elderly couple, although it did require a
certain suspension of disbelief to credit them with sustaining the
trauma of their youths to such an extent. I particularly like her old
woman—perhaps reader identification. Then Timothy Findley's *The
Telling of Lies* is a really good mystery, quite unlike anything else he
has done. Also read an Anita Brookner—one of her passive intellectual heroines who is into Balzac ends up devoting her life to a
particularly ineffectual pair of parents. I didn't think it quite came
off, but was great reading. Now I'm reading Saul Bellow's *More Die
of Heartbreak*, but am somewhat disappointed in it. I loved
Humboldt's Gift, but don't think this is nearly as centred (a substi-
tute word for focused which is being overworked these days). His
verbosity overwhelms, partly because I can't follow his train of
thought much of the time. Still worth reading though. What fun to
have such an orgy of novel-reading! Hope you are doing the same.

My novel is still sitting with Macmillan Publishing. I didn't
have any response to my query to General last March, but while
I was away Leslie and family were staying in the house and Don
Bastion from Stoddart phoned and said he'd like to see it and to
send it.

Leslie and Austin decided to do some renovations to their house
and had just nicely got the place torn up when they heard that poor

Bill [Clarke, Austin's stepfather], who was travelling in Russia and had been taken ill, had been diagnosed in London as having lung cancer. He flew back to Toronto where Austin's sister got him tested, etc., and the prognosis is very poor. He flew back here and is now in an apartment hotel downtown waiting to start treatment. In the meantime they had to cancel their holidays, but fortunately had another friend's house to move into—much as I love having the little ones around, the chaos is just a bit more than we are prepared for. My fingers have already stuck to the keyboard this morning [after the kids were using the computer with sticky fingers], and I am resigning myself to the necessity of doing some heavy-duty housework in the wake of the onslaught.

Would love to hear how France has been this time—we often think of the wonderful time we had with you last year.

Blanche

August 2, 1988

Dear Carol,

It's a long time since you sent your well-wishes, but I am just now getting to doing some writing.

I am recovering well, but get very impatient with the slowness of it all. I can now walk comfortably around the house with no canes and use one cane when I'm out and a back brace in the car. The numbness in various parts of my body remains, which is frustrating mainly because of having no idea of when and if it will end. However, overall I am doing well, the pain is usually not bad at all and I am actually enjoying having a summer off at home with the kids.

I loved your book, Carol. Your writing style was excellent—a work of art! I admire you for attacking a different genre so wholeheartedly.

Thank you for sending (God, my mind's gone blank) by Margaret Drabble.* I thought it was an interesting read, but had mixed feelings about the development (or lack of?) of the characters

---

The Radiant Way.

and the slow pace. I kept having a feeling of it being somewhat apocalyptic. Did you at all?

I have read a couple more excellent books of late—*Disturbances in the Field* by Lynne Sharon Schwartz and am currently reading *Anywhere But Here*, an excellent first novel by Mona Simpson.

Thank you again for your kind thoughts.

Love,
Allison

August 4, 1988
France

Dear Blanche,

Your card was here when we arrived—and I was very relieved to hear that Allison is making progress—and then your letter arrived a couple days ago. How welcome letters are. Your New England excursion sounds like what you both needed after the ordeal and worry this spring. I like your question: are impoverished people nourished by charming? We are reading a book about France at the moment, and apparently one of the things the nobles deplored in the peasantry was their non-appreciation of nature, the fact that they never took a walk or even paused to regard the surroundings. Around here, though, farmers are carefully restoring their charming brick and timber farmhouses and not—as I would have thought—opting for a little cement bungalow.

We attended Anne's graduation at Cambridge and found it marvellous and medieval. By an act of Senate she was allowed to graduate without taking her exams, but she had luckily completed her thesis before the accident. She has recovered, she thinks, almost completely, and says she has reordered her priorities as well. I can hardly bear to think about it, how much worse it might have been. We met her marvellous fellow students who saw her through the ordeal. Nine of them have lived together in a house, all Trinity Hall postgraduates, and the Hall Master told me—this was over strawberries and cream at the garden party—that he has never seen a group quite like this. She has been in Italy all month, and she and Tony will come here next week to spend a few days with us. She is pregnant—imagine that! And delighted, as we are too, to our surprise.

Both Anne and I have recently read a novel that I think you and Allison will like. It is Mona Simpson's *Anywhere But Here*, out in paper. She has found a new way to write a family saga, and has also—very important to me at the moment, in my thoughts—given voice to the inarticulate, a reliable voice.

Bella has "taken us out" of General—her phrase, and I am now with Random House, back to Ed Carson who will publish the short stories in the spring. I hope to heaven I never have to change again. I've been working on the novel all summer. It is called *Bodies of Water* and is, as of today, at page 133, a mere drop in the ocean though; this will be a long book. About love. Set in Winnipeg. Do you have some pithy observations about love? I would love to hear them.

I forgot to tell you we have bought a tiny stone house in a tiny hamlet of 30 people, most of them over eighty years of age. By next May we should have a bathroom, but for the moment we have only a lovely view of the Jura Mountains and green fields. We are a little shocked that we have actually done this.

We've been on a farm these last weeks, right in there with the chickens, goats, horses and crowing roosters. Oh, we will have to diet when we get home—all this butter and cream is doing us in.

My love to you both,

Carol

August 22, 1988

Dear Carol,

It was good to hear from you and know that the summer has gone well and that Anne is well—more than well, pregnant!

Everyone is well here. I enjoyed *The Radiant Way* although I have to agree that it was overwritten and that the characters were not terribly well fulfilled. However, I was fascinated with the insights into Maggie Thatcher's England—doing it without being judgmental, at least not obviously so.

Now I have almost finished Mona Simpson's wonderful novel *Anywhere But Here*. I gather Allison recommended it to you, even as you were writing to recommend it to us. It is engrossing. The character of the mother is beautifully drawn, and her technique of going back over the past never strikes a wrong note. The voices change perfectly with each change of character— incredible that she should have achieved all this with a first novel, isn't it?

Just read a wicked review of a novel of Jerzy Kosiński's in *The G and M*. Who is Don Coles? I don't think I'd warm to him too much just judging by the rather supercilious quality of the review.

Allison is continuing to make slow progress. Leslie and Austin are going quietly mad with house renovations that are stretching far beyond the designated time, since she has to keep the little ones somewhere else every day. Periodically she asks to come up and trash my house, and says she is running out of friends who may stay friends. Bill is sinking fast, still in his own apartment but the cancer is spreading fairly rapidly.

Welcome back to Canada. I was fascinated to hear of your purchase of a French home. I think it is quite exciting, and would love to hear more details.

Give my best to Don. Bruce is feeling better than he has in years, having finally overcome that infection that hung on for so long. I've even managed to haul him over to the tennis court, where he proceeds to trounce me thoroughly, but never mind.

Love,
Blanche

September 23, 1988
[Winnipeg]

Dear Blanche,

I was so happy to hear from you—and am anxious to know what happened re the workshop, did it happen? Was it useful? What next? I think these one-day sessions are excellent, that the full-scale workshops that last a week or more can lead to a too-many-cooks situation.

I recently came across a novel by a woman called Donna Steinberg, very light, labelled "an entertainment" in fact, published by Eden Press in Montreal. I wrote them at once to say *we* had a comic novel, and "entertainment," and were they interested in looking at it. I felt heartened to discover another [potential] publisher.

What I've been reading lately are my students' first batch of papers. By the way, what ever happened to general knowledge, known now as trivia? No one in a class of 28 had ever heard of McLuhan, global village or the medium is the message. Not one knew what prose meant—they thought it meant poetry. No one could define a sonnet. What are those high school teachers teaching? Lord, I'm becoming a curmudgeon.

Next week I go to my 35th high school reunion, and I'll be sure to send a report.

Everyone is well and happy in our far-flung family. There is a thin possibility of our getting to Vancouver for Christmas, but we may decide to huddle at home here.

Love,
Carol

September 27, 1988

Dear Carol,

Synchronicity! I came in the door tonight after my first session with Pamela Hawthorne [of the New Play Centre] thinking I would write to you immediately, and there was your letter. Today

I had an hour and a half with Pamela (who sends greetings) going over the things that bother her. She is very businesslike and we worked hard.

I'm sorry to say that Bella didn't want to read my [novel] manuscript. She read the short story I extracted from it—the one you read, but with a good deal of subsequent work done on it, and said she wasn't surprised about Veronica Geng.* She recommended that I change the name, which I have—to *Random Access Memory*—and that I try Denise Bukowski. I sent her the first and last chapters, but she declined with the following rather curious comments: "The style and attitude seem from a pre-computer era, from another generation. The sensibility seems more appropriate to an older woman OBSERVING this generation and trying to make sense of it. In fact, I would think that your talents might well be devoted to a portrait of an older woman of a certain background in the 1980s."

All from a couple of chapters! A bit of an age put-down, wouldn't you say? By the way, I had mentioned that our play was to be workshopped, and she asked me to send along her best to you, that you had worked together long ago when she was with McGraw-Hill.

Interested about your high school reunion—I did tell you about mine, didn't I? I've just had a week in Calgary—life in the slow lane, visiting my 85-year-old aunt who is in a lodge. I spent from 10 a.m. until 8 or 10 at night with her, played about 15 hours of bridge, and although she and her friends are still bright and interesting, the pace was terribly slow.

When is the grandchild due? Glad to hear that Anne is fine, after her frightening accident.

Love,
Blanche

---

*Fiction editor of *The New Yorker* who had me resubmit a couple of my previous short stories, although in the end they were not published.

October 1988

Dear Blanche,

The turkey is in the oven roasting, and we are about to set off for a walk. But I want to get this note off along with Eden Press's letter. My suggestion is 1) to send *C.S.* at once with a note saying we are open to editing to bring it up to date and 2) a paragraph saying who we are and what we've written. I feel guilty sticking you with this job—not to mention expense—but I think it would be so wonderful if our efforts saw print.

You ask if I think Denise's letter is an age put-down. AN AGE PUT-DOWN! Can you hear me shrieking? I think, as the French would say, this sort of comment is insupportable. An older woman of a certain background indeed. I am breathless with outrage. On to the next paragraph before I implode.

The high school reunion was both unsettling and euphoric. I was chagrined to find how much I had forgotten, names and faces both, I who have prided myself on my memory. But seeing my good friends, having time to talk, reverting to teenage hilarity—now that was worth the trip. I found I was being talked at a lot, the men assuring me of their financial success, women of their ongoing marriages, their children and grandchildren, and I wondered what aura of passivity I have that encourages this—this is oddly worrying. I kept wanting to yell—"My turn." But didn't.

We have a record fall, one golden day after another. We'll have eight for dinner tonight, a mix of family and friends.

Love to you both,
Carol

November 23, 1988

Dear Carol,

You must wonder what has happened to my usual garrulousness, and the answer is nothing, except busyness.

I worked quite hard during the election, having finally decided I didn't like the free trade deal, but all to no avail. It was disappointing, wasn't it? Also had a week of flu, encompassing my 65th birthday, and am not sure if the flu wasn't partly caused by my reaction to said awful event. Interested in your remarks about the reunion, and your question about why people tell you everything. No, it is not an aura of passivity as you surmise, but it is true that people do tell you everything. You have an enormously intelligent way of listening, which I have often remarked on—when somebody tells you something, you ask a question that is so insightful and interesting that the other person immediately launches into further exposition. At least *I* find this so, when we talk in the realm of ideas. Perhaps, though, the kind of talking-at that you got at the reunion may be because your successes have impressed these people, and they feel impelled to relate their own successes.

No change re Allison's legs. She is going to have some tests mid-December, although otherwise she is very well and thinking of returning to work part-time in January. Leslie and Austin are fine, but Bill is very bad and they are finding it a terrible strain. Mortality is awful. (An indisputably deep observation, *n'est-ce pas?*)

Must run. I'm having a dinner party Saturday night and haven't even vacuumed the house for a fortnight. Feet are sticking to the floor.

I'll let you know how the play goes. Keep your fingers crossed, that some rich producer will wander into the workshop and fall in love with it.

Love to Don.

Blanche

> *November 1988*
> *Carol Shields*
> *237 Wellington Cr.*
> *Winnipeg*

Dear Blanche,

You will be astounded at the technological advance this letter represents. Don and I've had our Mac for about a month now, and mostly we play with it and see what happens. I've lost pages of text twice—maddening—but I don't think I will again. I haven't done any "real" writing yet with it, but have done letters. My daughters believe my letters have been remarkably silly lately, so I am trying not to let this machine lead me into absurdity with all its clever tricks. But I do see why you love it.

This is a short note, since it is very late on a Sunday evening, the end of a social weekend. But I want you to know how delighted I am with the workshop and that I'll be thinking of you on the 8th— and I do think it is extraordinarily loyal of your family to be in atten- dance. I hope you'll have a chance before Christmas to let me know how it went and if there is anything further they will be able to do.

I'm also pleased and grateful that you've got the amended ms [of *A Celibate Season*] off to Eden Press. What can we lose—besides the postage, and I will contribute to that, I promise.

Carol

December 15, 1988

Dear Carol,

Bowled over by your word-processing debut—you seem to be doing remarkably well with it. I'll be interested to see whether your letters get longer, as mine have done since I got this alter ego.

Well, the workshop [*A Celibate Season*, the play] was an exciting day. My family *all* came, rather to my surprise, and, I'm sure, to Pamela's. Also Barbara Perrault came. I hadn't known that Barbara actually earned her living for a while before marriage as an actress, CBC and some stage, actually had an ACTRA—or whatever— membership.

The actors Pamela had gathered together were well-known professionals around the city, and some of them had studied the play enough to make a damn good presentation—especially the gal who played Davina. She *was* Davina—how I wish you could have heard her, everything we ever dreamed of in Davina, presuming either of us have ever so indulged. In any case, the reading went very well, and then visitors (except Bruce) left and we spent an hour with Pamela and the actors giving their criticisms and suggestions. It was interesting that they became so heated—about whether or not Jock would have got that mad about her wall being knocked out—that the supposedly controlled discussion erupted into shouts.

Yesterday Pamela and I met for a session of where to go from here. Everyone has found the character of Jock unsympathetic—a criticism of the novel that we had fairly often. Pamela says it invariably happens that the playwright has the most difficulty with the character that may be coming from her own experience or point of view. Have decided to make Jock a breezier, upbeat woman who *assumes*—as opposed to fussing [about whether]—Chas will manage fine on his own, and then is appalled when he doesn't. She has always been a take-charge kind of woman and hadn't realized that Chas tended to be a bit of a dreamer and simply wouldn't cope. Also I was criticized for a bit of verbiage that sounded novelistic, and was grateful for the way the actors zeroed in on just the spots to change. Having said all that, the actors and Pamela told me that it is a very good play, and that it wouldn't be meriting this barrage of criticism and suggestion if it weren't.

Since Bruce has decided to RETIRE February 4th, I too am going to retire, at least from accounting. How our lives are about to change!

Had a debilitating attack of nostalgia this morning—a state to be avoided like the plague, especially at Christmas—when cleaning out a drawer I found pictures of family in the Parliament Buildings. Everyone looks so young, especially Bruce and me. Sixty-five is a bad age for feeling the social pressure of negative expectations—I keep testing my brain to see if it's still working, have even taken to reading a complicated book on quantum physics theory to see if I can understand it. (And I don't completely, but I recall not understanding it when young as well.)

Allison's myelogram (yesterday) turned up no blockage, so now it is a question of waiting and hoping. Cases such as hers can take a couple of years before the nerves regrow. Delighted about

Catherine's move to Winnipeg—so great to have a daughter near. Why is Anne in Toronto? Do they live there now?

Love,
Blanche
P.S. The actors did a lot of guffawing and were unable to read for laughing, which was encouraging.

> *December 20, 1988*
> *Cold and Snowy*
> *Christmas Sneaking up*

Dear Blanche,

Ah, I know what you mean about nostalgia. We looked at some old family slides the other night with the idea of having them printed as photos. Oh, those young bodies, thick hair, unlined faces, dappled sunshine. It has plunged me into melancholy. I keep saying that the photos don't show the whole of that time, that it was, in fact, a stressful period in many ways, but Don and I think we were braver then, more decisive. I don't think we had time for introspection. Quantum physics may well be a good way to keep the brain monitored. I think I will try to memorize some short poems from a little anthology I have, make them mine. (I have tried reading critical theory, but it leaks out of my head as fast as I pour it in, and besides, I distrust a good deal of it.) Little things do give cheer though—such as this amazing machine. I plug it in in the morning and it seems to say: let's get going here. I don't know about it producing longer letters, but off-point ones, yes. Here I started to write about the play, and haven't even mentioned it.*

Am feeling remarkably unfrenzied, cards sent, baking done, gifts bought and even wrapped. Obviously there's something I've forgotten, but what?

Let's make a list of the good things about getting older. Here's one: I never worry about going to parties and running out of

---

*Carol includes several suggestions regarding submitting the play.

conversation. Social ease has more or less arrived, but what good is it? Onward 1989.

Much love to you both,
Carol
P.S. Another good thing about getting older. I've given up all pretense of being a well-rounded person. Recently, listing the organizations I belong to, I realized they were all literary in nature. So be it. Amen.

7

1989–1990

➤ There is something baffling about the Law of Probabilities. Flip a coin, it says, and there is a fifty–fifty chance you'll get heads. After five or even ten heads, our intuition tells us, we have more than an even chance that the next one will come up tails, yet those who decipher the future by probabilities tell us it doesn't work that way. Number eleven has just as much chance of being a head as number one had. The string of successes, they say, has nothing to do with the next toss.

What, then, accounts for the eleven heads in a row? No one seems to be able to tell us. It is a mystery. The ancients thought the gods were smiling on them; today's gamblers call it being on a roll. That's about all anyone can say.

Through 1989 and half of 1990, Carol and I were on a roll in our daily as well as our writerly lives. Carol joined me in learning to use a computer for writing—it seems quaint now to read how, less than twenty years ago, we felt daring and intrepid as we began to experiment with this wonderful new and extraordinary toy that saved us the wearing task of typing up entire manuscripts. Perhaps

I should say entire *drafts*, since there is no such thing—except for a few rare birds—as a finished first draft. And the miracle of cut-and-paste! Instead of using scissors to cut up our drafts, and liquid paste to reposition them, we could now metaphorically cut and paste with a few tweaks of a keyboard. And the joy of turning on a printer that spewed out copy, and whose only minor drawback in those computer Middle Ages was that the paper had to be fastened with notches on the edge of the printer and pulled apart afterwards! Not to mention the unmourned passing of carbon paper that smudged our fingers; now we could photocopy our precious manuscripts before we sent them to publishers.

Alas, rolls never last. I remember when I graduated from university, seeing a cartoon in the local newspaper of young mortar-boarded graduates marching off in the shadow of a university building, while just around the corner out of sight lurked the World with his big round head, carrying a baseball bat.

January 24, 1989

Dear Carol,

Your word processor seems to possess capabilities that are making mine quite envious—I'm referring to the classy heading. Mine doesn't possess graphics capabilities (if you'll pardon my computer-ese), but otherwise is completely endearing.

Smithers was great fun. Lovely scenery, beautiful cross-country skiing with powder snow and temperatures around minus-5 to minus-10. Irene is wonderfully organized—seven months pregnant, hardly shows, whipped up pecan pies Christmas morning, accompanied us on an hour's walk through deep snow, finished opening presents, then whipped up a dinner for twenty. Oh yes, and gathered two dozen eggs from her chickens (which Stephen hates), which she then sells to neighbours.

Good things about getting older? Yes, there are some—quite a few in fact, as long as the health holds out. I've never been so calm in my life—blood pressure so low now, it is hard to believe I was ever treated for it. I don't have the same urge to smarten the world up—notice how I've stayed out of the current Writers' Union controversy re the Women's Press issue? I've accepted the fact that there is no hope of my becoming a top-flight writer, but having accepted that, have made the decision to keep working as hard as ever at it, as it gives a focus to my life and prevents neurosis. Also there is the satisfaction of seeing the young well settled and the grandchildren growing and turning into very nice young persons. Also—with Bruce's pending retirement—there will be a lot more leisure things—plays, etc.—that we haven't been doing, because often Bruce has been tired in the evenings after long and arduous hearings. And of course the good old Old Age Pension and Canada Pension. The best argument for universality—it makes you feel so good to get that first cheque that it erases some of the anguish of wrinkles.

I was delighted, by the way, to see William French's nice remarks about a short story of yours that is appearing in a new anthology. He gives you high praise indeed. Also loved your review of Edna O'Brien's book. You write wonderful reviews— why don't you submit one to *The New York Times Book Review?* That one of *An American Childhood* [Annie Dillard] was outstanding—and, oh yes, I did read it after that, and loved every minute of it.

Oh yes, one other thing—Bruce and I are going on a long retirement trip, driving through the south—California, Arizona, Grand Canyon, Salt Lake City, etc., immediately after I finish being chairman of the church board, last week in March. We thought we'd take about a month. I am slowly resigning my community involvements, am down to the church board and the library board, and some residual work in the Liberal Party. Also have resigned all accounting, so feel Free, Free, Free! Must run.

Love,
Blanche

March 24, 1989
Eureka, California

Dear Carol,

A quick note to tell you that Bruce and I have joined the silver-haired wanderers who celebrate (?) the onslaught of old age with a sojourn by car to the great southern regions, the modern-day version of the elderly Hindu and begging bowl. (Probably apocryphal.) In any case here we are, in Eureka, in the rain, but hopeful palm trees out front. (Bruce speculates that the original namers of Eureka probably laughed themselves silly over the clever name.)

A positive note (you must need one now), Anna Hagan of the White Rock Summer Theatre phoned to say she *loved* the play, the characters, and everything about it. She was sorry they were rehearsing this year's play and asked if she might hold it for a while. (YES YES YES!)

Also sent it to the Canadian National Playwriting Competition—had to say it was by me, as it would (according to the person on the phone) work against us to have a joint authorship because part of the prize is a workshop in Victoria; however, if I won I could acknowledge the other person at the time. Hope this is okay by you.

As for the novel, nothing from Eden Press. I had hoped to write before I left, but life got too hectic. We celebrated Bruce's retirement in February by painting the upstairs (spurred on by new carpets) and then getting so carried away we did the living room. Then Stephen and Peggy (aged 2) arrived for a seminar for Stephen and after chasing Peggy for 4 days we were both quivering wrecks. Finished my year as board chair of the church (thank God, or Sweet Reason—being Unitarians) and then left.

Has Anne had her baby? Stephen and Irene had their second girl in February. (*Six* grandchildren.)

Have read *Days and Nights in Calcutta* [Clark Blais and Bharati Mukherjee]—most enjoyable. Also Michael Ondaatje's *In the Skin of a Lion*. Reminiscent of *Voss* [Patrick White]—not as stirring, of course, but a similar texture of language as well as the journeys

into the strange land, and the rather metaphorical repetition of
water imagery. I was impressed. Currently reading another White,
Riders in the Chariot. By the way, I thought the latest Margaret
Atwood (*Cat's Eye*) far superior to the others. Beautiful interplay
among the three young girls—almost Alice Munro, except for
Atwood's harshness.

Love,

B & B

P.S. Was about to mail this this morning, when I got an early
call from Vonnie Grindler (Arts Club Theatre Company). She
had just finished the script, LOVED it (!) and is recommending it to
the artistic director Bill Millerd for workshopping with a view
to production. (She also warns to be persistent.) She says it speaks
beautifully to the current dilemma of women and we have a wonderful ear for dialogue. We also talked about the fact that women like
the play terrifically and men not so much. That's a worry.

HURRAH (perhaps).

Love,

B

April 1, 1989

Dear Blanche,

Your delightful "On the Road" letter arrived yesterday, and though
you and Bruce won't be back home from your rambles for a few
weeks, I thought I'd write this morning and tell you our news.

We are now the grandparents of Joseph Aurilio, born 26th
February, 7 pounds, healthy down to the last fingernail, loads of
hair, lovely. Don saw him first, on a business trip to Toronto, and
reported that he was about the size of a coffee pot, and I spent
Easter weekend in Toronto, doting and patting. Anne is taking it
all in stride—though she certainly doesn't get much sleep what with
feeding little Joey every two hours. She and Tony have a houseful of
yuppie baby equipment, a high-tech high chair, Italian pram, and

a marvellous little swing that winds up. I expect you know all about this revolution.

We're off on the 25th—just as you and Bruce get home with your begging bowls—first to Scotland to see Sara, then to Paris for two weeks and then to our little house.

I read, and loved, *Days and Nights in Calcutta* some years ago, and am glad to see it getting some attention now. Have not read Ondaatje's *In the Skin of a Lion* yet. I wonder if I ever will—I find him to be such a fuzzball. This was my year to be a judge for the Governor General's awards, and so I have read nothing else but the 1988 list—a very long list too, though about half of it was genre fiction, mostly police novels. (Does this sound faintly disdainful?) I agree that Atwood's *Cat's Eye* is her best yet. The amazing details of the main character's childhood—they felt just right. And I was reminded how little I seem to have retained of this kind of atmospheric sense. The other judges, by the way, were Bill New, and Bill Percy—he is the sort of reader who likes "a good yarn." Hmmmm. You will understand. He is unable, really, to believe in the lives of women, their domestic lives, or their reflective powers, and their seeming unwillingness to get on with the story. Ah me! Gwen Hoover asked if I would serve again next year—they like to have some continuity—and I said no. In fact, I said never. It was interesting, but the time it took up! Boxes of books kept arriving and arriving, and I found it really disturbed my real reading life, which I came more and more to value.

Bruce—congratulations on your retirement—how does it feel? And congratulations to you both on your sixth grandchild. Why don't you start planning for next summer in Montjouvent. You'll love our setting—hills, cows, clear air, and our odd little village.

How I love my Mac! But it does encourage verbosity. I trust you as an old friend to be forgiving.

Love,
Carol

May 17, 1989
[North Vancouver]

Dear Carol,

It was so nice to have a letter from you waiting when we got back from our sojourn, which was successful throughout. Found a lovely place in Arizona, Sedona, which we liked so much we stayed five days, and got back about three weeks ago tanned and healthy and feeling that we had shed ten years, also resolved not to again become mired in the rat race, which resolve lasted twenty-four hours or thereabouts. We also had a five-day trip to a library trustee convention in Penticton, where we were wined and dined mightily by old friends, some of whom it was difficult to recognize due to the erosion of years. (And we haven't changed one bit.)

Another superb surprise—your story in Saturday Night. Excellent—inspires me to brag about our friendship. One of the outstanding things about it is your wonderful use of language—the best yet, in my opinion—I think you have reached some sort of pinnacle in this respect, and others of the family were equally impressed. I also enjoyed your two stories in Prairie Fire. It's fun for me to try to relate the settings to the places and events of your life. I think your new book must have come out while we were away.

But here is the good news: they* have funds this year to work with five or six playwrights. The co-ordinator has invited me to join this group, at the same time warning me that I may find them a bit overwhelming (a Marxist revolutionary, a New Yorker who is loud, articulate, opinionated and overbearing, to name a couple). Also (he warned) the language may be somewhat offensive. Ah me, bourgeois image again. I assured him that I thought I could hang in there and hold my own, and Bruce's comment was that maybe he (Bruce) should phone and warn *them* to watch out. In any case, I'm quite elated, as well as flattered to be asked, and intend to start work on another play immediately, to be ready for the fall. (In the nick of

---

*New Play Centre.

time, too, since I had been wondering if I should bother to continue
to write. A periodic angst that overtakes me.)

Your suggestion that we come to Montjouvent next year struck
rather a resonant chord, as we had definitely been talking of a
European holiday next summer. However, we do *not* want to
impose ourselves on you again, but what we have been thinking
is that maybe now while you're there you might look over the
pension or other rental situation, something small that we could
rent not too far from you, and then we could have the pleasure
of visiting without being intrusive. (We had such a wonderful
time just two years ago in Paris with you that I feel quite excited
at the prospect.)

Congrats on the new grandchild—we saw our new one when we
got back, she is as sweet as can be. Bruce loves retirement, and we
both have been working like beavers mending things which, after
fifteen years here (15!) have begun to rot or otherwise fade.

I can't tell you how wonderful it is to see your career taking off
as it is. Your writing now is as good as anything I read. I read Anita
Brookner's *Latecomers*, and was struck with the strong resemblance
in style to Henry James. There are whole passages on Fibich's development that would fit almost unnoticed into *The Ambassadors*. I am
enclosing a short bit that particularly struck me. Also was quite
overwhelmed by Patrick White's *Riders in the Chariot*. What remarkable work! And if you think your computer encourages verbosity,
how about this?

Blanche
P.S. HATED Janette Turner Hospital's *Borderline*.

> *June 12, 1989*
> *Montjouvent [France]*

Dear Blanche,

I am late replying to your wonderful letter with the news of
the whereabouts of the play and about your participation in
the worksop (not a Freudian slip—just bad typing)—we roared

reading about the warning they gave you—ah, this is going
to work its way into material, *n'est ce pas?* What a cast of
characters.

We are delighted that you would think of coming to France
next summer and spending time with us. It really is necessary
to book by about February though, for the *gites** in particular.

There are so many things that need doing that we hardly know
where to begin. Today Don is cleaning the beams in the kitchen, a
dreadful job. The bathroom was not in when we arrived, but is now,
at last, in place. The bedroom is functional, and the living
room–dining room will be left largely till next year. Our pride and
joy is the patio which is flagged with the stones taken from the
stable. The view is simply splendid. I wake up every morning and
think how lucky I am to be in France. Oh, we found the date of the
house carved on a beam in the stable—1792, just after the revolution. We will be planting a "revolution tree," as all French people are
being encouraged to do. We try not to work all the time, but to do
some sightseeing and some hiking—we walk for a good hour after
dinner most nights.

And I'm working on the novel, tentatively called *Bodies of
Water*. It is about that odd subject—love. But I'm trying to make
it a serious book. I think, fear, that love has come to be regarded
as a frivolity, or at least we must all pretend it is. Which brings
me to the subject of Anita Brookner and the passage you sent.
I think this must be the reason people have loved her books—
she has understood the importance of love in our lives and
insisted on it by writing about it *well.* I am not making myself
clear, I fear.

Do please excuse this typing. How I miss my beloved Mac.

Love,

C

---

*A *gite* is an inexpensive, rural vacation retreat.

July 4, 1989

Dear Carol,

I hope you got my telegram re the *gites*. The housekeeping aspect appeals, as we like to cook our own meals a certain amount and also like Spartan (within reason.) We phoned John [Shields] to ask him where Montjouvent is, and he tells us he thinks near Geneva. By the way, John sounds in great spirits, also sounds very proud of your recent successes—he said something like, you always think of somebody as just Mother, and it comes as a surprise to think of her in another context. Great to be able to impress your kids, isn't it? He also tells me that you are taking on a five-month stint at University of Ottawa, "with Dad following her around for a change."

The second reason I'm writing is to send the attached good and bad news. First the good. Remember when I mentioned that I was sending the play to Theatre BC's Canadian National Playwriting Competition, and had to use my name only because they advised against co-authors? (Sorry about that.) Anyway, it ended up as a finalist, and the critique has seen me walking on air all day. I phoned both the Arts Club Theatre (Bill Millerd still hasn't read it) and Paul Mears, who congratulated me enthusiastically. Will we see it staged, do you think?

The bad news is, of course, Eden Press. As you will see by the enclosed, it sounds as though they had intended to publish it [*A Celibate Season*] before they went out of fiction.

I got a copy of *The Orange Fish*—Duthie's, you'll be glad to know, was well stocked—and loved the stories. I think you have progressed a great deal over *Various Miracles*, although of course there are individual stories that are exceptions. One story that particularly gripped me in this new collection was "Hazel"—for some reason I found her odd courage quite touching. Bruce *loved* the collection, couldn't get over your wonderful use of language, and Allison is currently reading them and is finding them wonderful.

The reason we were in Calgary and Edmonton was that I took advantage of a library convention (I'm still on the board) to have the trip and visit Aunt Blanche. (Still doing well at 86.) We went to a reading by W.P. Kinsella, and who should I bump into but Merna Summers. She came up for a drink in our room, and we had a great talk. She told me about visiting you in Winnipeg and a great evening with Joan Clark and you. She is a very nice person, isn't she? I was pushing my way rather torturously through *Under the Volcano* (can see why it is considered to have traces of genius, but that doesn't make it inspired reading), but when I said this to Merna she was absolutely astonished, as it is a book she has adored since an early age—seems to have attained a mythological status in her mind. However, she felt as negative about a book *I* loved—*Voss*—and so we agreed to disagree (but both agreed about the excellence of *The Orange Fish*). Must close.

Blanche

P.S. Delighted to hear you are writing a novel about love, even if it is, as you say, somewhat out of style at the moment. It has been an implicit background in your novels but hasn't been the central theme. I look forward immensely to reading your treatment of it. The treatment of the question of love—its need of an object, can it exist without one?—in *The Cocktail Party* [T.S. Eliot] has always intrigued me.

A CELIBATE SEASON by Blanche Howard, North Vancouver—in FINALIST (Full-length)

A delightful play! Not an unfamiliar story, but also *not* laboriously presented. Full of wit and good lines. It is provocative and theatrically interesting. The play moves well with excellent characters—not self-indulgent, but believable. The play itself speaks, not the characters. Stageable! Witty, poignant, timely, moving. Good stuff!

Intelligent, well-written play about marriage, fidelity and betrayal. Very well crafted. Good, complex, well-realized characters within an interesting story. It is limited in scope and I wish it had something more significant to say, but otherwise very well done.

July 14, 1989
Winnipeg

Dear Blanche,

Can you imagine my delight opening your letter and reading about your placing in the top ten—lordy! And those comments, you want to gobble them up. "Witty." "Poignant" . . . "moving." And especially "stageable." Well, I can see this is going to open all kinds of new avenues. You mention getting started on something new, but what? I think we need more theatre about "older" people. After all, who makes up the audiences? And I can imagine a wonderful play about retirement. Or about spending time with friends aboard a boat. Ahem.

It's a shame about Eden Press. They did seem to be just what we were looking for. But I'll keep my eyes and ears open, and can talk to the people at Borealis when I'm in Ottawa. Or we could go back to one of our original houses—the people in these places have completely changed since our last assault, so we'll be coming afresh—and with the success of the play competition.

Don and I are off to Saskatchewan (Fort San) on Sunday for two weeks at the Saskatchewan Summer School of the Arts (D. is bringing two scientific papers to work on while I dally with budding novelists). And we've hardly unpacked from France. And I've just had three marvellous days in New York for the *Swann* launch there. Pretty heady, this. And rushed. But I wanted to make sure I told you about the *gite* we found in France that we think would be perfect for you and Bruce. It's in a village very close to us—so that if you decide not to have a car, we can pick you up in a trice. Legna is a small village in which the main occupation is woodworking and [it] is near the larger village of Arinthod (still very small). Our carpenter (and friend) lives in Legna, and we think you and Bruce would love it. The Bussillets have three *gites*, all in one old building. We looked at them all, and found them spotless, comfortable, much nicer, in fact, than any we have rented in the past. Mme. Bussillet is charming. If you write before Christmas it is best.

Shortly before we left France we had a telegram from Catherine announcing her engagement to the young man she's been seeing. (An engineer working in Pinawa [Manitoba], a nice man the same age she is—all is joy.) Another wedding this December. How our lives roll round.

Love,
Carol

September 7, 1989

Dear Carol,

A whole page in *The New York Times*, plus a picture! Isn't this the stuff that fantasies are made of (and if so, what more is there to fantasize about?). I'm thrilled for you, and my friends are tired of hearing about it. The reviewer said wonderful things about *Various Miracles*, and I kept thinking that he would be even more ecstatic over *The Orange Fish*, which I believe is, on the whole, a step forward from *Various Miracles*. (Although I will never forget Mrs. Turner and her grass. Also loved the one about the dying young man in France, and wonder that [the reviewer] didn't comment on it.) Too bad he wasn't altogether positive about *Swann*, I don't know what to attribute that to. Perhaps that you are now being compared to the best there are in North America and consequently he is applying exceptionally rigorous standards.

Bill Millerd of the Arts Club Theatre finally asked me to come in to see him, but dashed my hopes by saying they had decided against it, although he would be interested in seeing more of my work. I think one of the problems I'm up against is that all assistant artistic directors are women and they love the play, but artistic directors are men and don't regard Jock's dilemma as very high up the scale of human suffering. You will note Urjo Kareda's injunction against frivolity—I may become the only senior-citizen radical feminist extant.

Your life sounds frantic these days, what with little jaunts to South America and so on, interspersed between New York, France, Ottawa and Winnipeg. I do wish Vancouver would smarten up and get you out here! [With Bruce's] registration yesterday at SFU* in two credit courses, history and literature, I don't expect to go anywhere or even get to drive the good car until after Christmas exams.

Today sent off queries [re the novel] to Coteau Press and Quarry Press, recommended by Merna Summers.

Two books I've read lately that you would enjoy: *Dreams of Sleep*, by Josephine Humphreys. Excellent. Also a strange one, in paperback, *Hot Flashes* by Barbara Raskin. I particularly thought of you because it is about women born in your generation, attempting generalizations about their behaviour (which behaviour is rather outside the more modest experience of Canadian women—unless my life is more sheltered than I think). In any case, the people she deals with are all educated literary people, many of whom write fiction, and she writes with flair—although the steamier bits are obviously going to attract a wider audience than the subject matter would normally indicate. I would be interested to know what you think of it.

Margaret Atwood didn't fare too well with *Cat's Eye* in the *New Yorker* review, did she. He thought (or maybe it was she—can't remember) that the central tension of the children's play was superb, but the rest didn't ring true. (I agree.)

I told Mary Mahoney,** who was here recently, about your impending move [to Ottawa], and she would very much like to see you. Must close and think of something to feed the weary student when he returns.

Much love,
Blanche

---

*Simon Fraser University in Vancouver, B.C.

**Owner of Books on Beechwood in Ottawa, and wife of Pat Mahoney, a former Trudeau cabinet minister.

December 17, 1989

Dear Blanche,

Well, we are alive, back home in Winnipeg, and it is one week since Catherine's wedding—and now one week until Christmas. The fall has slipped by us quickly, too quickly, and I've enjoyed the writer-in-res job, meeting the people that is, but have pretty well decided against doing it again. I found myself reading manuscripts every evening and began to feel deprived of good prose. At times I actually found I was reading the first draft of someone's first effort—and I think it isn't very good for writers to be constantly assaulted by that kind of writing. I did have time to work on my novel, though never enough, and being in the middle of Ottawa was rather a lark. For about six weeks I was rather mysteriously struck with back and neck problems and spent a lot of time in physiotherapy. A humbling experience by the way. All in all, then, we're happy to be home, delighted with Catherine's young man (they are now in Florida honeymooning) and turning our thoughts to summer in the Jura.

I'm hoping you'll overlook my long silence and write me all your news—about family, about any progress with the play, about any new writing you've started since summer, about Bruce's courses and what you're reading. I did tell you, I think, about Jane Smiley's *The Greenlanders* (paper), which I think is quite a marvellous saga of 14th-century Greenland, not exactly the kind of book I usually read. I hope to read Margaret Drabble's new book too. I heard her read in Ottawa at the public library and found her to be a marvellous reader. Also heard Leon Rooke—what an actor! And afterwards someone told me he was more subdued than usual. About Richler's new book, I've heard all sorts of different opinions, but from women mainly negative reactions. I loved Michael Frayn's short book *The Trick of It* which was in *The New Yorker*. You mentioned the *New Yorker* review of *Cat's Eye*, which I found surprising—almost a wilful misreading of the book, it seemed, and the first time I've seen what looked like a personal attack in that magazine. (Of course *The New Yorker* is changing.) I'm teaching two courses next term to make up for the term I was away. One is an intro course to short story and poetry, and the other is creative writing. I think I'll enjoy both and still have time to get this novel finished by about March. It has grown rather long. I kept putting off the crisis. I had the feeling that I was meddling with the happiness of my characters for no very good reason, but also felt that no one would read the novel if I didn't brew up some kind of storm. All this has set me brooding about the constraints of the traditional novel, all that rising action prescriptiveness. There are so many things I'd rather put into the novel, and I'm having that marvellous experience lately of seeing ideas unfolding all around. A doctor I met at a party last night told me about some of the problems facing her thirtyish patients, and it was just what I needed.

All the kids were here for the wedding and can't afford to come back for Christmas, so it will be just Don and me, Grandma and Sara—she's just back from Scotland and thinking about graduate school, perhaps going on in philosophy. I imagine you'll be having your usual houseful. Please find a minute to drop a line and tell us your news.

Love to you both,
C
P.S. I've just bought a second Mac (for the office).

February 6, 1990

Dear Carol,

I have been waiting to write until I had news, but then feared it would be like waiting for Godot, perhaps you would never hear from me. I have phoned Coteau Books twice, and today they got back to me to say that when they accept a book, it must go through outside readers, then three board members, and then a final decision at a board meeting. I urged godspeed and tried a bit of a sales pitch about your success and the possibility of the play being produced, so it appears that there is still a good chance.

As for the play, I went to see the first play the Moodyville Theatre Company put on and it was very well done. Afterwards, dragged Bruce backstage so I could collar the director, Don Williams, whom I have known for some years in the Liberal Party. He has quite a background, having produced a number of [episodes of] *The Beachcombers* and quite a bit on the legitimate stage, and has recently founded this company to operate out of the very nice Centennial Theatre near here. Anyway, I asked him if he was still interested in *A Celibate Season* and he said very interested, he would be calling me very soon. (Two weeks ago.) Haven't had success with the many other people to whom I've sent the script, and was somewhat discouraged to read in *CanPlay** that only 13% of plays produced in Canada are written by women. (Getting paranoid.)

My next comedy, *The Lush Boat*, has been read by the group I told you about that I was asked to join at the New Play Centre, under John Lazarus, and very well received.

Now—France. After our three weeks are up, we are going to do some bumming around and spend about a week in Toronto, where we hope to see something of the Shaw Festival.** Needless to say, we are both looking forward immensely to spending this time near you and catching up on much visiting. I have been pondering your idea of a project, and so far have not had an inspiration. I did think of a whodunit, but not sure just how we would work it between us. On the other hand, perhaps we can think of something comic to work on. To my surprise, I think plays are turning out to be what I'm good at—maybe we can collaborate on a comedy, what do you think? Two couples in France, with attendant complications? (Considerably younger than at least one of the writers, goes without saying.)

---

*The Playwrights Guild of Canada quarterly newsmagazine.

**Named for George Bernard Shaw and held in Niagara-on-the-Lake, Ontario.

I was interested in what you had to say about the negatives of your writer-in-residence stint, and think you are right about the dangers of reading too much lousy prose. Not to mention the boredom of same. I was concerned to hear of your back and neck problems—would they be computer-related, do you think?

Bruce took literature and history the first semester, and I was intrigued with the former, also somewhat bemused by the reports I got back. It was an overview of modern writing—*A Passage to India* [E.M. Forster], *The Color Purple* [Alice Walker], *To the Lighthouse* [Virginia Woolf], Jean Rhys (can't remember what),* and Margaret Atwood, that one about the museum.** When I suggested that one of the themes of *A Passage to India* was sexual repression, the tutorial person was taken aback and allowed as how she'd never heard of such a thing and in fact marked his essay rather severely because of it. (Should have minded my own business.) I think the answer was racism. This semester he is only taking one course, history—thank goodness. (He was using my computer for his essays.)

What have I read? Much, as usual, but what I can remember— V.S. Naipaul, *A House for Mr. Biswas* (wonderful), Simone de Beauvoir's *The Coming of Age*—don't [read it], if you want to remain cheerful in the face of it. For a woman who inspired me with *The Second Sex*, many years ago—I was appalled to find that almost all her case histories of coping were about men, albeit famous ones, but still I think the approach here is quite different between men and women. Also read the delightful *The Writing Life* by Annie Dillard, and was given *Love Letters: An Illustrated Anthology*, edited by Antonia Fraser, a collection of delightful letters written by people like Keats, Byron, Victor Hugo, G.B.S., and Oscar Wilde (to Lord What's-his-name). Also got on a kick about Wilfrid Laurier, because I was fascinated by Sandra Gwyn's account of his liaison with Emilie Lavergne and thought it would make a good play. (One draft

---

* *Wide Sargasso Sea.*
** *Life Before Man.*

finished.) His letters to her were also published this year, and I have read a biography of Laurier, in which the French–English question and the pros and cons of free trade could have been written yesterday. Oh dear, is there little that doesn't repeat itself?

Love,
Blanche

February 21, 1990

Dear Blanche,

How I love your letters. Last week's was so full of news—all those various projects of yours (including coaching Bruce in his courses; and you certainly are right about sexual repression in *A Passage to India*, never mind what his prof had to say) up in the air at once. I'll be very anxious to hear what Coteau says. I *have* met Shelley [Sopher]*—who is married to Ven Begamudre who was at Fort San this summer. (The world is a village, as the French say.)

I too have been thinking about a project we might do in France, and have been told that two-handers work well in these money-tight days. I had a rather black idea the other day, an elderly couple who have promised each other to give the fatal injection that will end their mindless old age and suffering, but both become ill at the same time, neither can remember where the syringe is kept, etc. Is this a sick idea? Yes, I think it is. (Geriatic plays are in, someone told me.) Another idea—a man and woman in an aerobics class, chatting as they do their stretches. Why don't we start keeping a list of ideas. This is going to be fun. Maybe we can get Bruce and Don to contribute some gems of dialogue. At the very least we can get them to read lines, do our own work-shopping. (By the way, I am hoping to take this word processor along; I now have two; how is that for going from Luddite to two-machine owner in one year!)

Your story of "helping" Bruce reminded me of a time I "helped" John rewrite a short story for high school. I managed to talk

---

*Managing editor of Coteau Books.

him into reshaping the ending so that it was more "subtle," and his teacher returned it with the remark, "Great story, but you blew the ending with an anticlimax." (Of course I lost any credibility I had.)

My novel [*The Republic of Love*] is getting longer and longer, and naturally I wonder whether this machine is partly responsible. I have, too, a real reluctance to star-cross my pair of lovers, so fond of them have I become. I am hoping, Blanche, that you won't mind reading the ms. I remember with such gratitude how your changes in *Swann* saved that first chapter from coyness, and how much courage you fed into me at a dark moment. And to think you did it during a stay in Paris! Cath is reading the novel now—though I have three chapters to go, and her comments, mostly to do with overall tone, are invaluable. Anne is very good at details, and you are good at both. My three best editors.

Hope you can make sense of the two maps. These cold crusty mornings I'm thinking more and more about how wonderful it was to wake up with the sun in Montjouvent—to the sound of cowbells. It'll be hot and dry—at least that is the usual pattern. I can't wait to get some flowers blooming around our door.

Lordy, I'd better stop dreaming and get to work here. I have a class in an hour.

Love,
Carol
P.S. *Swann* has finally found a British publisher. A tiny firm, a tiny advance, but an editor who writes wholly charming letters and possesses the lovely British name of Christopher Potter. It comes out in August.

April 4, 1990

Dear Carol,

I'm ashamed to note that it is so long since I wrote, but I was Waiting for Coteau. The problem lies with grant money. (Groan.) In these days of Michael Wilson [finance minister] mentality, I don't know whether or not to allow myself a sliver of hope.

Thank you for the maps. Now we need a sketch of exactly how to find your farmhouse in Legna when we arrive. We have to supply our own sheets—I suppose the only sensible thing to do is to buy them in France. Any pointers on such problems? We have booked the car. As the time gallops nearer I am getting very excited about it.

I am ashamed to admit that I haven't had any good ideas of things we might write. All good ideas seem wonderful at the time and terrible two days later. I did think of something like a Jane Austen–like heroine set in the present, with a modern dilemma but the basic plot similar to the original, but probably too complicated for three weeks. I think your idea of a one-act play is good. My recently completed full-length play, *The Lush Boat*, has a stockbroker and his girlfriend (young, luscious) waiting on their boat for his old pal from law school, now dean, and the woman professor he is bringing, who turns out to be the stockbroker's ex-wife. Before they reveal all to the other two, they are adrift at sea. The play has a fairly feminist subtext, and it is interesting that in the NPC, the women love the play and the men don't. The group has been something of a disappointment to me—will tell you all the rather odd details when I see you. (Will we have time to cover everything *and* write besides?) From now on I shall concentrate more on trying to jot down ideas. I rather liked your sick geriatric idea, except that, having yesterday celebrated our *45th* anniversary, I fear becoming too personally identified.

Imagine you having two word processors! Is the one you are taking IBM compatible? If so, perhaps I should bring a copy of my program (WordStar—you probably don't use it—on 5¼–inch floppies.) (Sentences like that make me feel very modern—except that I keep thinking of all the things one says that wouldn't have been understandable ten years ago.)

I am delighted that you would like me to read the ms of your new novel. It is the sort of thing that I get a great kick out of doing, and although I think my modest contribution re the ending of *Swann* was far from crucial, I do feel happy that you liked it. So glad to hear that it has a British publisher, because it is far more a British novel than an American one. (I'm prejudiced—love British novels and only a few American ones.) At the moment am reading Tom Wolfe's *The Bonfire of the Vanities*, and my advice to you is don't. I read his interview of how he was driven to write the definitive novel about big bad New York [City] because none of the effete postmodernist writers could see what was under their very noses, but let me say that if he has written the definitive novel about NYC, then New York is a city without women. Except, of course, for the necessary sex kitten and the cuckolded wives. (Are women cuckolded? If not, what are they? Is it significant that there is no word for the feminine state?) I'm only halfway through it so perhaps it will improve—it would have to do so without me, except that I have made the mistake of being involved in two book clubs now and have to read it for one of them. However, I did love *Love in the Time of Cholera* (Gabriel Garcia Márquez). A wonderful story by Alice Munro in *The New Yorker* lately, about a friend of her dead mother's—did you read it?

A Celibate Season (play) is still getting wonderful comments but still not getting produced. Because of it I find myself on the board of the Moodyville Theatre Co., which I believe has little realistic hope of raising the necessary funds to mount a production.

Bruce has finished his semester and is enjoying the freedom. Last week we went over to Victoria for three days, and Kay Buchanan [friend from Ottawa] insisted that we cancel our hotel reservations and move into their lovely guest suite. They completely redid an old house on the ocean—in fact, it's hard to find a trace of the former house—and it is truly lovely. Kay has wonderful taste in decor and it was a bit like living in one of those pictures of homes that I would never even aspire to. We did enjoy ourselves, found them up to their ears in projects as we are, and had a discussion of why some of us are impelled to keep working so hard during retirement, instead of playing golf and bridge as more sensible souls do. They (and I) have been involved greatly with the back-stabbing that has gone on over delegate selection—to the point that I am overjoyed that we will be in France and therefore unable to go to the [Liberal] convention.

Must close. Don't these machines make one verbose? Ah, but how nice that is. Perhaps they will bring about a resurgence in the kind of letter-writing that went on in Victorian times as a matter of course.

Much love from both of us,
Blanche

April 10, 1990

Dear Blanche,

Your lovely verbose (your description) letter arrived yesterday. I'm still marking papers, a double set. Lordy. And I'm off to Germany and France on the 21st for eight days, two CanLit conferences— but I think I wrote you all about that. Thanks to the taxpayers of Canada.

If Coteau comes through, we won't have to worry about a summer writing project—we'll have to hunker down with our up-to-dating and other revisions. Cross fingers, cross toes.

I am anxious to hear all about your NPC when we see you—I'm sorry though that it's been a disappointment. People have very different ideas about what they want in a play and, yes, it does seem to split between men and women. And so, more and more, do novels. You mention Tom Wolfe's novel and his interview. We must discuss this. But what about *Solomon Gursky Was Here* [Mordecai Richler]—apparently it is another man-pleaser and woman-disappointer.

Thank you for so readily agreeing to look at the novel. I am worried that you will find this draft type, with its erratic spacing, too difficult to read. The chapters alternate between Fay and Tom (though Tom gets a prologue and Fay a little epilogue). I'm trying to do a couple of different things in this novel. I want it to "gesture" at the old romantic novel of the 19th century (and they've promised me I can have one of those frontispieces with a line of dialogue under it). But instead of isolating my characters, as is the case in romantic fiction, I want to show them in the midst of the whole big buzzing world.

Any comments, suggestions are welcome, as you know. I'm tough.

Love,

C

May 3, 1990

Dear Blanche,

Don was pleased to see you both, and delighted you're looking forward to your "stage" in the Jura. I've been longing during these last busy, crowded weeks for the kind of unstructured time we had there last summer, one day following the next. There's a good deal to be said for monotony, I think.

I think I'll probably bring my little Mac (as opposed to the big Mac with hard disk) though not the printer. Not only do I own two Macs now, but also, since yesterday, a new pair of "computer" spectacles. Ah, this technological age!

My eight days in Europe, in Germany and then in Strasbourg was interesting and enlightening. Very odd to sit in a room with European scholars and hear them discuss Canada as though it were as exotic a place as Ghana or Cambodia. They are strikingly theoretical in their approach, also earnest and stiff in the European way, but Simone Vauthier who organized the whole affair managed to get everyone to relax and loosen up. The other writers were John Metcalf, Ray Smith, David Arnason and Keith Fraser from Vancouver. A writer called Diane Schoemperlen was to have come, but apparently lost courage at the last minute, hence the gender imbalance.

There's snow on the ground here, little scraggly bits in the shadows of trees and shrubs, and we're all pretty mad and fed up about it.

C

May 3, 1990

Dear Carol,

I love what I've read [of the draft novel]. Your writing is marvellous, and I feel that I have a hell of a lot of temerity even daring to cavil about those things I've cavilled about. If a thing struck me as out of place or a false note I have mentioned it, but without analyzing my reaction—someone else might find it perfectly okay.*

Obviously Fay and Tom are going to meet and fall in love, and I am longing for them to do so. The buildup seems just right, like the romantic novel in some ways, but absolutely modern in the depiction of the bustle they live in. Oddly enough, Tom seems more interesting to me than Fay—perhaps depicting a male calls forth more extremes, but his reality is more present for me than Fay's is. Fay is somewhat elusive—not a bad thing, since she crystallizes more as the story goes on—but I find this slight removal a little disconcerting. Perhaps it is her youth, her viewpoint so different from the young women of my day, I don't know.

I do love the mermaid subtext. When Fay deals with it she comes alive, almost as though something about her is as hidden as the meaning of mermaids. Small things—your monologues of mothers and others talking are wonderful, arresting, ring completely true. The threatening quality of the parcel of shit to Tom is a lovely dark note in otherwise sunny material, and might almost be enlarged upon (not sure about this). I think the radio show is a touch of genius—something so familiar and yet so esoteric, everything about it seizes the imagination.**

I am looking forward enormously to finding out how you will tie it all up and what you have done with love (and mermaids). The type is fine—my eyes aren't failing, it's my ears. I'm going in tomorrow to the ear specialist and get myself a hearing aid before

---

*This letter is almost entirely devoted to a critique of Carol's novel, *The Republic of Love*. Most of it has been omitted.

**More comments have been omitted.

the trip, so that you won't have to be continually reminded about mumbling.

Allison had an operation ten days ago to remove one of the pins from her back as she was having a lot of pain and they thought the pin could be causing it. Her back fusion is now so strong that she can get along without the pin. She is progressing very well, although it is too soon to know whether the pain will disappear—so far it hasn't, but I think that's to be expected.

Love, also to Don,
Blanche

May 8, 1990

Dear Blanche,

A very quick note to say I am bubblingly, burblingly grateful for your comments which arrived last night. I've been sitting here happily all morning incorporating them—and I do mean all of them. You are GOOD at this. Cutting that paragraph on the first page (it hurt only a little) was exactly right. The things you pay attention to—authenticity of feeling and detail, tense, diction— are all the things that matter to me too, as reader and writer. But I don't trust my ear with my own ms, hence my gratitude. I am feeling guilty about the postage you're putting out, but Don says to tell you we will take the two of you to a most marvellous restaurant in Bresse (area next to the Jura) we found last summer where we can sit all afternoon on a terrace and indulge ourselves—I can't wait.

Hope this removing of the pin eases Allison's pain and I'm glad it went well, and that the spine has fused perfectly. I find this all amazing. Happy spring.

Love,
C

❧ Finally, the good news came from Coteau Books: *A Celibate Season* was accepted! I phoned Carol at once.

May 15, 1990

Dear Blanche,

I've been floating since getting your phone call yesterday. If you bring your copy to France we can work on it chapter by chapter. (I've an idea it isn't going to be all that hard for us to make these changes.) For me, it's going to be like reading a new novel since it's been so long since I read it in its entirety.

I forgot to tell you to bring clothes to France you can easily wash out. There are no laundromats nearby, and so I just rinse out a few things every morning—rather a chore. But your landlady may offer the use of her washer.

Love to all,

C

May 16, 1990

Dear Carol,

The mermaid theme in the novel is fascinating.* I was thinking today of the probably archetypal image that mermaids would represent in Jungian psychology. I think (although I could be dead wrong) that the emergence of a female figure from the deep water would represent the emergence of the anima figure from the subconscious. For Jung, the anima is the (physical) imprint with which the male is born and which accounts for the weird (numinous) character of the falling in love syndrome. I believe, in Jung's terms, that sailors who claim to have seen mermaids probably have indeed done so, since the brain will, when the psyche is in upheaval and poised for change, project the images of the subconscious. (At least that was his explanation for UFOs.)

Did I tell you I thought your review of Anita Brookner's book [*Latecomers*] was excellent? Bruce gave me *Solomon Gursky Was Here* for Mother's Day, so I guess I'll read it after all. I am so glad you find my help useful, and I enjoy doing it immensely. My only

---

*The novel being discussed that came out as *The Republic of Love*.

problem is a haunting fear that I may be completely wrong, so don't take my word for anything important.

Love,
Blanche

May 25, 1990

Dear Carol,

Leslie says to tell you she is touched by your sending a card and thanks you very much, and says if she weren't such a slob she'd get cracking and do the same.

MORE GOOD NEWS! The little Moodyville Theatre Co. is going to produce *A Celibate Season*, probably November, in the nice little theatre here in North Vancouver (seats about 500, very modern).* They are an actors' equity co-op, professional drama school grads trying to get established. We won't see any money from this either, needless to say—in fact wouldn't be surprised if it costs me a few pennies—but what the hell! I'm delighted and I remember you said you'd come if we got it produced. Hooray!

Am writing this as my printer is printing *A Celibate Season*.

Love,
Blanche

❧In later years, my daughter Leslie commented about Carol's wonderful faculty for remembering her birthday:

"Carol was a wonderfully warm-hearted person who had the rare ability to focus on the person she was talking with, to the exclusion of all others. As she grew more and more famous and in the public eye, this endearing quality remained. Carol carried the intense focus on individuals into all aspects of her life.

June 2 was the birthdate that I was fortunate to share with Carol, making us Geminis, the twins. I think our similarities ended there however. Every year a birthday card would arrive in the mail a few

---

*Centennial Theatre.

days before my birthday with a lovely handwritten note wishing me well. The arrival of this card would usually prompt me to rush out, buy and send a card to her, hoping it would arrive not too terribly late. One birthday particularly stands out in my mind, in that her card arrived right at my birthday, leaving me no time to send her one before the big day. Oh well, I thought, Carol will know how busy my life is, what with the kids, the job, etc. I stopped short, suddenly realizing that Carol's life was probably just a wee bit busier than mine, what with having recently been feted around the world as that year's recipient of the Pulitzer Prize for Literature." – Leslie Howard

May 30, 1990

Dear Blanche,

A quick note to tell you that the ms has arrived. It's been so long since I've seen it that it's like reading someone else's novel; there were whole scenes and situations I'd forgotten about. But I think you're right, it won't take long for our updating. After all, women and poverty is as much an issue today as in the early eighties, perhaps more so.

About the other ms, your comments were all wonderful, and I've taken each up in turn, from little notes on tense to large notes on gaps. At first I thought your suggestion that I move a large block forward in the book was impossible, but I woke up the next morning and did it—presto—and it is just right. Inspired! I feel very protective and uneasy about this book, and don't know whether it's the subject (the presumed fluff of love) or whether one's confidence erodes with age (I notice I have a hard time these days deciding on menus or picking out wallpaper— we must discuss this).

We must also discuss what (who?) we want for an editor. Do you think Allison might read it over again for us when we're done?—I remember how valuable her ideas were on our early draft.

Love and thanks,

C

P.S I forgot to tell you I did read *Bonfire of the Vanities*. I should have listened to you. Have also just read *The Chymical Wedding* [Lindsay Clarke], which I think you and Bruce would find fascinating.

June 1, 1990

Dear Blanche,

I am overwhelmed! My first impulse after getting your letter yesterday [with news of the play's acceptance] was to phone, but my puritan impulses (about phoning long distance in the middle of the day) prevailed. I couldn't be more delighted. Only 500 seats, you say! Don and I blinked at that. That is enormous! I'm very anxious to hear more about this theatre, who they are and so on. And of course I'll be there—somehow. I can apply to the Manitoba Arts Council here for funds for a first night (saying I was co-author of the book it was based upon) or, failing that, apply for a travel grant from the drama section of the Canada Council. I think I'll apply for both, quickly before we leave for France, just to cover the situation. Ah, show biz. Much more exciting than publishing books. I expect you'll be sitting in on rehearsals, at least I hope so.

Here is the final chapter [of *A Republic of Love*] plus "epilogue"— not that I intend to call it that. You will notice that I've plagiarized right from your letter with the Jung material, and as I typed it in I recalled Muriel Spark's novel *Loitering with Intent*, in which she talks about how, when one is in the stream of writing, things simply arrive at the right time and work in perfectly. Well, things arrived from North Vancouver. Once again, your comments are perfect—and I've paid attention to them all. I finished up last night, and could hardly sleep for the excitement—after two years and two months. Comes to 550 pages in all. I've taken a vow not to touch anything until my two editors have read it. One could fiddle forever.

Much love and thanks for the beautiful birthday card.

C

8

Fragility

1990–1992

I haven't been a faithful journal keeper throughout my life, but during our three weeks in the Jura Mountains staying in a *gite* near the Shieldses' country home I made a point of recording our days. Carol and I used the time to edit *A Celibate Season* for publication, but when we weren't working we gathered up the threads of a discourse that had been interrupted by the lengthy interstices between meetings.

My husband and I were well aware that Carol and Don had been leading a frantic life prior to heading for France, and so we did our best to be independent and leave them with days when they could savour the peacefulness of the area by themselves.

This, then, is a record of that time, one that I look back on as being highlighted with a singular radiance, as though in my memory the intensity of the sun's rays was magnified by the roiling storm clouds in the distance.

Saturday, June 23, 1990
We arrived *chez* Shields about 3 o'clock, having driven up and down strange alleys, unable to quite get to it for about an hour. By then the

car was hot and Bruce was obviously wearing out, herding the new and strange Renault through the unlikely *circulation* of France.

Anyway, there we were, embracing, exclaiming, accusing Don of lousy map-making, and soon taking a glass of wine in the sunshine. Brief sunshine, I'm told. The weather has been as bad as at home, and I brilliantly have brought almost all summer clothes. No sweaters.

Then time to take us to our rented *gite*. We followed Don and Carol the 8 kilometres to our quarters in the tiniest of villages, Legna, and to our quarters, but to our chagrin Don did not come in to translate for us. So we were treated to eloquence from Mme. Bussillet, who spoke in a strong local dialect, declining refreshment, coping with a bewildering treatise on a small impatiens plant that needed re-potting. And to wine and the *Sunday Times* left for us by Carol and Don, with Mme. wondering why they had left them here for us when we would be seeing our friends first. (*I* don't know.)

Finally she took us next door to our quarters (at first our sinking hearts had thought their tiny living room was ours—could see no bathroom, as Bruce pointed out). It is actually a house, beds all over the place, and she seemed surprised that we would be choosing the beds upstairs. Voluble explanations re the working of heater and stove and toilet and garbage, plus a lengthy inventory of dishes, spoons, etc., which I declined to count as she was going through. (Eight liqueur glasses? Six white wine glasses?) We also established that Mme. B's daughter—who stood by, smiling mutely, has 45 *ans* while my eldest has only 40. (Well, 41.) Finally alone. Bruce had only fifteen minutes' sleep before we headed back to the Shieldses' for dinner.

What a formidable task they've taken on! Reminds me of our disastrous boat venture—when we were about their ages. Large former barn, now stripped down and refinished, a nice adjoining kitchen and bathroom, and on the far end a little patio looking over the lovely hills of the Jura.

We sat out for drinks and Carol's delicious boeuf bourguignon. Much wonderful talk. Carol and I tried (but frequently failed) not to exclude the men in wonderful conversations re books and plays.

Carol had seemed tired when we first saw her this afternoon, aged more than I thought she should have, but tonight looked fine. We talked of aging (I professed to having lost ambition, but she caught me out re my novel), of the cheap politics of Canadian theatre, uncluttered by much intellectual depth, of our children and their children, of retirement, Canadian politics (will the Meech Lake Accord pass? Today was the day), and on and on until Bruce called a halt.

Sunday, June 24, 1990
Our conversation has turned a lot to aging. I said I think the problem is grief, the loss of the body that has served us well, and confided my own anxiety this year over sudden aging skin. Carol said I have a wonderful skin, but that she is finding hers going before it should. We talked of sun—which shines today—and the dangers, wrinkles and skin cancer. Yesterday we spoke of death.

C's father had died—he'd been out of it for some time—and we spoke of assisting a loved one when the time came. I said I couldn't do that, but found myself unable or unwilling to explain why. Because every aspect of consciousness may have a meaning? Because of not playing out the grand plan? Not sure if I think that, but I do think meaning resides somewhere, and that life, at whatever level, has meaning.

And we talked of Bruce's course on history through novels, and socialization, and of how some great writers—Munro, Laurence—have been able to observe the socialization, to step out of it. We marvelled and wished.

Tuesday June 26, 1990
Today we had a great expedition to Lyons to go to Ikea for furniture. The temp. climbed to nearly 40, and we nearly melted. We took our car—slightly larger—and came home with an entire chesterfield tied securely to the top and innumerable lamps, two chairs, rugs, etc., tucked in everywhere. Two large cardboard cartons separated C. and me in the back seat so we couldn't even talk—Don threatened to make this a permanent condition. I told C. of the acceptance process

I'd had to go through at 65, a moving away from my centre so that I view myself more dispassionately, as from a distance. We discussed the ego, and the need some aging people have to feed it—why? Did they never have the opportunity to develop, so that [their ego] is still trying for fulfilment? I said my philosophy is to carry on as though I would live forever, since what alternative is there? Make plans as always, see friends—Aunt Blanche has always done this. C. agreed.

She had a miserable time with her neck and back last year in Ottawa, which was, she thinks, brought on by a move she was forced to make from her office at the university. Her office was co-opted by an associate professor who, because he worked full-time to her part-time, has a higher status. The enormous rage she felt at this mean political manoeuvring surprises her still. This little pipsqueak has published almost nothing compared to C's enormous output and her reviews in U.S. papers (*N.Y. Times!*), but the department head refused to interfere. ("My hands are tied.")

Unloaded the furniture at Shieldses' and came back to a bowl of soup, and Bruce already in bed.

Thursday, June 28, 1990
Last night had Carol and Don to dinner and if I do say so myself I managed—given the limitations of our *gite*—to serve a delicious lamb dinner.

Went over this a.m. to work on the novel [one last edit of *A Celibate Season*] and Bruce—now feeling almost well again—helped Don plaster in the chinks of the building's stone wall.

C. and I made good progress. I was struck, once, by her admission that she has never felt jealousy. A miserable emotion to have escaped. She is one of the most well-balanced people I have ever known—unusual in someone so intelligent and hard-working. Also she is non-judgmental (unlike me). Sometimes I wonder if the absence of the darker side of human nature is a disadvantage to a novelist. We talked of Anne Tyler's novels and their lack of a dark side, except that *The Accidental Tourist* has a grief motif that makes it powerful and compelling.

Not that Carol doesn't have her dislikes. [A novelist], for instance, who suffers from overambition, and of course the pipsqueak who stole her office and to whom she doesn't speak. C. is quieter this year than in Paris. Probably because then they had been nearly a whole year away and needed stimulation, but now have come out of a pressure cooker of activity and need this space to wind down.

Sunday, July 1, 1990
Today the four of us took in the funny little fair in Orgelet, put on by the *pompiers.** Very chilly, but we wandered around, listened to bands (good) and watched pathetic little costumed dancers and drum majorettes (terrible).

C. is working on a paper on *Emma* for the Jane Austen Society, also on poems for a proposed book. We discussed Virginia Woolf's problems with abusive stepbrothers, and the excellent *New Yorker* review she is using for a talk. Also talked about whether the teaching of creative writing accomplishes anything. I had thought it might save the years of errors and learning to prune and avoid clichés; C. not so sure.

I told her about Joseph Campbell's statement that the body is merely the vehicle of consciousness, and also the theory or possibility that the brain may be a receptor of consciousness. As a matter of fact, I've started a short story on this theme [published as "A Good Day on a Minor Galaxy" in *The Antigonish Review*].

Monday, July 2, 1990
Off early with Carol and Don to wonderful market in Louhans. Live fowl of every description, rabbits, crowds—very interesting.

Then went to a wonderful dining room for lunch. Beautifully decorated interior, the kind of food France is famous for. Don showed us the little farm where they stayed when they bought their place, and we admired ancient buildings and the architecture of the Bresse area.

---

*French firefighters.

C. and I discussed our younger days with children, the happiness, our relations with our daughters (all of them wonderful, "signed, Mother") and great sons. I asked C. about her mother and she says she didn't feel they had ever developed the kind of relationship she has with her own children. [Carol was] too caught up in her own family to be devastated by her death—which was not the case with me at Dad's death. We talked of the difficulty we both have in writing autobiographically—why? Because we think of ourselves as uninteresting? (I think C. should. There are depths to be tapped.)

Tuesday, July 3, 1990
C. and I discussed whether or not we are intellectuals. She said I was because I like philosophical abstractions, but I said not in comparison with the true intellectual (Northrop Frye, Joseph Campbell, Hannah Arendt). I said I admired her ability in English Lit, particularly her ability to review books—point of view, use of language, insight. She says what she lacks is the philosophical approach—ability to hold disparate ideas and call on them. I said my problem was wide but shallow knowledge on a great range of subjects, while she felt hers is the lack of interest in many fields (they aren't music or dance people, marginally art), while at the same time great depth in her own field. My conclusion was we aren't intellectuals because of those great ones above us, but she says perhaps each layer feels this, because except for the very top layer there are always great minds above. (Matter left unresolved.)

Actually there are periods of silence now—we thought we would never run out of things to say, but the silence is comfortable.

We talked of young men and my belief that between about 18–28, most are unable to relate to women as people, only as objects. C. says that with only 2 or 3 exceptions she has never established a good rapport with male students.

These ideas and dozens of others I haven't touched on whirl about in my head. Lucky we have them because it is making the holiday. Especially on the fairly frequent days of "iffy" or soggy weather.

Thursday, July 5, 1990
Tried to do some exploring of the dam at Lac de Vouglans. Got caught in violent mountain storms and barely got back in time to get dinner for the Shieldses. I served stuffed chicken breasts.

Had a good time, although C. was tired from having had a sleepless night, during which she read Anne Tyler's *Celestial Navigation* and then passed it on to me. She told me the next day that sleeplessness may be caused by hormone replacement therapy—which I didn't do (because of phlebitis). Her doctor advises it because of the danger of osteoporosis.

Friday, July 6, 1990
In the a.m. Bruce helped Don with cement work on the stones of the house. C. and I went for a walk. She is anxious to do what I do— e.g., the 5-kilometre walk—because I was her age when I started and it seems to have kept me healthy. She is feeling much better today. Their friend Roger whom we met 3 years ago in Paris, arrived, so Bruce and I went back to the *gite* and got ready for our side trip tomorrow.

Had dinner at the Shields home. Very merry—Roger speaks excellent English, and we discussed Canadian politics and many other things. I told C. earlier how happy I am that we've "found" one another again. Friendships need more than an exchange of letters, and sometimes people change too much to continue a friendship in the former vein. She too feels that way. She told me of renewing and recapturing friendships at her high school reunion.

Tuesday July 10, 1990
Home home, home! At least insofar as the Legna *gite* can be made to feel like home. [We had decided to drive south for some sun and stayed near Cannes.] Today we bombed back all the way on freeways, bucking terrible winds in the Aix en Provence and Avignon areas. Got lost after leaving the freeway, stopped in Arinthod for wine, then checked our rear-view mirror and there were Carol and Don right behind us. We made them come in and share some wine while we recounted our adventures. C. has done good work on her poems.

Thursday, July 12, 1990
C. and I discussed many many books. She is the only person I know who has read everything I have and of course much more, and with her background in English literature she is highly informed. Her English copy of *Swann* comes out in August, then in February they are bringing out *Happenstance* and *A Fairly Conventional Woman* in paperback together. How her career is blossoming!

In an essay published in *Prairie Fire* I recorded a magical day we spent together in Burgundy:

One day we toured the wine caves of Burgundy and purchased a bottle of local champagne. We drank it at a sparkling picnic on a high hill with a deserted stone tower that overlooks a vista of fields and small villages. There was a mysterious square of concrete beside the tower, and when we got out of the car Don danced Carol around it to the hum of a Strauss waltz.

My mother used to say that nobody knows anything about the true state of a marriage except for two people, but on that magic day in the glistening heights above the painterly background, with the ragged hum of *The Blue Danube* and Carol's black sundress splashed with orange flowers and the two of them twirling on the cracked and weedy concrete, it seemed possible, probable, that sometimes we get it right the first time, and that these two incredibly lucky people do love one another romantically and passionately, even after thirty-some years together.

After we left the Shields place my husband and I spent a couple of weeks touring around France and working our way to the beaches of Normandy, where we explored the sites of the D-Day invasion and the area around Aramanches where the Canadian forces had done much of the fighting. As we drove through the frequently wild traffic of France I thought often of Carol, of our talks and of the things we had pondered, but for some reason I felt uneasy. I dismissed it as one does, and on our return I didn't write until mid-August when I knew they would be back in Winnipeg. I had no idea that a near-tragedy had befallen them.

August 1990

Dear Carol and Don,

When I got home there was a message from Shelley Sopher [ofCoteau Books]—she wondered what we had decided re an editor. I asked her about whether they were operating on grants or their own money, and it turns out to be their own money, so they are anxious not to hire anyone too expensive. I suggested that she come up with four or five names and fly them by you, since you are much better acquainted with the editorial marketplace than I am.

All is on track with the play. I couldn't help worrying, so dragged Bruce off to A *Midsummer Night's Dream*, being played in Vanier Park (beside the planetarium) in a tent, since our producer, Don Williams, is playing Bottom. Excellent production, and afterwards we talked with him and heard the good news that a fundraiser had raised $3,000 and so they will be able to afford a set designer. Yippee! Nothing more until *Midsummer* finishes on August 26th, then we'll be getting into rehearsals.

By the way, I was struck by a lovely speech of Oberon's, early on in the play, about mermaids. I would have looked it up for you but can't find my Shakespeare. Thought you might like it.

Now to non-business. We had a wonderful final spin around France. The weather, as you know, varied between perfect and too-perfect, and so the trip to Normandie was especially interesting. In fact, we loved Normandie, as you suggested we would. My favourite thing was the Bayeux Tapestry. We did climb Mont-Saint-Michel to the very top (on a hot day), and stayed a couple of days there at Hotel de la Poste nearby—excellent hotel. Took side trips all around and reconstructed D-Day—very interesting. We decided to splurge at a Michelin-recommended two-knife-and-fork place, the Rôtisserie de la Paix. The meal was absolutely wonderful—ranks up there with that wonderful lunch we had the day we went to Louhans.

Bruce left a drawer-full of clothes—sweaters, T-shirts, shorts, etc.—in Geneva. I wrote to the hotel, never again expecting to see any of it, and two days after we got home a parcel arrived at the door containing all the stuff, and freshly laundered at that!

We thank you both for taking so much time to show us around and feed us and wine us, etc. The whole trip was one of the most successful holidays we've had. French driving being what it is, I don't know if we will attempt a driving holiday again. Which is too bad, as we enjoyed all our exploration immensely, and found our French adequate as we got more into the spirit of things. We did hit one fierce day of heat as we travelled into Rouen—apparently it hit 40 degrees that day—and so we didn't see as much there as we had hoped.

Our week in Toronto was a great success. Saw a wonderful production of *Guys and Dolls* at the Stratford Festival and two plays at the Shaw Festival. Also spent time at a cottage in Muskoka. It's very hot. Thirty-six days without rain, and an official temperature yesterday of 32. (A record.)

Bruce sends greetings and thanks for the great visit to you both.

Love,
Blanche
P.S. Loved the two paperbacks, *Jubb* [Keith Waterhouse] and *Pasmore* [David Storey]. Loved both—had read the David Storey one year ago, and loved rereading it. Read a book *Perfume* [Patrick Süskind]—strange, well-written, not worth it. Agree *Witches of Eastwick* not Updike's best.

∿On September 3, 1990, I wrote in my journal:

After we left the Shieldses (July 14) I thought continually of them having a traffic accident. Two weeks ago [after getting my letter of August 13] Carol phoned and they had indeed been in a terrible accident on July 21. Don went through a stoplight. Carol and passengers were not hurt, but Don had severe internal injuries. They operated immediately, and after about three weeks

in the Chalon hospital he was taken by stretcher to the airport
and flown to Winnipeg (23 hours hospital to hospital). He was
there until a couple of days ago and is now home. Broken shoulder and broken hip, using a walker.

Carol was crying a bit when she told me. I wrote at once, and
phoned two nights ago.

August 22, 1990

Dear Don,

Carol phoned last night and told me all your very unpleasant
news. Poor you! It sounds as though you've had one hell of a time,
and with a ways to go yet. We're just terribly thankful that you are
going to knit together again without permanent damage.

I'm so glad that John managed to get to France, as it must have
been terrible for Carol (not to mention you) waiting alone at the
hospital. Isn't it wonderful to have family old enough to lean on?
When Allison was having such awful things happen to her [back
surgery], I don't know what we would have done without the
support of our young people.

As I mentioned in my note to Carol with the pictures, we were
delighted with Normandie and followed your advice (not to
mention your green Michelin). What a lovely area it is, especially in
the sunshine. No wonder France is so renowned—almost every area
is beautiful. Your instinct, when young, to establish an academic
base there was certainly sound. When we got to busy, uptight, and
somewhat smug Toronto, we missed the sidewalk cafés, the relaxed
atmosphere, the ability to buy a beer or a glass of wine anywhere,
and especially your company and Carol's.

I am sitting at my computer and looking at my bulletin board,
which is covered with pictures of us slurping champagne on a hillside
overlooking a little town, of Bruce, Don and Carol sampling the best
of the chèvres at Louhans, of us eating one of Carol's delicious (and
tasty) suppers on the patio at Montjouvent, and of Carol and me
posing as unlikely recruits for the Légion Étrangère. Happy memories!

Carol says you blame yourself for going through a stop sign, but I think it is important to remember that there are none of us who haven't occasionally made a major error in driving. Bruce went right through a red light in Rouen, and not long ago I turned left onto the Mount Seymour Parkway onto the wrong side of the cement dividers and found myself going the wrong way.

Well, Don, as they say in the best circles, I think I bugger off now.* Bruce joins me in hoping for a speedy recovery.

Blanche

August 22, 1990

Dear Carol,

I am still reeling a bit from the shock of your news last night. Bruce and I were both very shaken; in fact, neither of us could get to sleep for some time. Bruce asked a dozen questions I was too dazed to think of: How did you manage, while Don was in the hospital in Chalon? Did you find a good place to stay? Was the car a write-off? When did you actually come back to Canada, and how did you manage on the plane, with Don so ill? Of course we are both delighted that no permanent damage will be done, although I'm sure the healing process, with a broken shoulder and hip, will be arduous. I feel terribly sorry for him, and have just written to him. I also sympathize greatly with what you must have been through, and what you will yet go through as you deal with the enormity of the shock. Try to spare yourself as much as you can, as traumas like this take a lot out of a person. Thank heavens you escaped more or less unscathed! And there were no terrible head injuries, the most devastating thing of all.

---

*This refers to a story about the wife of the Japanese ambassador in Ottawa. She was an elegant woman who was working hard to master the intricacies of the English language, and who is reputed to have said, when it was time to leave, "I think we bugger off now."

Delighted that you will come on October 19th [for the play]. Maybe I'll have a small gathering after the play that night, family perhaps and a few mutual friends. Bruce sends love and we both send mounds of sympathy.

Love,
Blanche

August 26, 1990

Dear Blanche,

Thank you so much for your lovely caring letter. Yes, it has been an ordeal, but I'm glad to say it is mostly behind us. Don is home for weekend leave at the moment, and feeling stronger. He has been given a little wheeled walker to help him get his strength back, and will soon go on a cane.

You asked how we managed at the hospital in France. He had a private room, and I stayed with him, so for three weeks we were like little birds in our little nest. I slept—surprisingly well—in a chaise longue. When they delivered Don's sleeping pill every night, I asked for one too. We did have friends in Chalon, the couple we were going to have lunch with, and they picked me up every day at noon for lunch at their apartment. They had a bedroom for me, but their marriage was so volatile that I preferred my creaky chair. And they would have been terribly hurt had I found a hotel room. Don has had nightmares about the accident, but I haven't for some reason. He hopes to be back teaching by the end of September, and perhaps running again in six months, though he's talked about swimming instead. The photos cheered us enormously.

We were both distressed to hear about Bruce's diagnosis—though you mentioned it was not completely certain.* I'm glad you're feeling hopeful. It certainly is a disease that seems to be

---

*I had told Carol when I phoned that Bruce had been diagnosed with Parkinson's disease.

getting a lot of attention at the moment and all of it positive. I looked it up in our old encyclopedia, 1967, but everything is out of date. I expect you'll consult a specialist about the new treatments. Will they begin right away? And what is the effect of the treatment?

I'm so glad you're fired up about writing again. Much love to you both. I'm about to walk out into the sunshine to mail this.

C

September 17, 1990

Dear Carol,

I can't tell you how delighted I was to hear your wonderful news [Carol won the Marian Engel Award*]. Mum has been the word, but do let me know when I can start bragging. It would be nice to have you in Vancouver a little longer, but the Friday night is the main thing. I have been trying to draw up the list of people to come up after the play and am having trouble keeping it down to fifty, as this house isn't too well equipped to handle more.

My son Stephen is coming through this weekend, so I have the family coming for Sunday brunch. Suddenly things are rushed, and I find myself thinking of fields of poppies in Legna. John loved it there, didn't he? He tells me he is thinking of buying near you. Wouldn't that be wonderful?

Oh, I'm excited about your wonderful award. And I'm pleased to hear of Don's steady progress. Bruce is also much improved—the medication seems to have actually reversed many of the symptoms. He is studying Quebec history this year at SFU. Must close.

Much love to both of you,
Blanche

---

*The Marian Engel Award is presented annually by the Writers' Trust of Canada in memory of Canadian writer Marian Engel. It goes to a female Canadian novelist in mid-career and is awarded for the recipient's entire body of work.

November 19, 1990

Dear Carol,

It was a relief to see Don [in Vancouver] looking so well.

Saturday night was the municipal election. I worked hard for Barbara Perrault to be alderman in the City of North Van and am delighted to say that she did win.

[Bruce's] Parkinson's symptoms continue to retreat, so we are feeling very positive about it.

Blanche

P.S. I got Alice Munro's book [*Friend of My Youth*] for my birthday—am loving the new ones as well as the rereading of the old.

Try to see *The Company of Strangers*. A beautiful film, the exchange of stories among eight elderly women. For my money, I would advise you *not* to see *Henry and June*, which Marilyn took me to on my birthday. While it may be that Anaïs Nin's diary of that time was very erotic, I don't find portrayals of bodies intertwined right side up, upside down, and in and out particularly stimulating, at least not intellectually. Thanks to me we left before the end—I was enormously bored—although Marilyn claims to have not been bored. (Boy, am I getting old!) There was almost no conversation besides orgasmic grunts, and much viewing of the exquisite face of the actress who played Nin but nothing to give the uninitiated the idea that her diaries might actually claim the odd insight. As for Henry Miller, he was John Wayne with literary pretensions. So much for Jay Scott [the *Globe and Mail* reviewer], who adored it!

November 23, 1990

Dear Blanche,

We're off to a dance at the Faculty Club tonight—a sure test for Don's healed hipbone. I've been reading the play all afternoon with great delight and wanted to get my thoughts off to you before the nice warm feelings of pleasure fade.* I laughed out loud a number

---

*Carol had offered to go over *A Celibate Season* and perhaps help me with the ending, since I hadn't been satisfied with it when the play was produced.

of times, and of course, the play is so recent I was able to picture a good deal of it. Some of the things I'll mention are merely typos, some little places that "gave me pause." So onward:

[Two pages of detailed comments and criticisms have been omitted.]

Lordy, it's time to get dressed, so better dash. I've had a chance to do a little research on fertility saints, and will get off the opening piece in a few days. Much love to you both. And many thanks for everything.

C

P.S. Have finished A.S. Byatt—*Possession*—superb!

November 29, 1990

Dear Carol,

Have finished the Alice Munro book, and was struck with the recurring theme: walking away from a perfectly nice husband because of the revelation that a willingness or searching for a love affair signifies the end of the marriage. Interesting, isn't it? An attempt to come to terms, place it in perspective, do you think?

Glad you loved *Possession*.

Am anxious to know if the first chapter of *Fertility* [the mystery Carol and I had agreed to write] is the kind of thing you had in mind. Barbara and I are going to walk the West Van seawall and then put back all the calories with lunch at Peppi's.

Glad to hear Don can still dance! No matter how nice the Faculty Club is, you'll never dance more divinely than on a cement slab on a hilltop overlooking the Bourgoyne!

Love,
Blanche

December 4, 1990

Dear Blanche,

I was interested in your remarks about Alice's book. Joan Clark wrote me that she'd noticed Alice used the word "arse" a lot in this book (and that she used the word "serious" a lot in the last one). It reminded me of how you picked up the fact that I'd used "sweet" over and over again in *Swann*. Curious—too bad a computer can't pick up this kind of thing.

I must go do a few Christmas things today. What a lot of time Christmas takes, even when one's children are gone. All is well.

Love,
Carol

December 10, 1990

Dear Blanche,

I am mailing this in a terrific hurry—guessing at the postage too because the queues at the post office are a mile long.

I got a call from a dinner theatre in Cornwall who wants to do *Departures and Arrivals* in March. I will try to go, and will take a copy of *A Celibate Season* with me to show them—I do think it might work well for dinner theatre, what do you think? I don't want to send it now, though, for fear of looking pushy. (Why do women have to be the ones to worry about such stuff?—I'm sure men don't.)

Love to you both,
C

December 14, 1990

Dear Carol,

I am actually ready for Christmas! Although I wouldn't tell anyone I know, especially my own daughters, for fear of pulling down curses on my organized head.

As I said when I sent your card yesterday, I absolutely love what you did with the little saint in the prologue [for the mystery novel]. Far from thinking it too poetic, I think it is just right, and am now worrying that mine is too prosaic. Anyway, it won't hurt to have some contrast, and I don't think you should change a word of the little saint bit. Have just finished a Ruth Rendell book and wonder what the fuss is about. I thought the writing very mundane, although the sense of place was good and the plot properly convoluted. It seems that convoluted plots are what mystery readers like.

Yesterday my church book club read *A Celibate Season* [the play]. Lots of good discussion, but the recurring unhappiness with the ending. (They didn't read your new ending.) I like it.

Hope you have a great Christmas season. I've already eaten things like banana cream pie. Allison is doing the dinner this year—yippee!

Love to both of you,
Blanche

December 17, 1990

Dear Carol,

Would you believe I have already written *A Celibate Season* for dinner theatre? About a year ago a Calgary dinner theatre was advertising in the Writers' Union newsletter, so I rewrote it, but didn't get far.

I am flying high over your revisions to my chapter, because I love it! Lerner and Loewe, Gilbert and Sullivan, and now—Shields and Howard!

Love,
Blanche

December 19, 1990

Dear Blanche,

What am I doing writing a letter just before Christmas, you ask? Because, like you, I find I'm ready for Christmas. I can't believe it— and I'm not going to admit it either, not to anyone. How did this happen? What does it mean? (Actually I have a couple little notes to get off, but everything else is more or less in place!) I've loved my December holiday from the university, and wonder at times like this why I continue. I'm sitting here at a practically clear desk—what a joy. Maybe I'll spend a few minutes untangling my paper clips or dusting my stapler.

Maybe we should work on our new [mystery] novel, [sending it] back and forth, amending and re-amending—but if we do, we really should try to find a way of sending disks back and forth, otherwise it could be very time consuming, retyping and keeping track of drafts. Are our disks compatible? Blanche, you're the high-tech management part of this partnership—what do you suggest?

I've tried Ruth Rendell too—my brainiest friends read her—and I couldn't get interested. I agree with you—that convoluted plots appeal to mystery readers; they have concentration powers, it seems. Well, good, we can convolute all we want, then.

These last few days I've made a few wobbly steps into my new novel, what I hope will be a kind of saga, but with a different shape. I'm beginning in 1905 and setting it in a village just north of Winnipeg where there are some famous stone quarries (Tyndall stone—from which the Parliament Buildings are made). I'm nervous and dithery about it, but it feels good to be back into something, thinking about it anyway.

About theatres, I seem to be totally ignorant. They only seem interested in prairie realism here in Winnipeg. Or New York imports. Nothing in between. I'll keep my ear to the ground.

Love,
C

December 27, 1990

Dear Blanche,

Your letter was here when we got home from Toronto last night—after a most marvellous Christmas with the four girls plus sons-in-law plus our little Joseph—or Joe, as he is more and more called. My next few weeks will be a bit eaten up with a little piece I'm doing for the CBC and with visiting Don's mother in the hospital. While we were away she fell and broke her leg, pretty tricky business at age 85. Yes, I agree that our outline should not be rigidly adhered to, but it is rather nice to have a structure to turn to now and then.

I'll look forward to seeing the dinner theatre piece. We also have a dinner theatre here in Winnipeg, as you may know, and though I don't know the people involved (and have never been there), I could

always hurl myself at them. Could you run a Winnipeg version?
Do you have any handy Winnipeg jokes? Probably they involve mostly
weather, mosquitoes, North End ethnicity and left-wingedness—the
Winnipeg diaspora, especially in Toronto.

I got some lovely books for Christmas including, from Don, one
of those mighty dictionaries I've always craved. Hope your
Christmas was filled with joy.

Carol

January 21, 1991

Dear Carol,

Herewith many goodies, and I'm sorry to have taken so long, but
after a week of snowbound-ness with everything cancelled, I suddenly
got terribly busy with all the previously cancelled things.

I finished *Possession*, which was marvellous. What erudition!
Novels like that make me feel that I have a lot of temerity to even
continue writing. Much about it reminded me of *Swann*—which,
by the way, my church book club is doing in February, me leading,
of course. If you could direct me to any in-depth reviews that
I could search out in the library, I would appreciate it. I also—for
the book club—waded through *Satanic Verses* [Salman Rushdie].
While I admire the writing and imagination and erudition enormously, the magic realism was just a little too much for my linear
mind. (Although, I like Gabriel Garcia Márquez very much, but
this is even more fragmented.) It has an *Arabian Nights* quality, and
I am glad to have read it, and was considerably more enlightened as
to its theme by the time we'd gone through reviews and discussion.

I saw the most wonderful thing on PBS television the other
night. A British actress—I've forgotten her name—delivered
Virginia Woolf's famous essay, *A Room of One's Own*, as though she
were Woolf and making the original speech in Cambridge. She was
absolutely marvellous. I've taped it, and hope that if you missed it
(knowing your aversion to TV), I can play it for you some time
when you are out here.

I won't mention the Gulf War, since what is left to say about it that hasn't been said?

Love,
Blanche

January 29, 1991

Dear Blanche,

Well—we're on our way [in writing the mystery novel]!

These last weeks seem to have been taken up a good deal with Don's mother (who is now at home and doing quite well) and with my concern over my brother who is very ill with a vicious face and brain cancer (I don't know if I wrote you about this). However, work is a comfort—and a distraction—and I am back at my Mac once again. Don and I go to England on the 8th of February for a week (the book launch and tour), and so I don't know if I'll get Chapter 2 back to you before then, partly because I need to know from you about point of view. Whose heads do we want to be inside for this book?

I'm delighted you loved *Possession*—not all my friends have. Anne, too, adored it, and she even read every scrap of the poetry, which I didn't do. A friend has saved me a tape of the Virginia Woolf presentation and so I will be able to see it. I asked him if they tried to make the actress look like Woolf, and he said only a little, that no one would want to look that ugly??? I haven't tried *Satanic Verses*—my temples throb just thinking about it, but I think I'll at least read it diagonally, as the French say.

The war has me going about with clenched teeth. Be sure to read the piece in this week's *New Yorker*. I can't believe we are in the hands of such second-rate (fourth-rate?) leadership, these awful dumb generals, the impossibly ignorant Bush machine. Little boys craving adventure. Profiteers. Politicians. Whenever I hear that "title" Operation Desert Storm, I want to go out and kick pigeons.

I'm off to the university.

Much love to you both,
C

February 4, 1991

Dear Carol,

First—how exciting that you are off to England! Is this for *Various Miracles?*

I am terribly sorry to hear the news of your brother. I liked him so much when I met him—he seems a gentle man—and I know how fond you are of him. Such a dreadful thing to have. It seems that you are having some tough years, what with Don's accident, and now an illness like your brother's. These things take their toll, don't they?

[Several paragraphs regarding the joint book effort have been omitted.]

The Antigonish Review accepted "Let Me Compute the Ways," which you may or may not remember was excerpted from my novel about dreams, *Random Access Memory*. I finally phoned Penguin about the novel and was informed that the editor I'd been dealing with had left and they had sent back the ms.

I'm glad about the story being accepted, and apologize for moaning about the novel—these are the hazards of writing, after all. But, to quote from a wonderful play, "The insensitivity of the fucking inhabitants of this planet never ceases to astonish and confound me!"*

Saw a wonderful—though quite controversial—play by Michel Tremblay, *Hosanna.* I understand that many outraged citizens left before the end of the first act, uncomfortable with a man wandering around in black garter belt and stockings. But, although the language and specific sexuality could be construed as shocking and pornographic, the actor actually managed to convey the pathos and confusion in the mind of the drag queen protagonist, and both Bruce and I found ourselves quite moved. But then, what do I know? I hated *Henry and June* and did leave before the end, and found that *The New Yorker* loved it.

Hi to Don, and love to you both.
Blanche

---

*This is a quote from Chas in *A Celibate Season.*

April 8, 1991

Dear Blanche,

Whew! I wish I had time to go through the whole thing [*A Celibate Season*, the play] one more time—but I've got to get my class wound up, and get organized to leave on Friday [for England].

What a lot you have ahead—a whole wedding [Allison's to David Corbeil], and then finding your way through what has become a mess of little yellow flags [Post-its].

Winnipeg is brown but sunny, and the river is flowing by at a nice clip. We've already seen the first canoe out there, dodging the ice.

Love to all the family,

C

April 25, 1991

Dear Carol,

The final (?) draft went back to Margaret [Allen, the editor we were working with] yesterday, and thanks to your good ideas it wasn't nearly as horrendous to come to terms with Jock's short-comings as I had expected it to be.

Am enclosing a warm and reassuring letter from Margaret. She sounds like a terribly nice person, and I think we have been incredibly lucky.

I do hope your trip to see your brother wasn't too heart-wrenching. I thought of you often, knowing how awful such things are. I do hope the prognosis is encouraging.

Our wedding was delightful. The weather was unbelievable—two weeks of summer temperatures and clear skies. The ceremony was very moving, Allison and Dave faced the congregation, flanked on either side by his teenage daughter and son and Allison's same, girls dressed alike. Dave's daughter burst into tears, and so did half the wedding guests. (Not me—I feel terribly hard-boiled to admit this, but I almost never cry. I did actually feel that I might, however. A mini-breakthrough?) The party afterwards was one of those exceptionally happy ones, since Dave's friends are pretty well all

members of our Unitarian church, and Allison's should be.
(Compatible, I mean.) Dave's parents turned out to be delightful
people who live in Ottawa, also members of the Unitarian church,
who formerly, before his retirement, lived in Montreal. He is one of
those perfectly bilingual French Canadians, and we share similar
interests, viewpoints, etc., etc. A happy union.

You ask if I think the reviewer in the *Sunday Times* review [of *The
Orange Fish*] is a man. The only clue he/she gives is that sentence: "It is
impossible now to believe that women were like this." I find that
young women (thirtyish) do actually believe that there has been some
profound change in the behaviour and circumstances in which women
find themselves, although I don't think it is nearly as widespread as
they believe. For this reason I think it could be such a youngish
woman. These are truly wonderful reviews ("with brilliant formal skill,
each story is made to act as figure and ground to the other"). Wow!

I've read and am reading two wonderful stories. The first, a
"biographical novel," by Sybille Bedford, *Jigsaw*, is a fascinating
account of her growing up more or less all over Europe between the
two wars. I know you would love it. The second is that new one by Iris
Murdoch, *The Message to the Planet*. So far, I'm finding it fascinating.

My health returned quite suddenly—I don't know what to think of
the three-month bout with lingering shakiness, and suspect a mental
component but am at a loss to know what (or if) it was. At any rate,
the wedding, the exceptional summer weather, a lot of resting, or
whatever, saw the last of it. Now I have to get back to the three-mile
walks, which were cancelled or scaled down for the first time in years.

Love,
Blanche

May 16, 1991

Dear Blanche,

Blanche, you are absolutely right—Clare from *The Sunday
Times* is indeed a woman in her thirties (late thirties, a "little bird

of a woman," according to Christopher Potter*). I can picture her perfectly all of a sudden.

I was relieved to get your letter and learn you had completely got over your malaise, whatever it was. And that you are back walking. (I went today, too, for the first time in a while and came back not winded, but sore of foot.) I had a wonderful lunch with three cronies yesterday where the talk ranged from deconstruction theory to how many calories get burned while walking, and learned that 100 calories are burned per mile, regardless of how fast or slow one walks—can you believe this?

I was also pleased to hear that Allison's wedding was a joyous affair and that you felt happy and at ease with the "other" family. Re weeping at weddings: we went to my niece's wedding last weekend and she wept throughout, down the aisle, at the altar, choking on her vows. And she has lived with the groom for a year. We were all astonished, since we had never thought her sentimental.

I had a little note from Coteau Books—as you probably did— saying that they would soon be in touch about cover art [for *A Celibate Season*] and I'll be interested to see what they come up with.

At least the snow has finally melted and we are loving our glorious spring days. (Winnipeggers are so forgiving—give them one or two good days and they blot out whole months of misery.)

I loved your piece in the TWUC newsletter and was just slipping it into an envelope to send to *The Globe* when I remembered [the newsletter] was supposed to be confidential for members. [I had counted the number of letters to the editor and discovered that those from men far outnumbered those from women.] I think you must know that the Letters editor is a woman! O irony. I'll enclose the piece I wrote last fall for a program note for the Manitoba Theatre Centre, since it picks up the same theme, though not so thoroughly. You have me watching now every morning, and counting. And fuming. (My only attempt at a letter to *The Globe*, a correction to

*Publisher of 4th Estate, Carol's British publisher.

one of their recent Albania pieces, has NOT been printed.) We should try to get some of the women we know to write.

We are so glad we went to Indiana to see my brother. We were, of course, very worried about what we'd find, which was why it was so extraordinary to see how far he has come. There is not nearly the distortion to his face that we had imagined, and, despite the chemo and radiation, his hair is growing back quickly and covering the scars. (We used to tease him about being so hairy.) He has a long way to go, of course, and still naps quite a lot during the day. He was dashed to learn this week that he would not be able to drive for a year—I think driving must be much more important to men than to women.

Our days there were marvellous, very easy, and full of interesting things to look at. We visited some of the limestone quarries in the area and a stone finishing plant (the subject of my next novel) and that gave us a sense of purpose. From Indiana, I did a side spin, 2 readings and [visits to] 3 daughters, and then the reading in New York, which was fun. The theme of the night was Canadian humour, surely an oxymoron. Susan Swan did the introductions and told a few Canadian jokes, of which I can remember only: Why did the Canadian cross the road? To get to the middle.

I'm rereading Jane Austen's *Persuasion* for a paper I'm presenting at the Jane Austen Society conference in Ottawa next October. It will focus on her use of the body, her non-use I should say. In conjunction with this I've been reading some other books about the history of the body as it appears in literature and thought. Wonderful stuff, and how I'd love to chew it all over with you. I am making *Persuasion* sound like an academic chore, but in fact I'm finding it funny and sharp and full of sly pleasures I must have overlooked when I read it at twenty. I'll try to find *Jigsaw* to take to France this summer. As for Iris Murdoch's *The Message to the Planet*, I've tried to read it but got bogged down, though you know how much I love her books. For some reason there seemed too many men introduced all at once who all sounded alike, and all of them fuss-budgets. I suppose I should give it another run. I remember that I made a second attack on one of her other books and was very glad I did. Catherine's baby could arrive any time now. I jump when the phone rings. Don is fine; he's doing his exercises while listening to *Ideas* on CBC, a nightly ritual lately. Then we go for a walk, during which he summarizes what he's heard. (We seem to have fallen into all sorts of routines and rituals—what should I think of this?)

Love to you both,
C

May 30, 1991

Dear Blanche,

Hello from hot and sunny Winnipeg, dandelion/mosquito capital of the world.

I just had a letter, as I'm sure you did, from Shelley. I love her idea for a cover, but thought we (you and I) should discuss some of the details she's asked about. Did we decide the year of wedding would be about 1970? I do think, knowing Jock's mother, that there would have been a formal studio photo. I imagine Jock (dashing, eyes full of intelligence, maybe an expression of irony) in a very plain white dress, absolutely no veil, probably long straight hair(?) and Chas, with longish-but-not-long hair, medium brown, medium handsome, and, yes, a tux, I think, but not a fussy tux. I would imagine this photo to be in a very plain silver or black frame. A photo of their kids—to make sense—should be close to their own age in the novel, don't you think? Or maybe not. I think we might suggest to Shelley only to make sure the kids' faces match, if possible, the general physical characteristics of the parents. As for writing implements, Jock uses some kind of pen (a Bic?) and unornamented stationery—or would she use government paper? Chas would use a rather beat-up old manual portable, I should imagine. Wedding rings—very plain and rather wide, I think, so they'll show up.

Catherine is having her baby today—they're inducing it since it is a little late. I'd give anything to be closer. Have given myself an afternoon of numbing chores to keep my brain frozen.

Who are we going to dedicate our book to? Any ideas? Did you ever send Shelley the photo of us together?

Much love,
C

June 3, 1991
Dear Carol,

You have been on my mind since our talk on Friday, and I hope and pray that Catherine is well now [after a complication during childbirth]. It never occurred to me, when I had my own children, how hard it would be when grandchildren were born.

What a lot you've gone through lately! It does seem, as Jock's mother pointed out, that troubles come in batches. I know for a few years we seemed to have one thing after another, as you have of late. In any case, I was relieved to hear in your previous letter that your brother was not as badly disfigured as you had feared. I hope there was no brain damage, but from the way you spoke it sounds as though not.

I was envious of your wonderful talk with three cronies, who could discuss something like deconstruction theory. I have many friends who could do the calorie part you mentioned, but I seem to have a dearth of same interested in literature, at least at that level. Partly my fault, having not been attending meetings of the Writers' Union. Too far on rainy nights (most nights) in winter. However, I am pushing myself out to a Federation of BC Writers meeting on Saturday, so may renew a few old acquaintances. But I do feel starved for good conversation these days.

I can't accommodate my thinking to a woman being editor of the letters in *The G and M*. Must be one of those REAL women who believe men should run things. Actually, their Letters page is not very interesting any more—they used to publish on the basis of wit and style, but now it seems mostly to be merely the dreary presentation of factual matters that need correcting. I loved your program notes to *The Heidi Chronicles*. Your analysis about the

number of men in stage- and film-writing was excellent. It got me
wondering whether the whole thing is a function of power, whether,
if women were the powerful group in society, the reverse would
happen. Or is it a function of psyche, something different between
the sexes? I incline to a mix: men are powerful, they have the money
and operate via old-boys' networks. And even when conscious of it
and trying not to, they like the way other men think and write
more than the way women think and write. An alienation that
might have something to do with 20th-century society—reading
letters between the sexes in Victorian times, one doesn't get the same
feeling of the two sexes operating in completely different worlds. By
the way, saw the exceptionally good [stage play of] *Shirley Valentine*,
and was furious to think a man could write with a voice so true.
There go some of my better generalizations.

After that diatribe, I probably shouldn't admit that my latest
reading was *Rabbit Is Rich*, which I didn't read when it came out
because I found Updike's bawdy characters off-putting at that
time. This time, however, after initial resistance, I have to admit
that he is remarkable at putting you inside the head of Rabbit,
even though it is not a place I normally would care to be. The
upshot is, I think I'll now read *Rabbit at Rest*. (Certainly Updike
makes our own "daring" sex scenes in *C.S.* look like a Sunday
School picnic.)

Am glad you got me onto Iris Murdoch. I realized when I went to
the library that it wasn't she I had read and then found forgettable, it
was actually Ivy Compton-Burnett.

Thinking of you in France reminded me of the poems you were
writing last summer. Did you ever find a publisher for them?

Oh, about the dedication. Since you have done your children,
what would you think of us both doing two grandchildren this
time? I thought of it because of using the pictures of Gregory and
Jacqueline [Allison's children, who appear on the cover of *A Celibate
Season*]. Bruce and I send love and concern to you both.

Blanche

June 26, 1991

Dear Carol,

I picture you hunkered down in Montjouvent, the sun shining gloriously, eating your meals while looking out at the peaceful setting across the hills (cow lowing in the background). Tomorrow we are going to the Okanagan to the fortieth wedding anniversary of old and dear friends, so hopefully we will have some hot [weather]. Stephen is flying down with the 2- and 4-year-old, then driving with us to meet Irene there, who has some sort of school track meet. My enthusiasm is marginally tempered by anticipation of a trip of some four to five hours in heavy traffic with said darling grandchildren, who will probably become less darling at an exponential rate as we crawl through the miles. (Am I sounding curmudgeonly rather than grandmotherly? Find a tendency to this as the years fly by.)

Good news: [Coteau] expects to publish in September. Joy told me that they had put the book into "Books for Everybody," which I didn't know about, but which she says has a very wide circulation among distributors. She also said they were doing something about grocery chains—sounds as though these people are aggressive marketers.

I am enclosing various bits and pieces that I thought might interest you. I was a bit astonished to think that Jane Rule would retire from writing—it doesn't seem a vocation that one would ever retire from, does it? I mean, what would you do with your time?

I went to a Federation of BC Writers luncheon, which was a bust, but met an extremely nice woman named Fraidie Martz, who is writing a history of children who were let into Canada during WWII, and who lost their parents in the Holocaust. We are having lunch next week.

Have just finished Updike's *Roger's Version*, and don't know what to think of it. Full of sound and fury, but whether it signifies anything I don't know. Actually, I can't help suspecting that the verbal pyrotechnics concealed a certain emptiness at the core, but perhaps that is a bit uppity of me, given the marvellousness of his writing. Rather strange that he and Iris Murdoch wrote novels with such similar themes, isn't it? I do think hers came off better, although neither of them proved anything about the Unknowable (that I know of).

Canada seems to be in the doldrums, which is perhaps a better place for it than fighting Meech Lake. Allison is coming with me in mid-July to Calgary to visit Aunt Blanche, who is now 88 but has all her marbles. This will make the annual visit less burdensome for me, in fact, should be a lot of fun, since I get too little time with my daughters these days, as they rush from thing to thing to do with kids. Bruce and I have just been to a school awards thing for Grade 7 (Jacqueline) in which she got two awards. However, I bypassed Leslie's violin recital for Tommy (4) and Katherine (6), on the basis that I can't turn my hearing aid into the negative decibel spectrum.

Must go and fasten down the movables before the onslaught, which arrives on tonight's plane from Smithers. Bruce sends greetings.

Love,
Blanche

July 1, 1991 [Postcard]

We miss you! I'm about to go for my 5-kilometre walk, Blanche, and would love your company. The sun shines, the poppies are in bloom everywhere, all's well with the world (except Yugoslavia, Iraq, etc.). Hope you're getting a real summer in B.C.

Love,
Carol

July 12, 1991
Montjouvent, France

Dear Blanche,

Is there really someone called Fraidie Martz? Wonderful. (I've already appropriated "Fraidy" for my new novel, short for Elfreda.)

Your letter, with all its enclosures, was a joy, and made me miss you terribly, especially when I set off for my solitary walks. (With my amazing new Rockport sandals, I'm now doing a good 6k a day, and feeling the benefits, especially at night, falling asleep in minutes.)

I can't tell you how heavenly this summer has been. Near-perfect weather. The most marvellous flowers. The house is coming along too. I work every day on my new novel, and can't remember ever working with such happiness. It will be a rather odd "novel," a departure in several ways, but I hope there's enough narrative glue to hold it in place.

What good news about the September publication. It hardly seems possible. The U.K. house who has bought paperback rights to both *Swann* and *Happenstance* is Palladium Books. [Coteau] *might* be interested. About a dedication (maybe you've already decided something), I've been thinking of what we might do. My new novel coming out in February is already dedicated to Don, and, though he's a very nice husband, two dedications in one year might turn his head. I propose:

To Bruce (for Bruce)?
To friendship and to love (??)
To friendship
To the lost tradition of letter writing (only kidding)

Actually, Blanche, I'm not very good at these things, and I'm hoping you've already been struck by inspirations while reading the proofs.

I found *Roger's Version* a bore—though I read some stunning reviews, and wondered if it was just me! I think Updike struck out on this one, and suspect you are right about the reason. (Janette Turner Hospital also wrote on this theme in her last novel, *Charades*.) I've just read a most marvellous non-fiction book, *Dead Certainties (Unwarranted Speculations)* by Simon Schama, an investigation (enthralling) into that thin line between history and fiction.

You and Allison are probably in Calgary right now. I envy you having a daughter for a whole week. Hope you can read this scratching. Oh, for a printer.

Love to all,
Carol

~Fraidie Martz remembers her surprise when she saw her name in Carol's novel *The Stone Diaries*:

> Over the years my curious name had drawn a lot of attention, but I never imagined that one day it would enjoy a jewelled life between the covers of a great book. As they say, hanging out with writers can lead anywhere, or as Byron said, "the glory and the nothing of a name." In my immigrant parents' day, early in the century, it was not unusual for interrogating government officials to rename newcomers with English-sounding names before they took their first steps on the new promising land. A version of that practice took an original twist when my parents named me. In the Jewish tradition, a child is named after a deceased family member, in my case a beloved grandmother, the Bobba Fraida. How to retain its original phonetic tone, yet write it English-looking? "Fraidie" was their laboured solution, likely unaware that the letter "i" on either side of a consonant does not exist in the language.
>
> Soon after Carol Shields' award-winning novel *The Stone Dairies* became headline news across the continent, I was taken quite unawares by unexpected phone calls from far-flung friends. Did I know, they asked, that a character, albeit a minor one, sported my peculiar name? I hadn't given much thought to my friend Blanche Howard casually mentioning some time past that she had dropped my name in one of her frequent letters to Carol, and Carol asking if she might appropriate it for her novel."—Fraidie Martz

July 25, 1991

Dear Carol,

I gather that Winnipeg has suffered from an all-time terrible mosquito infestation, so you are doing well to be away from that.

Now re the book. I did the page-proofing yesterday—it did arrive about a week ago, but I had my Calgary trip so didn't get to it until I got back. The type is nice. They are printing it with unjustified margins, which actually looks rather nice, gives it the sort of informal feeling that letters would give.

[Shelley] wants me to make the decision [re the dedication]. We kicked around a few ideas and came up with the possibility of us dedicating it to one another and to our letters, which she felt might tie in rather nicely with the theme of the book. However, I'm not at all sure I like what I have come up with, but here it is:

To Carol from Blanche and to Blanche from Carol, and to the letters woven into the fabric of friendship.

I am terribly afraid you may think it too flowery, so I am hoping this will arrive in time for you to phone Shelley if you hate it, or to change the wording.

They are using that picture of us taken last year in Montjouvent. In fact, they are delighted with it. Shelley says the sales reps and everyone else want to know who wrote which character, and I said that while I was quite willing to tell Shelley, I thought it would be a good thing not to tell others. I thought this might add some mystery and therefore interest to the publicity, and I also thought it would make for more honest reviews. Do you agree? (Actually, I'm feeling a bit hesitant about making all these decisions on my own— just hope you are happy about them.)

Shelley agreed that secrecy might add a lot of interest from the publicity point of view, and so she won't tell the sales reps, so I expect that will be the number one question we will field. (Strange what turns people on, isn't it?)

She talked of publicity trips, saying the Canada Council would send us on one trip but not two, and that she was hoping there would be some with us together. (A chance for a visit?) She hoped that some of the publicity could be in Ottawa, where she thinks the book will be well accepted, with its Ottawa venue. Also thinks the Spicer Commission* has made commissions more high profile, to

---

*1991 Citizen's Forum on Canadian Unity.

our advantage. She asked about Vancouver book signings (generally lousy) and I suggested Vicki Gabereau, which she said she'd work on.

On the strength of the dialogue in *A Celibate Season* (the play), some video people asked for collaboration on a video about the elderly going into a nursing home. Worked with two interesting and nice men, brainstormed for about five hours straight—a strange way to write, but it was actually fun. And they paid me.

Our trip to Calgary was much pleasanter for me this year, having Allison along. Aunt Blanche is doing well, has retained her sense of humour, and I saw my brother for the first time in many years. He is an alcoholic and has been so bad that most of the family had retreated, but he is going through a dry spell and it was delightful to see him again. Seems remarkably untouched by years of abuse and (unjustly—smokes heavily as well) looks much younger than his 64 years.

Love to both,
Blanche

September 23, 1991

Dear Carol,

I've been meaning to write ever since our nice long phone chat, but seem distracted these days. Possibly because I've had such a long bout of labyrinthitis (ears), which comes and goes and has slowed me down. The doctors offer much sympathy but no cure, and I keep thinking that a school of thought believes that is why van Gogh cut off his ear. (If I am reduced to such drastic measures, I promise you won't be the recipient.) I do have hopes now that it's winding down.

I will stay over in Regina for a day as it will save them so much money if I don't fly Saturday, but I don't really mind as I have both a niece and a nephew there (nephew a well-paid petroleum geologist executive, niece runs her own tattoo parlour, so I have choices), and can probably nail one of them at least for the afternoon or evening. Unless, of course, you are staying over too,

I didn't get that too clear, in which case we can treat ourselves to a well-deserved huge and indulgent dinner somewhere. Pray God my ears are all better so I can go back to imbibing wine, the lack of which has caused me the greatest sense of deprivation during the whole indisposition—other than the slowdown in doing any work, of course.

I enjoyed your review of Anne Tyler's new book but haven't read it yet. Also glad to see that your *The Republic of Love* will be out in February. Exciting! Did I tell you how much I liked Updike's *S*? A novel of letters from a woman, and beautifully done, funny, gets into the head of his female heroine with no detectable wrong notes. Once again revised my opinion of Updike. Also read a paperback release of Mavis Gallant's seventies novel, *A Fairly Good Time*. At first I didn't think so highly of it, but as the novel progressed I realized it really is a masterpiece. Don't know how I missed it in the first place. Do read it if you haven't. Also read a last-century novel, *The Awakening* by Kate Chopin. Marvellous! And banned in its time, because it so disturbed Victorian sensibilities.

I see that you are on the jury this year for the CBC Literary Awards. Good for you—but I think it's fairly strenuous, isn't it?

Saw the article by your friend Joan Clark in *The Globe*, and wondered at her crying over rejections from *The New Yorker*. She must set great store by the *N.Y.* Interesting row over Mordecai's article [Richler's take on Quebec separation] in same, isn't it?

Family are all well. I had everyone over last night for an easy chili supper, to celebrate Allison's new husband having landed a job in building inspection for prospective house buyers. He had decided to pursue this relatively new field and had just written the first exam when he got an opportunity to start right in with a company. With my daughters and family and a young nephew and family, we now number 14 at the table. Gregory is now 17, very handsome, and I gave him my old ancient car, so he thinks he has the world by the tail.

Bruce is aggressively fighting Parkinson's by exercising, and is producing surprisingly good oil paintings. Speaking of exercising, we went to a wedding of one of the Angus offspring, and Michael, age 67, had just run that day from Port Coquitlam to Stanley Park, 26 miles. He is training for the Portland Marathon. Since he is a doctor, my brief lecture on the physical dangers left him singularly unimpressed.

Well, I started out to write just a few lines but seem to have rambled on about nothing. I hope yours are all well, and the grand-children thriving.

Love,
Blanche

September 26, 1991
Winnipeg

Dear Blanche,

[Pam James of Coteau Books] has me coming Friday morning to Regina, and I too will stay over till Sunday to save that chunk of money. And I've got a couple friends to visit too—so it should be fine. I'm trying to work out now what to read for the Toronto reading. I have half an hour, and I intend, never mind what Greg Gatenby has to say, to spend at least half my time introducing the book and talking about how we wrote it, etc., which, for some reason, I think may interest people. I have the book now and will tell you—though I don't intend ever to tell anyone else or even drop a hint—that I find the cover a little unsatisfying. Can't put my finger on the reasons; it is just a little un-booklike. It feels slippery in hand, like a catalogue or travel brochure or something, and the size "feels" non-bookish.

I've just finished two academic papers, one on Jane Austen for the Ottawa conference next month, and one on Margaret Laurence for a commemorative volume to be published in France. These two are now in the mail, a relief, and they've convinced me I don't have the bones to be a real academic. Now back to the novel—this feels heavenly, even though I don't know exactly where I'm going with it. At least it isn't a stitching together of other people's notions and quotes, all cautious glue and reverence. And reservation and equivo-cation and meek little forays into theory.

Grandchild 3 is coming toward the end of November. Don is busy and happy and in good health, though we seem to have heard of a lot of illness among our friends lately—cancer, heart attacks mainly.

I'm looking forward to lots of long talks.

Love to you and Bruce,

C

❧ In my journal about the launch of *A Celibate Season*, I wrote:

I went off to Winnipeg at the end of October, arrived during an ice storm and minus 17 and a blizzard. And was met by Carol (late, because she couldn't scrape the ice off her windshield). We did a reading at McNally Robinson Booksellers, a CBC interview, and then on to Regina in a scary little turbo-prop whose whirling propellers had to cut their way in the darkness through the driving snowflakes. The launch in Regina was at the Globe Theatre.

We talked of many things, perhaps more frankly than we have at other times—discussed sexual abuse, a topic of some attention at the moment. Also John Cheever's amazing bouts of homosexuality described in his journal, and his speculation about Updike's sexuality. *Updike! The great fictional womanizer?* We wondered about this mysterious sense of sexual disorientation, since both of us are so heterosexual it is difficult—impossible—to comprehend.

And in an essay in *Prairie Fire* I wrote:

Carol and I met—or rather, didn't meet—Gloria Steinem once. At breakfast the day after the launch we sputtered over an unpleasant *Globe and Mail* review whose main preoccupation was with the names of our protagonists. By way of restorative we hurled ourselves against an icy gale in minus-20-degree temperatures for several blocks to a bookstore. Almost nobody was there, except for a lone woman who was sitting in a chair waiting to sign books. "Who is it?" Carol whispered to me. "I think it's Gloria Steinem," I whispered back. It was. We didn't introduce ourselves. Carol thought it might be intrusive—and I agreed, since we hadn't read Steinem's new book. I regret it now.

November 3, 1991
Winnipeg

Blanche,

This letter is for you. A fan letter.

I met Carol at the airport and we went for coffee—a cappuccino. Out of loyalty—loneliness?—I had started *A Celibate Season* this morning and was halfway through. I told Carol how I regretted not having read the book before you came to Winnipeg. I had found your writing witty, intelligent and thoughtful. I wished I had discussed the feminization of poverty with you—particularly the middle class's views of the feminization of poverty. Not so much the issue itself, but the wonderful way you presented the issue from so many viewpoints.

Now, I have finished *A Celibate Season* —before a fire, with the love of my life close by and a bottle of champagne to celebrate. I was deeply moved by your writing the letter which was never sent. The powerful image of the child in the womb, the tenderness, and the Christmas bicycle. I am even more pissed off that I didn't know, and therefore couldn't say what a memorable experience it was, your book.

Love to you (and Bruce too),
Don

November 11, 1991

Dear Carol,

I see by the TV that Winnipeg today was a balmy 9 degrees—my timing was certainly off. In spite of which I had a great time, and was delighted to see your lovely apartment and go to your class. Nice to be able to visualize all these things when I write.

So far the Vancouver papers have ignored *A Celibate Season*. Have you fared any better in Winnipeg? I wrote Coteau Books and told them what a successful launch I thought they had, and thanked them for the great hotels, etc. They are nice people to work with, aren't they?

When I got home, I listened to your story on the radio. It is a lovely story, and now I would like to read it. It seems to me when I think over your short stories generally, that you have carved out an original niche in the genre—they are quite different from our other well-known short story writers, Munro, Gallant, Atwood, because for one thing you are able to tie together diverse elements with a humble common theme, as you did in "Keys," and keep it alive with your exceptional use of language.

My birthday was on Thursday, and although we did nothing to celebrate it on the day, Marilyn took me to lunch, and both Allison and Leslie have had dinners for me, and everyone is giving me discs for the CD player we have ordered (but not yet received). All family have glommed onto the idea of CDs as the perfect present, and I'm wondering if we should have kept quiet about it until after Christmas, since I will miss my usual complement of blouses, earrings, etc. Ah well, if music be the food of love, and so on.

Have finished *Rabbit Is Rich*, and I think it is one of Updike's best. Interesting that for a brief few pages he switches voices to Janice's—I don't recall him doing this in the previous Rabbit book, or anywhere else in this one. Rabbit finished by being, for all his sins, a sympathetic and endearing character, didn't you think?

I do hope we get a few more reviews, and that *A Celibate Season* repays Coteau for their investment at least. Austin was quite indignant that the *G and M* reviewer included "Austin" as an oddball name. However, others seem to be under the impression that it was a good review, so I think you are right, no one really reads them that carefully.

Bruce is well and was glad to see me back. We both send love to both of you.

Love,
Blanche

P.S. Wow! Just got Don's wonderful letter and it has (to quote Davina) shot me over the moon! Thank you, Don, and also thanks for all the chauffeuring about and general looking-after in Winnipeg. How I appreciate your thoughtful comments! Much love, Blanche

December 1, 1991

Dear Blanche,

Our first minus-20 day, but nevertheless we were out on our daily walk—you would not have recognized us, however, since our faces were well protected by our new L.L. Bean face masks—they're marvellous, some miracle fabric. And we're feeling very happy about the arrival of our new grandson, Nicholas, about ten days ago. The birth went without a hitch, and our tiny 100-pound Anne produced an eight-and-a-half pound child—how is this possible, we wonder. He is, from all reports, a wonderfully calm baby, and very beautiful.

I wanted to get these reviews and notices off to you. I don't know if you've seen *Quill and Quire*. The Winnipeg review came out yesterday, and there will be another mention next week in a column Dave Williamson is writing about what books to buy for Christmas. I don't know how sales are going since I don't seem to get to bookstores lately. I've had the first two advance reviews of *The Republic of Love* (*Publishers Weekly* and *Kirkus*) and they're both delicious. (I did almost eat them.)

Having told you Don doesn't always read my books, I was astonished to get home from Regina and find he had—and that he had been so moved by your description of the love scene. One never knows about the one one marries, does one? I too enjoyed our times and talks. You do have the most wonderful way, Blanche, of listening and sorting out and putting together odd little filaments of thought. While you were having your interesting Saturday evening with assorted rels, I went out for dinner (a lovely bistro) with Connie Gault and [playwright] Dianne Warren. We had one of those memorable gabfests women sometimes fall into, and in fact, we were having such a good time (gossip, theory, speculation) we decided not to go to the play, but to have a round of chocolate torte instead.

Now must spend a few days doing Christmas things—shopping, parcelling, cards, the pudding, and organizing the three separate supper parties we're having. Was I mad when I thought up this three-party nonsense? I must learn to ignore these little bursts of sociability when they strike. Children all well, everyone seems to be moving along in their various grooves. Don and I are going to California in February for our winter break!

Hope your Christmas is merry and warm and non-rainy.

Carol

P.S. My friend Marjorie was indignant too about her name being thought "quaint."

December 28, 1991

Dear Carol,

At last a break in the December madness. Although I didn't do three dinner parties, I did do one, plus family Christmas, plus neighbourly drop-in last night which was proffered as being eight to ten, but went on until about midnight. Plus, it was about the most social season we've had for some time, now have to walk off three pounds.

Unfortunately, the festivities were greatly dampened by Leslie contracting viral pneumonia, which I must confess I didn't know was so debilitating. It is now nearly four weeks, and she is still in bed and very weak. She caught flu as the pneumonia receded, so I suppose it isn't that surprising that it hit her so terribly, but it has been worrying. I have also done quite a bit of grandmotherly stuff, and expect to do more next week.

Thank you for the reviews, loved the one in *Quill and Quire* naturally, and also received some from Coteau Books as you no doubt did. I don't know why we have been ignored here in Vancouver. I do know that *The North Shore News*—given freely to all residents of the North Shore and read quite avidly—is sitting on one, and now I suppose they'll do it in the New Year after our chance at Christmas sales. On the plus side, our local bookstore said they had good sales, but I suspect they were largely to friends and acquaintances.

Also I discovered Alice Hoffman for the first time, the novel *Seventh Heaven*. She is marvellous, isn't she? And loved David Malouf's *The Great World*, although his voice is so much like that in Patrick White's earlier novels that I kept thinking I was reading the latter. I don't know why no reviewers seemed to mention that. Also read a charming little book called *Griffin & Sabine: An Extraordinary Correspondence*, which is an illustrated novel of letters. Have you seen it?

I was really and truly touched to get Don's lovely fan letter, and am enclosing a note to him. Certainly those are the most detailed and thoughtful remarks I've had about the novel (and the only ones in writing).

Did you happen to catch *The Journal* the other night, with Neil Bissoondath's nice little essay on fathers? The thing that fascinated me was the presence of Susan Cheever, who seems warm and articulate and remarkably untouched by what can only have been a strange upbringing. I've just read her seventies and eighties journal in *The New Yorker*, and find it strange that she could have emerged with such a wry and accepting view of a father who must have been hell to be around, with his self-obsessed whining and declarations of deep love (although hard not to forgive the lack of character when one reads such beautiful prose, just dashed off apparently often in drunken stupors). Also have been reading that V. Woolf *A Writer's Diary* I bought after we bumped into Gloria Steinem (literally), and find it, too, fascinating. Oh, and the other person on the *Journal* thing was Michael Ondaatje, who is most attractive in an early-Leonard-Cohen brooding way, and whose thoughts re his father were laced with melancholy musing on mortality.

You must be excited about *The Republic of Love*. I am excited about rereading it, and hope it will have wonderful good fortune. God, how those years speed by! But, having embarked on a positive outlook (for perhaps the hundredth time in my life—remember we discussed how one relearns over and over?), I'm living for the moment.

Bruce and I have now decided to do another driving trip through the U.S. We [hope to] work our way down to New Mexico and back. We only drive a couple of hundred miles (max) a day, and stay wherever it is warm and interesting.

Love,
Blanche

December 28, 1991

Dear Don,

This is a proper thank you for your wonderful (and only) fan letter. It is a great treat to have someone actually take the trouble to tell you what they liked about a novel. In particular, I was gratified that you found the letter that was never sent so moving, since I think Carol will tell you I found that the most difficult to do, without becoming too wordy and sentimental. It was chopped and changed and shortened innumerable times, but your comments give me hope that it did, finally, succeed in conveying what it was meant to convey without sloppiness and sentimentality.

Hope your 1992 brings good things. Bruce sends greetings and love, along with mine.

Blanche

January 7, 1992

Dear Blanche,

I hope Leslie in now on her feet. What an ordeal, and what a worry for you. (This species of worry over offspring never goes away, does it?) Christmas here was joyous, alternately quiet and hectic. Although only two of the children were here (Cath and Sara) we were in almost daily touch with the others by phone—and I've learned this last year to dial those long-distance numbers without a thought. The three parties went fine.

I had the simplest of menus and simply went through the same set of actions three times. Nevertheless, I wouldn't have been able to work up the social energy for a fourth. This exercise had me wondering what people hope for when they sail off for a social evening. Sometimes, I confess that when arriving at a party, I fantasize for a moment about it all being over and us on our way home to our beds. Do you think this is normal?

I've been reading too, Christmas books. *The Invisible Woman* by Claire Tomalin, about Charles Dickens' probable mistress— it's written as a sort of mystery—you'd like it. Also *Self Help* by the American writer Lorrie Moore, whom I discovered through *The New Yorker*—she's very funny and juggles language in a way that makes me madly jealous—though her material is a long way away from my life. Another friend has written me about *Griffin & Sabine*.

Like you, I am hearing the loveliest things about our book, particularly its unputdownableness. It seems half my friends here got it for Christmas from their husbands—hmm.

I'll be in Vancouver for the promo for *The Republic of Love* in February. I'm hoping your grandmotherly duties will have abated by early February so we can have time for [a] natter (I do like that word).

Love,
Carol

February 26, 1992

Dear Carol,

Well, I think you must have hit the jackpot with *The Republic of Love*, don't you? Note that in B.C., anyway, you are third from the top on the best-sellers list! It isn't long since you said to me, all you need is one best-seller, so maybe this is it. Also am enclosing an article by Ian Haysom, *The Vancouver Sun* top editor, which you may not have seen. Almost everyone here seems to have heard the Bill

Richardson* interview (which was wonderful, all agreed), and which was repeated. Heady days! (I'm basking in reflected glory, from *C.S.*) Speaking of *C.S.*, did you note that Coteau's newsletter indicated that the hardcover had sold out? Wonder how many were printed.

It was great seeing you here, and I thought the reading a real success.

I reread *Possession* for our book club, and found it much simpler on the second read. It is quite surprising, the number of parallels with *Swann*. Read Violet Keppel Trefusis' *Echo* for the first time, (you remember, Vita Sackville-West's paramour; they ran away from their husbands together) and was greatly impressed, wondered why it took so many years to translate her from French. Also am reading a fascinating book, *Falling Angels*, by Barbara Gowdy, a Canadian writer I hadn't even heard of until Allison lent me the book. A very interesting voice—have you read her?

Douglas & McIntyre (yes, them again, I just hope—what was his name?—has left) have expressed interest in my novel, so am frantically trying to do some rewriting before we go. Fraidie very kindly read it for me, and has some excellent suggestions, and I find on going back over it that there are some very weak areas. Also have had quite a bit of thoughtful feedback over the years. Just wish I had more time *and* energy, although I can't complain, since I'm feeling really well again.

I liked the thought of coming over to the Sechelt conference.** I haven't even mentioned the TWO enormous and positive articles in *The Globe*—wonderful! Your (our) enemy in the English department must have purple insides.

Must attack dinner, but without too much gusto, since I have acquired two extremely recalcitrant pounds. May not sound like much, but could be the fat end of the wedge.

---

*Author, humorist and radio personality who later become host of CBC Radio's *Richardson's Roundup*.

**Annual Sunshine Coast Festival of the Written Arts.

Much love, and everyone sends congratulations. Barbara Perrault told me to be sure and pass on her compliments on the Bill Richardson interview. My old book club threw a dinner for me (I didn't remember that they mentioned dinner when they asked me, and had already eaten mine, but I chomped my way through number two without anyone twigging to it—could this be the source of the two pounds?). They began the dinner with lentil soup, in honour of the book.

What of the movie offers? Perhaps you will be rich, a most unlikely result for a writer's career. If you ever have time to send any, I'd love to see some of the American reviews. Allison is sorry she missed the reading but is going like mad since her promotion to program director.*

Love,
Blanche

June 24, 1992

Dear Carol,

I imagine you are now ensconced in Montjouvent and relaxing after what must have been a fairly hectic few months [promoting *The Republic of Love* throughout the U.S.].

I got your card and will meet your plane. If all goes well we will be able to catch the 11:30 a.m. ferry to Sechelt—the earlier the better, as later ones tend to get crowded in summer.** Read Rohinton Mistry's *Such a Long Journey*, and was only lukewarm, although others in my book club loved it. Very much like V.S. Naipaul, except that the plight of the protagonist didn't grab me until more than halfway through. Also read Milan Kundera's *Immortality.*

I was pleased to get the money from Coteau, it was actually more than I had hoped for. Also found out when I phoned a new B.C. author book-prize group (VanCity Book Prize) that Coteau had already persuaded them to consider *A Celibate Season* on the basis that 50% of it is by a B.C. author. So they seem to be keeping on top of things.

---

*Allison had been promoted to program director for a large social services agency.

**Carol had asked me to join her and stay in the lodge when she went to Sechelt for the annual writers' festival. Sechelt is on the mainland, on what is known as the Sunshine Coast, but is accessible only by ferry.

Meant to send you a birthday card and Leslie asked me to convey her best wishes. She hit the dreaded 39 this year (my BABY!).

Have you ever read any Penelope Fitzgerald? Fraidie loves her but I found *Innocence* a strange book, not sure I liked it.

Love,
Blanche

July 2, 1992
Montjouvent, France

Dear Blanche,

How similarly we respond to books! (Though you're more generous.) Penelope Fitzgerald is a writer I always think I'm going to like, and never do—never got engaged in any way. I haven't read Mistry's book because someone told me it was full of lugubrious 19th-century prose. And, no, you did *not* tell me your response to *Immortality.* I loved the first part; then the whole thing seemed to recede. A chill-hearted man, I think. Here in Montjouvent I've been reading biography, Madame de Pompadour, Emily Brontë (a lovely book called *A Chainless Soul: A Life of Emily Brontë* by Katherine Frank).

I'm worried only about how I'll fill the 1¾ hours allotted to me [at the Sechelt writers' festival]. This seemed a marvellous chunk of time when Betty first proposed it. Now it seems unfillable. But we'll be there early enough to see what other writers do. Song and dance? Travel slides?

It's 3 weeks since we left home, and neither of us understands where the time goes. We're walking—often in the evening these days—making small improvements on the house; I work on my novel (about 8 days out of 10) and Don on his wall. We think of you two often, how much fun it was to exchange meals, all our walks and our *talks*. (We'll have a good chance to catch up at Sechelt.) We're thrilled that Bruce is feeling so well, doing so well. Is he especially fortunate, or is this medication a true step forward?

Love to you all,
Carol

July 18, 1992

Dear Carol,

A quick note to let you know I watched your interview with Danny Richler last night on the Knowledge Network. It was an excellent interview and you *looked* spiffy (as well as sounded). I thought you handled it beautifully, spoke well, and were wonderfully composed. Bruce and I were both amused that D.R. seemed nervous, a little awestruck in fact. Previously when I'd seen him on *The Journal* he had always struck me as the most self-assured young person I'd ever seen.

Loved getting your letter. Felt the same way about *Immortality*— decided you can't get away with that much speculation in a novel. On the other end, I used to think I knew what a novel should be, but halfway through *The Gates of Ivory* (Margaret Drabble) I have decided I don't know nuthin'. Sometimes I wonder if too much world angst (surely a good thing) is a bad thing in a novelist. Yet it is gripping, but more in a John le Carré way than as insight into the individual human condition, which I guess is what I used to think a novel is about—at least, the literary kind. Also read and was highly impressed with Jean Rhys' *Wide Sargasso Sea*. I haven't always liked her clipped style, but this, the product of her old age (encouraging), is quite different.

As for my own writing, not much except that an essay I wrote some time ago, then polished recently, is a finalist in the *Event* Creative Non-Fiction Contest. Won't know until November, Andreas Schroeder final judge.

Looking forward to good talk, etc., at Sechelt. I have tickets to Friday, Jeffrey Simpson, and Saturday, Andreas Schroeder and Tom Berger, and Sunday, of course yours. I gather [Peter] Gzowski is a huge draw—sold out long ago.

The Constitution drones on—and on and on. Triple-E Senate driving Quebec nuts (or nuttier). Love to Don from both of us— we think of glorious Montjouvent often.

Love,
Blanche

9

The Meaning of Life
1992–1994

In mid-August Carol and I went to the Sechelt writers' festival and on a sunny afternoon held court on the spacious grounds of Rockwood Lodge where we stayed. Carol's presentation went very well, and although it was about *The Republic of Love*, one of the members of the audience asked about co-authoring *A Celibate Season*. "Are you still friends?" she asked, and Carol assured her that we were and introduced me to the crowd.

When we caught the ferry home there was a tremendous lineup, and we parked on a sweltering hillside, unable to get near the boarding area. Carol was desperate for a bathroom and so, wearing only light, precarious sandals, she ran the approximately half-mile down to the terminal. She had no sooner disappeared than the lineup began to move, and I had no alternative but to move with it and park in the holding area. I knew that Carol would have no idea what had happened and so I raced to the washroom—I couldn't leave my car in case we were called to board. Fortunately I found her, and we finally got on the ferry a couple of hours after the scheduled time.

Carol tried to phone but her son John in Vancouver had already left to pick her up at our house in North Vancouver. When finally we got there, Bruce poured us a gin. Carol fell asleep and John almost had to carry her to the car.

Of the trip home I wrote in an essay for *Prairie Fire*: "On the ferry Carol was gently probing me about my thoughts on aging. 'Carol, are you asking me for the meaning of life?' I asked, and we both laughed, and then I said, 'I'll tell you what, if I find it I'll phone you,' and, after a pause, I added, 'and if you aren't in, I'll leave it on your answering machine.'"

From that time on "the meaning of life" became a half-teasing, half-serious running joke between us.

September 10, 1992

Dear Carol,

By now you must be heavily into the new university year, and, I hope, enjoying your new associate professor status.

I put aside Alberto Manguel's book [*News From a Foreign Country Came*] until after the trip to Smithers, then found it very hard going and was completely unprepared for the emotional wallop (I hadn't read the reviews) of the Captain's classroom. In fact, that was so beautifully (and painfully) done that I wrote to Manguel. I couldn't say that I thought the novel was great, because in fact its inability to engage one's attention until near the end is a major flaw, but I did talk to him about the wallop of the torture discussion, and the need for writers to bear witness, as he has. I see now what you meant by saying that it was too bad about it, because that is exactly what I felt.

Not a lot of news here. The trip to Smithers, in spite of the distance (700 miles) and the 5-year-old, was not nearly as bad as I had expected. She was very good, and slept quite a bit. We enjoyed our visit and the pleasant scenery through the Caribou. Up to my ears in political intrigues these days, and this weekend Bruce and I are off to the Liberal Party convention. Bruce and a lawyer friend are organizing a forum on the Constitution—people everywhere are of two minds, I think. I am concerned that the aboriginal government is going to have a notwithstanding clause so that it can opt out of the Charter, since I think that could be devastating for the women on the reserve. They used the Charter, as you probably recall, to get rid of the old sexist thing on the reserves about who is an Indian.

Ondaatje apparently is a good bet for the Booker Prize. Have you read his novel? I liked *In the Skin of a Lion*, but can't remember a single thing about it. I see that Janette Turner Hospital has a new book out, and a very favourable review. I haven't heard who won the Marian Engel Award.

I presume you got my message (not the meaning of life) re the "Hey Jude" error in *The Republic of Love*. Thanks again for including me on the Sechelt weekend.

Love,
Blanche

September 16, 1992

Dear Blanche,

What an odd coincidence—your letter arrived about five minutes after I sent off the corrections for the paperback, chief of them being the change of Beatles song—I have several letters about this, a couple of spankings in reviews and all kinds of comments from people I wouldn't expect to know about Beatles songs. (We had a spirited discussion in my class this morning about accuracy—can we invent our own worlds with our own rules, or must we adhere to certain forms of authenticity? It was a draw.)

I will treasure the photo of us in the sun. Don't we look like cats brimming with cream. What a wonderful time it was! Even the ride home was fun, despite our delays—always nice to discuss the meaning of life—but I don't know what Bruce put in my gin and tonic, or was it two gin and tonics? I fell sound asleep on the way into Vancouver anyway. Well, we'll look forward to February and seeing you both. It's funny, except for seeing you, I really didn't want to go, but it turned out to have been a joy. And I can say the same thing for the week in France. My daughter Meg came with me, and for both of us it was a week we'll never forget—so much time to talk at long last. She's just announced her engagement to Richard, her housemate, and wanted to talk about weddings chiefly. The week was full of incident, mostly of the delightful variety, lots of walking, some interviews, sightseeing, dinners with friends, the first reviews which are excellent, and the book launch itself, a genuinely bilingual affair. One small complaint: Cultural Affairs provided wine and—guess what else—pretzels. Not too classy.

I'm looking forward to reading Ondaatje's book, which is published tomorrow, I believe. Apparently the hype in the U.K. has been tremendous. I did read Janette Turner Hospital's book [*The Last Musician*] and seem to be about the only person who didn't like it. The *Globe* review was odd, a glowing tribute ending with the small admission that none of the characters actually came to life. As if this were a minor matter. I found it full of clichés and one in particular rubbed me raw: manicured lawns. As an exercise I had my class write one-sentence descriptions of manicured lawns, avoiding the cliché, and they came up with marvellous alternatives. A good class this year with wide age-spread, and none of them look as though they intend to write about dismembering women [a reference to a former student of Carol's whose subjects had made her nervous].

I've been reading all the books of Elinor Lipman, who reviewed my book in the States, and (no surprise here) I love them. Also the books of Francine Prose, [and] Beth Harvor's book of short stories called *Mothers & Children*. Will there ever be enough time to read! I wonder if I'm feeling bloody enough to tackle Susan Sontag's new book.

Please let me know what you think of 1) gender equality in the Senate and 2) the NAC [National Action Committee] "No" vote on the Constitution. The first is especially interesting to me, opening up all sorts of other questions. Isn't this just the affirmative action we practise at the U of Manitoba? The second embraces your reservations about aboriginal women. I grieve to see the last of Family Allowance, by the way, remembering how I looked forward to my cheques—and needed them too. Or did I really? The affluent poor, that was us.

Don's in Quebec City for a conference, home tomorrow, and then we both plan to stay home for a long time. Until February anyway.

Love,
Carol

September 29, 1992

Dear Carol,

What a treat to get a letter *and* a wonderful review [of *A Celibate Season*] all in the same mail, and wasn't it clever of us to zero in on St. Paul's letters to the Corinthians? (Who says there isn't a collective unconscious?)* The artistic director at what was formerly White Rock Summer Theatre (now Arena Theatre), which has a good reputation hereabouts, was practically ecstatic about *The Lush Boat* [a play I had written] when she phoned, and they may option it for next season. She also wants me to try film companies, but I don't know how to go about it. I hate to impose on people, but I think I'll phone Sandy Wilson ([director of] *My American Cousin*).

By the way, did you read the Backlist News in the latest Coteau Books newsletter? Seems *C.S.* has been "adopted," whatever that means, by the U of New Brunswick, U of Saskatchewan, Wilfrid Laurier U, and Western. I hope it means they've put it on the English reading list.

So glad that Meg was able to go with you to Paris. What a joy, to have a daughter all to one's self, and in Paris to boot!

---

*Meg Stainsby, in reviewing *A Celibate Season*, quoted St. Paul's letter in which he asserts that celibacy is desirable in a marriage, but only for a "season." As far as I know, neither Carol nor I were aware of this previously.

I have just finished *Maurice* [E.M. Forster], having never read it before. What a long way we've come in our attitudes in this century! Seems incredible that it wasn't even published until after his death. Am currently reading Carol Corbeil's book, *Voice-Over*, which is in both French and (mostly) English. So far am finding it interesting, seeing Quebec from a different perspective than the French-Canadian (Roy) or the Jewish-Canadian (You-know-who, plus Cohen).*

I have to say that I'm not in favour of gender equality in the Senate (as legislation), because I think if women are given a level playing field they will hold their own in elections. This has already happened here at the municipal level, where women do not have to cope with things like going somewhere else and leaving the family alone, or raising vast sums of money from old boy networks. It seems to me that if you entrench this sort of thing in what is supposed to be a democratic process, you open the gates to all sorts of resentment among other groups (men). In universities, however, the problem seemed to lie more in the tendency of an elite group to choose other members of their own elite group (men), whether consciously or unconsciously, and sometimes such groups have to be hit over the head via gender equality rules.

The truth is, I don't know where I stand on the BIG VOTE yet [the referendum on the Charlottetown Accord]. Bruce is leaning no, I'm leaning yes. Certainly, here in B.C., the unspelled-out question of aboriginal government is giving the most pause. The thing is a real can of worms. Would the Criminal Code in the rest of Canada apply on reserves? Would the Charter apply? Nobody seems to know the answer to these questions. However, Allison gave me the argument which may convince me to vote yes. If there's a hole in the centre of our country—which there would be, if Quebec left—would it be long until the Pacific Rim allied itself in a north–south way? Or the Atlantic, and Midwest, for that matter? There is a danger of being swallowed by the States, which

---

*Refers to Gabrielle Roy, Mordecai Richler and Leonard Cohen.

seems to have horrendous social problems at this time, which we
don't want to share in.

The preceding paragraphs may warn you never to ask questions
like this again in your letters. My life is immensely political these
days—Bruce's forum is going together well, he has Ray P. [Perrault],
Ted McWhinney (professor and constitutional expert), Gordon
Wilson, our provincial leader, and two women who are quite well
known around here.

I have been doing quite a bit of entertaining lately and have
switched to luncheons, because it is so pretty around here at this
time of year. My theory is that I'll soon have paid back everyone
I owe and can then sit back and enjoy being entertained over
Christmas. Am glad to hear that your life is going to be at Home
for a long time, as you say. Love to Don too.

Love,
Blanche
P.S. Am very impressed with Patrick Lane's stories. Instead of a
panel on violence against women, the government should just have
read them. (Can they read?)

October 8, 1992

Dear Blanche,

I've just this minute finished a glowy letter to the Canada
Council praising Blanche Howard's versatility, background,
talent, learnedness—and a word or two about your sense of
humour which seems to be a rare commodity in our literature.
I was delighted to do it, of course, and just hope they come
through for you.

And now I am about to send you something in two or three
days—the new novel [which eventually became *The Stone Diaries*],
which has rather quickly—well, two years—got itself to its end. Don
asked me whether I did indeed write "THE END" on the final page,
and I confess I did, centring it and putting it in caps. Feeling a mite
self-conscious, though. I am now in a very up-and-down stage about

it, more down than up today. Does one ever get over the writer's fragility! I do realize you won't be able even to look at it before the referendum [the Charlottetown Accord]. (This is the most amazing political time I can remember, and every day gets more interesting.)

Three of five children will be home for Thanksgiving weekend, and I'm spending tomorrow making pies, cakes, casseroles. We'll be fifteen counting Don's grad students, two big tables—lovely. And the weather has been incredibly beautiful.

Love,

C

October 28, 1992

Dear Carol,

Post-referendum, and we both voted NO in the end, after studying the document and listening to everyone in sight. Our family, however, voted yes, which resulted in a less-than-Rockwell-type Thanksgiving dinner. As the decibel level increased, Katherine (8), with tears in her eyes, suddenly said, "Why is everyone mad?" "Just because our faces are red and we're shouting at one another doesn't mean we're mad," Austin answered, and so we agreed to disagree. I was hung up on the new levels of aboriginal government having the notwithstanding clause, which would mean that where the band was run by traditional chiefs rather than democratic elections, the native women would not necessarily be protected by the Charter, since they could opt out. I found that as many constitutional lawyers agreed with me as disagreed, but never heard anything that convinced me. Also didn't like the Senate, because of the entrenched veto power. Otherwise could have lived with it, although I believe in a more federal state, but we weren't given a choice.* Bruce's forum was a big success—more than 300 turned out, and we had six distinguished speakers, including Mary Collins.**

---

*The referendum didn't pass.

**Minister of defence.

Anyway, it's over, and in the final days, having made up my mind and boggled my brain with conflicting views, I switched off, and then your ms came and I have read it carefully. IT'S WONDERFUL! You don't need to be afraid that the lack of plot will work against it, although I can see why you would be nervous, it's rather a radical departure from your previous work. I love the way you've started, the writing with its deceptive simplicity, exactly right for the era. The thumbnail sketches of the people are all so telling, and the final chapters are absolutely entrancing, and I don't think there is any danger of the reader flagging. As always, your writing facility alone is enough for the intelligent reader, but I know you need and want a wider audience than the dedicated. I feel sure you'll have it with this.

I suppose one of the things that made it especially appealing to me is that the date of Daisy's birth corresponds roughly to my mother's and to my Aunt Blanche's (about to be 90). She was very influential in my life, and because I went to live with her and my grandmother temporarily in Calgary when I was nearly 6, my memories of the era are very clear. (I think new experiences at that age evoke a lot of long-lasting memories, coupled with the home-sickness I suffered.) Anyway, you will see little pencilled suggestions of memories of that time sprinkled here and there in the work.

Now, having said (and meant) all those nice things, there *is* something I have a problem with. It is this: Daisy, the child, and the young woman, do not come through enough in the first four chapters to make for real identification with her, and therefore to sustain the story through her, which I think is necessary when she is the central thread. This may be a strictly personal opinion, but it did bother me. I know why you have done this, that as a young person the world sort of rolled over her, and as she aged there was more interplay between her mind and the world. But the interior passions of all the other characters come through very clearly (Cuyler and his tower, Barker and his lady-slippers). Chapter 1 sets the scene wonderfully, and Chapter 2 is full of the most inter-esting detail about the three people in her life, but I keep wanting to see a little something through the eyes of this little girl. Just something small, and here are a couple of possibilities. In the letters back and forth, wouldn't Daisy have been taught to write to her father? Perhaps one letter would reveal something of the child's feeling of rootlessness. And in the last chapter of the book you talk about her wanting and always having lacked a witness to her life.

Perhaps the lack starts as a child, when she doesn't find a special girl-friend, and perhaps, just before she is stricken with measles and immediately after leaves with her father, she has finally found that most treasured of childhood loves, a special friend. It could leave a lack in a life, and might account for the feeling of mourning she had as a child. During the long train trip, as Cuyler talked, she might have thought of herself confiding all this to the friend who might have been (Chapter 3). Or even drift in and out of wonderful dreams of playing with the friend.

One other thing that struck me is that she would have bonded with Barker as a father figure. This could introduce into their subsequent relationship a sense of—what?—danger, sin, the destruction of the male god of childhood, anger that this could be so, I don't know. But I think she has to, in this almost incestuous marriage, have more of a dramatic sense of what has occurred. (Subconscious, of course, but influential. Perhaps a driving force behind the anger that the cutting-off of her column sparked, and the subsequent depression?) The depression, by the way, is wonderful, and I loved seeing it through the eyes of the others, and her interior knowledge when she was cured.

From then on, I have no problems. It goes along, exactly right, wonderfully interesting, perfectly pulled together. I particularly loved the fulfillment she found in doing her own thing, writing the column. And the sense of betrayal when she lost it. And the final chapters of illness and decline simply can't be improved upon. Those chapters are enormously moving, I felt like crying myself. They move into the mind of the old woman in the most

Blanche Howard's photo taken for the jacket of *The Manipulator*, published in 1972. *The Manipulator* received wide acclaim and won the Canadian Bookseller's Award. *(Murray Mosher Photography)*

Carol's photo taken for the jacket of her first novel, *Small Ceremonies*, published in 1976 when she was forty-one. *(courtesy of Mary Lou Crerar)*

Carol and Blanche editing *A Celibate Season.*
(courtesy of Blanche Howard)

The cover of *A Celibate Season,*
first published by Coteau Books in 1990.
(photo courtesy of Don Hall)

Carol and Blanche signing books at the Vancouver launch
of the new edition of *A Celibate Season*, published
by Random House Canada in 1998.
(courtesy of Blanche Howard)

Blanche in 2000 while promoting her book *Penelope's Way*, which is set on the North Shore of Vancouver, shown in the background of this photo.

(Ian Lindsay/Vancouver Sun)

Carol holds the Bessie statue after winning the Orange Prize for Fiction for her book *Larry's Party*, presented at The Royal Festival Hall in London, England, May 19, 1998.
(AP Photo/Adrian Dennis)

Carol smiles as she arrives at the Giller Prize ceremony
at the Four Seasons Hotel in Toronto, November 5, 2002.
She was nominated for her novel *Unless*, which won several
awards including the Governor General's Award.
(CP PHOTO/Kevin Frayer)

Carol and Blanche spending time together in May 2001.
(courtesy of Blanche Howard)

sympathetic and believable way—I was reminded a bit of Hagar in *The Stone Angel*, although this is much more polished, with the use of changing viewpoints and letters.

And good for you, putting in the old Jew and the Mongoloid (that was perfect). I'm tired of newspeak.

I feel as though I have a lot of nerve (good old expression) in daring to criticize writing and structure as sophisticated and intelligent as yours, and hope you realize I'm not suggesting anything major, just some insights that will sustain our sympathy and curiosity regarding Daisy, until the story gets rolling.

Thank you so much for once again pleading my cause to the Canada Council. Also thank you for the $31. No, you didn't give me a cheque before because you thought you wouldn't bother to put in for expenses, and since I had so many freebies I was more than willing to pay for the ferry. However, I gather they must have sent it to you anyway, so thank you. Glad your Thanksgiving was so successful, and gather you didn't all shout around about the referendum in the uncivilized manner that we did.

And thank you for giving me the opportunity to comment on your novel. You should *not* feel fragile about it because it is by far the most moving thing you've written, and also it has enormous depth. It may be *the* winner; at any rate, it's a wonderful breather from all the glitziness, or disaffection, of the young that seems to be in novels lately. I made a note in the last chapter that the phrase "just let her life happen" might be worked up, or you might consider using just her name, Daisy Goodwill.

I hope I'm not completely out to lunch. It's a truly wonderful and moving novel. Oh yes, loved your Marni Jackson review, including the little blurb at the end. She's had an amazing amount of publicity, hasn't she?

Love,
Blanche

December 17, 1992

Dear Carol,

Yes, I'm more or less ready for Christmas, although a few more presents to get, and yours is the last card because I was waiting to take the time to write. A friend sent me the blurb about you from the Ottawa *Citizen* re your new book of poetry (which I will immediately look for) and accompanying picture—which is awfully good, by the way. Congratulations!

I did enjoy that review of *A Celibate Season* in *NeWest Review,* didn't you? I thought it awfully clever, but also thought I detected a hint of disquietment (disquietude?) that they, too, were young separated professionals. Also, the sudden realization towards the end that the criticisms they were making were based on gender assumptions.

I read *The English Patient* [Michael Ondaatje], and have been trying, ever since, to come to terms with my own thoughts about it. It is, of course, brilliantly written and very captivating. It is also—and I don't know how to say this and remain a feminist—a man's book. The hero as Cool Hand Luke, with a total concentration on the work at hand to the exclusion of the possibility of his immediate death. (Kip, by the way, I found the most sympathetic of the characters.) The woman, nurturing and needy, yet quite believable, but I never felt close. The writing, by the way, reminded me of Salman Rushdie's in the ability to paint somewhat surreal word pictures, so that the Italian villa seems both dreamlike and possible—although Rushdie is far further into the realm of the magical. I wonder if you agree with any of this.

Reread *The Latecomers* [Anita Brookner] for our book club, and loved it as much the second time. Oh, how I enjoy her careful delineation of change, so like Henry James! But it struck me, as I reread it, that her theme of the hole in lives that a broken childhood leaves is somewhat parallel to the same theme in your new novel. The one refugee (his name escapes me—oh dear!)* was

---

*Hartmann.

pulled away from his childhood at age 12, while Fibich was only 7. The 12-year-old one built a careful life, based on his modest pleasures, while Fibich sank into melancholy. Wasn't Daisy 12 when her father spirited her away? I thought of this when rereading my last letter to you, where I commented on Daisy's feeling of rootlessness and her having lacked a witness.

By the way, I have pondered a lot since our talk, and I don't think I've changed my mind at all from the initial impressions. I find myself thinking again and again of the poignancy of the ending. DON'T TOUCH IT! I think this is by far the best thing you've written, even though it doesn't have the fireworks of *Swann* or the sparkle of *The Republic of Love*. What it does have—that most necessary ingredient of great classics—is wonderful empathy with the human condition, as exemplified by one person. I often still find myself thinking about Kazuo Ishiguro's *The Remains of the Day*, where the writing was simple almost to the point of monotony, but the effect was profoundly moving.

Had great visits last week with old Ottawans—Kay Buchanan stayed two nights, and she, Mary Mahoney and I spent pleasant time together, then the Mahoneys (both) were here for dinner with Kay. Leslie met us for lunch, as she was friendly with them in the Ottawa days (babysat for Kay, Christmased with the Mahoneys). Now Leslie has been scouted for a wonderful part-time broker's job. She has decided to step out to this new challenge.

Must go and attend to those things still undone, since (horrors, gasp) it is supposed to snow tomorrow.

Love to Don, and any others of yours there for Christmas,
Blanche

January 22, 1993

Dear Blanche,

I'm writing this between two interesting events on campus. This morning I attended Di Brandt's doctoral defence. I'll enclose the announcement so that you'll see just how radical we're becoming here in Manitoba. Full of interesting ideas touching on all sorts of issues, the killing of the mother figure through witch trials, through bungled deliveries, through suppression. (One could get pretty worked up about these issues.) It's a beautiful thesis, and she handled the questions of the committee with bravado, or is that bravada?

In an hour I'm attending a colloquium on women writers and humour from a visiting prof from the U of T. When Don asked me at breakfast what I'd be doing today, I told him I'd be listening to women's ideas all day long. (He looked distinctly envious, though he claims he does not—never mind Di Brandt's assertion—envy women's ability to bear children.) Be sure to ask Bruce about this—but he'll have to search his subconscious. Deep, deep down.

I put on some speed to finish the novel before Christmas, actually took four copies to Toronto in my hand luggage. I want to thank you again for all your comments and encouragement—I needed both. Your idea of "normalizing" Cuyler's wedding speech was exactly right, and I quite enjoyed bringing down the rhetoric to a more realistic level. The current title is *Monument.* A little heavy, but "they" seem to prefer it to my other suggestions.

Since January 1st, I've been involved with rehearsals for the play [*Departures and Arrivals*]. An involving and very intense experience, also a joyous one. It opens next Thursday. I'm far too close to it at the moment to know how it will succeed. But I love the actors, the music, the director, the composer, the set, and I am thrilled with the process, making something three-dimensional out of a two-dimensional script. You've had this experience and so will understand what I'm nattering about. How I wish we could sit down for a good talk. The hardest part was cutting out one scene that I rather liked. But once the amputation was made, it felt perfectly clean and logical, and the scenes flanking it soared (see how theatrical my language has become in just four weeks).

I'm reading *The English Patient* now, and probably shouldn't comment until I'm done, but—I find it awfully studied, terribly solemn, taking itself incredibly seriously, and as for the dialogue??? "Wooden" isn't the word. And the worship of the beautiful male body is getting to me a bit. As a matter of fact, I'm having trouble with a lot of men's books lately. Do you think it will get worse and worse? Oh, I hope not. I can feel the tug of all this gender warring and am a little afraid of it.

To our disappointment we will not be coming in February. Don's interview at Concordia U comes in the middle of that week, our only free week, and so we'll be hip-deep in Montreal snow instead of strolling along a B.C. beach. He is not at all sure he wants this job. The department is demoralized, as you can imagine, following the murders of the four profs.* And who in their right mind is moving to Quebec anyway?

We both adore having Evan [Catherine's child] overnight. There is something wonderful about waking up in the morning with a baby in the house. (He's a beautiful and responsive child, at least we think so.)

Write me your news, thoughts, let me know if you've stumbled on the meaning of life.

Love,
Carol

February 17, 1993

Dear Carol,

What a treat, to come home from Florida and find your goodly package waiting for me, especially the book of poems. So far I have read only the "Coming to Canada" poems (I am slow at poetry reading, always fearful and suspicious that I don't understand) but perhaps I can venture a couple of amateur's comments anyway. The poem "Daddy" I found enormously moving. The lines "holding the garden hose/in soft padded hands" evoke a shivery, sexual almost shame, and are beautifully rescued by the next two lines, and the delicious irony of "of all things." Still, I felt an underlying sadness,

---

*On August 24, 1992, in what became known as the Concordia University massacre, a disgruntled former associate professor of mechanical engineering murdered four of his colleagues.

about not knowing another, and about unknowability. I loved "Learning to Read," witty and perceptive, that about the unlocked code. Also loved the haunting questions behind "Easter," the enormous humour in "Vision," and in "Dog Days," I could feel that humid eastern heat in my bones, and remember so clearly "banking coolness for another day" when we lived in the hot Okanagan. This is the kind of small precious book that I keep beside my reading table and dip into in the evenings, and thank you again, and congratulations.

Loved the book club's comments on *C.S.* As you say, people like it but critics don't—wasn't that a misogynist treatise in the U of T quarterly? "Lacks focus, style and credibility"—what is left? And I'm sure no one has ever before accused *you* of using bland language. However, from what I can see of the other reviews, e.g., Anne Cameron's, he (probably a he) doesn't like anything anyone writes. Is Leo Simpson still alive? Could he be the rat?* On the plus side, isn't that good news about the Literary Press Group including us in their push into the U.S.? I am not sure, from the thing Coteau Books sent, whether we are among the 20 frontlist titles, or just among the other 54 titles, which "have strong, continuing sales established without an advertising campaign, major promotions or publicity." Do you understand it?

And now your play. Can't tell you how delighted I am for you—I heard your interview with [Peter] Gzowski, and thought the *G and M* review most encouraging. It really is a fun process, isn't it? I still send *A Celibate Season* (the play) around, and continue to get lavish praise but no takers. I don't suppose I ever mentioned our sudden decision to go to Florida—old Toronto friends wrote at Christmas to say they had decided for the first time to spend four months at their new condo there, and asked us to come down if possible. We did, went for ten days, had a marvellous relaxed sun-filled time.

---

*Refers to a misogynistic review Simpson gave of my first novel.

I'm sure you are wondering what on earth possesses me to send you this snapshot taken in Florida. The reason is going to sound very trivial to you, but I am getting so much attention since I cut off my hair and let it go its natural colour, that I'm beginning to feel like an adolescent convinced that everyone is looking at her. I don't know if I told you the story of why I went through this rather radical change. One day I was down at Allison's, and Jacqueline [granddaughter], aged 14, sat down beside me and said, "Grandma, I want you to look at this magazine with me, it's called *Vogue.*" I allowed as how I had heard of it, and we turned page after page of models whose hipbones threatened to poke through their unflawed skin. At the end I asked what the point had been, and she replied, "You see? Nobody wears orange hair any more."

The result is as you see. I never dreamed I would look okay in this chopped-off style, but to my surprise it suits me, and the response is so surprising—one scarcely expects, at 69, to be inundated with compliments, but maybe I looked like hell before. It is actually not as white as the picture looks, but is rather a pretty colour if I do say so myself. Anyway, I don't feel invisible any more.

Before Christmas I rewrote the dream novel, suddenly seeing a theme I'd missed, that of the Sleepwalker. (The new title, actually.) This seems to hold it together and I really like it now. I sent it to a couple of agents and had a long and heartening phone call from Beverley Slopen. She says she loves it and wants to represent it, but has been having trouble lately with placing fiction. However, after further talk, she says that if I would get two or three endorsements from writers, she would take a whirl at it. Now I know you do not write endorsements so I'm not asking you, although maybe what I am asking is too similar for you to agree to it. I wonder if I could quote what you said when you wrote me, some years ago after reading the first draft. You said, "I'm reading and enjoying it. You have found a good sharp, amusing voice to tell this." Maybe this is an endorsement by another name, and please don't feel that a "no" will endanger our friendship, because you did explain your reasons to me for having decided not to do endorsements.

I've been trying to think of who else I might approach. Do you think Merna Summers would feel put-upon? Sarah Ellis? I wish I hadn't drifted so far from the writing community. (Up to my ears in politics lately.) I loathe asking people to do things for me, but it sounds as though I don't have much choice. I do like this novel and would love to have it see the light of day. By the way, when I was looking through my file called "Carol" for the above response, I got caught up in the letters we've exchanged now for nearly twenty years. We have talked a lot about literature and politics, and I suddenly thought, if we should ever have some time, these (edited) letters would make a nice little, reasonably erudite book—especially since everyone seems to like non-fiction better than fiction these days. I not only have your letters, but I seem to have saved most copies of mine as well. If the idea appeals at all to you, try to have some spare time when you come and we'll take a look together at the file and see if it is feasible.

What else? Kim Selody said that the New Play Centre had decided against *The Lush Boat*, but were keeping a copy on file at the office for anyone who might be interested. He said he thinks I am caught in a catch-22 position, that it is just right for summer theatre, but that summer theatre doesn't like doing new things. I phoned Anna Hagan at the Arena Theatre. She is as enthusiastic about it as ever but couldn't convince the producer to do it. She thinks I should turn it into a screenplay and wants me to work on that and not let it die (wants to have lunch and discuss it, actually). She asked me who I knew in film and when I said, only Sandy Wilson, she thought I should phone her and ask her to look at it. I hate to impose on poor Sandy as she might feel obligated, but perhaps I'll just send it to her (known her since she was a child, a friend of her parents) on the basis of the repeated advice I am getting lately to be more pushy.

Stephen came down right after we returned, as he had to write five three-hour exams if, as a land surveyor, he wants to get any federal government work when they settle the Indian land claims (one of exams on constitutional law, of all things). He brought 4-year-old Stephanie, so I had my hands full, especially since Bruce was laid up with a hernia incurred when shovelling snow before we left. (He has to get surgery—fairly minor, I'm told.) My aunt in Calgary went into a nursing home and in the middle of child-caring, bedroom furniture I had admired twenty years ago suddenly arrived, requiring certified cheques and instant decision-making, so it was a bit hectic for a few days. (Loved having the little girl though.) I am going out to see Aunt Blanche the first part of April. She is 90 now.

Well, this is a long, rambly letter. Excited about the news of your novel, I truly believe it is a winner.

Much love,
Blanche

April 26, 1993

Dear Blanche,

After hanging up the other night I, of course, remembered all sorts of things we forgot to discuss—do you think we'll ever get caught up? Probably not, and probably that's a good thing—but I do want to get back to letter writing. The telephone is an insidious invader; I sense it trying to take over (in much the same way this word processor put my dear old IBM Selectric out of business). When it comes to letters and phone calls, though, I think we need both, since different kinds of exchanges seem to require different airwaves. (A friend of mine here is trying to introduce me to e-mail, but I'm resisting.)

Let me know as soon as you hear from Beverley Slopen—she sounds so enthusiastic, and it seems likely she'll be able to convey that enthusiasm to a publisher. I had lunch with her some years ago, and thought she was lovely—intelligent, warm-hearted, very very knowledgeable about books and book marketing. She's also very chic, and who knows? maybe chicness helps in this business. I had a facial before the Manitoba Literary Awards night on Saturday, and the woman who "did" me said, "It's not how you play the game, it's how you look when you play the game." How's that for a morsel of wisdom. By the way, I did not win [for

The Republic of Love]; Sandra Birdsell did, for *The Chrome Suite*. This was done in Academy Award style with no advance announcements and envelopes opened on stage. I gave in to a momentary gnashing of teeth—but did manage to keep a big good-sport smile firmly in place under my professionally applied makeup. Timothy Findley was there reading from his new novel, which I do not intend to buy. The section he read was all about Peter Rabbit and other creatures popping out of literature, etc. He does read well, but this does not appeal. Too fey. Twee. How did I get on this subject?

The promotion trip to the U.S. was a lot of fun, though I don't know if I'll ever get used to travelling alone—those lonely hotel rooms. But I saw Sara in New York. She and her partner, Dave, love to drive down from Halifax. I think I told you she did a journalism course at Dalhousie U after she discovered the philosophy degree was not negotiable on the job market. She went into the course to pursue print journalism, then got hooked on radio. Last summer she worked for the CBC in Moncton, and now she's got a job in Halifax on Community Radio. She produces public affairs shows, concentrating on marginalized groups, women, prisoners and so on, and also hosts three shows a week of her own, one public affairs and two music. Why am I telling you all this?—I guess because I'm feeling proud of her. I loved the American bookstores with their range of books and coffee bars and music, and couldn't help feeling a blast of despair thinking of our poor Winnipeg stores—which are, in any case, better than they were ten years ago.

My latest discovery is the American writer Alice McDermott. Her most recent is out in paperback, *At Weddings and Wakes*. Her first is called *That Night* (I loved it) and the second is *A Bigamist's Daughter*—haven't read that one. Her sentences are long and complex and rhythmic, and the books are filled with original psychological insights and period details, a lovely writer.

I also loved [John] Updike's *Memories of the Ford Administration*, or at least I loved most of it. There were a few arid stretches toward the end, but he does dazzle, and in this one I think he comes as close as he's ever come to understanding women. I'm trying to read some Australian novels before we go; Don's reading travel books, so between us we'll have assembled a kind of image of what it looks like. By the way, Peter Carey was at my reading in New York, but I think he must be a friend of Mary Morris, with whom the reading was shared. (Australians seem to go in for length.)

Much love to you both. Please keep writing. But don't forget to phone if you discover the purpose of life.

C

June 10, 1993
Montjouvent, France

Dear Blanche,

We're not really in France, but we will be by the time you get this note, sweeping ourselves out and settling in. The weather is supposed to be heavenly at the moment.

I was delighted with the lovely birthday card and with your note, but sorry to hear Allison has had to put up with so much misery [following some minor surgery]—hope she's mending now. How our bodies let us down! Do you feel, as I do, that the world is filling up with new bacterial and viral torments and new ways for our bodily mechanics to go wrong? Don and I have to laugh at ourselves: he has one eye in which the tear gland is overactive and thus leaky, and I have one eye which I have to dose daily with drops because it's too dry. What will become of us?

I'm enclosing our schedule for the next 14 months. It was exhausting just typing it out. Following through will take all our strength. One day at a time I suppose we'll manage, but the thought of all those beds we'll be occupying is overwhelming.

I have a great stack of books to take along, many of them Australian novels, and I plan to keep a sort of reader's diary for a year. I hope to write some stories, work on the screenplay, and think about a play about families that Catherine and I want to write together. I've been thinking lately about the idea of dramatic conflict, and how our notions of conflict need redefining and set into a feminist context. I suppose I'd like to see conflict as being less polarized, more subtle, more emotional and psychological. The old patriarchal binaries of good and evil, virtue and sin, tragedy and comedy, etc., seem hopelessly clumsy and crude.

The PC leadership race is going to be dramatic, we think. Did you think the *Globe* profile on Kim Campbell was extraordinarily intrusive?

Love to you both, birthday wishes to Leslie and a hug to Allison.

Carol

❧ The schedule Carol enclosed had them going from France in mid-August 1993 to Scotland, England, Australia and Greece, touching down in Winnipeg in late September for two days, then to California, followed by two days in Winnipeg, Toronto for Meg's wedding, Vancouver, Berkeley, India, France, and in August 1994 back to Winnipeg.

June 19, 1993

Dear Carol,

Delighted to get your second letter and *The Schedule*, which made me feel faint merely contemplating it.

And the good news: Beverley Slopen phoned a week ago, and has decided to take on *Random Access*. (She didn't like my rename to *The Sleepwalker*, and I told her it had been *Random Access Memory*, and we settled on *Random Access*, which you thought last summer would be good.) Anyway, she gave me the most enthusiastic phone call, which is such a far cry from what I'm used to that I was on the ceiling all morning. Said she got so caught up in the novel she forgot she was working and couldn't put it down, had almost no quibbles (except that "miniscule" is actually spelled "minuscule," and appears in *Webster's* under "miniscule" with the notation: "Frequent misspelling of minuscule." I expect you knew that).

Anyway, at my own expense I am required to send her ten copies with spiral binding and plastic covers, which gets a bit expensive, but Zippy Print will have it done today and I'll send it off. Says she wants to blanket all sorts of places, so I'm keeping my fingers and all other accessible parts of my anatomy crossed. Oddly enough, my biggest worry is that when they find out how old I am, publishers might back off because they would be afraid I wouldn't be good for much publicity, especially on a novel about a 34-year-old woman. Do you think I'm suffering a touch of paranoia, or reality? I carefully omitted all reference to my age in my bio, but these things are easily ascertained.

I mentioned to you before about how odd it is to look back at the letters we have exchanged over the years. It is almost like reading an old journal, a history of things I'd forgotten all about. Even if we never do anything with them, perhaps someday we'll be able to find time to browse through them together. Which, unfortunately, won't be in October. Wouldn't you know, when you are finally going to be in Vancouver, we are going to be in Europe? Bruce's health has improved so dramatically with this new drug he's on that we decided we'd better get on with the Italian trip we've always wanted to take, so, finding a two-week Mediterranean Princess cruise on a two-for-one sale, we are going to sail from Barcelona to Venice, with stops in many cities, starting October 4th. Then we are going to stay on for two weeks in Italy and just bum around. Very excited about it, but it looks as though we won't be home until about the 29th.

I was interested to hear of your Manitoba Literary Awards night and the opening of the envelopes and the whole bit. They did the same thing for the B.C. Book Prizes this year, in Penticton the last night of the B.C. Library Association conference. Bruce and I went to the convention and to the dinner, and W.D. Valgardson won the book award and gave an interesting little talk about how he wakened at three every night and had to get up and write the book, it was almost as though something was writing it for him. He hopes his Muse will rouse him again soon. Rather unusual, don't you think? Sorry to hear Sandra Birdsell beat you out, by the way. I don't even know her work, but must read it.

I am enclosing something you might have missed, an interview with your friend Beth Harvor in *The Antigonish Review* (who have, by the way, taken another of my short stories). After I read this, I got *Women & Children* and *If Only We Could Drive Like This Forever*, and without knowing which was which, I thought *Women & Children* was the most modern. I was then surprised to find the reverse was true, that some of the stories in *Women & Children* went back to the fifties. It seemed almost as though some lightness of heart had gone out of her in the second volume, leaving a sadness, not quite bitterness, but something more stripped down. I then reread the interview and noted that she, too, thought the first book was more dazzling. Of course, I know nothing about her, except that she is your friend and has had some troubles (as she mentions in the interview). I found the stories wonderful, and think she has been badly neglected in Canadian Lit. Allison liked them too.

Allison is *very* slowly starting to recover. It has been a scary time for us. Her weight dropped about 15 lbs., to 120, and no one could figure out why, after a relatively minor operation. I think I told you that they finally found her thyroid is hyperactive, which accounts for pretty well all the symptoms. It is amazing how much it takes out of one when a daughter is sick. She has been spending the days up here, rather than home alone, and I have been very worried. Now that she is recovering, I am finding my energy returning. The time since Christmas seems to have been crisis-driven (Bruce's surgery, Aunt B.'s death in March, many complications with being the executor, Leslie and Austin moving, various political upheavals, and then Allison's sickness). I feel out of control, and am hoping for a return to our little structured environment and some time to actually write. Yes, as you say, the world seems to be filling up with new viruses and environmental pollution, not to mention age-related aches and pains. (I mustn't complain, in case I am Overheard.)

I had a birthday party for Leslie's fortieth and invited just her old Penticton friends that live in Vancouver now. It was quite successful, except Allison was sick and the star was exhausted, having just moved house the weekend before. Leslie is back in the stockbroker business and feeling enormously ambivalent about it, because she wants to be home with the children—is there a solution to this? The job was supposed to be part time, but pressure is on her to put in more hours and the money is seductive. I advised her to give it a year, then say the hell with it, life is too short to do what doesn't turn you on if you can avoid it.

What have I read? Barbara Gowdy's short stories, *We So Seldom Look on Love*, were beautifully crafted but not for the weak-stomached. Necrophilia, in charming detail? But she is enormously talented, nonetheless. An old Barbara Pym I'd missed, and now an old Iris Murdoch. I know there have been many more—oh yes, those short stories of Patrick Lane's I got last year in Sechelt, some of them are excellent. At the moment nothing has fired me up too much, although I read a couple of lovely Penelope Fitzgerald gems. I will follow your Alice McDermott advice.

Much love, and to Don. Bruce, Allison and Leslie send greetings.

Blanche

July 26, 1993
Montjouvent, France

Dear Blanche,

First a word about "minuscule." It was misspelled on the *first* page of *The Box Garden*—by me—and overlooked right into the paperback. The error was gently pointed out to me by a *Vancouver Sun* reporter, of all people. It is also one of the few typos I've seen in *The New Yorker*, though these are now multiplying.

Second—I am overjoyed about Beverley taking *Random Access*. And when an agent is enthusiastic, it sells! My theory, anyway. Me, I wouldn't worry about your age or PR possibilities. You know how to be forceful; you certainly aren't going to attend interviews with a lapful of knitting. Having said this so bravely, I'm busy trying to lose 5 pounds and get my legs tan for the author tour in the U.K., less than a month away. This image/age thing! It might be an idea to think about an anthology of essays by women on this issue. (But there are so many such projects floating around these days.)

Third—yes, do use the suggested quote [re Carol's endorsement].

Fourth—I'm sorry we'll miss you in Vancouver, but thrilled about your Italian adventure. And even more thrilled that you're feeling *up* to it. About Christmas—it's so far away and so blurred by intervening events that it seems an abstraction—I've a feeling I'll want to be in the "bosom" of family, so we may make a trip to Winnipeg.

I thoroughly enjoyed reading Beth's [Harvor] interview and appreciate your sending it. Why can't we simply cut off the hurts of childhood and get on with it? But it seems we can't. Our resourcefulness is somehow damaged, though I can't help thinking a good marriage (whatever that is) can give one a fresh start. Is this true? Or not?

The summer is passing too quickly. But how can this be, I ask myself, when there are no demands on us? I'm walking, every day, and following your advice about taking the same route. (I forget your rationale, but you know I always do everything you say anyway.) And I've written 3 short stories and 3 book reviews (one of them for *The Boston Globe*—on Gowdy's stories). I'll be meeting her next month in the U.K., where we're scheduled for a joint reading.

I have thought of Allison often, and also of the toll taken by a sick daughter—Oh yes! that marvellous bond threatened. By the time you get this nearly illegible note, she will no doubt be herself again. Love to all of you. We are sitting here in a burst of glorious sun.

Love,
Carol

August 5, 1993

Dear Carol,

Last time you wrote, you mentioned keeping a list of the books you read, and I thought it such a good idea that I promptly started. June 2—Iris Murdoch, *The Sacred and Profane Love Machine*, which I liked, but not nearly as much as *An Accidental Man*, which I then read. It is such a beautifully understated study of a man who seems purely evil more by inadvertence than Machiavellianism, so that you wonder again if, as Hannah Arendt said, Evil is banal. Then I took your advice and read *That Night* by Alice McDermott—yes, she is impressive, wound so much out of one night's happening. *Itsuka* by Joy Kogawa was a mistake, a novel that was really a political polemic and didn't come off at either level, disappointing, and a waste of time and a basic good talent.

Then I read *The Chrome Suite* to try to understand how Sandra Birdsell could possibly have beaten you out at the literary night. I didn't figure that out, but I do understand her attraction. It is undoubtedly autobiographical, and yet she is so unsparing of her [character] (and thus of herself) that it exerts quite a pull. Having said that, there is no comparison with the way you write. I got thinking afterwards that it was a bit like comparing an impressionist painter with a top-flight photographer; you are working in two different mediums, one of reality filtered through the imagination (yours), the other of a clearly delineated image of the reality, seen through a pretty cold lens.

Then I read Anita Brookner, *A Closed Eye*, and finished it just as your letter arrived with what you said about a good marriage and the way it can give a fresh start. Have you read it? Here is a case of the reverse (well not quite, only a passable marriage) being true, but with just enough questions about what does constitute a good marriage to give one pause. I found it interesting, and loved getting lost again in her careful buildup of change.

Besides that, I'm halfway through a book on mathematics (the theory of), also read a lot of *New Yorkers*, including an old one with a lovely Alice Munro story I hadn't seen before, about an old journal of the life of a man who cleared a homestead for himself in Ontario in the 1800s, with a curious twist. I thought it was wonderfully done.

Well, that makes 6½ in about six weeks, so perhaps it isn't surprising that I don't get as much other stuff done as I intend to. Although, I only read in the evenings, but it does make me wonder what all these people who don't have time to read do with all that time? (The boob tube, I know.)

Am glad you are obeying me in the matter of daily walks—the same route was to stop having to think about where you are going. A mixed, sometimes, blessing. I've written some more short stories too, another one excerpted from the novel and accepted by the *Prairie Journal of Canadian Fiction* (first one I sent it to). Interested to hear you are meeting Barbara Gowdy—still think of the totally arresting scenes where they stay in the bunker for two weeks. The classic childhood fear, buried in the dark. She must be strange— I will be interested in what you think of her.

The U.K. tour sounds exciting. Hope your legs are sufficiently tanned to pass muster. Actually, the British climate being what it is, tanned legs will probably be regarded as something that just isn't done. Our best to Don as well.

Love,
Blanche

～ *The Stone Diaries* was short-listed for the Booker Prize and I sent Carol this handwritten note:

September 23, 1993

Dear Carol,

Absolutely *over the moon* (Chas) re the Booker short-listing! Merna phoned yesterday, having heard it on *Arts Report,* and I gave her the fax number in Athens, but it must be wrong—in any case, hope she got through somehow. Then Bruce rushed in, having heard it in the car.

This morning I phoned John, and *he hadn't heard it yet*! So he was dashing out for a *G and M*—said he'd got his copy [of the book] two days ago and was loving it (even though, as he pointed out, it has no guns, cars, or chases). I also got my copy and was delighted and grateful (not to mention over the moon) at seeing my name first among the thankees. Thank *you*! Loved the pictures—Bruce and I had fun identifying your children. Then (two days ago) Fraidie phoned and had got a copy downtown. How come? Wasn't due for release until the 30th.

Bruce sends delighted, enthusiastic congrats also!

Love,
Blanche

∿Carol and Don stopped to visit us briefly on their way to California.

> *November 1, 1993 [Postcard]*
> *Berkeley*

Blanche,
A long and newsy letter will shortly be on its way, but this is just to say HAPPY BIRTHDAY. You continue to stand as a model to me, your energy and human warmth. Hope you and Bruce returned from your trip full of good memories and adventures. With thanks for your wonderful card. Thrilled to see Allison looking so well!

∿ *The Stone Diaries* won the Governor General's Literary Award for Fiction.

> *November 17, 1993*

Dear Carol,
Congratulations and more congratulations! Am delighted about the GG's Literary Award (although I would have been furious if you hadn't got it, but was a little afraid that the temptation of Thomas King as an aboriginal might be too much for them).

And how you deserve it! On the cruise I reread *The Stone Diaries*, savouring it this time instead of trying to cast a critical eye. How I loved it! I'm ashamed to say that I misread it the first time—I remember urging you to tell more from Daisy's p.o.v., when of course that is precisely the point, that Daisy couldn't define herself (except at the junctures when you do give her a voice), and that as a child she was conscious of the space within her that she must fill. I guess that is one of the hazards of reading in ms form.

Then Bruce read it, and it is a long time since I have seen him so fully entranced with a novel. He loved it, and I think this says something about universal appeal, men and women. (Enclosing a short thing by M. Atwood on this subject that I thought you might find amusing.)

Next, Allison. (Not making a heck of a lot from the Howards, are you?) Marilyn, however, got tired of waiting and bought it. Both Marilyn and Allison are deliberately going slowly because they don't want it to end. Marilyn says it is a long time since she's felt that way about a novel.

Fraidie bought it at once, then bought six more for Christmas gifts. She, too, "adores" it. She told me quite a funny story, about a brother-in-law who phoned her and said, "Guess what. This new Carol Shields novel has a name just like yours in it."

I was incensed by the *Globe and Mail* review. Who the hell does Geraldine Sherman think she is? Typically Canadian, that our national newspaper should dump on both Booker nominees instead of patting ourselves all over our backs.

Your picture this morning in said *G and M* is, however, lovely, and I was proud of you that you spoke out with [Allan] Gotleib on the Canada Council cuts.

The one amazing thing I felt about the award was that Jane Jacobs [*Systems of Survival*] didn't win [under Nonfiction]. I read a lengthy excerpt and intend to read the book. I was enormously impressed with the new light she shed on behaviour, and I can't imagine the other book being so academically stimulating. However, they may have been judging on quality of writing, so who knows.

Thank you so much for the birthday card—I was touched that, in the middle of what must be a frantic time for you, you thought of it. And thank you for all those nice things you said about me. We seem to stand in relation to one another as mutual mentors, since I am always in awe of your talent and studying your work and methods for enlightenment. Odd to have a relationship where mentorship works both ways, isn't it?

The daughters threw a wonderful afternoon surprise party for me, practically everyone I know at it, and I *was* absolutely surprised. For one thing, who expects a party in mid-afternoon? I thought I was going to a children's play. In any case, I am one of those rare mortals who actually *like* surprise parties (how Davina [from *A Celibate Season*] would have disapproved), and I was in a state of high excitement.

I must be resigned to old age (what choice, at 70?), because I have not gone to bed, ill, for a week as I did after 65. Actually, although one's interior states are slippery and fairly undefinable, some pleasant and peaceful psychic breakthrough seems to have occurred with the gradual subsidence of my ear problems. (Related? Who knows.) I thought I must be imagining this new calmness, but was given solid evidence of it when I wasn't frightened by my old flying phobia on this trip. I sat there, expecting to be overwhelmed by the usual anxiety attacks, and nothing happened except for slight nervousness, easily dissipated with a glass of wine. Farewell the days of g-and-t's and eventual hangovers! At least I hope so.

The trip was marvellous. The cruise was enough to make a work-ethic nut feel like a participant in the decline of the Roman Empire, with wonderful day trips to relaxed and warm Greek islands. The ensuing bus trip was, however, fairly strenuous and not something we are likely to repeat, although it was an excellent way of getting Italy in a capsule. You will be relieved to know that the Sistine Chapel is everything it's cracked up to be, especially since it has been restored.

I feel terribly lucky that I am really well again, old energy restored, old hair gone (from the picture yours looks nearly as short as mine), and old psyche smartened up (or dead). A few small victories in my writing: do you remember us discussing the short story I was writing around the chaos theory last summer at Sechelt? The editor of *Queen's Quarterly* likes it so much that when she wrote, she said she already knows that it will be their entry in this year's Journey Prize contest. And *The Lush Boat* was in the top seven entries in this year's Canadian National Playwriting Competition of 98 full-length plays, although it didn't win. But the novel isn't sold yet.

Naturally we are delighted that the Natural Governing Party is back in charge. I worked quite a bit before leaving, and was glad to miss the last three weeks. Now I am involved in helping Barbara [Perrault] with her campaign for a second city councillor term (this Saturday).

I forgot to mention that I saw both your interview with Eleanor Wachtel and the one last night on Newsworld. You certainly handle those interviews wonderfully now.

I'm looking forward to the long letter you promised but you may find yourself even busier now, since the GG thing.

Love,
Blanche

December 17, 1993
University of California at Berkeley

Dear Blanche,

Our "affairs" are rather in a muddle; it seems I can't find your last letter anywhere—though it must be here—nor can I remember whether or not I wrote after getting the letter. This isn't senility, I hope, but lack of a proper filing system, and the fact that we're about to move out of this place in a few days, then off to India, and back into another house in late January when we return. So where to begin?

I'm hoping, when I hear from you next, that Beverley has placed your novel. But I'm delighted with your other successes, which you must find very encouraging.

You'd never know it was Christmas here. I don't have one sprig of greenery, not one decorated cookie. We did put a little Christmas music on last night to bring some sense of festivity. But it's hard to believe in Christmas when there are flowers blooming—though you must have accommodated this oddity by now. Our gift to each other was our yellow fever injections. And a book each for the trip. I have the new Margaret Atwood, bought at 30% discount, of course, as all American books seem to be. Have peeked already. Don has *Consciousness Explained* [Daniel C. Dennett], which strikes me as being a book you and Bruce would like too. We're thriving, though Don is suffering from a very familiar sabbatical frustration, that so much work has followed him here, theses to read and supervise mainly. However, he's got a couple of new ideas using fractal theory. And there's nothing like having a brand-new idea! I'm working on little things, little articles, little book reviews, and finding it oddly satisfying, tasks completed and put away. Now I'm back working on both the film and a play about families in our era. Have you any nuggets about family politics to contribute? Everyone blames the family for the ills in the world, yet it's all we have to sustain us. How is this paradox to be dealt with? You can't stand back and objectively view your place in your family.

Never again, we say about our three months of wandering, though we have some sparkling memories and were royally treated. My, I did grow weary of my blabbing postulating self. The hardest part for Don was being unable to concentrate on anything, even reading, while travelling. I felt much the same. But how can you say no to opportunities that may not come again. (Won't even bother putting a question mark here.)

I think I told you we'd be in Vancouver late May/early June, looking seriously for a place to buy—for the future. We also plan to have a look at Victoria, which I liked very much (I know you don't) during my 24-hour stay in September, a real literary community, not that that's the only consideration. By the way, Anne and family are moving to Kamloops. It may just give her the time she wants to pursue writing; she's had quite a number of law articles published this year, and she has all sorts of ideas for children's books.

I'm off to meet Don for our gamma globulin injection. And lunch. Grilled eggplant on sourdough is the in California thing. Merry Christmas to you both, and to all the family too.

Love,

C

March 2, 1994

Dear Carol,

I was delighted to get your letter—at that time you were just off
to India, so hope it turned out to be a good trip. I am actually
wading through the thousand and some pages of *A Suitable Boy*
[Vikram Seth], having got it for Christmas and unable to waste
a present. At first I found it heavy going, but now that I'm thoroughly indoctrinated with the characters, am enjoying it. Finding it
a bit like *War and Peace*, during which I had to keep looking up the
characters also. But not just that, it has the same involving quality
of getting into the depths of the interlocking families. In any case, it
does make me think I know something of middle-class India and
the terrible trials after partition.

I am enclosing a couple of things for you, one a review of your
friend Beth Harvor's new poems, which you may have missed, and
the other the review of your novel in our little local *North Shore
News*. A good review, I think. Merna sent me her excellent review
written for *The Canadian Forum*, I'm sure you saw it. And speaking
of your novel, hasn't it done wonderfully in Canada? About 20 weeks
on the *G and M* best-seller list, mostly at the top, having displaced
Atwood. I keep wondering how it is doing in the U.S. The only new
thing that has happened to me was the considerable shock of receiving a small anthology-type booklet from the Canadian Authors
Association and finding an earlier version of a short story of mine,
"Chaos," that was already sold to *Queen's Quarterly* and about to be
published. Printed without my permission! Turns out that they had
decided to print the honorable mentions along with the winners of
their contest, when more funds became available, and didn't bother
to inform said honorable mentions. When I phoned the sappy-
sounding president he was most aggrieved. "I thought you'd be
thrilled to see your story in print" is what he said, and couldn't grasp
my problem. The happy ending: the *Queen's Quarterly* editor, after
she heard that the book wouldn't be available in retail outlets, said
not to worry, they would publish anyway.

How about the Writers' Union? Have you followed the strange June Callwood saga in which June was attacked by one of the Writers' Union members on racist grounds? Has everyone taken leave of their (common) senses? I wrote what I hope is a comforting note to June.

We are delighted to hear that you will be in these parts late May or early June. Isn't it wonderful that Anne will be in Kamloops? I'm hoping that that will slant your minds towards Vancouver rather than Victoria, since Kamloops is such an easy drive now from here.

I am giving my kitchen an update by painting the cupboards white. Would have preferred to just have the kitchen razed and redone, but the choice between that and last fall's cruise had already been taken (without regrets). Also as usual am fiddling about with politics, organizing a forum on education for the North Shore. In other words, busy about many things and still writing. Beverley urged me to start another novel and I have done so, but find it hard to keep my enthusiasm when the last one is not getting published.

Bruce is keeping well too, although the Parkinson's means he doesn't have as much energy as I do. I saw a movie the other day which reassured me that it is possible for the U.S. to produce a comedy of manners every bit as funny and witty as the stuff that comes out of the U.K., namely *Six Degrees of Separation*.

Our best to Don.

Love,
Blanche

March 13, 1994
Berkeley, California

Dear Blanche,

It was wonderful to get your letter—with enclosures—last week. First, I am so glad you're working on a new novel, the very best thing, I think, you can do while waiting for a novel to find a home. (And I think Beverley will do it eventually.) I'd love to know a little about it if you feel like divulging, but perhaps you're superstitious, as many people are. I can't wait to get back into one—it's where I hope to be in September. I've been doing short projects, some articles, book reviews, the play script which is shaping, and now the movie script, all very engrossing, and satisfying to tick off, but not deeply satisfying in the way that writing a novel is, building up a world brick by brick.

India turned out to be one of the great adventures of my life, though I was reluctant to go, as I think I told you, and fully expected to be appalled 24 hours a day, and we simply weren't. We saw lots of temples and tombs, including the Taj Mahal (which lived up to its billing), went to Benares,* the old city, where we saw people bathing in the Ganges, burning their dead, doing their yoga, and thwacking their laundry on rocks—all this mingled together somehow. It was here our hotel caught fire, an adventure of another sort, and certainly a bonding experience with the others on our tour. Then off to Nepal for a few days. Certainly there was some inefficiency, but everyone we met was so well intentioned, so polite, so smiling and anxious to chat. We spent our final week in the southernmost state, Kerala, where I gave two lectures at the university on Canadian women writers. A young Indian, who had been at the U of Manitoba the previous year doing his doctorate, was our guide and mentor. He took us to the tip of India where three oceans meet, the Bay of Bengal, the Arabian Sea and the Indian Ocean, and there we sat on the beach and watched the sun set, along with about a thousand other people, all of them silent and wonderfully appreciative. Then it was up at 5 a.m. for the sunrise, which we watched from the roof of our little hotel, some of the crowd—all Indian tourists—wrapped in their bedsheets to keep off the chill. This seemed such a peaceful and sane thing to be doing. I'll always remember it. And I'll remember seeing women pounding rocks all day to make gravel. Think of that

---

*Now Varanasi.

when your daily round seems tedious. Don and I were extremely diligent and thus managed to stay healthy, despite eating some strange and wonderful things. My recollections are still, as you can see, unsorted—and overwhelming. I had a chat with Vikram Seth in Delhi. We got to know each other at the three literary festivals last summer, and both Don and I are fond of him, an extremely warm and witty man. I read the first hundred pages of his book last summer, then was interrupted, and realized I'd have to begin over again. So it is to be my project in France next summer. I did read *Such a Long Journey* [Rohinton Mistry] while we were in India, and it seemed to make perfect sense there; even the rather wooden writing had a kind of Indian-ness.

We had to leave right away for Winnipeg to see Don's mother in hospital. Two weeks later she died, and we were back for the funeral. She was 88, and simply worn out and ready. Catherine was by her side when she died, and we were terribly grateful for that. We think she had a happy life, though the last years may have been a little lonely and a little more confused than we realized at the time.

Joan Clark sent me all the information re June Callwood, since I was rather out of touch with all the happenings, and like you, I will send her a note. I don't know what else one can do—it is all so unfortunate and confusing and sad. Political correctness has been shown in all its foolishness. Did you hear about the U.K. teacher who refused to take her kids to *Romeo and Juliet* because it celebrated heterosexual love and might, therefore, offend gay people? Oh my.

The Stone Diaries comes out officially in the U.S. this week, but there've already been a number of reviews. *The New York Times* is coming at the end of the month. I'm about to do a city-a-day tour, with a couple of breaks in the middle. Portland, Seattle, three stores here in the Bay Area, Los Angeles, Chicago, New York, Philadelphia, Washington, then up to Halifax, Ottawa, Kingston, Toronto and Winnipeg, then home to Berkeley. The Canadian part of the tour is for the reissue of *Happenstance* and *A Fairly*

Conventional Woman, all in one back-to-back paperback volume
now. Yes, I'm delighted, and also astonished, at the success of the
book, and want to thank you once again—I really mean this,
Blanche—for all your support and spot-on suggestions, especially
that one scene where I had the tone way off.

About the Canadian Authors Association publishing your
story—it's shocking. I'm so glad you didn't just let it go. I get the
Queen's Quarterly, so I'll be seeing your story—not sure when it
comes out, but it sounds as though it's soon. A good place to be
published. Heavens, that magazine has had a new shot of life,
hasn't it?

We'd love some advice about retirement and houses and what we
need, want, can afford. I feel lucky to have counsel from those
who have done it so successfully. I think it's a major life problem,
what you do when your active, structured employment ceases.
And engineers seem to have real difficulties facing the work void for
some reason.

Love to you and Bruce, and to the "children" too.
C

April 13, 1994

Dear Carol,

I loved getting your nice long letter, and have been waiting to
answer until I got the *New York Times* book review. Marvellous! You
must be walking on air, and a full page plus, as well as a very
discerning review. Congrats! And hope this means you'll be on the
best-seller list there too, followed by riches as well as fame. Also I
liked the interview bits with you, they seemed a bit different from
other quotes, especially the bit about the Russian dolls.

I'm not surprised that you weren't appalled, as you'd expected to
be, in India. By the time I finished Vikram Seth, I had also found
that the appalling aspects of India have been greatly harped on, to the
detriment of the ordinariness of their ex-British life. So much of their
lives in the fifties were greatly like our lives, and the women actually

seemed to have more freedom in some ways—upper-middle-class women, that is, and of course not Muslim women, who were subjected to *purdah* then, even in India. He does an excellent job with his women, by the way. It is quite a remarkable book and by the time I finished it I felt I had a fairly clear picture of that stage of India's existence. Nor does he gloss over the truly awful stuff; he deals with it in a straightforward manner, and we learn that many Indians were socially conscious and many weren't, which is about what is the case everywhere.

June Callwood sent back the warmest imaginable letter, in which she said that my letter had lifted her up and made her feel warm all day. I didn't think I'd been that eloquent, but I suppose thoughts from others when you go through bad times are more important than one realizes. One thing she did say was that the kerfuffle at the Writers' Union had faded to an annoyance in the background because her son had been paralyzed since some brain surgery last year. The poor woman!

I think Beverley S. is probably about ready to give up. She has done a great job in showing the book around, but I guess it just isn't striking a chord with what is in at the moment. However, I am writing more short stories. I told you I started a novel, but my heart isn't in it—it was more or less at Beverley's behest, to have something ready should she sell the book. I think I'll stick with doing some more short stories about the woman (age 70, surprise) in the short story I told you about. Actually, have done one more and Fraidie Martz has looked at it and thinks it's great.

It's lucky that computers don't yet have listening facilities, as I have just inherited a new (relatively) one from Allison and all the commands are in slightly different places so that I keep hitting control when aiming at "shift," and then sending my deepest thoughts into the limbo where such thoughts go. (Where is it?)

Bruce is well and sends love.

Blanche

May 18, 1994 [Postcard]
Berkeley

Dear Blanche,

Just reread your splendid last letter, and am looking forward to catching up. We'll be in Vancouver, staying at John's May 28–30. We will spend 3 days in Victoria too first, tho John says we'll be bored after! We leave here on the 22nd and drive north, our California idyll over. What a rest to the spirit to have a year of fine weather.

Love to you both,
Carol

July 8, 1994

Dear Carol,

It was lovely seeing you both, as well as seeing John—who is a great host, by the way—and hope the rest of your trip went well. When I phoned to thank John, he mentioned that you had put an offer in on the Victoria place.

The day after you left I did go to the airport to see Merna, and we had an hour together. She looked wonderful, and was delighted to hear that I'd seen you. I did get a card from Hawaii and she was having a wonderful time at her writers' retreat. She said she had a nice hut to herself, a bit primitive but delightful anyway, so I was glad I'd made the effort.

The other day I went to a friend's birthday party at SFU, a retired biology prof, and bumped into Sandra, formerly Djwa. Anyway, she said, Guess what I'm reading? And it turned out to be *A Celibate Season*, for the simple reason that she has been assigned to do it, *The Stone Diaries*, and *Happenstance* for the update for *The Oxford Companion to Canadian Literature*. She said she really liked *C.S.*, and I noticed that it sold a few more copies this year—also that their new catalogue calls it a best-seller among their previous titles.

I've just finished reading Anita Brookner's *Dolly*. As always, an enormous treat, although I didn't find it quite as captivating as

Fraud. Also am reading Josef Škvorecký, *Dvorak in Love: A Light-Hearted Dream*, and although it isn't my usual type of book, it is pleasant going, extremely well written, and I think I'm going to find it quite worthwhile. Have you read him? Oh, and came across a *wonderful* Alice Munro story, "Vandals," in an old Oct. 1993 *New Yorker*. I thought it a tour de force, the kind you don't immediately understand and then go back and find the wonderful little clues scattered throughout, and it all falls into place.

Bruce is doing quite well, although friends say they see a deterioration in the last months. I made a big mistake, the night we were visiting with you, when I said that I doubted we would go to France again, as now he is determined we should go next spring. I am not sure if I want to tackle it, although his idea of finding a place to rent in Provence or some such idyllic spot doesn't sound too taxing.

I do hope Montjouvent is as lovely as I remember, and that you are sitting out every night on your lovely patio with the mountain view and drinking *beaucoup excellent vin locale*.

Love to both, also from Bruce,
Blanche

July 9, 1994
Montjouvent, France

Dear Blanche,

A Saturday morning in Montjouvent. Don is working on the masonry in our cave; the back wall is finally finished—and we thought it would be the work of a lifetime. I'm doing odds and ends, keep running out and measuring the growth of the two grapevines we've planted; the tendrils have been growing one and a half inches per day, which seems hardly possible.

Our days have fallen into a pleasing rhythm, though I suppose it would sound dull to anyone else. I still take my daily walk, and think of you every single time I set out, imagining how nice it would be to have some scintillating conversation.

Our big news is that Don has been made Dean of Engineering at the U of M [Manitoba]—he was ready for something lovely to happen to him, I think, but very surprised nevertheless when the news came. There is a cost; they want us to cut our summers in France down to one month, but we think we can perhaps nibble away at that during the five years of the appointment. (In my first book, *Others*, there is a poem titled "The Dean's Wife." Never in a million years did I think I would become . . .)

Our condo purchase in Victoria has gone through, and it seems strange to me to think that we'll be moving in at the "turn of the century," such a beguiling phrase. We fully intend to come to Vancouver frequently.

There are a number of projects humming along for me—the film script which is now three-quarters finished. I work away at it dutifully, not passionately, every morning. I've just finished a review of a Richard Bausch book, *Rare & Endangered Species*, 8 stories and an extraordinary novella. And now I'm into my major summer project which is Eudora Welty [writer and photographer]. I have four books to review for a piece in *The Times Literary Supplement*, one rather plodding memoir of her (she is still alive), two of her novels and a collection of her book reviews. At first I thought a collection of book reviews was of no interest to anyone, but, in fact, it provides a most compelling profile of her life. She reviewed books, both important and marginal, for fifty years, and this "places" her in the century. And her application to the books she reviewed says so much about her and the liveliness of her intelligence and the courage she was capable of—she was not at all the isolated Southerner I had imagined. I had not read much of her before now, but these days I'm living inside her head. I fear Don will soon weary of my "Eudora believes . . . or "Eudora once said that . . ."

I haven't even mentioned the paperback launch in England or the week's teaching in Paris, but both went well. Signing books in Cambridge, I met three Winnipeggers in the queue, which I found oddly thrilling. All these adventures seem far away as we tend our geraniums here in remote Montjouvent. Five more weeks. Much love to you both,

C

August 17, 1994
University of Manitoba

Dear Blanche and Bruce,

A brief note to tell you Don turns 60 on September 2. There will be a surprise (sort of) party for family and friends here in Winnipeg, and we would love to have a message from you. Could you fax something very short to me here at the Arts Faculty?

We have just returned home after fifteen months of wandering! Heaven!

All best,
C

❧ The following message was sent by fax:

DEAR DON,

CONGRATULATIONS! YOU'VE COME OF AGE. I STILL REMEMBER SIXTY (BARELY) AND THERE'S LOTS OF GOOD STUFF AHEAD. MAY IT ALL BE YOURS. WITH LOVE AND BEST WISHES, BLANCHE HOWARD.

THE FOLLOWING FACTS TAKEN NOTE OF THIS 2nd DAY OF SEPTEMBER, 1994:

THERE IS A BOFFIN NAMED DON
WHO WILL SOILS ENGINEER YOUR FRONT LAWN
ALL MORNING AND NIGHT
WITH ENDLESS DELIGHT
HE WONDERS AT SIXTY YEARS GONE.

HAPPY BIRTHDAY! BRUCE HOWARD

September 1, 1994

Dear Carol,

I hope our fax arrived all right and that the birthday party was a surprise (in spite of surprises being a form of concealed aggression).*

We haven't even sent our very heartfelt congratulations to Don on becoming Dean of Engineering! We are both delighted, impressed actually, and think this is a wonderful and prestigious way of ending the formal part of a career. Congratulations, Don!

You must have loved returning home from foreign strands (". . . whose heart hath ne'er within him burn'd . . ."etc.**) and finally settling back among your own things. Your life sounds, as always, extraordinarily busy, while mine—which seems to me at all times to be super-busy—sounds quite plodding by comparison. We had a good trip north and down to Vancouver Island on the ferry, then took a small freight boat down Barclay Sound (out of Port Alberni) to Bamfield on the west coast of the island, all with the Boston cousins. With time to contemplate the larger issues—eternity, immortality, politics, etc. Al talks up a storm and we had some great visits. Came close to the meaning of life.

I was interested in your Eudora Welty reviews. It's a long time since I read her stuff, but I seem to remember it as somewhat Faulknerian—or am I remembering correctly? By the way, I *loved* your Erica Jong review [of *Fear of Fifty: A Mid-Life Memoir*]—couldn't help but think of those critics who accuse you of too much niceness, since you managed to convey pretty much how you feel about the excesses of people like that without ever indulging in the kind of hostility that goes under the name of reviewing. Acerbic but restrained, and subtle. (Sounds like a good wine.) I did finally read *The Robber Bride* [Margaret Atwood], and to my astonishment—had heard a number of negatives, including from Allison—I got very caught up in it and loved it. I couldn't finish the Josef Škvorecký I had begun when I last

---

*A quote from *A Celibate Season*.
**Sir Walter Scott, *Lay of the Last Minstrel*, canto 6, stanza 1.

wrote—too convoluted, my brain isn't what it once was, or maybe his isn't. And here is a must for you if you haven't already read her: Susan Minot, in a remarkable collection of related stories called *Monkeys*. She writes sparingly but extremely movingly. (Is movingly a word?)

Mary Mahoney's bookstore should have just opened by now. It is called Books on Beechwood, and I sent her a great list of suggested titles and told her what you said about coffee in the U.S. shops. She wrote a couple of weeks ago and said to tell you that she has two wicker chairs and a coffee pot in their very small quarters.

I loved that *New Yorker* that was devoted to writing, didn't you? Oh, and thank you for suggesting that I might do a piece for the issue of *Prairie Fire* on you. I told your professor [Neil K. Besner] that I would be delighted.* He suggested the story of our collaboration on *C.S.* and I think that will be a wonderful vehicle for me to reveal all (just kidding). Seriously, I will make use of our letters I've kept and I think I can do something reasonably interesting about how *A Celibate Season* grew.

I have finished another short story about my 70-year-old doppelgänger. The one for *Queen's Quarterly* still hasn't been published.

All the best to both of you from both of us.

Love,
Blanche

September 10, 1994
Winnipeg

Dear Blanche and Bruce,

Thank you for the birthday greetings. If you'd been here—and I very much wish you had been—the celebration would have included existential elements, I am sure.

---

*Neil K. Besner was dean of Humanities at the University of Winnipeg. He also edited the Spring 1995 edition of *Prairie Fire*, which was devoted to Carol's writing and in which I wrote a piece titled "Collaborating with Carol."

It was a wonderful celebration, nevertheless. Our youngest, Sara, came up from Dartmouth, Nova Scotia, for five days. Our two oldest, Anne and John, were here for a full day from British Columbia (the yuppies). Daughter Meg, and her husband, Richard, came early from Toronto. Anne and Meg are both pregnant (with our fourth and fifth grandchildren) but Carol may have told you all that. John brought his current love, Audrey, who managed very well in spite of the number of strangers.

Daughter Catherine, her husband, Ed, and Evan, my pal and grandson, hosted the Saturday evening party. So there I was a week ago surrounded by a wife, my five children, one grandson and friends, being feted and toasted and paid attention to. And now that I am really old, my wife has left me (for four days in Montreal, where she and Sara will be a team act at a reading), as have four of my five kids. Evan remains my pal.

Carol was number one today with *The Stone Diaries* at the top of the paperback fiction list in *The Globe and Mail.* Last week she was off their hardcover list for the first time in nearly a year.

Love to you both—in spite of (or perhaps because of) Bruce's doggerel. (Blanche, it's easy to see which one of you is the writer.) We are pleased that you are thinking of France next year. We intend to be there all of July.

Don

September 20, 1994

Dear Blanche,

This is a very short note and a sort of SOS too. Remember this summer you wrote me about one of Alice Munro's stories in *The New Yorker*, that you hadn't understood it at first, and then all the pieces suddenly fell together? I think it was the story "Vandals" that ends her new collection. Can you write me, right away if possible, about what you figured out. I'm a little mystified, more than a little, and am trying to write a review for the *Ottawa Citizen.* I remember you cracked the code, as it were, on her story "Fits." Sharon Butala's review in *The Globe* did shed a little light on the new stories, but not quite enough.

I'm trying to get into a new novel and am having trouble finding the right voice, though I think I have the structure at last. I want to write about what it's like being a man in the last quarter of this century. All pithy or unpithy thoughts are welcome.

Don's deandom is still in the honeymoon stage, but he's starting to wake up during the night and write little notes to himself. Is this a good or bad sign? He has a couple of priorities. One, to hire women on staff and even, audacious thought, as department heads. Two, to persuade engineering students to join the human race and reduce their beer-chugging, women-baiting, arts-hating loutism. (I think they're waiting for a little adult leadership on this.) Over the weekend he joined several from the engineering society in painting over their more obscene lockers. We had to go out and buy him a bunch of suits!

This is awfully rushed. But I would love a thought or two about Alice's puzzling story if you can spare a minute. Love to Bruce. Provence will be marvellous.

Love,
C

October 4, 1994

Dear Blanche,

A very brief note to say thank you for your "key" to "Vandals," which, as you can see, I've used. And thanks too for letting me know about the Alice Munro interview on CBC, which I caught.

I think I told you I'd be reading with her in New York next Monday—so it will be a chance, perhaps. I'll have to feel this out to ask her a few questions. However, I am absolutely sure you're right: I tracked it through, numbering the clues as I went.

We had a glorious weekend, taking Evan to our local conservation area where we saw geese, cattails, swamps, deer—it was heaven, and he never missed a thing.

Love,
Carol

❧Here is an excerpt of Carol's review of *Open Secrets* by Alice Munro:

The final story, "Vandals," concludes with a bizarre event: a young woman trashes the house of a couple who befriended her in her childhood. Why? Munro is not a writer to tease her audience. In this case she provides a sub-story of sexual abuse—and the condoning of abuse. The nearly hidden narrative flickers on and off the page, partial, suggestive, and mimicking the way in which an unspeakable memory can surface and fade in the consciousness. This psychological acuity becomes a form of embracing insight; men and women struggle with old injuries, amending their histories, devising alternate strategies—all so they can go on with their lives.

October 18, 1994

Dear Carol,
After all that modern communicating via telephone it is about time to get back to what we feel comfortable with. But first of all, thank you again for that wonderful excerpt re Alice Munro from *The Paris Review.* Those ruminations on aging are exactly what I need for this thing I am doing for the ElderCollege at Capilano College. Also, as I said, I think your review for the *Ottawa Citizen* excellent, especially the insight about how the terrible things happen in Munro's stories. I got thinking about "The Albanian Virgin" after hearing her on CBC, and I remember that when I read it I was quite

convinced that the strange couple (Albanian virgin and lover) were the ones who had committed the robbery and—was it a murder? Did you think that? I'll be glad when I get the book.

I sent off the piece about you to Neil Besner last week. Haven't heard yet whether he wants me to shorten it. I sent him a couple more snapshots, a nice one of us at the picnic on the hill. I know you were a little surprised that I wanted you to vet it first, but I was nervous that I might reveal something you might not want revealed. You and I both tend to be rather private people, at least about some things. (What are we guarding? Do we know?) We'd never make it on *Oprah*, or so I hear. Haven't actually seen it.

I like your idea for the new novel. It interests me that so many men have become defensive under the onslaught of feminism, although I suppose it isn't surprising. But when you consider how long women put up with various forms of discrimination and abuse, it is almost bizarre sometimes reading the ranting of Michael Coren (who the hell is he, anyway? He must be the most prodigious producer on the planet, I read him everywhere. Do you know him?) Somebody gave me *Frank* magazine on my last birthday—a lascivious and frightful rag—and he was so front and centre in it that I've been wondering if he is one of the principals. I happened to see Margaret, formerly Trudeau, on *Front Page Challenge* last week and she blew up at the mention of *Frank*, claimed that you can't sue them because they have a new numbered company for every issue. I note in the last issue of *Frank* that Coren announced he would no longer be doing Michael Coren's Diary, which is a smutty and malicious look at everybody and everything on the Hill. Especially Sheila Copps, whom he appears to hate.

I'm still plugging away at Iris Murdoch and *Metaphysics as a Guide to Morals*. Much that I don't understand, but I was quite fascinated with a discussion about consciousness and Sartre's description of consciousness as "gluey, liquid, jumbled, cloudy," which, Murdoch says, "is intended to illustrate the senseless messiness of the 'inner' by contrast with the clear clean effective visible nature of outer commitments and choices." As I was going through *The Stone Diaries* again for the book club, I couldn't help thinking about how this so often applied to Daisy and the way she was shaped by external influences. Also why, although there is an essential nihilism in this viewpoint, it so exactly reflects much of current philosophical thinking. Perhaps it is this recognition that makes the book so gripping—I'll fly the idea past the group on Thursday and see what they come up with.

Tomorrow night I'm going with Joanne Tait to the Vancouver International Writers' Festival readings. I think we have Mordecai Richler, among others, and under normal circumstances I wouldn't be busting my back to hear him—I don't care that much for him, do you?—but there will be others, Roch Carrier, for one, and it should be fun.

Do you remember me telling you once that I was working on a short story set in Legna?* I sent it to *The Antigonish Review* and they have accepted it. When it is published I'll send you a copy.

Bruce is quite well, and tonight we are going to the opera. So must hunt out some glad rags—there's an obsolete expression for you. Hi to Don.

Love,
Blanche

December 12, 1994
Winnipeg

Dear Blanche,

I've been pondering these days about the continuing joy of children. No one told me that children would grow up and be so funny and so thoughtful. John, and Audrey, his fiancée (for want of a better word), came from Vancouver for the weekend, and it was heaven to have them with us. They'll be married in Vancouver on June 25th, so we'll be there—and looking forward to seeing you and Bruce. We like her very much. She has an absolutely positive spirit, and fits right in with us.

---

*Legna was the small village Bruce and I stayed in when we visited Carol and Don in the Jura.

I think you know that Catherine and I have written a play together about the politics of families, and the Prairie Theatre Exchange here is putting it on in March. I can't tell you how much fun this collaboration has been. (Almost as much as ours.) Most of the funny lines are hers, but she also kept a brake on some of the scenes that would have gone wildly out of hand. Other news: Meg is expecting next week, and Anne at the end of January. Sara has been rather ill with malaria, but is now recovering and will be home for ten days at Christmas.

At the moment I'm working very, very hard postponing getting into a new novel. What to write about, how to begin? Something like paralysis has taken over, but I'm planning to sit down the morning of January 1st, unplug the phone, and actually put words on paper. I have a wonderful title: *Unless.*

Don's deaning has changed our lives. There are lots of functions and, for him, a much longer day. Sometimes we wonder why at our age we're working harder than we ever have in our lives. Does this sound sensible to you? He loves it though.

I've just mailed off a baby gift for the daughter of my English publisher. She is married to someone (an aristocrat actually) named Nick Howard, and they've named the baby Blanche. And so—are you ready for this?—I'm addressing the gift to Blanche Howard! I can't tell you how much pleasure this gave me.

Much, much love to you and Bruce.
C

January 9, 1995

Dear Carol,

Yesterday I was putting the pictures in an album of our wonderful visit in the Jura with you (only five years behind on this) and decided to write *before* we leave for Arizona on Sunday—I had meant to write there, when no doubt leisure time will begin to hang heavily on my hands. But then I thought I would be reduced to actually *writing* the letter—by hand—shades of obsolescence! Will it be e-mail next?

I'm delighted to hear the good news about John, but awfully disappointed that we will be in France in June. I think I told you we have rented a house in the Languedoc region, north of Béziers, for the month. I had been hoping that you and Don might arrive early on your annual trek and perhaps let us return some hospitality for a few days, or whatever, but I suppose now you won't be going until after the wedding. The area sounds interesting—the small town of Roujan, 55 km west of Montpellier, town has 1,600 inhabitants, *boucheries*, *boulangeries*, etc. The house is two floors, and a couple we have known for many years are going to share.

I was very interested to hear of the play you have done with Catherine. What fun! And also to be getting it produced! I suppose Meg has had her baby by now.

I hope you followed up on your New Year's resolution and are now into your new novel, also hope that I may still be a reader when it gets to that stage. I love the title, and immediately thought of all the things that will happen or could have happened . . . unless.

You ask what I am reading, and I must say mostly old *New Yorker*s while I finally finished Iris Murdoch's daunting *Metaphysics* . . . It took me three renewals from the library, as it is so many years since I studied philosophy at U. that I couldn't relate to the concepts—in any case, it stretched the remaining brain cells and was good for me, I suppose. One thing it did do was demolish the logical base of [Jacques] Derrida's deconstructionism, but since I hadn't understood him in the first place, this is a doubtful advantage. Glad I didn't waste time understanding him. Now Allison has given me Jane Jacobs' new book, so I won't turn completely to mush on the holiday. Also Bruce gave me Harold Bloom's *The Western Canon*, and with all this on my plate I'm almost guilty when I relax into the pleasure of a novel—intend to find the nearest library in Phoenix and read nothing but, all month.

I loved your story of the baby gift to Blanche Howard. I had an interesting dinner party for daughters and husbands to meet Ross Howard of *The G and M*, who is transferred here now and is Bruce's cousin's son. He and his wife Peggy are delightful people and we had a great time, and also picked up much gossip about the *G and M* people that one wonders about. Small world (six degrees of separation) but they turn out to be best friends of Marilyn's daughter Gail and her husband.

I got bogged down in my next short story about Penelope Stevens and rewrote the damn thing about five times, and it still sounds as though I am beating the reader over the head about ideas. Bruce said, sensibly, don't send it to anyone, just put it away until we return and by then you might be able to see what's wrong with it. While away I will do some writing—I often think about Alice Munro's story "Vandals" and would like to write a short analytical piece on it, something I've never tried before. Other than that, *Prairie Fire* has taken a piece I wrote some years ago called "The Interstices of Time" (reworked it since; it was the one that was a finalist in *Event* magazine's contest) for their life-writing issue.

Our Christmas was lovely, and I was the holder of same this year. The only time I cook a turkey, and then it was complicated by the poison scare,* as I had bought mine in the designated week at the designated store. So much scrambling around at the last minute for another turkey, plus joining the lineups for returning turkey. All "kids" were with us—Gregory, twenty now and finishing his commercial pilot's training, and probably going to finish the two additional years needed to get a degree, Jacqueline, now sixteen and tall and lanky and looking like a model, plus Leslie's little ones, Katherine now ten, and Tommy at eight devouring books and reading past a grade twelve level, according to the assessment they had done. Stephen and Irene don't try to come down because flying in and out of Smithers in winter isn't wonderful, but they have a couple of horses and gave themselves a sleigh for Christmas! Shades of Kamouraska! Doesn't that sound heavenly, over the frozen lake they live on?

Love,
Blanche

---

*Christmas turkeys were withdrawn from grocery store shelves due to a report that they had been innoculated with poison. This turned out to be a hoax, but it created a turkey shortage.

February 20, 1995

Dear Blanche,

It has been ages since I've written, and for this I must plead lack of organization and also overload. But I was thrilled to get the Picasso postcard, *The Race*, conveying the news that the grant had come through. Congratulations. Onward!

Item: Granddaughter 1 (Grandchild 4) Rebecca Rachel, born 30 December, ten days late, in Toronto, 9 pounds.

And Granddaughter 2 (Grandchild 5) Sofia Frances, born February 4, one week late, in Kamloops, 9 pounds 3 ounces (to a 98-pound mother yet!)

And, one more, (Grandchild 6) expected in September, here in Winnipeg, Cath and Ed.

What a year, biologically speaking!

Besides grandmothering, I've also been doing some book reviews (Peter Carey for one), two articles (one, oddly enough, on divorce, an issue I've had not a lot of experience with, ahem, but seem to have written quite a lot about; curious!). And the new play which opens in Winnipeg on March 9, written with Catherine. All this means that the new novel has not had much attention, but I hope to get back to it properly in April. I think I have the "pattern" in mind at last, and some notion of what it will be about: before dinner, dinner, and after dinner—that's the plan. A sort of triptych, extremely modest in scale.

A the moment I'm absorbed in reading [for review] the Anne Tyler *Ladder of Years*, which comes out in April. I am full of admiration at how quickly she gathered me in with her first five or six pages. There's a loving innocence about this book, but she seems always to be standing back, blinking at the foolishness of much of the contemporary world. And she is terribly funny. And taps straight into that fantasy about the wife walking out, impulsively, from a long marriage. Remember Constance Beresford-Howe? And Joan Barfoot. And Doris Lessing?

Love, to you both,
Carol

10

Turning Point

1995–1996

Carol became famous, and she handled Fame's seductive nature with happiness and seeming gratitude. I asked her once how she felt about the deluge of adulation and she answered, with her usual modesty, that she kept thinking it must be some mistake, that she would eventually be unmasked as a fraud.

Nevertheless, her celebrity did come with a price. Nobody under the pressure of its constant demands could maintain the same level of involvement with family and friends as before. Now she had the world at her door. Yet she managed to juggle it all so that the occasional threads of loss we felt—or at least that *I* felt—were not fuelled by any egregious neglect on her part. My uncertainty was akin to the ambivalent feeling that descends on parents when the young leave home. Once the most important persons in the lives of their children, parents find themselves increasingly superfluous, and into that vacuum inevitably creeps a measure of sorrow.

Over the years, as Carol's achievements grew, I had become afflicted with a form of hero-worship. Awe is scarcely the underpinning for a robust relationship. I thought that perhaps I had moved to a place on the periphery of her regard and others of greater renown were replacing me—those with lives infinitely more glamorous than anything I could pretend to.

In the end I was wrong, of course. Carol made it clear that she valued our long-held ritual of appraising each other's manuscripts, and she mentioned often that she loved getting my letters. Somehow she found time to respond with the warmth she had always manifested. And when my own writing began again to get more serious consideration, my self-confidence returned. If our friendship stumbled briefly, when it picked itself up and dusted itself off it emerged stronger, perhaps, than before.

March 27, 1995

Dear Carol,

Your full life must be even fuller since the National Book Award! How wonderful. Several people heard your interview on *Morningside* and your mention of our collaboration (many thanks) and I'm sorry I missed it, but I did hear you on *Definitely Not the Opera*, and immediately went out and rented *Truly Madly Deeply*. It is lovely, isn't it? Also we share liking of Mahalia Jackson.

Delighted to hear of all your grandchildren now—do you realize that when #6 comes along, you will be up to us?

You mentioned reading Anne Tyler's new book. I'm sure we did talk about her before, as I am also a long-time admirer—actually, I went and got *Saint Maybe* from the library, and found it wonderfully touching, the young man giving up his career to raise the three orphans. What a different take on men from, say, Atwood. Speaking of whom, I reread *The Robber Bride* and it is one of the few books I've ever completely changed my mind on. I had liked it first time through, but disliked it second time through, found the women stereotyped and the men babbling nonentities when not downright awful. Clever dialogue, of course, but empty.

My own writing is going well. In Arizona I wrote another Penelope story, which clipped right along in my mind, as though desert cactus and open spaces was all I needed. I also wrote an analysis of Alice Munro's "Vandals"—something I haven't tried before—and I think it is pretty good, so will try sending it out. However, Barbara [Perrault] persuaded me to go on the North Shore Arts Commission here as it was floundering badly, and it has been taking precious time. Also we decided the old house badly needed an update and so have repainted and re-floored and re-applianced the kitchen and balcony area.

Did I tell you that Allison and Dave sold their house and are going to live in a townhouse condominium? Still in North Vancouver, but they have adapted a very vigorous biking and hiking lifestyle, and with children nearly raised, want to simplify their workloads.

You have no doubt received our fiftieth anniversary invitation, and needless to say we are looking forward to the party, which will be at Leslie's house. Stephen and Irene will be down for it, along with assorted friends, relatives, nieces, nephews, cousins, etc. How I wish the Shieldses were going to be here!

I'm reading Stevie Cameron now*—Bruce has been in some sort of shock about all the revelations. Also just bought Jane Urquhart's *Away* today.

Finally the sun came out and daffodils are blooming and blossoms are blossoming once more. What is it about this renewal that makes everything seem so hopeful? Because if the press is to be believed, we should all be in the depths of despair and rotting away with fumes, radiation, and skin cancer (perhaps we are). Anyway, my walk today was lovely and blossomy, and the ocean and mountains dazzling, and it was almost enough to make me forget that I'm old enough to know better.

Much love to you both. Don't work too hard!

Blanche

On the Take: Crime, Corruption and Greed in the Mulroney Years.

April 2, 1995

Dear Blanche,

We've had your wedding photo up in the kitchen all these weeks.* I should tell you that I burst into tears when I first saw it—don't know why, just suffused with affection, I think. And how we'd love to be there. I'm going to try to reach you the morning of. You'll be surrounded by all the people you love most in the world!

I'm anxious to tell you my response to "A Good Day on a Minor Galaxy" [the story I set in Legna, France]. I read it with a sense of wonderment. Enchanting in its substance, very much in control too, but what really struck me was the INTELLIGENCE of it, the non-compromise of vocabulary and of ideas. And that made me think about the stories I've been reading lately, how they're dumbed down, and why should that be? Well, I loved it. And I'm anxious to see how the Penelope stories are working out. About your Alice piece,** I'd love to see a copy of it.

I was interested to hear about your reread of *The Robber Bride*. A friend told me she had had a similar experience with *The English Patient*, swept away on first reading, and then beaming in with her feminist eye, and seeing, she says, a wholly different book. I'm going to try to read *Paddy Clark Ha Ha Ha* [Roddy Doyle] again, now that we're further from the Booker Prize.

New York was smashing, like the Academy Awards only high seriousness instead of glitter and glitz. I had fantasized about meeting John Updike, but he wasn't there. However, William Maxwell† was, getting a lifetime achievement award. I have loved his books, and have been interested in knowing that he was a major influence on Alice Munro. A wonderful occasion, and I kept pinching myself and reminding myself to enjoy it all. I kept thinking what Muriel Spark

---

*Our invitation to our fiftieth anniversary featured Bruce's and my wedding photo, taken in 1945 when I was 21 and he was 22.

**"The Vandals of Stratton Township" was an analysis of Alice Munro's "Vandals."

†Author and editor of *The New Yorker*.

says in *Loitering with Intent*, "What a fortunate thing it is to be
a woman and an artist in the 20th century." Yes!

The river has broken up—I feel that spring is coming, even
though we're being pelted with freezing rain today. But, yes, it is
amazing, isn't it, how we allow ourselves, every spring, to feel the
miracle of regeneration. I might even do some spring cleaning,
some sprucing up.

Have just finished, for review, reading a book of diaries called
*Ruby, An Ordinary Woman,** which comes out next month in
the States—I found it an amazing document, one that breaks
a dozen stereotypes of women's lives in this century. Also read,
also for review, a ditzy and dumb novel called *The Love Letter*,
by Cathleen Schine. No wit, nor warmth—just thudding
clichés, and I ended up writing "around" the book rather than
"at" it. I seem to lack the courage for demolishment, knowing
how it feels, I suppose.

We'll think of you this week, and I'll try to phone on the big day.
Our love to you both—fifty years!!

Carol

❧I sent a postcard to Carol immediately after getting the astounding
news that she had won the Pulitzer Prize for Fiction with *The Stone
Diaries*, then followed it later with a letter:

May 8, 1995

Dear Carol,

I'm ashamed that it should have taken me this long to write a
proper congratulatory letter re the Pulitzer. Then I got wondering if
you have yet waded through your mail to where you could possibly
even notice, and in my mind's eyes I picture your mail under your
mail slot like little mounds of snow leaking through in a blizzard.

---

*Written by Ruby Alice Side Thompson, and edited by Bonnie Glaser and Ann
Worster.

(I suppose you don't even have a mail slot.) And no doubt it has been like a blizzard around your place, ever since the big win! Needless to say we are enormously proud of you, and I have even basked in a fair amount of reflected glory.

Thank you so much for your lovely phone call the day of the party. It was a wonderful party, about sixty people, I think. When I look at the white-haired elderly woman I have become, I feel no sense of identification (as you perhaps felt over being the Dean's wife.) Isn't that rather odd? I don't think that about Bruce, he has changed gradually before my eyes, but my internal picture of myself is back somewhere when I was about 50.

Speaking of which, if I am not mistaken, this birthday card signals your advent into 60. How can that be? Just the other day, it seems, I was writing you my little thing about 50 being the old age of youth and the youth of old age. What, then, is 60? 70?

Your last letter was lovely, and thank you, thank you for the soul-enhancing remarks about "A Good Day on a Minor Galaxy." Hope you don't mind, but I passed them on to George Sanderson, editor of *The Antigonish Review*, as I often think these good souls, editors of literary magazines, labour away without a lot of feedback on their choices. You said you would be interested in seeing the Alice Munro article I did, and so am enclosing it. I took your advice and have sent it to *Canadian Literature*.

I'm still hoping we can have that dinner in Paris on July 3rd, although I realize that the Pulitzer may have changed your life and plans completely. After I sent off the final payment for the rental house, I got a long letter from Mrs. Stephen Davis with her own name on the envelope this time, and she turns out to be—guess who? Lysiane Gagnon [columnist for *The Globe and Mail*].

John phoned me the day you won the prize to make sure I'd heard, and I said to him, John, do you realize your mother will probably be a rich woman? And he said, Well, let's hope so, there are five of us. He really is funny, a real sweetie. He tells me they will be visiting you this summer in the Jura.

As for the short story collection, I decided to try for a mix rather than doing all Penelope Stevens stories. I read Jane Urquhart's *Away* and was enormously impressed. She has an engaging, almost dream-like style, and I thought her blending of history and superstition quite masterful.

Bruce and I went with Fraidie and Ben Martz to the BC Book Prizes the other night, because Fraidie had been instrumental in getting Lillian Boraks-Nemetz's book for young adults, *The Old Brown Suitcase*, published. Lillian did win in her category, and we had a merry evening. Saw some of the old crowd, all of whom asked to be remembered to you with congratulations. Andy Schroeder, and do you remember Mona Fertig who worked in the Writers' Union office? Then this week saw (briefly) Joan Drabek. After Jan finished his stint as Czech ambassador to Kenya, Jan was appointed chief protocol person for Czechoslovakia and is presently engaged in organizing the Pope's visit. Isn't it astonishing how lives change? They were living most humbly in Prague, teaching English and scraping by, when Havel took over and honoured Jan as the son of one of his old wartime resistance fighter friends. Just as this prestigious prize will no doubt change your life.

I managed to catch some of the interviews with you right after the prize, you sounded so excited and somewhat astonished. I see by *The Globe* this morning that the National Film Board will be doing *The Stone Diaries*. Wonderful!

Well, I must run before I run out of memory—I mean the computer, I don't admit to that happening to me. Heartfelt congratulations from all of my family as well—Leslie was the first to phone me, and when I picked up the phone, she said, How does it feel to be on the acknowledgement page of the Pulitzer Prize–winning book? (Great.)

Hope [Don] isn't feeling overshadowed by all this, although I suppose it would be hard not to. I often think of your character in one of the books about whom somebody said, "She's a person in her own right." You are truly that now.

Oh yes, the Federation of BC Writers have asked if they might reprint "Collaborating with Carol" after it comes out in *Prairie Fire*. I was happy to agree (subject to *P.F.*'s agreement, of course.)

Love,

Blanche

May 24, 1995

Dear Blanche,

Yes, we'll be in Paris July 3, and look forward to meeting you for a dinner. Don proposes we meet at a restaurant called Café Bistro Champêtre.

Sixty! I prefer to call it *soixante*. Thank you for the beautiful card. I don't believe it, of course. The passage will be infinitely sweetened by the honourary doctorate my old alma mater, the U of Ottawa, will give me on the 3rd. And by lunch on the 2nd with my friend Mary Huband, sister of Charles, whose birthday is also June 2nd.

We are only just back from New York, freshly Pulitzerized. Don was there, and also Anne and little Sofia. It was nicely low-key. Another Pulitzer winner [for criticism], Margo Jefferson, a journalist, sat at our table with her proud parents. She told me a Pulitzer will follow one all through life, and be the opening sentence of one's obituary. I find that just a little spooky.

This business of age! I hope we'll have time to talk about it a little.

Life has been just a little overwhelming, but I know it will slow down soon. And I certainly don't want to go into whining mode. Lordy.

Much love to all,

C

❧ Bruce's and my French trip was difficult. Bruce was not well, also disoriented much of the time. When we got to Paris, I studied the maps and managed to get him from the Charles de Gaulle airport by train and then by Metro and finally by cab to the centre of Paris, where we had agreed to meet the Shieldses. Carol took one look at the situation and said, "I can't believe you did this!" Don drove us back to the train station afterwards, sacrificing his hard-won street parking spot to do so.

I told Carol about my plans to publish my series of Penelope short stories—I had had encouragement from Coteau Books—but she advised me to work them into a novel instead. This turned out to be a fairly momentous piece of advice.

July 9, 1995

Dear Carol,

I'm writing not even a week after our lovely visit in Paris to thank Don for driving us to the train station—I do think we would have found the return journey somewhat formidable, since Bruce was getting pretty tired. (Okay, so was I.) And to thank both of you for a merry evening, especially when, with your busy schedule, you probably longed for simple peace and quiet, not to mention losing your parking space. I hope Don found another one. Anyway, it was wonderful to catch up on things and to see you both looking so well and happy.

The next day we went into Paris and exhausted ourselves strolling along the Champs-Élysées and watching the Parisiens and dodging traffic. It was a lovely day.

My, though, it is nice to be home! In spite of mail stacked to the ceiling and weeds to my eyeballs.

The Vancouver Sun has a large picture of you on the front cover of the Weekend section, and an article on "The Spiritual Side of Carol Shields." Douglas Todd who did it is a nice man (spoke at our church), sensitive and somewhat shy, I thought, and he did a wonderful job of the article. And what a treat to read someone saying the true things, that love is what matters and what holds us together, instead of all the *angst* and confrontation that the twentieth century seems to have spawned. Isn't it odd that it takes courage these days to affirm the ancient verities? I am very impressed with Anne's piece in *Prairie Fire*.* I couldn't believe the maturity and insight she brought, for one so young, as well as her ability to get across what is really a complex relationship, between mother and daughter. It is a fine bit of writing, and I think she will do very well if she pursues writing as a career.

We both agreed, however, that some of the critical pieces suffer from density and are not easy reads. (I remember your remarks on academics.) "On the other hand, nemesis develops as construction, where the concept of nonrepresentational is understood as the replication of perceptual processes rather than surface appearances, an insistence on the volatile and assailable nature of possible correspondences and competing terms of reference." That has taken its place in my mind alongside the meaning of life and Heidegger's Uncertainty Principle. However, Perry Nodleman's piece on "Carol Shields' Winnipeg" is delightful, and that is as far as I've got. Thank you so much for your suggestion about working my short stories into a novel on Penelope. The idea is so perfect, I actually spent my wakeful jet-lag nights being so excited by it that I wanted to get out of bed and start then and there. Ideas are tumbling in from every direction—thank you, thank you, don't know why it didn't occur to me.

I see from the *Sun* article that you are interested in saints, so I want to mention one that has been, strangely enough, influential in my life, namely Thomas Aquinas. In my last year of university I had to take, besides science, one arts course, and instead of English (regret, regret) I chose a course on Thomas Aquinas given by an *elderly* Jesuit brother (he was all of 33, I was 19). For reasons to do, I think, with religious intolerance, I ended up being the only pupil of this very erudite man, and had a wonderful year of testing my wits against the harsh logic of Aquinas. But the interesting thing behind all this background was something I read not long ago, that some epiphany took place in the last months of Aquinas' life that silenced him—he who had devised about 14 proofs for the existence

---

*"Reading My Mother," which appeared in the special edition of *Prairie Fire*, vol.16, no.1, Spring 1995.

of God, etc. I intend, some time, to do some research and try to find out what it was that happened.

Much love,
Blanche

July 28, 1995

Dear Anne,

Writing about one's own mother can't be easy, and yet you've managed to do this without sentimentality but with love. Not an inconsiderable feat! I laughed out loud at your anecdote about the facts of life—it sounded so like her!—and my daughter Allison (who read yours before I did, since we were in France, and who had already told me how good your piece is) was fascinated by your description of how Carol did all the usual household things and painted walls, etc. I remember, too, that she used to sew her own clothes, and I remember the two of us once exclaiming in surprise that we dreamed the same dream, that we were in a clothing store and trying on dresses, and were allowed to buy anything and everything we wanted.

Blanche

August 29, 1995

Dear Carol,

Went up to Whistler with Leslie and Austin, who were taking Katherine (now 11) to riding camp. I thought we weren't going to be able to get Leslie and Austin to actually leave her, and even Katherine was dislodging their third final embraces and saying, "I'll be all right, Mom and Dad." And she was. Leslie and I went the following weekend and she had had a wonderful time, riding, rock climbing, even overnighting at the top of the mountain in a tent. In the first ten minutes all the girls sang all their camp songs to us, collapsing in giggles at the end of each verse. Is there anything more wonderful than little girls that age?

Your suggestion re the Penelope novel was inspired—I had no idea it would be so easy to stitch the stories together into the general whole.

It does seem that writing is the source of happiness, or at any rate a measure of tranquility, as I am finding with the new novel going together so well. Logically at my age and with my track record a new novel should be bringing me nothing but despair, but instead when I feel really good about what I've done I am practically waltzing about the house.

Mary's [Mahoney] bookstore is thriving in spite of Ottawa's recession. I hear rumours that bookstores are thriving all over the country. My own theory is that this is a spinoff from computer use, even dreadful Internet, since people are being turned away from visual intake of information to the printed word again (don't know of anyone who shares this theory).

The best to Don from both of us.

Love,
Blanche

October 2, 1995

Dear Blanche,

I was most interested in your remarks about Thomas Aquinas and his final silence. I think you were suggesting a loss of faith, that after all his many proofs of God's existence, he finally ran out. But my next-door neighbour here at the university, a Catholic philosopher (ex-priest, I suspect), says it was almost certainly a stroke he suffered. He had been working terribly hard, giving whole days of lectures in Paris, and was exhausted. He did speak during the final weeks, but not officially, and couldn't, it seems, write. I suppose we'll never really know, but Don McCarthy says it is extremely unlikely that he lost his faith. Ah, if only we lived closer . . .

Much love to you both,
Carol

October 24, 1995

Dear Carol,

Congratulations on your lecture [at the Vancouver Arts Club Theatre]. You gave just the right mix of humour and seriousness, and handled the questions like a pro (which I suppose you are). I remembered back to the days when you hated having to do public things. How our lives can change our inclinations!

I've thought quite a bit about our thesis that the written word can never approach "reality," and it occurred to me that there are instances when the written word actually enhances reality. I'm thinking of the mythical relationship we sometimes feel we have with the geography of the place that the book was about. For instance, the moors where Heathcliff cavorted would have for me an eerie desolation if I visited them, and Alexandria (after reading The Alexandria Quartet*) would seem more than a bustling and dirty city. Sometimes I think this ability to mythologize places, and people as well, is one of the things we lose as we grow older, and may account for the sense of disillusionment often encountered in the elderly. "Larger than life," which is one of the things that makes life interesting, somehow shrinks to quotidian dullness (seen it all).

It was lovely of Audrey and John (isn't she nice?) to include us in the family party, and we enjoyed ourselves thoroughly. I got my note off to Helen Buss** to thank her for the remarks she made about my essay in *Prairie Fire*. The line that struck me is where she talks of the audacity of assuming that mothers/grandmothers have intellectual lives and can tackle scientific inquiry. It does seem to me that this is one of the areas where it has been assumed that women have no business intruding. Strange, isn't it, the cultural assumptions.

In the *Globe*'s Social Studies column I noted a funny bit of trivia: the worst male criminals have almost no activity in their prefrontal lobes. I don't think that has much to do with anything, but for

---

*By Lawrence Durrell.

**Editor of the special edition of *Prairie Fire*, "Life Writing," Autumn 1995.

some reason the relationship between the physical brain and evil has come to the fore of late, with all the genetic stuff.

I'm glad to hear that you aren't going to teach next year. Will you still be able to use your office at the university, or will you want to?

Love,
Blanche

November 2, 1995

Dear Blanche,

It was good to see you, but, as always, too short, much too short; when will we ever catch up? The only thing to do is get back to serious letter writing, and here I have been negligent.

Yes, I suppose language can "fix" a scene in a way that an experienced sensation can't—fix in the photographic chemical sense, and even to the point where it is unalterable. We see what we want to see. I certainly have blotted out modern Rome successfully. Of course I was only there half a day!

Someone else offered an interesting comment on my notion that we don't put enough "work" in our writing. His thesis is that literary fiction may skip over work, but that trash fiction takes it seriously: those doctor TV programs, vet programs, police shows. There people are always in their working environments. Now, isn't that curious. On the other hand, I haven't seen many lathe operators plying their trade on TV.

Our book group did Gail Godwin's *The Good Husband*, which is not a very good book, but it does deal with matters spiritual, and provoked a lively discussion about what exactly a good husband (or wife) is. Sad to say, we came to no conclusions. It was a long book, and something kept reminding me of Stan Persky's comment on the new Josef Škvorecký book, that it was "mildly interesting." And is that enough to claim our time? Don's just finished the lost Camus novel,* which was a bit rough but still quite wonderful. Lordy, there's so much

---

A Happy Death.

to read. My NY editor has sent me two Tim O'Brien books. I met him in Toronto and found him a real guy, hence, I suppose, these will be guy novels. But maybe I'll be surprised.

Much love to you both,
Carol
Vive le Canada, sort of.*

December 12, 1995

Dear Carol,

Another Christmas almost upon us! There is no doubt about it, time is speeding up. We've Christmased in this house 22 times and yet I still think of it as my new house.

I don't know if you remember your advice to me in Paris that I should put my short stories together into a novel. Using pages of writing already done certainly speeds things up, and I find that my themes are more interrelated than I had realized. In any case today I finished the first rough draft, all chopped and pasted together (computer pasted, that is), and I'm hoping to be able to go through it before we go to Arizona in February, where I'll have days of sun-filled time to work away and think.

Our book club is doing Barbara Kingsolver's *Pigs in Heaven.* The tale is light, perhaps a bit overly sweetness and light, but her writing is as witty as any I've read and her bizarre characters beautifully sketched. Unfortunately everyone operates only from a centre of humanity, even the misguided ones, which would be lovely if only it were true. Happy ending too.

Something you said in your lecture struck me. You said, you can put anything in a novel, and I thought a lot about this and about how you often do just that, and I've found myself doing it now and it really is great, the stuff you can talk about.

Did I tell you that Fraidie Martz had her documentary book on the Canadian children of the Holocaust accepted? By a Montreal

---

*A reference to the Quebec referendum, in which voters in Quebec voted by a narrow margin to remain part of Canada.

publisher. We went together to a Susan Crean book signing the other night and she is over the moon. She was looking for a way to end it, and as I had just taken a class on Martin Buber at our church, I suggested that a great Jewish thinker and the I/Thou spirit might be just the things for acts of such compassion as those young people received here in Canada from the Jewish community.

I must get on with my Christmas cards. Allison is doing Christmas this year, I'm happy to say. Gregory [grandson] is suffering through his first real winter in Yellowknife, where he is working his way up from baggage handler to pilot—hopefully, after that awfully expensive training he took. Baggage handling in temperatures that have been below 50 and days that have scarcely any daylight will certainly be the test of whether flying is truly worth it, but he is a very directed person.

Bruce is doing well and keeping busy, although he has days when his energy runs out completely. I never like to mention my own good health as I am afraid Someone may notice.

Much love,
Blanche
P.S. Have officiated at 2 book clubs on the strength of knowing you. Almost have *The Stone Diaries* memorized.

April 2, 1996

Dear Carol,

By now I expect you have dug out from under the mountain of mail that I always envisage as your lot now, after your N.Z. trip.

Bruce was not well, as I think I told you, after and during our Arizona trip, but last week he saw his neurologist and had his medication readjusted (a periodic necessity for Parkinson's patients) and is picking up now and—thank God—driving again. His energy is returning nicely and so we feel that that crisis is behind us, although it does appear that travelling is too strenuous for him, so we may limit ourselves to B.C. forays in future.

I just finished rereading *A Celibate Season*, and wonder if you managed to do so [Carol was talking to Random House about re-releasing it]. Actually I was quite pleased with how well it still reads, and found parts of it refreshingly funny.

I have done my registration for the Writers' Union AGM and asked them to book an extra night for me at the Marlborough [in Winnipeg], which will be June 2nd. It would be wonderful to actually have time for some chin wagging, besides the necessary book discussion, if you can manage it.

In case you haven't seen this review [enclosed]. I was bemused more than amused that a failure to bow in the direction of lesbianism could constitute literary criticism, but what do I know?

My novel is going apace. I did a lot of work in Arizona (with pencil, paper and scissors) because of Bruce being sick, and since then have been revising and putting it on the computer. Fraidie and Allison have both offered to have a look. I think it's good, but that's only this evening. Tomorrow I may think it's awful. Tentatively titled *Penelope Stevens and the Meaning of Life*.

Stephen is convinced that Bruce needs diversion so is sending us a computer that will take Windows and Internet and e-mail and God knows what else, so that he can keep himself in communication with outer space. Do you people already have all these sophisticated things?

Love, and Bruce adds his, and to Don also,
Blanche

April 5, 1996 – Good Friday

Dear Blanche,

Good Friday is such an odd day, no mail, nothing open, awfully awfully quiet, and so I sat down and read through *A Celibate Season* and have just now, almost 4:00, finished. I haven't read it since it was in proofs, and I was surprised that it holds up so well, is funny, more intelligent than I remembered, and that it has lots of nice light ironic points.

I do think the play [*A Celibate Season*] should be yours, though. I've thought a good deal about this, and this is the only way I'd feel right about it. I feel sure it won't affect the Vancouver Arts Club decision about *C.S.*

Sara is working as a reporter on a rural Manitoba newspaper just an hour away. She's had wonderful adventures, which she related for our amusement. Anne and family are moving to Vancouver in just two weeks. Cath and I go to Toronto next week for a sneak preview of *Swann* [the film]—we can't wait. Don is fine, but up to his neck in doing taxes this weekend, a job he loathes. So we're about to sally forth for a restorative cappuccino. By the way, you might be interested in Jonathan Franzen's article on novel writing in April's *Harper's Magazine*.

Love,
Carol

April 18, 1996

Dear Carol,

A quick note to catch you before you take off to France.

It will be fun to update it [*A Celibate Season*], and I'm so relieved they are going ahead with it, at least in Canada. At BC Book Prizes night (Audrey Thomas won), I bumped into Bill Schermbrucker* and wife, and his first statement was, "Oh, I finally read *Celibate Season* and enjoyed it," then, turning to his very nice wife (musician, also teaches at Capilano College), he told her I was the co-author. Her reaction was *very* effusive—she apparently loved the book.

I've made my plane reservations to Winnipeg. At the moment I'm feeling good about my novel, as Bruce loved it and both Allison and Fraidie have phoned with words of much enthusiasm. How right you were to suggest I use my stories! The odd thing is that they fit together as though somehow they had been planned that way, in my subconscious or wherever it is that such things germinate.

---

*Writer, founding member of Capilano College, and former editor of *The Capilano Review*.

Got started on *No Ordinary Time** about the Roosevelt era, that won the Pulitzer the year you did, and it is fascinating reading but somewhat big.

I was surprised that you are getting off to France in May. Is this for a start on the summer stay, or is it to do with the other degrees you are getting? I am looking forward to our visit.

Love,
Blanche

❧I went to the Writers' Union AGM in May in Winnipeg. Carol wasn't able to attend as she was giving the address to the graduating students at the University of Manitoba and had been asked to be chancellor of the University of Winnipeg. I stayed over for a day and in the morning went with her to inspect the University of Winnipeg and her office there, and in the afternoon we worked steadily at updating *A Celibate Season*, sitting in a small glassed-in balcony off the living room in their Winnipeg apartment. We decided that we had to make a bow in the direction of new technology, so references to telegrams were taken out and faxes found their way in.

July 1, 1996 – Oh Canada!

Dear Carol,

Belated thanks for all your hospitality in Winnipeg. I enjoyed the good conversation, the work, the excellent food and wine, the coffee, and the tour of Winnipeg U (not necessarily in that order). I do hope your life has become a little less hectic and that you are sitting in Montjouvent enjoying the gentle lowing of the beasts next door and the lack of human contact.

We had great visits from Pat and Mary Mahoney. Her little bookstore in Ottawa is doing very well in spite of Chapters. I think there is hope yet for literacy.

No Ordinary Time: Franklin and Eleanor Roosevelt: The Home Front in WWII, by Doris Kearns Goodwin.

One thing I have concluded is that the Internet is mostly hype. Since Bruce got it, I have spent a bit of time and he has spent a lot of time, and find that what we access is usually minimal. For instance, I finished Iris Murdoch's *The Green Knight* and wanted to know what people thought about it (very obscure) and all I could find on the Web was her name, a brief biog, and a listing of novels. However under your name I found a couple of excellent reviews of *The Stone Diaries*, particularly one by Ann Cowan at SFU, but under novels written by you there were just two, *The Stone Diaries* and *The Garden Box* (no, I'm not kidding, that's the way they have it). Perhaps we don't yet understand it sufficiently, but what I think is that in five years it will be infinitely more efficient so that information will be immediately retrievable by a simple question. Ever optimistic.

Love,
Blanche

July 13, 1996
Montjouvent, France

Dear Blanche,

Bless you for remembering how I ache for mail at Montjouvent!

I sent Doug Pepper [of Random House] our revised *A Celibate Season*, and spoke to him on the phone about it the same day.

Your comments about the Internet reinforced my (totally instinctive) feelings. Namely, that the information available will be targeted to the famous common denominator, just as TV is. I remember my astonishment when learning that Patrick Watson's series* made history because it was aimed at a grade 12 audience, rather than the usual grade 8. Food for thought. Frightening.

We began the summer with a glorious week in Spain when the translation (two actually, since they also did a Catalan version) of *The Stone Diaries* was launched. We simply and purely loved our

---

*The PBS series *The Struggle for Democracy*.

Spanish hosts, who were funny, articulate, stylish, graceful, and open in a way that the French don't quite manage. We also loved both Madrid and Barcelona, especially Barcelona, which I felt was a little piece of heaven, and as interesting in its way as Paris. There is a wonderful pedestrian walkway called The Rambla, where we sat late in the afternoons watching the world go by, and this, for me, was the highlight of our Spanish week. All the variables of human form on parade.

Our time in France has zipped by, with a couple short side trips, and nice long days of writing. The novel is shaping, and I'm developing, slowly, more confidence in it as a project. I expect you are feeling this even more than I, since I think you're further along and can see how all the parts work together. I would like to be done by mid-September, and then have four whole months to tinker (and to have you look at it with your astute critical eye). This tinkering/polishing/pressing period is something I look forward to enormously, and I'm pleased with my decision to stop teaching.

Time to make us some lunch. We're going heavy on goat cheese these days, since it's so *cher chez nous.*

Much love to you both,
Carol

August 4, 1996

Dear Carol,

I have some good news for a change, which you may already know: I got a Canada Council B grant based on fifty pages of the new novel! I didn't mention to you that I'd applied because of your position on the council, and this time they didn't require three sponsors, which is a relief, and you can imagine I was over the moon, since real money for writing has been scarce in this household.

Anne phoned a week or so ago and is on the short list for the Western Magazine Awards (I didn't make the cut with mine). I hope she wins! Also Austin told me she had won the *The Advocate* [published by the Canadian Bar Association, B.C. branch] short story contest, so looks as though she has inherited her mother's talent, or a facsimile thereof.

Your Spanish trip sounds wonderful. Glad you are making such good progress on your novel, and, yes, I would love to look at it at the looking-at stage. Given your fame I felt it was perhaps presumptuous of me to offer, but I do enjoy doing it very much. Fraidie's book is coming out in the fall and is slated for the centrepiece of the big Holocaust memorials this year, already booked to go on Gzowski.

We have just had five great days in Smithers, complete with horses and buggies and—for the children—water sports and trampolines and whatever else you can think of. Leslie and Austin and kids went at the same time and that was great.

I got a new printer. It took me three hours to finally track down the command that will make it work (this is progress?) but now am turning out pages of much beauty. (Typographically, that is.) Observe the printing of this letter if you don't believe me. By the way, International Readers' Theatre (Blizzard Publishing's thing, I'm sure you know) needed your assurance that *A Celibate Season* (the play) is mine, so I managed to fold the letter you sent saying you wanted it to be that way in such a way that nothing else showed and photocopy it, and I guess that was sufficient.

Searched through my own books recently to make sure I'd read everything there and found Balzac's *Cousin Bette* unread, so am now reading it. No wonder Balzac has such a reputation! His delineation of character is surprisingly good and very modern, although his disquisitions on the female character sound a bit like those of the judge in Quebec, who was disciplined, about how bad women are very very bad indeed. Have my hold in the library for Anita Brookner's latest, having reread several of her older ones when I really feel the need to lose myself for a while. Her first novel, *The Debut*, is as surprisingly finished as all her others, it's as though her talent arrived fully blown and needing no practice.

The stuff Don is reading on consciousness and memory sounds fascinating. Would love to hear what he has learned. Penelope (in novel) contemplates this sort of thing too, and she could use the odd insight. I know what you mean about the tinkering process being so much fun.

Must go.

Love,
Blanche

∿ Carol and I now had acquired e-mail and we took a while to adjust to it. The printed-out versions suffer from all the faults of early e-mail, the inability of sentences to fit within the parameters of the paper so that a word or two sits on the next line by itself.

There is a long gap here between letters, probably due to the fact that we had begun to be less cautious about phone calls.

Date: November 11, 1996
Subject: Larry's Party

Dear Blanche,

Thank you, thank you. It is early on Wednesday morning, and I'm going to get busy right away with your suggestions [for Carol's new novel, which she had sent me]. I do so appreciate your warm words too. This is a rather crazy métier, isn't it? We expose ourselves so, our ignorance, everything. I had lunch with a friend yesterday who told me he'd always been suspicious of people so naïve as to hold him in respect.

When I suggested that maybe we all harbour this secret belief, he said, quite sensibly, how do we know this if no one talks about it. (I think women DO talk about it.)

Love,
Carol

Date: December 2, 1996
Subject: Botulism

Dear Carol,

Wonderful to see you and have a good chat. I've just started your ms and so far love it—it drags you right in and immediately I found myself reading eagerly to find out what is happening.

When reading about the poisoning with rhubarb sauce I thought I remembered from my own extensive years of canning fruit in the Okanagan that it was non-acid food, meats and vegetables that are at risk of botulism. I looked it up in my faithful old bible, *The Joy of Cooking*, and that is what she says quite specifically, listing rhubarb among the acid foods and therefore not at risk. You probably have a more up-to-date source but just thought I'd bring it to your attention in case it is an error that everyone will feel impelled to bring to your attention.

The writing in this novel reminds me much more of *The Republic of Love* than *The Stone Diaries* or *Swann* (although the treatment of the subject matter is very different). So far I love it. I can't tell you how much I appreciate your offer [to read my manuscript]—I truly felt that your life is so hectic in comparison to mine that I shouldn't impose.

That was a great fun evening at Anne's.

Much love,
Blanche

Date: December 3, 1996
Subject: Botulism

Dear Blanche,

Many thanks for your information, which has my head spinning. Now I must think of something else. What about pears? Many people have pear trees in England. Too acidic? I could do green beans, I suppose. Does *The Joy of Cooking* mention them? How I appreciate this.

Carol

Date: December 3, 1996
Subject: Greenbeans

Carol,

This [e-mail] is fun, isn't it? Anyway, I think you'll have to go with green beans—I'm perfectly sure they are okay, as I remember a story I read years ago about a woman who wanted to get rid of her husband

and at a dinner party fed him and her guests poisoned beans and ate them herself so no one could prove anything. The theory was that she had inoculated herself by ingesting small amounts every day over a period of time, but the prosecution couldn't prove it (naturally).

I LOVE this book! Am at about Chapter 7 and haven't hit an off note. What else is there for you to win?

Sent off mine to you today—am feeling nervous, Beverley [Slopen] wrote today to say that McClelland & Stewart will give a definitive answer on the 13th. That's Friday the 13th! Am reminding myself that I'm not superstitious.

Love,
Blanche

Date: December 4, 1996
Subject: Greenbeans

Dear Blanche,

God bless e-mail! I mean it. What joy.

Green beans it is. And how I appreciate finding out now, since changing later might be awkward and also make me look like a sloppy researcher. And I have a feeling my 3 editors aren't up on botulism.

Thank you, too, for your supporting words up to Chapter 7. I'm feeling awfully nervous about its first exposure "out there."

Love,
Carol

Date: December 8, 1996
Subject: Larry's Party

Hi Carol!

Had a couple of days of flu and the bad news is I missed a couple of parties, but the good news is I finished your manuscript.

Loved it. Even better than *The Stone Diaries*, because I have a great partiality to being on the inside of the head looking out rather than the outside looking in. Perhaps why Anita Brookner and Henry James are great favourites. (When I thought of H. James and your chapter on Larry's penis I burst out laughing about what the old boy would have thought.) And you've taken it further, since Brookner and James develop their characters' consciousness-awakening in a linear path, but you've gone back and back over familiar territory and developed new insights, which is much more the way it is in real life.

It is courageous, though, and I can see why you're nervous. After all Brookner and James are not big among the masses. However, I don't think you have a problem there, as you have used modern idiom so successfully that it just breezes right along so that a superficial reading is satisfying as well as delving deeper. I thought your subtle examination of social differences and the crossing of social divides beautifully done—when I went recently at a friend's invitation to hear the twin act of P.D. James and Ruth Rendell (I'm not a mystery fan but they were very interesting), Rendell was asked about the use of so much class difference in her novels, and she replied that being set in England you couldn't avoid writing about class. Here we pretend it doesn't exist, but you've done a wonderful job of delineating the below-the-surface stuff.

I have a couple of caveats for what they're worth [several specific comments regarding the book have been omitted].

This zings right along with a great sense of immediacy. Amazing quality of truthfulness about the family dinner, reminds me of Alice Munro (is there higher praise?).

One thing about the poisoning (now beans). Wouldn't Dot have been ashamed at the great relief she felt that her own child hadn't been poisoned? And she herself?

I'm going to stop now, temporarily, so as not to overload the circuits (mine, not the e-mail's). I will finish this tomorrow, but can't resist skipping ahead and saying that I absolutely adored the ending. Bowled over and very satisfied, plus your great ability to get a dinner party like that so exactly.

Love,
Blanche

Date: December 9, 1996
Subject: Infinite

Dear Blanche,

It is not quite ten in the morning and I've ALREADY incorporated all your suggestions. All your points were right on. Of course Dot would feel, if not shame, her gratitude for passing up the green beans.

About beans, I was moaning to someone how sorry I'd been to have to give up rhubarb for beans, but she said, "But beans are funnier." Which is true in a way. Is there a funny side to this? Perhaps. I feel rotten that this was your sickbed entertainment.

Penelope is here, and I'm enjoying it enormously. I do think this will find an audience. You've given her brains. And a sensual history. So many nice turns of phrase too.

You've given me courage! Cath is going to give me her comments today, so little by little, I'm putting in the revisions. Each person approaches it slightly differently, and so I feel lucky to have a sort of super-critic. I think I told you Meg said, "Oh, Mum, you've made a cultural boob. You have to say 'heavy metal,' not 'hard metal.'"

It's rather thrilling, giving a ms a "final coat of varnish." I think it was Anne Tyler who used that phrase.

Love and thanks,
Carol

Date: December 9, 1996
Subject: Larry's Party

Dear Carol,

Got your lovely letter this morning and am so encouraged that you like Penelope so far. Yes, the final revisions are the most fun, aren't they?

[A sampling of two pages of comments follows.]

Chapter 4. pg. 3. Does anyone say "Good gravy" any more?

Chapter 15. A superb chapter! A superb ending! Leaves the reader feeling enormously satisfied—which is the way to leave them. (Leave 'em laughing. Who used to say that?)

You aren't going to suffer the fate of Annie Proulx, whose first post-Pulitzer novel was apparently not great.

Love,
Blanche

Date: December 11, 1996
Subject: Re: Larry's Party

Dear Carol,

What an interesting remark, about him [Larry] being suspicious of people who hold him in respect. Made me think of another side to this. The person with low self-respect sometimes devalues the person who respects her, thus reinforcing her own poor self-image. Has side effects, like the accepting abuse syndrome and kicking out the kindly nerd. You are lucky to have male friends who think about such things, as I said to Barbara the other day, most of our male friends in politics spend their time swinging their antlers at one another and showing them off to us.

How wonderful your treatment of the party itself is—the progress of the party by means of the little conversation bites was superb, and I remember that that was one of the things that first impressed me about *Small Ceremonies*. All the conversation rang true.

Love,
Blanche

Date: December 11, 1996
Subject: Re: Larry's Party

Oh, bless e-mail! You've buoyed my spirits.

My good male friend is gay; perhaps that explains why he isn't into antler swinging (can I use that?). I think what he was talking about was the imposter syndrome that we women know all too well.

It's getting dark. Time to walk across to Don's office and end the day.

Much love and abundant thanks.
Carol

Date: December 12, 1996
Subject: Pen's Way

Dear Carol,

Use all the antler swinging you want. Just got disappointing news from Beverley S.—Ellen Seligman (M&S) has decided against *Pen's Way* [which is how Carol and I referred to *Penelope's Way*] because it isn't "literary enough." Oh dear, I like Penelope so much I do want to see her born.

Sorry to unburden my unpleasant news so quickly, but it does feel better to shift the burden. Wonder why that is?

Finally got all my Christmas cards done—why do women take on all those things? The whole holiday would die out if left to men. In the genes, no doubt.

Love,
Blanche

Date: December 12, 1996
Subject: Pen's Way

Never mind, you'll find a good editor who loves Penelope—and what she stands for. Like all the other millions of people "at the cheese course of life"—can't remember where I read that.

Yes, the cards, the cards. I've been doing ten a day. I suggested to Don that we give up cards this year, but he couldn't bear the thought. Yet I notice he hasn't rushed to help. Yes, Christmas is a woman's responsibility. In fact, as you suggest, [so is] almost all human interaction. And as for the Christmas pudding, which I've just assembled, that would certainly go.

I'm almost done with Penelope and her year of reflection, and love it.

Meanwhile, this day by day exchange is rather addictive.

Love,
Carol

Date: December 13, 1996
Subject: Thanks

Thanks for the kind words—yes, I think *Pen's Way* will come alive sometime and I don't feel too dashed, much to my own surprise.

Yes, this e-mail is addictive, isn't it? (Don wouldn't be surprised at how much we gab on it, would he?)

Love,
Blanche

Date: December 16, 1996
Subject: Re: Thanks

Dear Blanche,

I've just finished *Penelope*, while sitting in a café waiting for Don to have his annual checkup. Wow! What an ending. Final chapter superb, and epilogue too. I will send ms back because there are too many little notes to summarize, and I'm afraid I do typos too, since I can't seem to separate small things from large as I read along.

The university is deserted, and I plan to spend most of the day going over *Larry* again, incorporating suggestions and also additional thoughts which seem to come and come. This book is getting longer than I'd intended.

Snow, snow, snow. Ah, to be in beautiful rain forest!

And love,
Carol

Date: December 16, 1996
Subject: Pen's Way

Dear Carol,

I'm so glad you like the ending. We both pulled off great endings this time—I love that party [in *Larry's Party*]!

Descant asked me to rewrite a short story I took out of *Pen's Way*, about the Spoiler and Kate, and today I got one of the fanciest rejections I've had so far. Three members of the editorial board decided against it "with some back and forth, some wavering, and some hesitation, since the story is very good." Turns out they didn't like the Freud and Jung stuff which just goes to show, because I thought that bit of real-life stuff was interesting. *Chacun à son goût.*

I wrote a couple of good (I think) stories recently and was going to submit them to the annual CBC Literary Awards contest, only to find that it has been cancelled. Oh, these lean and mean times.

Have a wonderful Christmas. We are going to Leslie's this year and all are coming here on Sunday for brunch. *Quel* madness! Hi to Don.

Love,
Blanche
P.S. Finally finished Harold Bloom's *The Western Canon.* Took me two years and all I am is older but not necessarily wiser.

Date: December 17, 1996
Subject: Return of

Dear Blanche,

No! The CBC competition cancelled! It's an institution, for heaven's sake. Enjoy your Christmas. I am trying to relax and get into the spirit of things, not easy as one gets older. I wonder why. Tomorrow I go with two women friends to Carmen, Manitoba, to a church lunch, and then we do an annual visit to an enormous greenhouse which at this time of year has acres of poinsettias under glass, a most wonderful and somehow unexpected sight.

A dark stormy day here, utterly bleak, blowing snow. But I'm ready to go on revisions to *Larry.*

Love to you all,
Carol

11

Trust
1997–1998

❧ Every time a birthday rolled around, Carol and I would fret about another year slipping past. Writers are like that; honing the writerly skills is such a long apprenticeship, probably on average about twenty years, that each birthday represents another daunting notch on the belt of time.

Carol particularly was dismayed by aging. She asked me often what insights I had, how I was reacting to my slipping-by life, whether I had discerned any meaning, as though each step in my journey might be a signpost that would soothe her as she followed in my footsteps. Her anxiety sometimes now makes me wonder if she had some presentiment that her time would be short. She did work and travel at an increasingly hectic pace, for all the world like a person who knows there will be no tomorrow.

I, too, with caregiving eroding my time and consuming my energy, pushed hard against my diminished life as I tried to make every moment count. Yet we still wrote to each other, no longer laboriously finding envelopes and stamps and mailboxes, but using the electronic age's speeded-up version. "I love e-mail," Carol once wrote, and so did I. Maybe we saved a bit of time, who knows? For we still found the hours we needed to accommodate our great shared love, that of reading.

A T-shirt I was once given said it all: *So many books. So little time.* We both craved that delicious chunk of time when we could remove ourselves and settle into the lives of others, as though in those lives we found a nourishment without which we would wither and fade. So little time. So many books.

Date: January 1, 1997
Subject: Thanks

Dear Carol,

I can't thank you enough for your careful editing job. You have an acute eye and all of your suggestions will be incorporated.

When I get better, that is. Saturday I was whacked with what seemed like the worst flu I'd had in years, fever, chills, sweats, no appetite—the most startling symptom—and when not hugely better, Leslie urged me into the local clinic this morning and the doc there thinks I have a mild case of pneumonia!! Somehow, as Chas said, this makes me feel legitimate so that I can recline in queenly style on my kitchen couch and read Anne Tyler's book (the one where she walks out of her life). I'm loving it, although it is a darker book than Tyler's others, cuts closer to the bone, doesn't have the sweet, lovable, generous characters that attempt at least to restore one's belief in the ultimate goodness of human nature. But it is wonderful, wonderful!

I have been doing more thinking about *Larry's Party.* I do think that some reflection in Larry's mind, something (just a sentence or two maybe in a couple of places) along the lines of "Larry, if asked, would have been hard-pressed to explain the sense of anticipation, or completion"—you know the sort of thing.

I do hope this is some help.* Carol, I can't tell you how much I appreciate your editing in the precious moments of your probably fractured leisure hours. Oh, that last chapter that you thought

---

*Paragraph with some further thoughts on *Larry's Party* has been omitted.

I should send out as a short story actually started out as such before Pen was conceived. Life and fiction work in mysterious ways, *n'est-ce pas?* Much love to you both in the New Year!

Blanche

Date: January 7, 1997
Subject: Your health

Dear Blanche,

Look after yourself, read and sleep and don't feel guilty. It sounds as if that first bout lowered your resistance and left you open to THIS. I hope January is not filled with obligations and plans; it's a good month to "gird one's loins"—though I don't suppose women get in on this exercise, or do they?

Larry has gone off to the publishers yesterday, but I did do a lot more work on it, including an absolutely crucial little scene in the last chapter. And I did add something about the use of words.

I have the altogether happy task in the next few days of putting together a paper on Canadian literature to be given in Boston in February. Have you any pithy thoughts about CanLit, where it is at the moment? I'm calling my talk "A Report from the Frontier." Which is, in a sense, what I think literature is, a sort of dispatch.

Have just read my Christmas book, Margaret Drabble's *The Witch of Exmore*. Daring and also irritating. But I loved every minute of it. Thank goodness you got to a doctor.

Much love,
Carol

Date: January 8, 1997
Subject: Not much

Dear Carol,

I am very slowly getting better. Have only one more day of horse pills and off to the doctor for an all-clear. I am quite surprised at the tiny bit of energy that comes edging back each day—or would that be due to years?

Your paper on CanLit sounds interesting. I've always thought part of the resurgence of women writers throughout the world was precisely because of the strictures of the fifties and sixties. Young women with brains, education and talent could find no socially sanctioned outlet for their abilities and many turned to writing, and some had the genuine talent.

Of course that's beside the point re CanLit, which I'm sure was given its biggest momentum by the Canada Council. I like the dispatch from the frontier idea, makes me think of *Voss* [Patrick White], which was very much frontier exploration, and I think a parallel can be drawn about literature from former British colonies. Right now Indian writers are emerging as quite a force. Also, I don't think such writing clicks until the native writer begins to write about the unique experience of that frontier—Margaret Laurence led the way for us to a large extent, as did Patrick White in Australia, and what's-his-name who wrote *A House for Mr. Biswas* [V.S. Naipaul]. I also think of the riveting descriptions of Winnipeg in your books, esp. *The Republic of Love*.

Pamela Banting from U of Calgary just accepted a piece of mine for an anthology she is putting together, *Writing the Land.* (Cumbersome title.)

Much love,
Blanche

Date: *January 14, 1997*
Subject: *Your health*

Dear Blanche,

Are you getting your strength back? Looking after yourself? Reading?

I've just read William Trevor's *Felicia's Journey* for my book club. Powerful and also chilling. Now I'm reading the letters of T.S. Eliot. For some reason I'm in the mood to read letters. I love the way they set up a period in time. And I guess I love reading between the lines. Example: his terrible health problems all seem to be about his terrible marriage.

Love and keep well,
Carol

Date: January 14, 1997
Subject: Good health

Dear Carol,

Thank you for the phone call the other night. Tomorrow I go to the doc's to confirm that my lungs have cleared up and get off the antibiotics, so hopefully that is all behind me now. It was a bit scary, needless to say, not because I was so terribly sick but because health news keeps stressing that pneumonia is dangerous "in the elderly." Am I in that category now? Why don't interior feelings match what is happening? What is the meaning of life? (I often think of a remark you made once, that one is old for a very long time. How true, how true!)

I am loving Mavis Gallant's collection; don't forget to read the marvellous preface. Interested to hear of the T.S. Eliot letters. A couple of years ago I read an excellent biog of him and, yes, his marriage was terrible, and it seemed to me he behaved exceptionally well throughout most of it until he reached the breaking point. Although I am not a knowledgeable or even very enlightened poetry reader I do like his stuff, and have reread *The Cocktail Party* several times—it has a mystical flavour that appeals to the Penelope in me. Also often take out *The Waste Land* and browse through it.

I was interested to hear that Pam Banting used to be in the forefront of the postmodern movement. She must have gotten over it, as she was effusive in her praise of my writing, which, as you know, is situated at the opposite pole to postmodern. I think—never really understood it that well.

Must run. Thanks again for all your concern and your wonderful suggestions for *Pen's Way*, as well as the encouragement.

Much love,
Blanche

Date: January 14, 1997
Subject: Re: Good health

Dear Blanche,
   Onward! Here's to clear lungs by tomorrow.

Love,
C

Date: January 16, 1997
Subject: Healthy me

Hi Carol,
   Just thought I'd let you know that the doc thinks all that remains
is a bit of bronchitis and will check me next week to ensure that
all is well. Still a bit tired, but went to my book club this morning
where we discussed Edna O'Brien's *House of Splendid Isolation*.
A strange book, didn't quite come off, but there are passages of
wonderful writing and an extraordinary character development of
an old woman named Josie. I don't usually read books about the
Irish and their dreadful troubles as for some reason I find it infuriating, but I was impressed with this, though not wildly entertained.
Next month I am subjecting the group to Honore de Balzac's
Cousin Bette.
   Thanks for all your concern.

Love,
Blanche

Date: January 21, 1997
Subject: Healthy

Dear Blanche,
   Just to say welcome back to the land of the healthy.
   Yes, I find the Irish troubles infuriating too. It all seems for nothing,
so childish somehow. But I do often love Edna O'Brien's books. Now
I'm reading a rather light book called *Mail* [Mameve Medwed], with a
serious subtext which is class. A Harvard-educated writer falls in love

with her mailman. What will happen? I'll find out tonight when I read the last chapter. Do these kind of love affairs pan out?

Stay well.

Love,
Carol

Date: *January 25, 1997*
Subject: *Celibate Season*

Dear Carol,

Last night Bruce and I were watching the quiz on *The Journal* and were delighted to see (and hear) you as the mystery guest. Can't understand how the contestants missed it, since Bruce and I were prompting loudly enough to be heard in Toronto.

After a three- or four-month delay Coteau Books finally got back to me re *A Celibate Season* yesterday—I think they just got e-mail. That's one thing that has improved a lot in the electronic age—all sorts of people like Coteau write to me now that formerly never got around to it. Anyway, a pleasant-sounding person named Nik Burton says that although the contract isn't actually signed yet, Random House is taking Canadian rights only for $2,000. Of that Coteau gets half and we share the other, payment 50% on signing the contract and the rest on publication.

Was interested in the book you are reading where she falls in love with the mailman. Shades of *Lady Chatterley's Lover*? Isn't it interesting how fascinated we all are with the subject of class. Jane Austen, *Masterpiece Theatre*, etc. Perhaps that's why American short stories don't appeal as much—at least to me—they adhere so strongly to the democratic idea, or else they overdo it with recounting the lives of illiterates living on chicken farms. Mavis Gallant's enormous tome is so fascinating I am halfway through. One unexpected thing I've noticed, because of the way she has arranged the stories, is that her writing hasn't changed over the years, at least so I can spot it. For instance the stories of the thirties were mostly written around the thirties, but one of them was written in the nineties and I can't detect any difference in tone or any falsity of recollection of that decade. It is as though her talent arrived full-fledged and completely matured. I can mark the changing quite easily in Alice Munro, for instance, or your writing, and in fact in most writers. What do you think?

I love e-mail.

Hi to Don, and love,
Blanche

Date: January 28, 1997
Subject: Re: Celibate Season

Dear Blanche,

I've just spoken to Doug Pepper [of Random House] on the phone. *A Celibate Season* will come out early in the new year, that is January or February 1998. Doug went for Canadian rights only, since he didn't want to offer the book in open markets in the States or the U.K.

Love,
Carol

Date: March 13, 1997
Subject: Your reading

Hi Carol,

A note to say how much I'm looking forward to hearing you read on the 23rd. Leslie's daughter Katherine (now 12) is showing much writing promise, so she and Leslie are coming with us. Also looking forward to seeing *Thirteen Hands* [Carol's play] on the 25th. Anne did all the work in organizing a great group to go, and Allison and Dave are going with us.

You will be surprised to hear that we have made the decision to move to an apartment. Bruce has been having some problems with mobility and also may not be able to drive much longer. Starting the awful business of looking tomorrow with diverse opinions bombarding us from every side. And the horror of cleaning those storage spaces that have been accumulating for nigh onto 24 years! (Yes, it has been that long.)

Pen's Way has been resting at Knopf Canada for about a month with the decision pending. Am afraid to even write that down in case (superstitious), so please send positive accepting vibes!

Am back to my usual 4-kilometre walk now and suspect that wrestling with moving will develop many new muscles. I wrote a blistering letter to *The Vancouver Sun* re the parachuting of a (male) candidate into our riding, and got myself into all sorts of hot water with the party brass. Why is it that entire novels evoke scarcely a murmur and one lousy little letter has made my name mud, at least for the time being?

Love,
Blanche

P.S. Felt a terrible personal loss when I read not long ago that Iris Murdoch is suffering from Alzheimer's. So much for the theory that using the brain is some protection!

P.P.S. I read *Felicia's Journey* and absolutely loved it. I was amazed that William Trevor had written that kind of book, it wasn't a bit what I expected. It is one of the few books that I've ever felt such an unbearable tension that I had to glance at the ending partway through.

Date: March 19, 1997
Subject: Life changes

Dear Blanche,

I am not the least surprised about your decision to move, nor was Don when I told him at lunch. Of course, we came to this decision a long time ago. Don has never missed our house; I do at times, but it is because I didn't think out clearly enough what we wanted. I did try at the time to think about the parts of my life I wanted to continue in an apartment. So we got the fireplace. What I miss is a better dining space, since we love to have dinner parties. So if I had it to do over again—and if I were to pass on some advice—think of what you love to do. Your walks, for instance, and a balcony so you can have a little garden. And as much light as you can get.

In our case the big payoff was the view of the river—only the muddy Assiniboine, but still water. The task of moving is daunting, but I'm sure the daughters will help. Now might be a good time to find a place for your papers. Where have you tried? What about UBC, UVic, U of Calgary or U of Manitoba?

Yes, I feel terribly sad about Iris too. A friend sent me a clipping—awful. "Time's arrow," etc.

Our book club did *Felicia's Journey*. When I was reading it, curled up on the sofa on a Sunday afternoon, I felt cold. First I turned the heat up, then I found a blanket to wrap myself in. I think I was just SCARED TO DEATH. The way he drew out the suspense with the repeating of those women's names! I'll be heading back to Winnipeg soon after the talk [in Vancouver]. So why don't we try to get there a bit early.

Love to you both,
Carol

Date: April 4, 1997
Subject: House sold

Hi Carol,

We sold the house yesterday, although the market is soft and we didn't get as much as we had expected. Also now everyone wants huge houses with small lots, instead of small houses with big beautiful lots like ours. Nevertheless it is a relief and I'm glad we bought first [before the house was sold], even though it is trickier, as we got the apartment we wanted.

I haven't written about *Thirteen Hands* because I was waiting for my own reactions to gel. I thought the play wonderfully imaginative and beautifully written, but I didn't care for the way the actors played it. A little too hyper, I thought. However, I seem to be the only person who thought so as several people have come up to me, knowing we are friends, and told me they loved it. Anne tells me that the Manitoba Theatre production was much subtler and worked a great deal better, and I can see that that would be the case. It is also possible that since then they have softened it a bit. The lead woman was wonderful.

Your reading that day was wonderful—I loved your sly little joke about "We know what sells books, don't we?" [sex scenes]. A great bit of theatre too, since it invites the audience into your circle and respects their judgment. Everywhere I go, people speak of you so warmly. And wasn't it fun to have a little get-together in the pub afterwards? Your family are always so warm towards us, it makes it even more special.

I don't think this decision to move is a moment too soon. Bruce's health, esp. the ability to walk, is deteriorating quickly, and the Lonsdale Quay area has many little shops and other advantages as you may remember. Other more troubling deterioration I hesitate to put on e-mail, but it isn't encouraging [referring to progressive dementia].

Recently read Anita Brookner's *Altered States*. A thoroughly believable portrait of a man by a woman—your discussion of that at your reading was most amusing and on the mark. I love Brookner, and don't think she is still writing the same novel as many smart-aleck reviewers keep suggesting. Also for our book club just read W.D. Valgardson's *The Girl with the Botticelli Face* and have very mixed feelings about it. The writing is lively and quite compelling, but the subject matter seemed to me to be somewhat overwrought, histrionic perhaps. It reminded me of how a few years ago women's novels suffered under the accusation that they were repetitive voyages of self-discovery. Will anyone make that accusation at a male writer?

I won't tell you about the magnolias and camellias as I know you've had some rotten storms—saw it on the news. Best to Don.

Love,
Blanche

Date: April 30, 1997
Subject: Floods

Dear Blanche,

I was thrilled, Don too, that your house sold so quickly. I hope they'll appreciate your garden—and also hope that the next few weeks go easily.

Viking in New York has just put in a bid to Coteau for
A Celibate Season.

This is short. It's terribly hard to concentrate on anything but the flood which is coming very quickly, the crest that is. What a terrible mess. Loads of people evacuated. The U of Winnipeg has set up 200 cots. We're dry on the 7th floor but lost our elevator this morning because of flooding in the basement.

C

Date: April 30, 1997
Subject: Re: Floods

Dear Carol,

I was so glad to hear from you this morning as I have been watching the flood coverage avidly to see how you are doing. One day when they talked about flooded basements I was sure it was a picture of your apartment building, and perhaps it was. What an unholy mess! I do hope all goes well with you and nothing is lost. You must be getting very fit having to hike up seven floors.

Thank you too about the news re *A Celibate Season.*

I followed your good advice about contacting UBC over my archival stuff, and to my surprise George Brandak, the archivist, phoned back most enthusiastically. Wants me to come and meet him when I deliver it, so I will time it with one of Bruce's appoint-ments out there as it is a lot of driving and Bruce isn't driving much any more. The doctor doesn't want him to drive at all, so I am adding chauffeur to my credits. He has been failing quite a bit lately, and after we move I think I will try and get a homemaker a couple of days a week and give myself a bit more breathing space.

Right now Stephen's little Stephanie is visiting us for a couple of days, then gets passed on to Allison and Leslie. She is 8 and very sweet, but with a highly active mind hooked directly to an active tongue. Today she grilled me on whether it had hurt when I had her daddy—a subject I'm sure her daddy would just as soon bypass.

Take care and be careful during all this awful time.

Love to Don.
Blanche

Date: May 3, 1997
Subject: Celibate Season

Hi Carol,

Thank God the flood throughway is holding—we are all out here keeping our fingers crossed that Winnipeg continues with good luck. I do hope by now your elevator service is restored. I had a brief talk today with your Audrey [John's wife] and she tells me you've just been to Copenhagen.

After your letter I wrote to Nik Burton at Coteau, and today he e-mailed me to say that the Random House offer is signed and sealed ($2,000 for Canadian rights) and Viking/Penguin have offered US$7,000 for U.S. and Philippine rights.

This is a big morale boost about *A Celibate Season*. As I point out to those asking my advice (not numbering in the thousands, I might add), if you decide to collaborate with anyone, pick someone who will win the Pulitzer Prize. Much love to you both, and hope the worst is over in Winnipeg.

Blanche

Date: May 6, 1997
Subject: Louise Dennys

Dear Blanche,

I saw Louise Dennys briefly on Sunday evening at the PEN benefit; she says she has the ms of a friend of mine on her desk, covered with glowing recommendations. Well! It looks as though this may go!

And I'm pleased about your papers; I'm sure you have boxes and boxes, and it will be good to have them off your hands.

What would you think of my phoning Louise Dennys and being your advocate, muttering on about how we need novels that appeal to the "mature sector"? Anyway, my bet is on this one, she spoke so glowingly about the readers' comments.

Love to you both,
Carol

Date: May 8, 1997
Subject: Louise Dennys

Dear Blanche,

Tenterhook: a sharp nail or hook attached to a tenter.

Tenter: a frame for stretching and drying cloth (I'll bet it has to do with dying cloth).

We go to France on May 16, returning on May 25. We'll have four days in our new house, and the rest in Paris where Don is giving some lectures.

I've been working all day on a little magazine piece about Orkney [Scotland], and have only squeezed out about 800 words—200 to go.

Love to you both,
Carol

Date: May 13, 1997
Subject: Thank you

Dear Carol,

You are an angel (or the humanist version thereof) to take this on [offering to fax Louise Dennys about *Penelope's Way*].

I am running like a bat out of hell (a peculiar expression—where did that originate?) Today we signed the final papers for our new apartment and for a while will own both places.

We went to the opening of the new Chan Centre for the Performing Arts at UBC on Sunday. They did an oratorio about Job, and Bruce couldn't last past intermission, which wasn't that heartbreaking for me because oratorios as an art form have a rather limited appeal. The Chan Centre is beautiful and large windows look out on rhododendrons (now gorgeous) and the spectacular view of the mountains.

Much love and again many thanks,
Blanche

Date: May 15, 1997
Subject: Louise Dennys

Dear Blanche,

I faxed [Louise] on Tuesday, telling her I loved the book, that I thought it was time for older readers to see themselves in their fiction, and not as cute old codgers (probable variation of cadger, one who cadges or begs). I'm optimistic about it, Blanche.

Wonder what you thought of the debates. I'm afraid our Prime Minister did not look prime-ministerial at all, or not even very bright. Oh dear.

Love,
Carol

Date: June 2, 1997
Subject: HAPPY HAPPY BIRTHDAY!

Carol, have a wonderful birthday. I mailed a card to you over a week ago and with exquisite timing it came back today—I had forgotten to put the postage on.

Your card to Leslie arrived today. She and Austin had a wonderful time at Audrey and John's, they couldn't get over how much everyone hit it off (Anne and Tony were there too, and I think she said Sara). A nice feeling that our young are establishing rapport.

Loved the little bit in *The Globe* Saturday, about your upbring-ing. We await the evening's entertainment eagerly—dear God! Will it be Preston [Manning]?*

I'll toast you this evening—am reduced to drinking my supper glass alone.

Blanche

Date: June 2, 1997 [France]
Subject: Birthday

Dear Blanche,

Just got your nice e-mail. About your book, no news is good news. My, what an original way to put it, Carol. And, yes, I was really pleased to think our children now know each other.

My birthday resolution is to lose the 15 pounds that has gathered the last two years. Any advice for me? Eat less, move more—ah yes. I've read that women are constructed to store fat in their hips in case of famine, so perhaps I'm only obeying the evolutionary laws.

I've had a splendid birthday so far, mostly just sitting here writing a review of Cynthia Ozick's new novel [*The Puttermesser Papers*], which is a marvel. And lunch with a visiting academic from Boston. Now back to work. And this evening to go to Lloyd Axworthy's party to watch the results come in.

Much love,
Carol

∿Carol sent a postcard to Allison from England, dated August 3, 1997, with a picture of Jane Austen's donkey cart at Chawton Cottage. Under the picture was this quote from Austen: "I do not think it worth while to wait for enjoyment until there is some real opportunity for it."

---

*Leader of the Reform Party of Canada, running in the federal election.

Allison,

Jane Austen had it right, see reverse.

I loved the clippings you sent—esp. "Woman Shocked in Shower"—and have added them to my clipping file.* Perhaps we'll see you on the 22–23rd.

All best,
Carol

Date: June 16, 1997
Subject: We made it!

Hi Carol,

Just a note to let you know that in spite of doubts and misgivings we did get moved and absolutely LOVE our new apartment! The move was exhausting and could never have been accomplished without our young. Dave helped me with the actual directing of movers on Friday, and then on Saturday, Leslie, Allison and Dave spent all day helping me unpack.

The new apartment has all the things I truly like. It looks down on the beautiful treed courtyard around which the unit is built, and has a very large balcony that is almost divided into three by the angles of the apartment, so that each of the major rooms—living room, den and bedroom—have sliding doors onto their own little section. Then off to the right is the ocean, and since we are on the far end of the quad we get very little noise. Bruce loves it and I think it will make a big difference to his life. How I'd love you to see it! Do try to find time on your next visit.

Must run. Hope you are keeping well, and Don too.

Much love,
Blanche

---

*Allison often sent amusing newspaper clippings to Carol.

Date: June 16, 1997
Subject: Congratulations

Dear Blanche,

Brava. Also bravo! You did do it, and it worked your muscle tone up at the same time. It sounds wonderful; there's something joyous, isn't there, about waking up each morning with a new set of arrangements, especially when they are agreeable and you feel the right choice has been made. You'll have some new corners to explore, and will soon be meeting your neighbours, if you haven't already. How wonderful to have your family there to pitch in. I do hope to see it, and let's see if we can organize it when I come through in the fall.

Thank you for your kind words about the review. I love having written reviews, but feel a good deal of anxiety while in the midst of writing them—I don't quite understand this, but it makes me reluctant to take on too many.

We're thriving here. I've lost 6 pounds—thanks for your advice—and weigh in every morning, think about every gram of fat, do I need it or not, and have even learned how to eat in restaurants sensibly. I'd like to lose 4 more by next week when the Canadian Booksellers Association meets in Toronto—I'm going to talk about *Larry* for 20 minutes. I have a new dress made by my quilter friend, and would like to look not too stubby. Years ago Val Ross described me in *The Globe* as "still slender." Her next piece, a couple of years later, described me as "fiftyish." So you see, I am doing this for Val's eyes. Oh, dear. And for me, too. Buying clothes was starting to be a problem. Do women ever give up on this one!

Love,
Carol

Date: July 2, 1997
Subject: Celibate Season

Hi Carol,

June was the month from hell. After the move, Bruce's mobility began to decline by leaps and bounds (a singularly inept description, given the subject), he had three falls, and I have had innumerable types like occupational therapists and family service souls in, bars put on everywhere in sight, and finally the kids came in Saturday and just unpacked everything left to be unpacked and hung the pictures. Last week I did manage to get homemaker help for three days, as I couldn't even leave the apartment otherwise, and tomorrow we are looking at an electric wheelchair, which will help a lot. However, the worst seems to be over now. I am expecting to get help on a regular basis and the sun finally decided to shine and we love our new apartment.

Love,
Blanche

Date: July 3, 1997
Subject: Nik et al.

Dear Carol,

Am reading Pat Barker's *Regeneration*, the beginning of the trilogy that ended with the Booker Prize. She has a deceptively simple style that paints the picture with surprising clarity.

Wish you could see our ever-changing balcony view, with freighters changing the landscape on their way by and the SeaBus plying its trade. The wheelchair people came by today with an electric one for Bruce to try out (many jokes about pushing him into an "electric chair") but he is strangely nervous of it, and will probably opt for a scooter and maybe an ordinary wheelchair for the apartment. Believe me, they do nothing for the decor! The new Indian rug (yes! replacing the one of film fame) buckles like waves of the sea before the onslaught.*

---

*The Indian rug was an Aubusson rug we bought in the sixties and with which we were so enthralled that we took movies of it. Carol found this so amusing that she asked if she might include it in a novel.

Date: July 3, 1997
Subject: More

Dear Blanche,

Blanche, I am so sorry about Bruce, but glad you are getting help. Bless those kids of yours too. I did feel earlier that the move would be dislocation for him, but never dreamt this much. Keep me up to date on everything. That terrible disease, what misery it causes. I was pleased to hear you had arranged some home care and that you are easing into your new life, and finding some time after the awfulness of June.

We go to Kamloops for the weekend for a family reunion, Don's mother's side, the Icelandic branch. Her two very old brothers are there, both in their nineties. We leave for France on the 26th. Toward the end of the month we go directly to Edinburgh for the festival—where I'm doing a talk/reading, then the rest of the week in England for the book tour, then home for the end of August. September and October will be a blur with the U.S. and Canadian tours, but I will get to Vancouver, and will let you know when later.

I have an odd and interesting summer "job." An American publisher puts out an anthology of short stories every year by the cream of the students in creative writing programs in the States and Canada. I am to pick 20 out of 40—they did the original cutting down from 350—and write a short intro. The only problem is that so many of the stories are about the drug culture, which I find excruciatingly boring. Do you?

Love,
Carol

Date: July 7, 1997
Subject: Reviews C.S

Hi Carol,

My life has improved radically since the advent of home care. What a relief to be able to get out to do what I must do, without struggling with walkers and exhaustion (Bruce's, not mine). For the first time since Christmas I am going to have time to sit down and actually write and revise and do such things. Beverley [Slopen] has been after me to incorporate your suggested changes in *Pen's Way*, a thing I would love to do but haven't had the time until—I hope—now.

And, yes, I hate stories about the drug culture—a lot of the stories in the little mags bore me rigid for that reason. Why do Americans think they must write about what is seamiest in life, while the Brits write about interesting gossipy things like class distinction and the preoccupations of the privileged classes? (Yes, a wild generalization, but you know what I mean.) I actually think that *The Stone Diaries* was such a great hit there partly because people do want to read about ordinary, intelligent, educated people.

Have a great time in France (and Kamloops, unless that is an oxymoron).

Blanche

July 15, 1997 [handwritten note]

Carol Shields
Department of English, University of Manitoba

Dear Blanche,

I read a review of this book in *The Globe* a couple of weeks ago [Carolyn Heilbrun's *The Last Gift of Time: Life Beyond Sixty*] and went straight out and bought it. About getting older. About long marriages. I don't agree with her about everything, but I did feel, often, a sense of correspondence. And admiration, especially for the way in which she was able to "jump track." Let me know what you think.

Love,
Carol

Date: July 22, 1997
Subject: Book received

Dear Carol,

What a sweetie you are to send me that book!

Life is much more manageable here now with the homemakers coming in three times a week—all three are bright Filipino young women who are terrific with Bruce. I actually got back to my writing—first time in about six months that I've had time for my own work. One of my short stories rated the comment from *The New Yorker* "Some good moments. Thanks!" Don't know whether to be happy or sad, since I thought it had a lot of good moments. At least they almost always write me a little teasing aside—but never invite me to actually hop into bed.

We love our new place! Pat Mahoney is coming to lunch tomorrow. Living so close to the market, making lunch now consists of walking over and buying a gourmet quiche from La Baguette et L'Echalotte (sp?) and pre-rinsed salad and something yummy like a great pavlova one of the shops make, and fresh rolls. I feel spoiled.

Must close. *Bon voyage et merci, merci encore.*

Love,
Blanche

August 6, 1997

Dear Carol,

I finished Carolyn Heilbrun last night and can't thank you enough. Much of what she said, I could have said (although not so elegantly), and yet other things I didn't agree with at all. I did find it a bit uneven, did you? I do think though, as I ponder it a certain amount, that there is a change in the pattern of consciousness in one's sixties, a sort of stepping-back and summing-up that isn't done at all deliberately. What she said about unwanted detailed memories of scenes from earlier times was right on, something that has surprised me occasionally. It is as though much of my life—high school, early motherhood, etc.—had all but been forgotten, and then suddenly has begun to intrude, as though they were all part of an unfolding. (Pattern? Probably not.) The small, solitary house was lovely, although the husband's return the first night bordered on the "heart-warming," but a delightful anecdote. I particularly loved the way she brought in the poems and the viewpoints of others, such a well-stocked mind! Her experiences of academia sound bitter. She did an excellent job of musing about solitude and its biggest danger, loneliness. I thought of you during her musings on e-mail, and loved what she had to say about [poet and novelist] May Sarton.

Some of it, though, I found a bit thin. Her rejection of wearing dresses, the family lost and found—but least revealing of all were her discussions of men and marriage. The essay on living with men is a bit too Erma Bombeck, amusing but not terribly pene-trating. If felt as though the quality of essays tapered off toward the end.

Altogether she comes through as a delightful person that I would love to meet, self-deprecating, secure in her own place, humorous, aware of the advantages and privileges she has enjoyed. When I began the book, however, I thought I wouldn't like her because of her strange resolve to commit suicide at 70. That uncovered in me a rigid puritanical streak I had thought I'd left with my youth, at which time I believed suicide to be an immoral act. Perhaps I still do. (I have trouble with abortion on demand, although I'd hate my feminist friends to find out.) Heilbrun says that she agrees with Blake, that all life is holy, and that seems to me to set up a deep contradiction in one who would so cavalierly consider taking her own life. And what of the husband? By the way, I liked her observation that marriages that have endured over decades seem to earn a mutual mellowness. I think this is true. But suicide, one would think, would devastate husband and children, which no one would want to do. I wished that she had dealt a little more with the thinking that changed her mind. Another observation that I found true was that anger and small resentments in marriages suddenly evaporate.

I hope this long disquisition won't give you pause in asking for my opinion again. Must go. Hope Don is well, hope you are too.

Much love,
Blanche

August 17, 1997
La Roche Vineuse, France

Dear Blanche,

Thank you for your wonderful letter, full of reflection and wisdom. Yes, I do agree that the book is very uneven, not just the writing but the weight of importance of the various essays. And I disagreed with her about her wish to lose her gender distinction; on the contrary I seem to be anxious to hang on to a sense of femininity, hence my rather new interest in expensive silk lingerie, an older interest in silk blouses (I am silk mad, I suppose), flowers on the coffee table, pretty dresses rather than jackets, though they are terribly hard to find, at least the kind that don't turn us into aging milkmaids. And I differed from her in liking to cook, to set a table, to make an arrangement of furniture and lighting. But I agreed on many points, one of which is a disinclination to travel, other than in France, that is. And to appreciate the friendship of grown children, who learn to look after us a bit, and this I welcome and value and never, never resent. And to stand back from my life a little as you once told me you'd done in your sixties, asking yourself what you really wanted, that taboo question for women.

About the suicide, I am as perplexed and disturbed as you, though Don wasn't. He feels each of us has that right, at any time, in any situation. But I don't, since it seems a cruel rejection of the living. It's another thing in old age, in terrible pain, to think of some sort of assisted farewell. I wonder if she, our Carolyn, didn't pronounce her suicide impulse offhandedly one day, and it somehow got written into her script to the point where she couldn't withdraw it.* She certainly does not DEAL with it in this book. Nor with her painful university problems, which are only hinted at. Yes, she is too jolly at times—you call it Erma Bombeckish—but I think we women get cornered into performing that kind of coziness. By the way, there is a new biography on

---

*Carolyn Heilbrun committed suicide in October 2003 at the age of 77.

May Sarton, which is said to reveal her as manipulative and selfish and impossible.

Still—and I did not mean to write such a long expository paragraph (you call it a disquisition), I appreciate someone who writes about women's experience in growing old. In a sense you have done this with *Pen's Way*, and this is one reason, among others, that I feel it would be a welcome and useful and illuminating book to readers. Why are [Knopf] taking so long? But I have good vibrations about it, that it will happen.

We will spend a week in England on the book tour, having dinner one night with the publisher Vicki Barnes, married to a member of the nobility, Nick Howard, whose three-year-old daughter is named Blanche Howard. My, my.

I'll stop here, though there's loads of other news.

Love to you both,

C

Date: September 7, 1997
Subject: Everything

Hi Carol,

Welcome back to Canada! And thank you for the lovely long letter you wrote from France. What a treat to hear your views on the Heilbrun book. I love the idea that you hang on to your sense of femininity, because so do I (many years down the road from you) and have been quite proud of myself lately for adopting a more modern hairstyle (exactly like the one I wore when six years old, which may be why it makes me feel so young; bangs and short, almost straight). And new glasses (the girls hated the large round old ones). Yes, I too like to cook and set a nice table and make an interesting centrepiece of flowers, etc.

Last night, thanks to being alerted by Fraidie, I was able to rent *Swann* in video. Fraidie loved it and I found it totally engrossing and very well done. I particularly liked the casting for Sarah and Rose (Sarah kept reminding both Bruce and me of you). I loved the low-key looks at Canada, the background for Sarah's life in the fast lane, her outfits, Rose's straight-on look at life. I thought the director did a good thing in the innovation of incipient violence in the Brownie character, especially with its implicit comment on the violence done to Mary Swann. Where I think the director went terribly wrong was in not using your final scene at the symposium. That was delightful and funny, and when he had Rose and Sarah in the hotel room, I was looking forward to the very funny scenes of everyone gathered in the separate bedrooms and the final chase. It needed that at the end, although the gentler ending was satisfactory but not quite right. It held our attention from beginning to end.

And now for your hectic life—I know this because I just read your schedule in *The Globe*. I'm glad they didn't review your book this weekend, because Princess Di* rather usurped the media waves, didn't she? Didn't you find this whole thing quite extraordinary?

On to the reviews I have read of *Larry's Party*. I loved the *Times Literary Supplement* review. Candice Ross is a wonderful reviewer, isn't she? (Never heard of her before.) Although some of what she wrote is taken directly from your novel without quotation marks— but I may be wrong about this. Now, *The New York Times*. I hate reviewers who spend two paragraphs on the only negative they can think of, right at the beginning. Also I quarrel with his belief that Larry in any way resembles Rabbit. I was also quite sure he was wrong that your style was like Updike's, although there are some similarities. I am usually rather good at spotting influences and I have never read Updike into your prose. In fact I have never actually found that you write like anyone else.

Bruce is suddenly way better than he was, I don't know why, easing of stress or a slight increase in medication. And the three lovely home-makers each week have made my life like something in the rich lane.

Love,
Blanche

---

*Diana died in a Paris car crash.

Date: October 14, 1997
Subject: Good to hear from you

Dear Blanche,

First, I'm so sorry about the no from Knopf. I guess I've always believed publishers are the last people who know what readers want. I think this novel would have very wide appeal.

Hope your turkey dinner went well. We had one *chez nous* last night, just us and Cath and her family, so we have piles of wonderful leftovers. I bought the pumpkin pie this year, first time. I'm getting smarter. It was better than I could have made, too.

Yes, I'm exhausted with the tour and there's a little more to do, but I'm having ten days at home, much needed. There is so much interaction with people, and also the need to be "up." Lordy. When it's over I will have done 10 U.S. cities (New York twice) and 8 Canadian and 6 U.K. I have sworn never to do it again.

And I AM thrilled about the Giller Prize [short-listing] though certainly not counting on winning. I'd have hated to miss that great party, for which I've just bought a spangly top, my first real glamour thingamajig in years. I've had the Governor General's Literary Awards list leaked to me, and it is totally different than the Giller. (I am not eligible this year for the GG because I haven't been off the Canada Council for six months.) Jane Urquhart is on, also Sandra Birdsell and Matt Cohen (for a book that should have been eligible last year but got missed). And someone called Elizabeth Hay. Can't think of the other at the moment. No Mordecai or Nino. I've just finished *Barney's Version** and found the end very moving—but, my, it is politically incorrect throughout. Have we ever discussed him?

Carol

---

*By Mordecai Richler.

Date: October 15, 1997
Subject: Your tour, etc.

Dear Carol,

Lordy! What a tour. I know what you mean about having to be "up"—I sometimes think energy is something that one person can pull out of another (no, I'm not getting New Age—especially at my age). What I mean is that if I have to be up I feel as though others have pulled all the energy out of me, and yet using the energy for a walk can be restorative. So it's a different kind of same.

Also pleased that you've bought a sparkly top. I still have one in a drawer someplace that I bought for the first GG's party we attended, I can't bear to throw out all those sequins. I envy you the party (you know how I love parties). However, our local North Shore Arts Commission, of which I'm a member, threw a gala party the other night, honouring three North Shore artists, and it was a great success. Thank heaven!

As for Mordecai, no I haven't read the book and haven't rushed out to do so. The truth is that with the exception of *The Apprenticeship of Duddy Kravitz*, I've never liked him, although I love his political columns. He has a gift for dialogue, I suppose it's his view of life that I dislike. I thought the one about the Franklin expedition was quite awful (not to put too fine a point on it), and yet it was short-listed for the Booker Prize!*

Our Thanksgiving dinner went very well—I was relieved that our apartment seemed to have no difficulty with nine people and it does boast a lovely big kitchen. I too bought the pumpkin pie, although in this case it wasn't as good as I make. Allison brought a home-baked lemon meringue and everybody opted for that, so Bruce and I have to mush through a lot of pumpkin, not to mention reams of turkey and mashed potatoes. Farewell diet!

---

* Solomon Gursky Was Here.

Did you ever read *The Cure for Death by Lightning?** It is a pretty amazing novel for a first effort. Bruce sends greetings.

Much love,
Blanche

Date: November 5, 1997
Subject: Commiseration

Dear Carol,

I'm so sorry you didn't win the Giller, and am inclined to agree with Richler's remark about it being a lottery. There are probably as many shades of judgment as there are readers. I hope you weren't too disappointed, but (as I well know) that's life.

Friday is my birthday, and I find it impossible to credit that the youthful person rattling around inside somewhere is actually trapped in a body about to be 74. On the other hand, looking at those in my peer group, I feel too lucky to risk any complaining on the subject.

I am looking forward to seeing you in December. Have been reading *Birdsong* by Sebastian Faulks. It is wonderfully written but almost too painful to read in parts. World War I. Cheers for now!

Love,
Blanche

Date: November 5, 1997
Subject: Thanks, Blanche

Dear Blanche,

Many thanks for your words of sympathy. I did expect this to happen, given the jury. And I think I told you that I found Mordecai's book rather moving at the end. But politically incorrect! Wow! Ever so slightly refreshing. He was very sweet to me, and his wife is simply lovely. The party was great, and we were able to change our plane tickets and come home early this morning. It really is more fun to win! So I decided on the way home.

---

*By Gail Anderson-Dargatz.

By great luck, though, two wonderful bits of news reached me yesterday: *Larry's Party* has been nominated for The Guardian Fiction Prize [U.K.] and chosen by *Publishers Weekly* as one of their favourite novels of the year. A little bit of sweetness to console the heart.

Yes, I do like the cover of *C.S.* Classy.

Blanche, we'd love to come for lunch at Christmas. A happy, happy birthday. I am hoping you're giving yourself a treat of some kind, something extravagant. I remember thinking 54 was old (thank you again for telling me not to waste my fifties). One of MY little age resentments is the amount of time looking after the bod, and the diminishing rewards of doing so. My morning and evening routine has stretched, new items all the time. Such as checking for facial hairs. Oh dear.

I've read the Margaret Laurence bio with interest. I'm a little lost as to why it is so controversial, though I don't like the way he matched up her weight gain to loss of interest in sex as though it were axiomatic. Have also read with great pleasure David Nokes' new bio of Jane Austen.* It reads like a novel (what higher praise!)—a friend of mine says she doesn't like biography because the language seldom does anything interesting, all that listing and dating and explication. Whereas all these new memoirs seem to offer more.

I think I told you I reread *Mansfield Park*** this summer to see if I could figure out why Jane loved Fanny when no one else could. I found a few clues, not many, and have done a short essay for the Salon.com on it.

Back to the subject of age. I read the *Globe* article about Jane Jacobs by that irresponsible young man—forget his name—in which he called her "a little old lady" and referred to her "applehead doll appearance." I wanted to rip his ears off. And was too wimpy to write in and complain.

Much love to you and to Bruce,
Carol

Jane Austen: A Life.
**By Jane Austen.

Date: November 6, 1997
Subject: Christmas (tempted to write, Christ! Christmas!)

Hi Carol,

Thank you for the lovely long letter and the birthday wishes, and also for supplying me with my belly-laugh for the day; the mental image of you ripping the ears off the young man who wrote about Jane Jacobs. How I admire her work! Her *Systems of Survival* would have guaranteed her immortality in the pantheon of philosophers if only she'd been a man. This lemony statement comes from reading too many letters from frustrated writers on the Writers' Union chat line, on the subject of only 15% of reviews being by women, much less about women's books. Many good suggestions but I sensibly kept my mouth and computer shut. Some torches I pass on gladly to future generations.

I tracked down Meg Stainsby with ease and she was THRILLED to be asked [to have her review included in the new version of *A Celibate Season*], and she has already e-mailed her permission to Random House. Meg says she teaches *C.S.* every other year! I'm blessed if I can see what there is to teach in *C.S.*, other than that abstinence makes the heart grow fonder (of someone), but the world of academe is destined to remain a closed mystery to me.

Yes, it's wonderful to read a biog that is as good as a novel. The best example I ever came across was *Capote: A Biography,** even though the subject was not lovable and his stories seem terribly dated now. But the biog was so fascinating I could hardly put it down. *Nora: A Biography of Nora Joyce* (wife of James Joyce; by Brenda Maddox) was also a good one, not quite as articulate but with lots of insight.

Must stop rambling on. Daughters took me to lunch last Saturday at the Ferguson Point Teahouse Restaurant and we walked on the

---

*By Gerald Clarke.

beach afterwards, and I expect to continue to get as much out of this birthday as possible. How I've rambled!

Much love, to Don too.
Blanche

Date: November 7, 1997
Subject: Re: Christmas (tempted to write, Christ! Christmas!)

Started Don DeLillo's novel *Underworld* last night during a rare bout of insomnia. It seems it's destined to win all the awards this year. I gave up on *The God of Small Things*,* which struck me as high trash and terribly preciously written. (She compares—to give an example—the secondary teeth in one's gums to words in a pen. Hmm.) By the way, my plan is to stick with the DeLillo book for 100 pages, and if there aren't any significant women, I'll quit.

I'm writing a little radio play for CBC and must see if I can wind it up today.

Carol

Date: November 7, 1997
Subject: Visit

Hi Carol,
Just back from my [birthday] lunch with Marilyn at The Prow (which is at the Pan Pacific [hotel]). It was lovely and the entertainment unusual—a large submarine came in and docked right below the window where we were, getting in place for the major APEC conference which will disrupt Vancouver traffic and tempers starting on the 20th. Major arterial routes blocked for the entire time (about ten days, I believe) and security prowling everywhere. They will have 50 divers around the waterfront by the Pan Pacific.

I know you must adore grandchildren stories, but bear with me; this one has literary content. When we moved, I gave Tommy

---

*By Arundhati Roy.

(age 10) a copy I was given at about the same age of *A Tale of Two Cities.* He has soldiered on in the meantime and read it all, and used it as the subject of a book report, in which he wrote, "In spite of their aristocratic training, they screamed all the way to the guillotine."

Tomorrow I'm going to *The Overcoat** at the Vancouver Playhouse and to Allison's for dinner. I'm certainly squeezing a lot out of this birthday. Must run.

Love,
Blanche

Date: November 27, 1997
Subject: The Guardian

Dear Carol,

See by *The G and M* that Anne Michaels won The Guardian Fiction Prize [U.K.]. I'm so sorry it wasn't you, but a terrific honour to have been on the short list. I haven't read *Fugitive Pieces,* but Fraidie tells me it is excellent. I do hope you didn't go to England [for The Guardian Prize].

I get out a lot now with the homemakers three times a week, and am very involved with the arts commission here. Haven't had any time to write for some time as I've had a lot of trouble with computer programs and have finally straightened and figured everything out, I sincerely hope.

Finished the Margaret Laurence biog—at first I was disappointed that his language was so pedestrian and insights a bit superficial, especially during her young years, but became fascinated as I went along and thought he had done a very fair-minded job of putting together a complex (and terribly sad) life. In other words, well worth reading. I was disappointed, though, that he had little to say about her school years and interests, and whether ideas were important to her at university, and if so,

---

*From a short story titled "The Overcoat," by Nikolai Gogol.

which ideas. But as I say, he more than made up for it in his analysis of her later life.

Much love,
Blanche

Date: December 1, 1997
Subject: Re: The Guardian

Dear Blanche,

No, I didn't go to England—good thing too! I'd be interested to know what you think of *Fugitive Pieces*. An odd book, not satisfying to me. In fact it made me a little cross (but then I have trouble with books that LEAN on the Holocaust for their importance. Also trouble with the wise man and insipid woman thing.)

We're looking forward to Vancouver and seeing the two of you. I wake up every morning smiling, happy to be in my own bed. Am just finishing a rather odd little story about the Window Tax, which I'm sure you know about. But I set it in contemporary times.

Much love to you both,
C

Date: December 31, 1997
Subject: Thank you, thank you

Dear Friends,

Thank you, both of you, for a marvellous lunch and a chance to see your new surroundings—I can picture it now as your e-mail comes in. We both think you've made a brilliant choice, next to the water, the SeaBus and the market.

Our time in Vancouver whizzed by and we had a most restful and also exhilarating time. Still—it's always good to be home, and we had a long winter's nap last night in our own bed.

Much love to you both and all good wishes in the new year,

Carol

Date: December 31, 1997
Subject: Your note

Dear Carol,

Thank you for your nice note. (Isn't e-mail great? Remember thank-you notes the old way?)

I'm so glad you liked our apartment and choice. We're awfully glad we made it.

It bothered me a bit after you left that I began to tell you about Bruce and the possibility of a lodge. I should have added that this was his idea, I don't want to leave the impression that the family would decide anything like that. He has a horror of having what happened to his brother happen to him. There was a three-month wait for his brother after he needed care, until he could get into a place, and he had to spend it in a hospital room. The decision will be up to Bruce—it does have the advantage that you can come home three nights a week if you want a part-time arrangement.

Thank you for setting aside the time to see us. We both enjoyed it immensely. By the way, I meant to give you a copy of *Queen's Quarterly* that has a wonderful interview between Eleanor Wachtel and John Updike. I'll send it on, as his thoughts on mortality, etc., are interesting.

Allison read an in-flight mag on her way from Yellowknife and there was a short story of yours in it. Great!

Much love to you both, and the best in '98.
Blanche

Date: January 25, 1998
Subject: E-mail, visit, stuff

Hi Carol,

First of all, are you still coming out here this weekend? If so, will you have time for a walk, lunch, visit?

I am partway through *Alias Grace* (behind the times) and very impressed with it. I would say it is one of Atwood's best, and I like the fact that (so far) the men aren't a bunch of jerks but seem fully fleshed out. Am also impressed with her research and knowledge of day-to-day life then—reminds me somewhat of the good scenes in *The Stone Diaries* of Daisy Goodwill's mother and the birth. Glad to see that *Larry's Party* is holding up on the best-sellers list. Also liked the piece about you on the Salon.com thing that was in yesterday's *G and M*.

Love,
Blanche

Date: February 3, 1998
Subject: Great to see you

Hi Carol,
  The lunch was lovely and thank you so much. The conversation was even lovelier—triple thanks for that.

Love, Blanche

Date: February 3, 1998
Subject: Re: Great to see you

Dear Blanche,
  I'm really pleased that you have volunteered to cast your careful eye over the proofs [of *Unless*]. My ambition is to have an error-free book someday, and perhaps this will be it.
  The Vancouver sojourn was too short, a little rushed—that feeling of fragmentation one feels in the midst of family—but our lunch was an isle of calm. I value your friendship more every time we are together. It is wonderful for one thing for two people to talk and feel that all their references more or less match. And I appreciate your asking the kinds of questions that require me to think about important matters. Getting older, for one thing, a fairly constant preoccupation these days.

Love to you both,
Carol

Date: February 5, 1998
Subject: Thanks again!

Dear Carol,

I wanted to thank you for letting me know that you value our friendship more as time goes on (as I do). I have to admit that I found that reassuring. It is hard not to wonder, when an old friend has moved into circles where she meets fascinating and famous people, whether or not one still has much to contribute, especially someone who perforce leads a fairly humdrum existence. I hope this doesn't strike you as a bit Uriah Heep-ish (remember, I'm so 'umble?), but I know that I find it marvellous to have someone who, as you say, carries the same reference points, but I often think you must meet a lot of such people. And I also value terrifically the fact that we have and can confide things to one another over the years, so that the other can bring insights into times past as well as present. This is beginning to sound mushy, but you know what I mean. You probably have no idea what a support the knowledge of our friendship has been to me through the tough times of recent date.

Have started *Fugitive Pieces* and at first was a little put off by the exceptionally lyrical prose, but like it well enough now. I find it rather surprising that it should make best-seller lists, just as once I was bowled over that *The Name of the Rose* [Umberto Eco] did. It struck me as too obscure, and I'm not sure that so far there aren't quite a number of obscure parts in this. I know what it reminds me of—did you read The Alexandria Quartet (Lawrence Durrell)? The final volume about Clea, can't remember the name, had this same quality of almost being under water and viewing things from a prismatic angle.

Bruce continues to improve and my spirits react in tandem.

Love,
Blanche

Date: Februrary 9, 1998
Subject: Re: Thanks again!

Dear Blanche,

It looks as though we might do a promo thing in April [for the
new edition of *A Celibate Season*], probably at Zebra Books, which
I adore. I've suggested Saturday afternoon, since the talk is in the
evening. How does this sit with you?

When you finish *Fugitive Pieces* let me know what you think.
I get very itchy when I find writers using the Holocaust as a theme.
There's something just a little reductive about it, though she is at
least Jewish. Cynthia Ozick swears she will never write fiction about
it again; though it does come in slightly in her last book.

Love,
Carol

Date: February 19, 1998
Subject: Fugitive Pieces

Hi Carol,

Our book club was today so will try and give you some idea of the
feelings re *Fugitive Pieces*. Firstly, my own response, before listening to
the others. The novel was written like a long poem, and I have never
felt myself to be a person who sufficiently understands and appreci-
ates poetry. At first I found the lyrical prose disorienting enough that
I had some difficulty grasping the story, but eventually got quite caught
up with Athos and the touching closeness with Jacob. Thought she
brought this off very well. However, the final part of the book about
Ben seemed rather like an add-on, or afterthought. I can see that she
wanted to explore the impact of the Holocaust on the next generation,
but I think the structure was bad. Ben should have been introduced, if
only in a small way, sooner, or else omitted. I thought she did a marvellous job of writing the women through the eyes of men, but found the
secondary characters insufficiently developed and somewhat hazy.

After the group discussion, I modified a number of my views. The woman who led us absolutely loved the book, almost wept when she talked about some of the more moving parts, especially re children. After some discussion I realized that I am too linear in my thinking, and that those who loved the novel tended to be perhaps more lateral thinkers, at home with the disconcerting unfolding of the story. We touched on the Holocaust theme briefly. After the war, the Holocaust was seldom mentioned in fiction for about twenty years—I'm not sure why this was, perhaps no one could come sufficiently to terms with it to deal with it in any depth. One of the things that struck me was that I had never before heard of some of the atrocities she cited, and others agreed. One person was dazzled by the extent of [Michaels'] erudition, discounting the possibility that you could put it all down to research when there were many throwaway lines about music and a few other things that indicated her wide range of knowledge.

The consensus was that it was a book that needed two readings, to sufficiently understand and appreciate the prose. We all remarked on the parallel lives of Ben and Jacob—perhaps a bit too pat, I thought anyway. In the end I was taken aback at the level of awe with which everyone approached it, and rather unsure of my own reservations.

I don't think this addresses the things that bothered you. I am back to writing and enjoying it.

Much love,
Blanche

P.S. Glad to see you've joined the chat line [of the Writers' Union]. Good old Public Lending Rights!

Date: March 9, 1998
Subject: Ozick

Dear Blanche,

I loved the piece on Cynthia Ozick in *The G and M*, and am fascinated enough to order the book. What amazes me is that she regrets so deeply that period of her life, her thirties, when she got sidetracked in her writing. Surely this was the time she was raising children, but James Wood never mentions this and perhaps she doesn't either. I am somewhat in awe of the seriousness certain writers possess about their work—and I wonder if I ever had it. If so, it is slipping away.

Love to you both,
Carol

Date: March 11, 1998
Subject: Our reading

Hi Carol,
   Re our reading here [*A Celibate Season*], Sunday, April 5th, is fine by me. Random House wanted at least a hundred people so they aren't going to have it in the bookstore after all. Zebra's have arranged to have it in the ballroom of the Sheraton Vancouver Wall Centre Hotel.

   That's the good news. The bad news is that the books won't be ready until just before and they are going to fly enough out to have them there for the occasion. They thought we should read about half an hour. So what we have to decide is what to read. I'll see what I think. Looking forward to seeing you.

Love,
Blanche

Date: March 25, 1998
Subject: Re: Our reading

Dear Blanche,
   Forgive this slow reply. We have been to Jamaica for a work/holiday. We're not tanned but we are relaxed and we did meet the most amazing people.

   I think the Sunday affair sounds very nice, though I can't imagine who will be there. I'll put some energy into thinking what to read.

It would be nice if we could orchestrate it a bit, picking out paragraphs and reading back and forth, more like a little play, but how will we have time to plan?? Should I wear a man's tie so they'll remember my gender? Or maybe a big rumpled, badly pilled sweater. You could have your swish briefcase.

C

Date: March 26, 1998
Subject: Re: Our reading

Dear Blanche,

I've read the article about the failure of books [to entrance us as they once did], read it twice, in fact, and recognized many familiar feelings. If only one could go back to our teenage years when we were bonded to the books we read (it does happen sometimes in France). Or to the exuberance of certain literature classes. And to the moment when I finally saw Hamlet at age 22 and thought: So this is what all the excitement is about.

Members of our book group complain that it's been a while since we've LOVED a book, really loved it, and I wonder if we aren't suffering from what Arthur Krystal is talking about, exhaustion, distrust, and the feeling, as he says, that we've been along that road too. I think he's right about the private and public statement, that we've lost the sense of privacy that books were once able to interrupt and penetrate.

Love,
Carol

Date: March 27, 1998
Subject: Re: Reading, etc.

Hi Carol,

You've been short-listed for the Orange Prize! My God, girl, how far can you go (as in how far is up)? Wonderful, wonderful, I'm so thrilled for you. Also so glad you had a little getaway in Jamaica.

Bruce and I just had four days in Victoria. The occasion was a reception for former parliamentarians, so had fun renewing old ties, etc. Had dinner with Kay and Judd [Buchanan], who I accused of being Dorian Grey. The first time we've had a little holiday in two years, I think it did me good.

I think you are right about the reasons reading loses some of its enchantment, some of the time. There is another thing that just occurred to me while reading Doris Lessing's book *Love, Again*. It has had mixed reviews and I started by disliking it, then got completely caught up in some truly wonderful stuff about the theatre and interactions that bypassed age, and love whose carnality had bygone roots. At the same time I'm reading Anita Brookner's new book, *Visitors*, which also deals with an aging woman from quite another perspective, and finding it too almost un-put-down-able. So much has to do with relating to the problems currently being addressed in our lives, as we search for clues as to how to live each new chapter—and aging is a new chapter, whose misfortune it is to have only one outcome no matter how one chooses. But that's another bleat.

I bought a feminine spring-like skirt and top for the reading in the hope that Jock would give some semblance of (relative) youth. I like the tie idea. We could do a lot with this if it was a first go-around, couldn't we? Must run.

Love,
Blanche

Date: April 6, 1998
Subject: Tired

Dear Carol,

I hope you aren't wiped today. Everyone thought the reading very successful, and people said they Had Fun. I had fun doing it—and I particularly want to thank you for doing it. My friends all wanted to meet you and my family were pleased to renew acquaintance. And nice seeing Audrey and John.

One thing I meant to mention to you yesterday but forgot—I had an e-mail from Beverley the other day. She said she had bumped into Bella [Pomer], who had told her that the Chinese (!) are interested in *C.S.* I find this almost incomprehensible, but let me know if you hear anything. Thank you again.

Love,
Blanche

Date: April 6, 1998
Subject: Re: Tired

Dear Blanche,

I loved the whole event, seeing old friends and all of the Howard family. Yes, people did laugh, didn't they? And quite a lot bought books. It'll be interesting to see how sales go.

And, yes, I am tired today. It's caught up with me, but tonight is an at-home night, a fire, a book, and early to bed, heaven. I must be a little more careful about pacing myself. Is this the beginning of old age? This "taking care" of one's self?

Love,
Carol

Date: April 29, 1998
Subject: Orange Prize!

Dear Carol,

I see you are short-listed! AND going to England! Heartfelt congratulations, and fingers well-crossed for the big day. We're all terribly proud of you.

Had a great lunch with the "girls" [daughter Leslie and Carol's daughter Anne]—dim sum which I smeared all over the white tablecloth. Anne pretended not to notice but Leslie wiped up after me and I felt doddery.

All well here. Bruce continues to make astounding progress [thanks to a new drug, Aricept] and we are actually contemplating an Ottawa trip for the thirtieth anniversary of Trudeau's election as prime minister. Allison has written a couple of short stories which are excellent.

Wonderful luck—I'll be thinking of you!

Blanche

Date : April 30, 1998
Subject: Re: Orange Prize!

Dear Blanche,

I am about to do a number of Orange Prize interviews and preparing for that question about women-only events. Did you know that Nadine Gordimer has withdrawn because it is a women-only thing? I need you, Blanche. What shall I offer as arguments?

Love,
Carol

Date: April 30, 1998
Subject: Arguments

Dear Carol,

As it happened, I had been thinking about that very thing after reading that A.S. Byatt once refused to participate. I have always believed that any sort of organization can have exclusivity, especially where private money is concerned—naturally you can't have exclusivity where government funding is concerned. All sorts of men's clubs are men only, as are women's clubs. Private donors can spend their money as they wish, just as anyone is free to leave their money to whomever they wish (generally). It is kind of like an eccentric inheritance from a distant aunt, and while it might not be the way you would choose to leave your money, I don't know of anyone who would walk away from it on the principle that it should have been given to someone else.

The Commonwealth Writers' Prize is limited to the Commonwealth, the Pulitzer Prize to American citizens, the Marian

Engel Award to women at midpoint in their career. There are first
writers' prizes and young people's prizes and Native writers' prizes,
and so on. Then there is the argument that for countless centuries
up until and including the early part of this century, women's voices
were not heard. George Sands and George Eliot had to change
their names to get recognition. It is quite possible (this might be
worth finding out) that the donors of the Orange Prize may have
been attempting to redress this inequity to some extent—a sort of
affirmative action.

   Finally, you would have no objection to the existence of a men
writers' only prize (or maybe you would. Would you?). In any case,
you could always say that if it had been you setting up the prize,
you wouldn't have chosen to do it in that particular way, but that
everyone is entitled to do what seems right to them with their money.

   I don't know if any of this is any help. I keep thinking there must
be some small cogent statement that would put it all in perspective.
All I can say is, like Mordecai and the gin ad, Go for it kid! The
world of political correctness is destroying our critical thinking.

   All the luck in the world, and don't be intimidated by the
hypocrisy of the media, all of whom would give their right arms
to be short-listed.

Love,
Blanche

Date: April 30, 1998
Subject: Re: Arguments

Dear wise friend Blanche,

   A wonderful set (brace, legion?) of arguments. Thank you, thank
you. I have printed your letter out, and will carry it in my purse for
interviews. And for courage. By the way, I always feel I should like
Nadine Gordimer's books, but hardly ever do.

Love,
Carol

Date: May 6, 1998
Subject: Interview with The Guardian

Hi Carol,

Had rather an odd interview with a young man from
The Guardian this morning, re you. Odd because either he hasn't
mastered the intricacies of Canadian phone systems or
The Guardian is strapped for cash. I was getting into the spirit of
the thing when he said, "I hate to rush you, but I've got this
charge card thing from the hotel for $10 and it is flashing that
I only have a minute left. Perhaps if you think of anything
else you could phone me. My number is—" and then with
impeccable timing it went dead.

He seemed especially interested in your marriage (glowing
reviews) and your feminism (glowing reviews). I told him you had
the courage to write about the lives of ordinary women when at
that time they were held to be of no interest, and I told him I
thought Don considered your two careers as a partnership, and
was exceptionally supportive of your career and very fair in making
sure you had your chance to return to university and do your own
things. (More or less.)

My fingers are still very crossed. Oh, I do hope you win!

Much love,
Blanche

Date: May 6, 1998
Subject: Re: Interview with The Guardian

Dear Blanche,

Yes, the interviewer did tell me he had a most interesting chat
with you. Odd. I'm not counting on winning, shall go for the sport
of it all, ha ha. How do we get into such things.

Never mind, I'm thriving.

Love on a cold, windy, dark day,
Carol

Date: May 25, 1998
Subject: Wonderful!

Dear Carol,

I don't know whether you would be home yet, but couldn't wait any longer to express my delight that you WON! Wonderful, wonderful. *The Vancouver Sun* gave you a lovely colour photo right on the front page, so everyone in these parts knows!

Loved your comment about it being a great chance to visit England—you should have been in politics (too. Not excluding writing, which would have been a disservice to womankind). Also liked your comment about honouring women.

Anyway, Carol, we are all immensely proud of you, and I am grabbing a few wisps of trailing glory.

Much love,
Blanche
P.S. Did you read an Alice Munro story about two years ago in *The New Yorker*, about an optometrist who is found in his car in the river? If you missed it, I'll send it, as it is truly Alice at her most intriguing.

May 25, 1998
Subject: Re: Wonderful

Dear Blanche,

Yes, I do remember that haunting Alice story. How good she is at the kind of sensual details that stick with one.

And thank you for the good wishes. Well, it was super-glam and wonderful fun, and I several times used the discussion points you sent me. ALL the interviews asked me about the fairness of the prize. Did I feel it was a lesser award because men were excluded, etc. So much to talk and think about. We are off to China one week from today, and so I must work on my talk a bit.

Love
Carol

May 26, 1998
Subject: China!

Dear Carol,

China!—how fascinating. I gather you are giving a talk? To whom?

Bruce and I will be in Ottawa longer than I had expected, but there are a lot of functions and very dear old friends want us to stay with them at their lakeside home for the last weekend. Still feeling a bit nervous about it, but the worst that can happen (I suppose) is that Bruce won't feel well. Just so he gets to the numerous rather glam functions we have been invited to, to celebrate the thirtieth anniversary. (Speaker's dinner, GG reception, caucus meetings, etc.)

By the way, I adored Anne-Marie MacDonald's *Fall on Your Knees*. What a talent! And so young. Have a wonderful time.

Love,
Blanche

July 7, 1998

Dear Carol,

I keep thinking of you in your new pad in France, vegging out—although I have a little trouble getting that into focus.

We had a lovely trip to Ottawa. Bruce surprised us all by having quite an energetic time there, in fact we managed the whole Picasso exhibit which is a feat of endurance even for the non-afflicted. Spent a great weekend in the country with our old friends the Hills, who have built a country home where their cottage used to be, on Otty Lake. Lorraine found the painting equivalent of her voice about ten years ago and has done extraordinarily well since. This time I bought one of her paintings that I had admired many years ago, and am delighted with it. Also they were in the midst of neighbourhood work gangs cleaning up the debris from the ice storm. I found the devastation quite incredible—birch trees bent backward.

Pamela Banting, who I e-mailed after a piece of mine came out in an anthology of western landscape writing that she edited, tells me that *A Celibate Season* got a good review in the *Calgary Herald*. This is encouraging.

Reading. I am reading A.S. Byatt's *Angels and Insects*, slightly spoiled by the fact that I rather inadvertently watched it on *American Playhouse* and therefore know the more salacious elements of the plot. However, the novel is wonderfully written and great enjoyment anyway. Other than that, all reading has been sporadic—even stooped to *A Year in Provence*,* which wasn't nearly as entertaining as I had thought it would be after watching the film. In fact I fail to see why it swept best-seller lists, although it is several cuts above *Bridges of Madison County*.** (What isn't?)

B.C. politics continues to alarm, appall, and astound. Allison was part of a team that wrote, in a one-month time slot before Christmas, a comprehensive restructuring of the social services department, which the government proceeded to install while forgetting to consult with any of the users (or as we say in the lingo, the stakeholders). She ran herself ragged over this, and now the government, halfway through the restructuring with many employees laid off and re-allocated, suddenly decided tonight to abandon the whole thing. I haven't talked to Allison since I heard the news, but I suspect despair reigns.

Do have a lovely restful time, and write if you have time.

Love,
Blanche

July 18, 1998
En Linde, France

Dear Blanche,

What unadulterated joy to receive a stamped letter. Especially a letter which has now become traditional, your summer letter, six o'clock—Don and I are about to go out for a dinner in the

---

*By Peter Mayle.
**By Robert James Waller.

town of Igy (how to pronounce?) 6 kilometres away, to celebrate our
41st wedding anniversary. We also celebrate, or lament is closer to
the spirit, the fact that we have only two weeks left.

I too have wondered about the curious success of *A Year in
Provence.* I find he condescends to his French neighbours, but that
his troubles dealing with craftsmen are very true to life.

Did you see the film *Angels and Insects*? We went with friends—all
four of us loved it. But we came out into the lobby and met our
local film guru—also prof of film at U of M—who hated it. "Too
much moral clarity," he pronounced, and I laugh every time I think
of it. Applies to so many situations.

I've written 3 stories since being here, 3 speeches, one article for
Canadian Living (they offered too much money to turn down) and
an intro to a library thingamajig. I want to do one more story—a
sort of fable about the housewife, as I imagine her, who invented
the steering wheel muff. Just whipped it up one night with her
crochet needles. Any suggestions? Do you remember your first
encounter with a steering wheel muff?

Wish you were around the corner at the ivy-covered *gite.*

Carol

July 31, 1998 [Winnipeg]
Subject: Home

Dear Blanche,

Home again. We got to Winnipeg last night, fairly exhausted, but
as always happy to be home.

I'm spending the day going through some mail, and came across
this letter. I don't know who Laurence is, but thought you might.
In any case, you'll be interested in his letter and might want to reply.

Much love,
C

∾ Carol enclosed a lovely three-page handwritten letter from
Lasqueti Island, B.C., about *A Celibate Season.* "You told our story,"

Laurence wrote. "Strange to me that without having experienced it (according to the forward) you got it so right. I suppose that's your job; but though I have come to expect writers to be able to plunge in and plumb the depth of our human condition I find it tantalizing that you have managed it in the relative ordinariness of our domestic reality."

When I answered I added, "I'm so glad that we 'got it right' in telling of the pain of separation, even though neither of us has experienced it as such. Right now I think I'm experiencing a variety of it, since my husband is deteriorating with Parkinson's disease. It is as though a dearly loved and understood person slips away now and then to an unknown country, and sometimes I feel bereft."

Date: August 12, 1998
Subject: Welcome home!

Dear Carol,

Why is it that I feel better when you're on this continent?

Belated happy anniversary—41 years! Are you catching up to us, or have I quit counting? You asked if we saw *Angels and Insects*, and we did, and loved it as you did. However, reading the book later, I was much more circumspect. Not to put too fine a point on it, I did not love the book. Somewhat didactic, ponderous, and all those bad things—although I did like the Angels part much more than the Insects part. I flatter myself that there is a closer genetic tie to the former than the latter.

I had meant to send you an old *New Yorker* article by Updike, called "Me and My Books," about his relationship with his old books. In the next day or two I'll send it on.

Your friend Marjorie [Anderson] asked me to contribute to the anthology you may do this year, and I am flattered to be asked. *Quill and Quire* liked [the anthology *Writing the Land*], and singled out my contribution, "Evening in Paris," for special mention. How perceptive they are!

Yes, I will reply to Laurence, whom I suspect of being female, don't you? Probably last name. Also perceptive.

Much love,
Blanche

Date: August 13, 1998
Subject: Re: Welcome home!

Blanche,
     Two things before I forget. Viking Penguin will be doing *C.S.* in May of '99 [for the U.S. market]. I have a hunch they'll do rather well with it, sales I mean. Also it is to be translated into Chinese. I'll find out more about that. I can't quite imagine what the Chinese will make of it, but they do have major career separations.
     I'm going to Ottawa on Tuesday for the Association of Commonwealth Universities and am just finishing my speech. About why universities are not great workplaces, and why academics are usually whining about something or other. Wouldn't you think they would be the best places in the world to work?

Much love,
Carol

August 14, 1998
Subject: Great about C.S.

Hi Carol,
     Did I tell you I read two Jennifer Johnston novels, *The Illusionist* and *The Invisible Worm*, and absolutely loved them both? Have you read them?

Love,
Blanche

September 2, 1998

Dear Blanche,
     It's Don's birthday, the 64th—remember the song! "Will ya still love me, will ya still need me, da da da da da." I'm having a small

dinner party tonight, his favourite thing. Seven guests, my favourite number for around the table these days.

We're all fine, launching into the new term somewhat nostalgically, since this is our last Winnipeg year. We had a weekend in Stratford, another occasion when I had to sing for our supper, but well worth it. We were enchanted by *Winter's Tale*, in particular, and I had a lovely brunch with Joan Barfoot and Bonnie Burnard (excellent women both) at the rather eccentric bed-and-breakfast where they put us up.

I've read Alice Munro's new book for review in *Mirabella* magazine [*The Love of a Good Woman*] and am full, once again, of admiration. How boldly and darkly she steps out. Have also read for review vol. 4 of L.M. Montgomery's journals which I've been following since. I feel I know the inside of her head, and maybe that's what I'll end up saying. Also reading Elizabeth Hardwick's new book of essays.

Isn't it amazing that we should both have sent Merna [Summers] a copy of *C.S.* Don and I had dinner with her when she came to Winnipeg for a jury. We adore her, but I honestly don't think she's doing much writing, which is a pity. But who has decreed how many books a writer need write! She is VERY busy living.

Much love to you both,
C

Date: October 9, 1998
Subject: Thanks for the books

Dear Carol,

There was a story of Alice Munro's in a recent *New Yorker* about an abortion doctor and his daughter. I found it so immediate as to be painful—wonder if it is in the new collection. It could be read as a bit of a polemic by the anti-abortion crowd. On the other hand, the ability to create that type of immediacy is a superb talent. So deceptively simple.

Happy 64th to Don. I remember on mine that the kids had a party and played that Beatles song you mentioned—guess

the Beatles thought they'd never get near that age. Ha ha,
everyone!

Love,
Blanche

Date: September 10, 1999
Subject: Re: Iris Murdoch

Dear Blanche,
   Yes, I did read the piece on Iris Murdoch, moving sad, funny.
I was a little uncomfortable about his reporting that he had written
part of a novel of hers [referring to John Bayley, Iris's husband]. My
friend Dave Williamson (who has interviewed them both) looked it
up, and it was only a paragraph or so. I guess, too, I was rattled
that he should write this while she is still alive, but I'm at a loss
to understand my own reaction. I had always heard theirs was a
celibate marriage, but it didn't read that way, did it?
   Be sure to see this month's *Harper's Magazine*, in which several
people—men and women—reply to Francine Prose's piece last
spring on women writers and their general neglect. I'd love to know
your reaction. One of the letters made my feminist hair stand on
end. I don't need all that hair-on-end.

Much love,
Carol

Date: September 24, 1998
Subject: Re: Penguin

Dear Carol,
   At the moment I have an invitation to a book club re *A Celibate
Season*, and three places have asked for readings. Barbara [Perrault]
is going to read Chas's part—the local library here, and Barbara as
city councillor representative who is chairman of the board. So it is
a happy confluence. Also a bookstore in Tofino wants us to read,
and the Women's Liberal Commission. *A Celibate Season* is turning

out to be the sleeper of the year! It will be interesting to find out
how it did, if we ever do.

At the moment we have house guests (make that apartment guests),
Bruce's well-loved cousins from Boston that we enjoy greatly.

Must run. Actually made breakfast! Trauma.

Love,
Blanche

October 1, 1998
Subject: Re: Penguin

Hi Carol,

I'm going this weekend with Leslie, Austin and family to Victoria to
see the da Vinci exhibit. Although I am getting a caregiver in, I feel
guilty about leaving Bruce, but the daughters are quite determined that
I should get a break. The thing is, he's so well now I don't have the
pressing need for a break, hence the guilt. Ah well, some hang-ups never
change.

Recently read a wonderful thing in an old *New Yorker* about the
Koestler marriage,* and the ramifications not only of his wife's suicide
but of the complete abdication of a personal life on her part which
was the harbinger of her suicide. He ties it, rather eerily, to the plot of
Arthur Koestler's much earlier novel, *Darkness at Noon*, which deals
with precisely this conundrum, the morality or otherwise of exercising
such power over another person. Strange but interesting.

Love,
Blanche

Date: October 1, 1998
Subject: Re: Penguin

Blanche,
Of course you need a break. Don't please feel guilty.

---

*Author Arthur Koestler and his wife, Cynthia, committed suicide in March 1983.

I'm starting a new story called "My Mother's Friends." Do you remember your mother's friends? They are so vivid to me, even the ones I never actually met.

Yes, I did read the Koestler piece and found it haunting. I adored *Darkness at Noon* when I first read it, but understand that he went through strange personality changes.

Love,

C

Date: October 1, 1998
Subject: My Mother's Friends

Carol,

Your line "even the ones I never actually met" brought to mind Bruce's story of his mother's telephone friend—I don't think any of them ever met her—named, I believe, Hattie, to whom his mother would talk for a solid hour on all subjects from recipes to how the kids were doing. Love the concept!

Blanche

Date: October 14, 1998
Subject: Book Club

Hi Carol,

Last night I went to West Van to a book club—15 women showed up—and we discussed *A Celibate Season*. They all LOVED IT. They thought it was so current. I wonder if we have tapped some hidden vein that's finally come into its own.

In any case, unbridled enthusiasm. They asked me questions about Jock's motivations and Chas's motivations (I'm not sure what Carol had in mind there, I said, sidestepping neatly, and was furiously inventive over Jock). One thing that did amuse me— they were terribly prudish about Chas's "slip," or whatever. Shocked, not to put too fine a point on it. Has the world passed West Van by? They were ages 35 to 65, I'd say, and I pointed out to them that with Monica Lewinsky* and all, the world is a changed place, but they had their own view of Chas as some sort of paragon and weren't about to allow it. The woman who drove me home asked me what three people could possibly do together, and would one of them have to be a lesbian? Can't say I'd ever thought it through.

Oh yes, and some of the more homemaker types were upset about Jock leaving the children and distancing herself in her job so readily. I asked what they would have thought had it been a man, and they all agreed readily that they would have excused it, and were quite fascinated with the business of role reversal.

These weren't born and bred West Vaners. They were from all over as it was a newcomers' club (up to 4 years' residence), a really nice, interested, empathetic bunch. Who knows? The Yanks may love it.

Cheers!
Blanche

Date: October 15, 1998
Subject: Re: Book club

Dear Blanche,

Aren't people curious in their expectations, at least those of a certain age. I had an e-mail exchange from a local theology student who wondered why we had to resolve the novel with adultery at all. I tried to explain that I thought it was a reality in the world (but then, how would I know!).

Life is a little bit too hectic at the moment, but I'm reading Updike's new book in odd moments. It's delicious. Also *plein de noir.*

Love,
Carol

---

*The woman around whom scandal erupted because of her sexual involvement with U.S. president Bill Clinton.

Date: November 1, 1998
Subject: Updike review, etc.

Hi Carol,

That was a wonderful review in yesterday's *Globe*, but I must say I was relieved when you said that his story about murdering the reviewers was "squirm-inducing" [the Updike novel Carol had reviewed]. I had just finished reading an excerpt from the novel in *The New Yorker* and found the planned murders so squirm-inducing that I couldn't read the details of the final one, but skipped to the end for whatever comeuppance may have come Bech's way.* Which made me wonder at my own reaction— perhaps we identify with characters in stories to such an extent that the absence of normal moral compunction makes us fear our own dark sides. You were so right to say that goodness makes too small a sound in the world.

Oh, and I loved your little finger-wag about voice appropriation. One of the sillier side issues that has surfaced in recent times.

I am reading *Angela's Ashes* **—halfway through, but to my surprise I am not as entranced as the rest of the world seems to be. What did you think? It is of course a wonderfully written and precisely observed memoir, but I have to keep reminding myself that it isn't fiction and therefore different standards apply. I don't know what to think, and may change my mind before finishing.

The girls (my middle-aged daughters, that is) took me to lunch at a superb restaurant today to celebrate my 75th (next Saturday). Oh God! But I can't complain—or, yes, I can and do, but shouldn't.

Love and hi to Don.
Blanche

---

*The protagonist of the story.
**By Frank McCourt.

November 2, 1998
Subject: Re: Updike review, etc.

Dear Blanche,

About squirming over Updike, I think I was made uneasy by the yoking of violence with eroticism, that one drove the other. I kept looking for remorse, but found none. And did you notice that the kind of criticism Bech objected to was exactly what might have been tossed at Mr. Updike? Each example fits beautifully. I asked my French prof friend why the French word *voulu* would have been inflammatory. We finally figured that it has a tertiary meaning: studied. Hardly grounds for murder, but then . . .

Anne went to hear Frank McCourt in Vancouver and was quite thrilled, went home and finished the book, and remains impressed. Our whole book club loved it except for one member (an English prof at U of Winnipeg) who thought the material had not been "processed." It was just dished out without a sense of reflection or an attempt to fit it into the larger world. I wonder if that might have been your objection. I suppose it was the survival element that most people have reacted to. Having lived in England in the early sixties, I do know that these conditions existed then. People in Manchester wore newspapers under their clothes, slept under their overcoats, were hideously superstitious, etc.

In some ways it does have a similar narrative arc to fiction—the worsening condition and then the break to the New World. Interesting that he used criminal means to escape, and felt entirely unreflective about it.

Happy, happy birthday. Are you and Marilyn doing your regular swish lunch? I do hate getting older. I've had a trick knee all week (much improved today) and couldn't help thinking—here we go, into infirmity.

I'm reading, for review, Tom Wolfe's new novel [*A Man in Full*], which is really very carelessly written. And he got $5 million for it. Do I sound jealous?

What do you think of *The National Post?* Did you know Anne is now a columnist, every Tuesday.

Love,
Carol

Date: November 2, 1998
Subject: Cover

Hi Carol,

Thank you for your nice long letter this morning, and I was delighted to hear about Anne's column, will buy the *Post* tomorrow. Actually I was quite impressed with the first couple of editions, although would still stick with *The Globe.* It seems to me that the *National Post* is doing a little more sensational and international stuff, while *The Globe* has quite a Canadian presence now. Time will tell, but that is great for Anne.

Your thoughts about Frank McCourt were revealing to me about myself. I think you are quite right that I've been trying to fit it into some larger context or pattern, a habit I think I picked up from my proximity to the 19th century and its literature. Also have to keep reminding myself that this is autobiography, not fiction. I am getting far more caught up in it at halfway through, and will no doubt do a 180-degree turn in thinking. The poverty I do believe in, and that is exceptionally well done. Comparing it to Urquhart's *Away,* one can see the enormous distance the country has come in social support since the Great Famine. Also the drunken father reminds me of my alcoholic brother, who once replied to a question of why he would do such a thing (drink up long-awaited money) by saying that if he only knew the answer to that one he wouldn't be what he was.

I wrote to say that Penguin sent me the cover [the U.S. edition of *A Celibate Season*] this morning and I think it is great. I like the soft gold autumn colour. What do you think?

All best,
Blanche

Date: November 6, 1998
Subject: Celibate Season

Dear Carol,

Would you believe twenty people turned out to the reading last night in our small local library? And twenty books sold. Also two more engagements on the calendar and an interview with *The North Shore News*. Is this significant, do you think?

Blanche
P.S. Anne's column was great. Good for her!

Date: November 16, 1998
Subject: Re: Celibate Season

Blanche,

I was thrilled to hear about the good turnout. Yes, I have an inkling that we may do well in the States, but who knows?

I'm writing the Tom Wolfe review today. He keeps referring to loins. What are loins, Blanche? Any idea?

Love,
Carol
P.S. Yes, I do like the cover.

Date: November 16, 1998
Subject: Loins

Hi Carol,

The Bible, as I recall, was big on loins, as in someone being the fruit of someone's (usually male) loins. I rather vaguely assumed it was the area "down there." I hope you can think of something nice to say about Tom Wolfe, although if you can't it won't break my heart. I hated *The Bonfire of the Vanities*.

Blanche

12

Journeys

1998–1999

∾And now, with that malevolent timing for which the gods are noted, and with Carol at the summit of what she often referred to as "a very lucky life," I received a devastating phone call. Carol had been diagnosed with an aggressive form of breast cancer.

As I struggled to come to grips with this sideswiping of fate, phone calls and e-mails flew back and forth.

It is a lonely journey we embark on, when illness strikes. Carol was surrounded by a loving and supportive family, friends who cared deeply, a public that made its respect and extraordinary fondness known on every occasion, and even a media that responded with gratitude to her gentleness and to the respect and civility with which she treated everyone, including those most dreaded of beings, the critics. She was one of those rare people about whom one could say with truth: everyone loved her. Love and friendship are the true gifts; they make the aloneness bearable. They cannot dispel it.

As I was writing this I came across a line in *The Globe and Mail* by Rebecca Gagne, the mother of a three-year-old cut down by cancer. "Life is not measured by the breaths that you take, but by the moments that take your breath away," she wrote. Carol too discovered this; she spoke of how she cherished flashes of transcendence each day and of how their radiance lit for a time the path she must follow.

The words to use, the words of comfort, do not come trippingly to the tongues of we who watch. And I too was on a journey of loss, as the drug that had brought my husband back from the confusion of dementia began to lose its power. Nevertheless, knowing Carol's love of letters, I resolved to send her as many as I could manage, full of the kind of light anecdotes she enjoyed.

Sometimes sufferers complain that people do not want to talk about what they are up against. I tried my best to deal directly with her illness. She herself spoke of it without equivocation. Over the years we discussed her treatment, her symptoms, her reactions, her fears and hopes. In deference to the Shields family's wishes many of these passages, both in Carol's letters and in mine, have been deleted.

December 2, 1998

Dear Carol,

I just had an e-mail an hour or two ago from Anne to say that you came through the surgery with flying colours and that everything looks very good. Oh, I'm glad! I had lunch with Anne today and I think it was a good thing, as she was obviously feeling a lot of stress. We talked up a storm about all sorts of things not related to what we were worrying about, and I know I felt much better and I think Anne did.

Now the worst is over. Isn't it odd about Time, the way we plan our future with the assumption that it will all work as laid out. Something like this is a reminder that even the next second is behind an uncertain curtain. I'm sure you felt something like that leading up to the surgery, and now you can plan again for the future without that nagging "what if."

I was telling Anne about last night, when I went to another book club that is doing *A Celibate Season*. This time they were quite young, Anne's age or younger, and unlike the previous book club which was 40- to 50-year-olds, this one thought Jock quite justified in her career wishes. The older crowd were unable to hide their shock that she would behave with the indifference that one would only expect of a man, and yet this younger crowd hadn't even thought of her behaving in any untoward way until I put it to them. Both groups were in West Van and very few of the women in either group worked outside the home. The younger women had small children, and in fact part of my words of wisdom were drowned out by a pet 4-month-old that was being passed from hand to hand.

Interesting how book clubs have now burst upon the scene, attributable, I'm given to understand, to Oprah Winfrey. (I've never watched her, but after seeing her intelligent performance in *Beloved* I must try to do so.) Anyway, it appears that at long last publishers and booksellers are realizing that the female book club is a force to be reckoned with.

I haven't read anything worth noting for some time but hope to remedy that. I know there is a new Anita Brookner book out. I have written a couple of short stories that I entered in the *Prairie Fire* contest, and have a good first draft of the essay for your anthology. Did you find a publisher? I'm assuming that the plan is still on.

Must go and will write again in a day or two. Don't try to answer, conserve your strength and be ready to gallop around at Christmas. Or rather, trot.

Much love,
Blanche

Date: December, 7 1998
Subject: Home e-mail

Dear Blanche,
Your letter just came, and with it, thank goodness, your e-mail. I now have an at-home system (sort of), but must build up my address book again.

I must reread *C.S.* to see how shocking our 3-person scene is! I do remember being mildly worried about it. By the way, I heard someone say yesterday that worry is a form of self-mutilation.

You can see my thoughts are scattered. Anne asked if I minded her appropriating my friend—you—for herself. I replied that I was thrilled. I suppose this used to happen often in a more settled society.

Much love, Blanche, and many thanks for your good, kind, thoughtful and useful words.

Carol

Date: December 8, 1998
Subject: Rotten

Dear Carol,

Anne just e-mailed me to say the news was not what you had hoped. I'm so sorry. I know they are doing wonderful things these days, however, and I am far from discouraged. I feel strongly that you will come through this intact.

I was puzzled at your comment about your being deeply shallow. In fact I burst out laughing, but when you said you did mean this I began to wonder what shallow is. Emotionally shallow—unable to love—scarcely the attribute of a woman with five loving children and a deeply loving husband. Intellectually shallow—I don't think we need to chew that one over much.

If you want deeply shallow, read Sondra Gotleib in Saturday's *Globe.* At the same time, the sneaky little knowledge that we all hate being left out of good parties.

Oh, Carol, what silly ramblings at a time of crisis. I wish I had perfect words, but who does? I will sit down and write another proper letter—I always have the feeling that e-mail is out there for everyone to read, and just because I'm paranoid doesn't mean nobody's following me.

Much love,
Blanche

Date: December 8, 1998
Subject: Re: Rotten

Dear Blanche,

Thanks for your good thoughts.

Anne and I discussed how to keep our senses ironic during an illness, when it is so easy to turn sappy. She suggests I tell people I'm taking it three days at a time, rather than one day at a time. All thoughts welcome.

I have already developed a sort of routine. I used to give the following exam question to my students. "Routine is the killer of the soul." Discuss. Never once did anyone try to defend routine. Perhaps it was the way I posed the question that led to such obedient rebellion.

Love,
Carol

December 10, 1998

Dear Carol,

Routine is the killer of the soul. Isn't it odd that none of your students ever disputed this, as I have always found that routine is what frees me to do the things I want. Perhaps such a belief is a function of the young, when spontaneity is seen to be the exclusive purview of those who haven't yet acquired dreaded responsibilities.

Anyway, I think you are wise to develop a routine, that it could be a salvation, keeping your thoughts focused on tasks at hand and tasks to be done. Also taking it three days at a time is a good idea. On a soberer note, the old saw (one day at a time) has a certain merit. When Bruce was so bad last year I used to try to remind myself that I only had to get through that day, and it did seem to help. The downside is, of course, that one must blank out the future in order to do so, and since the future often contains more excitement than the present, life can get boringly concentrated.

Yesterday was a misty, rainy day, and I trudged on my daily walk with my umbrella, straight white hair flying, wearing my none-too-new Mountain Equipment Co-op jacket and sporting beat-up runners. I wondered if passersby thought I was some sort of zany old crone (I'm not. Am I?). Besides your bad news I was also coping with the death of the woman who was part of the couple we spent that last time with in France. He died a year ago, and she died Tuesday. It wasn't entirely unexpected as she had a dreadful lymphoma, and yet it was unexpected, catching us both off guard. I was very fond of her in spite of our little differences on the trip; we go back fifty years. Once when she was very young she worked for Bruce. Anyway, I was feeling calm and a bit self-congratulatory about how mature I have become in my ability to cope with life's reverses, and went into the market on my way by. A group of kids in about grade 3 were singing, proud parents in silent adoration, a woman conductor bouncing spirit-edly on the soles of her feet, whites, Natives, Chinese, East Indians, a great mixture all praising what they believe is a common God.

As I stood there my eyes suddenly filled with tears, which may sound unremarkable except that I am not inclined to cheap (or even expensive) sentimentality. As I continued on my way I wondered if there are other hormonal changes that affect one in old age, and it wasn't until I was home that the obvious reason hit me: that while I was coping well with the slings and arrows of outrageous fortune, something roiling around below everyday consciousness was grieving. I think this happens; I think people, like my friend who seemed to be making a wonderful adjustment after her husband's death so that everyone exclaimed about it, sometimes grieve at a subterranean level.

I hope this kind of discussion isn't a downer for you, since I am trying for the opposite. Leslie was telling me of an article she read recently about a survey of people who had gone through what you are going through, and the biggest percentage felt that the greatest negative in their treatment was a lack of emotional support from friends and family. I don't know what this says. Is it that friends and family don't know what to say? Or is it that there is no magic thing to say, and platitudes leave the recipient wounded, when what they really need is something for the soul.

Carol, don't try to answer my ramblings except to let me know by e-mail if you get them. Also I wish you would let me know if you are finding my letters at all distracting, or would you rather I went back to occasional e-mails? I guarantee I won't be offended. The name of the game is helping you through a rotten time in your life, as your words of comfort have helped me through bad times. When I had pneumonia, your e-mail was something I looked forward to greatly.

Love,
Blanche

December 16, 1998
Subject: Fan letter

Dear Carol,

Thank you for sending the letter re *A Celibate Season* [a fan letter that questioned the scenes of infidelity]. Maybe we should have left Jock and Chas in the double bed together where they belonged—this seems to be coming back to haunt us. Where is the damned sexual revolution when we need it? From my vantage point via the literature of the day, I thought such shenanigans would merit no more than a discreet yawn or a superior smile at the naïveté of the authors. Does no one believe Updike? Is this a Canadian phenomenon?

I'll write another letter shortly, but for now must decorate the one-foot Norway Pine I bought at vast expense. Should take 3 or 4 minutes.

Much love,
Blanche
P.S. Oh, and many thanks are due you. The archivist at UBC phoned today and said they had evaluated my papers for a donation receipt at $12,000! He took some wind out of my sails by saying, Of course it is the Shields/Howard correspondence that makes it so valuable. I'm grateful, believe me!

Date: December 17, 1998
Subject: Re: Fan letter

Blanche,

I think the problem with the shockable audience is that they've been reading Maeve Binchy and not Martin Amis or Updike. Also the fact that the shocking material comes from two sweet ladies like us—that must take a moment's digestion.

I am happy to have contributed to the economy—re your archive evaluation. Congratulations. We must rev up our correspondence. Happiness arrives in small increments following small deprivations.

Love,
Carol

December 17, 1998

Dear Carol,

Memory rises up at unexpected moments. I suddenly remembered the time when I was 35 and home after having a large benign breast tumour removed. As I went under the anaesthetic, they were convinced that it was cancer—diagnosis wasn't as advanced in those days. They did the biopsy while I was under, after removing the tumour. Imagine, I stayed in the hospital three days! But after your letter I suddenly remembered the little rubber tube that poked out beneath, and my own doctor back in Penticton removing it (had come here to Vancouver for the operation) and how glad I was to be rid of it. Something I hadn't remembered in years.

Out in the middle of the inner harbour there is a barge anchored with three houses on it. I know forestry workers live in houses like this when working in areas near the ocean, and I presumed the houses were just resting there until spring. Then today I saw lights on in the houses—neat little places, complete with gables—and I wondered what it would be like to be out there all winter with water all around, unable to step off to go for a walk. Then I remembered you telling me about the time you lived with five little children in a houseboat

on the Seine. How did you keep everyone afloat? All of which
is *a propos* of nothing, but amusing the way forgotten tidbits surface.

As I walked past the cafeteria attached to an office building,
smokers were huddled outside under the awning, blue hands around
warm coffee cups, and it occurred to me that they are the group
that gets out every day in the fresh air, rain or shine. In about
twenty years, are scientists going to be puzzled about why smokers
are living longer than non-smokers?

As you say, each increment can bring unexpected joy, which should
make one realize something about relativity, although I can't put my
finger on what it is. Much love, and each increment brings us joy too.

Blanche

December 26, 1998

Dear Carol,

The big day yesterday, with its feeling that something magical
should be happening but isn't quite, so that all day one goes about
wrapped in anticipation and not quite living in the normal way.

I have never been able to take Christmas in my stride. As a child
I was wild with the excitement, and when my own children were
young I could scarcely bear the expectation of their excitement when
they opened their presents—the quantity of which I was unable to
curb, with the result that Christmas often resulted in near bankruptcy.
It has taken me years to shed an uneasiness as the day approaches,
with the underlying despair that it means very little now.

I'm making progress, but I think my family finds me trying.
About five years ago I quit doing the dinner, so we all gathered at
Allison's this time. Gregory, now 24, was home for the first time
for Christmas in four years. As you know I am impossibly social
and want everyone to join in merriment, and unfortunately everyone doesn't share my exuberance. Bruce puts it down to the
French ancestry—my father was like that, and his father before, so
I'm told, and my son has these tendencies. The rest of the family
are quieter, more like Bruce. The grandchildren, I'm sure, find me

awfully uncool but they are more tolerant. I suppose to them old age is an unimaginable territory and therefore prone to breed strange creatures. When it is all over I wonder why on earth an illusion like Christmas should muddle an otherwise sensible brain (mine, at least, so I believe). I wonder how you managed yesterday, with children and little ones about when you are probably feeling fairly rotten. I do hope it was a blessing and a distraction.

I have been reading the *Norton Book of Women's Lives* (edited by Phyllis Rose), and this morning was struck by Anaïs Nin and her infatuation with June Miller. What a strange little creature Anaïs was! All of her relations with people were erotic before they were anything else, then friendship might or might not develop. I think with other people it is the other way around, and I doubt that many can swing from man to woman with scarcely a pause as she did. I find it quite unimaginable. What an endless variety of human responses about us!

The women's stories are fascinating, but the smallness of the excerpts drives me mad sometimes. For instance, there is a wonderful bit by Janet Frame, the New Zealand writer, and I could scarcely bear not to know what happened next. I shall get her book out of the library. I guess that's why I like novels, because they go on and on and tell you everything you need to know. The other evening we had quite a fascinating visit with two people that came back into our lives because of Parkinson's. John Nichol was once a senator (Trudeau's first campaign manager) but resigned because he found it boring, and his wife has a dreadful immobilizing form of the disease, so we have made contact because John is fundraising for research. Anyway, we went in for drinks the other night, and he had invited Fran Andras, the widow of Bob Andras who was once a power in the Trudeau cabinet. Both John and Fran are quick-witted, highly amusing, as noisy and opinionated as I am, and we had a quite wonderful time. Old people can be fun! John's daughter Barbara Nichol wrote the wonderful *Beethoven Lives Upstairs*, and another daughter (or maybe the same) often does *Ideas* on CBC. John used to write a syndicated column for many years, and he continues to write. He read us an amusing Gilbert and Sullivan–ish poem he had just finished.

Must go. Hope my babbling is distracting for you, and I wish I could think of the perfect thing to say, but I know there is no perfect thing. Keep fighting, and I'll keep rooting for you. Bruce sends love too, to you both.

Blanche

Date: December 27, 1998
Subject: Re: Greetings returned

Dear friends on 27th December,

What a joy to hear from you. We are loving having our children here, though there is never quite enough time to talk to each one separately—but I have a couple of days to try to establish some time. The girls and I went to a movie last night—imagine? Called *You've Got Mail*, a remake of a 1940s film called *The Shop Around the Corner*. It was corny and charming, but the most fun has been sitting about deconstructing it. Anne and I believe we should have been called in at the last minute for a "story conference." It strikes me that the discourse about films is better and more worthwhile than the films themselves.

Love,
Carol

December 31, 1998

Dear Carol,

I'm sure you read the article in today's *Globe*, about John Bayley and Iris Murdoch. I was quite struck by his statement, "She didn't have a great deal of consciousness of her own," comparing her interior being to what he believes was the case

with Shakespeare, who seemed to live a complex external life
inside his own creations. This had never occurred to me before,
that an imagination could be so fierce and all-encompassing
that the ordinary ego-consciousness was not much in evidence.
Did this seem a strange take on the subject to you? Or have you
thought about it before?

I was also struck (I don't suppose one is stricken—the two
words seem to have evolved quite different meanings) by something in a *New Yorker* article about Elizabeth Hardwick, where
she is quoted as saying, "Women are certainly physically inferior
to men and if this were not the case the whole history of the
world would be different. Any woman who has ever had her wrist
twisted by a man recognizes a fact of nature as humbling as
a cyclone to a frail tree branch." An interesting take on the roots
of feminism and discrimination. It has occurred to me before that
in tracing the lineage of sexual discrimination backwards one
would come up against the undeniable physical fact, the one that
would keep women in their places, but I used to think it too
simplistic. Perhaps not.

Which brings me to the subject matter of the book you and
Marjorie [Anderson] are editing [*Dropped Threads*]. I am
impressed, and also, and probably in common with everyone
who isn't Margaret Atwood, anxious that mine will not suffer
too greatly by comparison. I can't wait to find out what Sharon
Butala will have to say about hypersensitivity to the supernatural
following menopause, or Helen Fogwill Porter on the effects of
being labelled dirty.

I expect the daughters are leaving by now, and I think it was great
that you had the comfort of them while you are adjusting to a new
take on living. The good part is that the new drugs are so much
more effective—I'm hearing heartening stories all over the place.

A very happy New Year to you both.

Much love,
Blanche

Date: December 31, 1998
Subject: Re: Anthology

Dear Blanche,

Your wonderful letter arrived today—and I must tell you that they do cheer me enormously. Christmas! I remember, too, being addled at the thought of Christmas, and nowadays I only feel a quiver of the old enchantment, usually through music. I have a real dislike of Santa Claus, the whole idea, and the representation of the idea. I love cards and notes, though, and perhaps that's reason enough to celebrate the solstice. Such dark and cold days— we need relief.

We are actually going to the New Year's Dinner Dance tonight with a group of very old friends (I can say that after 20 years in Winnipeg). Doubt if we'll make it to midnight, but then I'm not sure we did last year either.

There are so many things in my head these days. I'm grateful that I sleep well.

Much love and thanks. Especially for your shared skepticism about Christmas joy, and for the observation that old people can be fun. And have fun.

Onward,
Carol

Date: January 1, 1999
Subject: New Year's

Dear Carol,

Thank you for your yesterday's e-mail. Imagine you going to the dinner dance! We were in bed by ten-thirty, having slept through *The National,* but I was wakened by ships' horns and shouting at midnight. Promptly went back to sleep—old age has increased one talent in me, that for sleeping.

Wonderful long tribute to Lloyd Axworthy in today's *Globe.* He is a fine person.

I'm so glad you like my letters, as I just fired another one off
yesterday. I feel more comfortable with saying things I don't
necessarily want the world to know in letters rather than on e-mail.
Mistrust of ether, I suppose it's called. So Happy New Year, and
I am glad your head is full of things these days. As it is bound to be,
with the great challenge facing you.

Love as always,
Blanche

January 6, 1999

Dear Carol,

This enclosure is not funny, in fact so unfunny that at first I
debated whether it might be a downer. But on rereading I found so
many astonishing takes on the business of aging that I thought you
would like it. (Mind you, she [Florida Scott-Maxwell] was nearly
ten years older than me when she wrote this, and much older than
you.) I found that her musings about the energy and passions of the
elderly hit a resonance in me, and others of her musing entirely new
and unthought of. What a lovely essay! ["1883–1979," from *The
Measure of My Days*].

I was able to find that *Harper's Magazine* from last September
that you mentioned. The letters regarding women's writing were
extraordinarily thoughtful and most points (the ones I agreed with)
extremely well taken. I liked the idea that a whole body of culture
had been built up around men's writing, giving them a base on
which to build, along with a laid groundwork in the minds of those
who had come to understand that particular take on life. And that
women had been denied this. Yes, it was something to once more
make one froth at the mouth and at the computer and all other
frothing points.

Someone gave us Edith Piaf on CD for Christmas, and as she
belted out "*Rien! Je ne regrette rien!*" I couldn't help wondering if it
could be true that there are people who regret nothing. Even
someone with the chutzpah of Piaf. (Mind you, the things she

wasn't regretting were probably far more exhilarating than the things nice ladies like us don't regret.)

To my surprise, I am finding *Burden of Desire** a really interesting book. It is one of those books that is a page-turner but *sans* clichés and bad writing, which is an achievement. While the writing isn't superb, it is clear and to the point. And his women are believable! (At least so far—only one-fifth of the way through.)

Much love,
Blanche

Date: January 9, 1999
Subject: Your letter

Blanche, your wonderful letter of December 31 arrived, full of ideas and issues and your own self. I was delighted.

The John Bayley piece** is wonderfully interesting. So why am I so uneasy about it? Because she's still alive. And I resented the place where he said he had written a part of one of her books. That should not have been revealed. Yes, I do think people have more or less self-consciousness, the weight and pressure of it. Which is better? It's self-absorption I fear.

[I have] a wonderful book at hand. It is by Diane Johnson and called *Le Divorce*. You will love it. I feel like writing her a fan letter, but settled for naming her as my recent fave book in an *Atlantic Monthly* interview I did yesterday. It is delightful— almost dangerously darling, in fact, which may be why it didn't win a lot of awards. It is clearly written for a reader, to amuse and inform.

Love to you both,
Carol

---

*By Robert MacNeil.
**Regarding looking after Iris Murdoch.

January 13, 1999

Dear Carol,

Last night, as I mentioned in my e-mail, another book club, this time teachers from a local school. All were upset at the infidelity—what is it with this modern world? I doubt that much has changed since Jane Austen.

I agree with you that the John Bayley piece was disturbing. For some reason it bothers one's sense of loyalty, especially while she is still alive. I wouldn't be able to do that either. And yet nowadays people seem to have entered a period when it is considered just fine to tell all. As John Major's cabinet minister (rotten Robin) is finding out.

You mentioned the fear that self-consciousness might turn into self-absorption. I think with a narcissistic temperament that is more than possible (Anaïs Nin again; the journals of Sylvia Plath). However, I think there is the self-awareness of the examined life, surely a good thing. One of the things that attracted me to Jung was his belief that consciousness was the human ability to express the universal unconscious, a sort of raising of awareness of the instinctual life, and he enlarges on this in a strange essay called "Answer to Job."

I do know now, as I get older, that my fascination with things psychological was precisely because of the factors that had caused much mental anguish—panic attacks since a child, anxiety, exaggerated and pervasive fears, extreme lack of self-esteem—and which culminated in a black dogs postpartum depression bordering on psychotic when I was 27. At that time it seemed to me that reading was a tiny lifeline in a universe of unremitting pain, and so I pursued Freud and Jung and anyone else who had a thought in their heads. I know that much of their teachings are now pooh-poohed, and I don't know what helped me, but I do know that gradually one ravening beast after another dropped away. There was no moment when I could have said, Aha! so that was it! Instead there were times when facets of the bad stuff just disappeared, and gradually as my need decreased I lost interest in the search. Was it a journey I made, and have I come out the other end? Or was it a biochemical accident or series of same? Who knows, I don't, only that the inside of my head is peaceful these days. (Also I don't know why I'm telling you this, don't think I have ever told anyone before.)

I finished *Burden of Desire* and thought it workmanlike and quite good, but not superb. Oddly enough his women were strong and believable and the men weren't.

Must go. Bruce's thoughts are with mine in praying for quick recovery.

Love,
Blanche

Date: January 20, 1999
Subject: Re: Florida's wisdom

Dear Blanche,

I am deeply grateful you sent the wonderful essay of Florida's. You thought it might sadden me, but in fact, the only sad part was that she eventually lost faith in books. Her composure struck me as extraordinary, and her honesty and intelligence. One doesn't often see these qualities in combination.

Your letter, arrived yesterday, had so many interesting questions, and don't you think you must be unusual in your age bracket to still be asking questions? Life as a biochemical journey?—of course, a good deal of it must be. Pushed by chemicals and responding to them. Perhaps even impulses of love and goodness occur in particular chemical circumstances. I hate to believe any of this, don't you?

I'm going with a friend this afternoon for a manicure and pedicure, which I honestly believe will be restorative to my spirit.

I loved Rick Mercer's "Talking to Americans" segment this week, when they were on the Harvard campus asking biology students what they thought about the resuming of the seal hunt in Saskatchewan. Oh my.

Love,
Carol

January 24, 1999

Dear Carol,

The other evening Leslie phoned to tell me that you were on television, and I tuned in to our Knowledge Network and was treated to that lovely hour about Susanna Moodie. It was delightful, and I thought everything you had to say was interesting and eminently sensible. Also what M. Atwood said, although I am always bemused, when listening to her, with that flat flat expressionless voice. It is not an accent I recognize as belonging to any part of Canada. I wonder where she got it. You always sound lovely, more Canadian than Atwood. Odd that the reverse is true. Timothy Findley didn't seem quite in the same league.

Yes, I think there is much more to life than a biochemical journey. I think the biochemicals are the modus operandi, just as pentium crystals are for the computer, but I do believe there is some sort of executive director in each of us giving the nod or pulling switches on the required circuit. You wonder if I am unusual in my age bracket in asking questions, and I don't think so. I think what one did while young is what one still does, although less energetically and with a different perspective. Although there are some things I'm less excited about. I used to love to learn things, especially ideas; now I find less intellectual curiosity. Not entirely because I won't be there to know the answer, although that figures in it, but because some vital energy that wanted to figure it all out before I die seems to have given way to a resignation that I won't achieve that goal. You once laughed about my capacity for indignation, and that has weakened.

I am halfway through *Le Divorce* and am grateful to you for telling me about it. It is amusing, literate, totally absorbing and all those good things. Love it. I can see that there is going to be a dark side to it. I love the character that she is writing through. How differently the young look at things compared to my day!

Speaking of which, I don't think I told you that I finally suggested to Beverley [Slopen] that she send *Pen's Way* to Coteau Books. She agreed. I think what I ran into was a form of ageism.

This possibility was brought home to me by those *Globe and Mail* and *Elm Street* magazine articles about the search by young publishers for young authors. When I'm out to these various book clubs re *A Celibate Season,* they always ask what I'm doing lately, and this adds to the frustration. I'd like to see it published in my lifetime, or so I tell myself. The truth is that one is never satisfied with whatever goal one sets. I can remember at one time thinking if only I had one story published in a literary mag, I would be satisfied, but now, having had many, I'm not. Do you feel satisfied, having won all the prestigious prizes you have? Or do you think you'll have to do the Booker Prize to be truly satisfied? Dissatisfaction, the human condition, probably a great evolutionary prod.

Well, must stop rambling. If you get tired of my longish missives, do say so, otherwise I do enjoy this rare chance to keep up to date. Hope the manicure and pedicure were restorative. I don't think I've ever had the latter, and can scarcely remember ever having the former, but I think you are wise to do anything you can to make yourself feel better.

All love, and hi to Don.
Blanche

February 1, 1999

Dear Blanche,

How I do adore your wonderful letters—you call them rambling, but that is what the best conversation is, don't you think? I'm so glad you are liking *Le Divorce,* since I always feel that suggesting books to people is like blowing in the wind. She smudges the ending, I think. Why must a writer bring on the guns?

I'm glad you liked the Susanna Moodie film. I was just a talking head, but I am now a sort of partner with Patrick Crowe, the director, who wants to do a feature film (Jane Austen kinda thing) on Moodie. I don't know why I get into the projects in my current state of health, but somehow one has to go forward.

Each incremental step toward normalcy is meaningful. Don and I plan 6 days in La Jolla. I've never looked forward to a holiday so much. The days go.

Much love,
Carol

February 1, 1999

Dear Carol,

I was so glad to hear from you and know you are soldiering on with spirit.

I'm also glad that you like my rambling letters, as I find I look forward to writing them and sort of gather odd thoughts during the week. I was waiting to write until this evening because this morning I was invited to talk about the creative process (what do I know?) to a creative writing group at the West Van Seniors Centre. As I knew they wouldn't necessarily have read *A Celibate Season* (I was right), I asked Barbara [Perrault] if she would like to come along, and we did our little gig in two parts, opening and closing. This gave them something tangible to ask questions about, and they were interesting and some of them quite knowledgeable. They put together a booklet of their own writings each year and gave me one, so I'll be interested to read it.

Saturday night we went to an anniversary party for old friends. Their son, Charlie Campbell Jr., has been editor of *The Georgia Straight* and has now moved to take the editorship of *Queue*, which will combine with the former *Vancouver Review* that Max Wyman used to edit. By the way, Wyman wrote a sprightly column lately of his fight to outwit the heart problems that pushed him into retirement (exercise, health food, etc.). Anyway, Charlie Jr. was asking me about books and I told him about the Chinese buying *A Celibate Season* and he said to me, "Oh, did you know Carol Shields has cancer?" I answered that I knew it but was astonished that he did, and he said that the press knew but had decided to keep quiet about it. Which shows a great deal more principle on the part of the media than I've been inclined to give them. I am glad that they are going to be circumspect; I'm sure these things are tough enough to deal with. (Also shows how well liked you must be. If you were at all threatening, they'd be on it like gangbusters.)

I did love *Le Divorce* all the way through, but like you I thought the plot a little too contrived at the end. She didn't need to do that; it held up beautifully on its own. But, oh, what a wonderful study in sociology it is! The take on the French and the Americans, the assumptions held by different cultures. Loved it.

Wonderful that you are off to La Jolla. I can believe that you are looking forward to it! I just hope that sun shines and shines and that you laze around the pool and find reams of great novels to pass the time. I suppose until chemo is over I can't wish you nice accompanying gin and tonics, but that will come.

I think that is great that you are going to work on a film about Susanna Moodie. It is a perfect antidote to get into those projects that really interest you, while avoiding all that might be put in the duty category (good works, sitting on commissions, that sort of thing). In my opinion—which is not generally sought by the medical profession, but what the hell—as long as you don't push yourself too much, interesting projects will be good for your health. Nothing could be more detrimental than having too much time to think about it. I'm a great believer in listening to your body so that you know when you're getting too tired or taking on too much, and otherwise have always thought one should go for whatever is going.

I am reading the book of short stories that Denise Chong edited and just finished "Bluebeard's Egg" by Atwood. Of course I'd read it years ago, but I was struck again by how very good it is. Most of the other stories in the collection are truly wonderful. I am looking forward to rereading your "Hazel" story, which I remember quite vividly from the collection it was in originally. Also a wonderful story.

Speaking of anthologies, I have pretty well finished my essay and am now nitpicking. So will send it off [for the anthology *Dropped Threads*]. Anne e-mailed me to say she was getting on to hers now.

I thought her column in which she talks (obliquely) about the effect of cancer on the family was a wonderful, warm and moving piece of work.

Much love,
Blanche

February 12, 1999

Dear Carol,
    When I reread "Hazel" in the anthology I told you about, I loved it! Had forgotten some of the details, but my, that is an accomplished story. I had always thought "Mrs. Turner Cutting the Grass" was my favourite, but this is a close second.
    I am reading *The God of Small Things** and have mixed feelings. Perhaps it is unfair, but the dark cloud of premonition with just enough hints to know how devastating they will be to the protagonists I'm finding quite pressuring. It's interesting that now that I'm older I am less able to handle the sadness of life (I think) than when younger. I seem to remember breezing through Raskolnikov murdering the old lady in *Crime and Punishment* with scarcely a tremor, and yet now I don't want terrible personal things to happen. Books like *Le Divorce*, treated with wry humour and social satire, are far more my cup of tea. I wonder why that is? Perhaps as one gets older there is a greater feel about the preciousness of life and the importance of children, and more awareness of the fleeting nature of happiness, whatever. The writing is, of course, great, and the background in India a suitable mix of squalor and detachment, but . . . I may feel differently by the time I finish.
    Well, Congress gave us a great Valentine present in finishing off the impeachment trial. What a strange melodrama that has been! Many learned articles on what all that will mean and does mean, but I was quite struck by one today that said it was a good-sized blow to the Christian right, that it shows the U.S.

---

*By Arundhati Roy.

is shedding its puritan background and this may mean a great depletion in their power. Also a great *New Yorker* article from September of '98 about how Clinton courted votes from a feminist lawyer named Molinari who wanted amendments that would allow the background of the accused to be admissible in court. If he hadn't helped her to get that legislation through, his own previous records, Paula Jones et al., wouldn't have been allowed as evidence in the case. Something vaguely Shakespearean about that.

We are off to the Vancouver Playhouse tomorrow to see *Skylight* by David Hare. Everyone tells me it is excellent—Fraidie said it had intelligent dialogue and things to make you think, which is both good and bad.

Am busy looking into the geriatric cruise scene—I figure Bruce could do nicely on an Alaska cruise that starts and ends in Vancouver, not much hassle when the cruise ships do their thing just across the harbour from us. And I could use a holiday myself.

Well, must go and phone my youngest granddaughter who is ten today. (Stephen's youngest.) The others are shooting through the roof and regard us with tactful (but polite) amusement. Jacqueline, who is 21 now, helped me bottle my wine this week, in return for two bottles. Sounds a bit cheap, I know, but I loan her the car too when I'm not using it. Look after yourself and e-mail me when you are safely home.

Much love,
B

Date: February 16, 1999
Subject: Re: My essay

Don and I are packing for CALIFORNIA, YIPPIE. Six days in the sun (we hope).

Love to you both,
Carol

March 2, 1999

Dear Carol,

I thought the enclosed (and ancient) *New Yorker* article about the re-emergence of the narrative short story was very interesting. The only thing is, this was written in 1996 and I don't recall seeing a lot of such stories in the *N.Y.* in the meantime, although there have been some.

The play I told you we were going to see, *Skylight*, by David Hare, was exceptionally good. It's rare to go to a play these days with witty social commentary about class and poverty and all that stuff, the antagonist to the teacher-type lady in London slums being the capitalist and his flaunting of the obvious success of capitalism in enhancing societies, and reminded me of Shaw, except that he kept enough sexual tension going in it to rivet eyes and ears.

Our social life these days is modest. Tuesday night I gave The Dinner Party From Hell. It started with coming events casting their shadows before, in that Monday I went shopping for TDPFH. It was one of our wild storm days, wind and rain, so I went early to Park Royal where I knew a nice little parking place quite sheltered from both, and lo—a good spot. After piling $183 in a shopping buggy I whipped open my purse for my Visa and—no Visa. (I had left it in a restaurant that Fraidie and I went to on Saturday.) They said they would take a cheque, so with antagonistic looks piercing my uncalm from those lined up at the checkout, I wrote the cheque and dived into my purse for my driver's licence, and lo!—you guessed it. I had put it in another purse last week. They said they would keep the stuff in the cooler, and I went out to the car and stared at the rain and did angst, when I thought, I'll bet they will accept the insurance documents, and they did.

The next night the guests arrived very promptly. One couple who are usually the meekest and mildest people in the world arrived with very flushed faces, and I suspect an argument had taken place on the way. [The other man drank] a lot of red wine. A whole lot.

Bruce can't help me much now, as you know, and he got up to say something to me and the guests all thought I wanted them at the table. En masse they rushed to the table, and I got rattled and pushed the buns into the oven where they immediately burst into flame and little bits of carbonized paper bag flew about and into the chicken. I slammed the oven shut before the smoke alarm went off and was able to rescue all but two irretrievably burned buns, and by now flapped completely I served the (baked, previously frozen) potatoes and chicken in the kitchen, [the] salad and vegs on the table. Everyone attacked the food as though recently released from a concentration camp, and I poured more wine and dug my fork into my potato—ice cold. Chicken only barely warm. (Bruce thinks he accidentally turned the oven down when he thought he was turning off the timer.) No one would let me warm them in the microwave, and the dinner proceeded in temporary masticating silence.

The odd thing is that usually, knowing Bruce can't help much, the guests at least look after pouring wine, helping with coffee, and serving dessert, but tempers had risen to the point where everyone just sat and handed me glasses, cups, plates, etc. Soon the noise level was such that I expected neighbours to knock at any moment, and then, to my subsequent sorrow, the mild woman of the sensible couple started, quite uncharacteristically, to dump all over the Nisga'a treaty [the breakthrough land claims settlement with the Nisga'a tribe in B.C., which was to be settled by referendum]. It is one of the remaining things I feel strongly about, and soon the battle was joined by all. In the end nobody seemed able to leave without a declared winner, and it was nearly 11 (started at 6:30) when they edged towards the door. Our final view was of them still shouting as they made their way down the corridor. Needless to say I couldn't sleep worth a damn, and also needless to say no one has phoned to thank me for the lovely party.

Had an interesting e-mail today from the archivist at UBC who said that one of your daughters works at UBC now and has been looking at our letters, deposited there by me. Did you tell me that Meg (or was it Catherine) is now at UBC? Anyway, I don't think we ever wrote anything we wouldn't want daughters to read, but in case you didn't know or are uneasy about this,

I thought I would let you know. It is fine with me, although
I guess I misunderstood the rules when I sent my stuff to UBC. It
was such a bad time and we were moving, so I didn't clarify things
like how long before researchers could look at them. Let me know
if you have any problem (not with daughters, I'm sure you don't,
but with others) because I believe copyright rests in the hands of
those who wrote letters, not received them (or have I got it
backwards?) and I will try to put some restrictions at least on your
letters. (I do mean this, that I am perfectly comfortable with it, so
not to worry unless you aren't.)

I mentioned to you that I was reading *The God of Small Things*,
and I never did find myself entranced, although thought it well
done. A little pretentious and overwritten in places. But a book
I was absolutely fascinated with—although it is difficult reading at
times, so wrenching—is *Blindness*, by José Saramago who won the
Nobel Prize. My, it is masterful.

I have gone along at length. Am longing to know if you are
doing well, or at least bearing up under all the awfulness.

Love,
Blanche

Date: March 10, 1999
Subject: Re: Anxious

Dear Blanche,

A ton of stuff accumulates when one is away. But I'm doing just
fine. We're heading off to Victoria on Friday for a deans' conference
and coming over to West Van for Sunday and Monday night.
Sunday night all the children will be there for a housewarming. I'm
hoping you can drive over on the Monday sometime, but know this
isn't always easy. I'll phone you when we arrive. Your letters cheer
me on, dear friend.

Love,
C

March 23, 1999

Dear Carol,

I was so glad to see you and felt mightily reassured to find you
bearing up so well and looking fit.

Last night I was at another book club for *C.S.*, this time a small
group of about seven highly intelligent teachers. I thoroughly
enjoyed myself, found they are discerning readers, and also found—
to occasional chagrin—that they are close readers, given to quoting
Chas and Jock all over the place and with their books stuffed with
yellow Post-it markers. The average age would be between 40 and
50, boomers all. They all were greatly sympathetic to Jock and her
ambitions, although there were some who thought she should have
been less eager to leave home and family. They thought Chas the
perfect husband, although one of them exploded in wrath at the way
everyone rushed in to help him. Interestingly, just as other groups
have done, they wondered how on earth we had got it so right,
about the perils and occasional growth brought about by separation.
One woman who does face a good deal of separation when her
husband works elsewhere thought we were dead-on, and this has
been a common theme with every group. Are we smart, or what?

Again, the adultery hurt them. I was going to say shocked, but
they weren't shocked, they agreed that this would be a hazard, so I
think *hurt* is the right word. They didn't want it to happen. One
woman complained that there wasn't enough foreshadowing and she
felt cheated, but another woman jumped in with chapter and verse of
all the foreshadowing she had found in each of their lives, instances of
Austin being helpful beyond the normal call of duty, etc. They were
all curious about our process and felt that it was exceptionally timely
(this after the 12 or so years since we wrote it), especially the use of
letters as a vehicle for the story. Everyone tried to get me to say that
the marriage was saved, but I managed to hedge and say that their
guesses were as good as mine, but I thought probably it was saved.
Anyway *C.S.* seems to have hit a resonance here in Vancouver.

We went to a couple of good plays, one an amateur production
of *A Funny Thing Happened on the Way to the Forum* (exceptionally

well done) and the other the Playhouse production of *Tartuffe*, which was funny and original. Somebody named David King had rewritten it in a modern idiom and it was very funny.

Am between novels now, which leaves me feeling as though friends have deserted me. I want to try to get Anita Brookner's *Visitors*, which I understand is finally out in paper.

The weather continues unsettled but not quite as unsettled as before, and a few brave cherry blossoms have ventured to open. Much love and get well!

Blanche

April 10, 1999

Dear Carol,

Another book club Wednesday night re *C.S.* Our favourite little bookstore has now sold 60, with 12 on order! For her this is some sort of record. This crowd were boomers all, and a very hyper lot so that I was tired out before long, as they got so enthusiastic they interrupted one another and me with arguments and carried on private feuds in the corner. They weren't unlike the others, again hurt by the adultery. One woman seemed to express what the rest thought when she said, of course that's what one would expect, but they hadn't wanted the illusion to be destroyed, they wanted to believe in possible perfection. The death of the romantic myth sort of stuff. When I said, how about Updike? they said, oh, yes, but they didn't identify with Updike the way they had with Chas and Jock. To them Chas and Jock seemed like real people, next-door neighbours, friends, and so they wanted everything to turn out right for them. I'm beginning to think the average person in Canada, and probably the U.S. too, is nowhere as world-weary and disillusioned as the media would have us believe, and that happy fifties myths are alive and well, along with a decent quota of faithfulness and integrity and honesty.

When I got Brookner's *Visitors* I realized I'd already read it, but I reread it with, if anything, more satisfaction than the first time. She got the boredom that often accompanies age just about right.

It made me think that the thing I miss most is plain ordinary fun, whether the fun of intelligent conversation about books or anything else, or the plain fun of parties and being able to laugh and drink and not worry about the unpleasantness of the middle of the night nor whether one is upholding sufficiently the dignity of age. I think that I of all people shouldn't be whining, especially to you, but there is a dearth of the kind of things that are fun when young, like suddenly deciding on a nice day to hike through the woods or tear off to a show or whatever.

Never mind, bleat finished. We have done some good things lately. Allison and Dave took us to a charming Brazilian movie called *Central Station*, if you get a chance to see it it's worth it. Tomorrow Bruce and I will try for the matinee of *Shakespeare in Love*, which I hear is very good.

At the moment I'm reading *Madame Bovary* once more for our book club. I am astonished at how well Flaubert got into the mind of a young and rather shallow woman, and how well he understood the boredom she must have felt and that many young women must have felt, when their options were so limited. Especially the shallow ones— no, maybe that's unfair. Anybody without some external interests is going to be bored in the constricted environments they were forced to live in. I thought of the woman in *Palace Walk* [Naguib Mahfouz] who was not in the least shallow, but who also yearned for a bit of stimulation of the outside world. Strange, the threat that women's freedom posed in that world, and still does, to some extent. Oh dear, isn't this Kosovo thing heart-wrenching? I feel for Lloyd Axworthy, who must hate the necessity of dropping the bombs, and yet I understand the futility and necessity of dealing with dictators like Milošević. There is never any easy answer, in the face of human nature at its worst.

We both think of you both much of the time, and pray that all is proceeding well and that your strength will return quickly once this is over.

Much love,
Blanche

Date: April 16, 1999
Re: Order of Canada

Blanche! Thank you for liking my swish black hat [as shown in a newspaper photo of Carol receiving the Order of Canada] designed and made here in Winnipeg by our famous Maria.*

I am thrilled that you are seeing so many readers for *Celibate Season*. Did we misunderstand the impact of adultery, do you think? Or the readership who hungers, apparently, for innocence?

I was interested in what you said about the boredom that sometimes comes with age, the lack of exuberant moments. I really appreciate your telling me this, since it seems to be a forbidden subject. Why? I wonder. It was once forbidden to talk about labour pains as real pain. In the same way, perhaps someone (???) believes we must perceive old age as a jolly and contemplative time of small cherished moments. Hmm.

Love to you both,
C

Date: April 22, 1999
Subject: Honours and C.S.

Dear Carol,

A lovely little article about you in this morning's *Vancouver Sun*, re the first Carol Shields Winnipeg Book Award. How lovely to have that happen! And Merna [Summers] tells me she heard via Joan Clark that you had received a Guggenheim Fellowship. Is that right? Wonderful.

Yesterday I got the *Celibate Season* from New York, and initially I was a little disappointed that it seems so slight in comparison to the Canadian version. Smaller, and finer paper. Allison, however, thinks it is just right to grab and put in the purse.

Amanda says there will be a great ad in *The New York Times* on May 9th. I owe you, Carol, Big Time! I had never hoped to have

---

*Maria's Hat Design.

my name appear in the N.Y. Times, paid ad or otherwise. Much love to you both.

Blanche

April 25, 1999

Dear Carol,

After my gut-wrenching bout of stomach flu I'm finally back in the letter-writing mode. Interesting, when one gets deathly ill like that and especially at my advanced age, all of a sudden the face-to-face intimations of mortality attack. It made me think of the first time I realized how alone one is after all, in spite of all the loving and concerned dear ones. It was during my first labour, when Allison was born, a long and very painful back labour, and all of a sudden the starkness of that knowledge, that in the long run these things are faced alone, confronted me for the first time. When you are young there has always seemed to be an interventionist body or bodies between you and that certainty, parents, husband, dear friends, concerned relatives, and suddenly they drop away and leave you with nothing but your faith or lack of it. Odd how such forgotten memories will surface, like Proust's madeleine, when sights and smells or retching bring them back.

Does the time come, I wonder, when a philosophical distancing actually takes place? I'm sure it does, since my Aunt Blanche in her last years kept saying she was ready and more than ready, but I realize that I am most definitely not sanguine about it yet.

Leslie phoned today to say that they had accessed Amazon.com and there is an early review of *A Celibate Season*, mostly positive. They say the writing is interesting enough to overcome the difficulties of the epistolary novel, and several other nice things (this second-hand over the phone). She says it ends by saying that even though the plot is mediocre (ha!) it is definitely worth reading for the writing.

I'm so glad to know that you are proceeding with your plans for England this coming year, and then what a nice feeling of closeness it will give me to know that you are in Victoria.

I'm reading *The River Midnight* by Lilian Nattel and am enormously impressed. She has reconstructed village life in Poland at the turn of the last century so remarkably that you feel as though you know and understand the motivations of men and women, and about their day-by-day living. She has also done a remarkable job of interweaving plots, forward and backward, and yet never letting them become confusing.

Spring is raising morale and probably lowering morals. (Go for it while you can, I say.) I hope the new novel is struggling along through all this—I can hardly wait for the first read.

Much love,
Blanche

Date: April 30, 1999
Subject: Jane Austen

Dear Blanche,
Your wonderful letter arrived via classic mail yesterday. Hope you're really over that terrible flu; the misery of ordinary flu is astonishing.

We go from day to day, and I have to say that the time is rushing by. The weather is heavenly, which makes me feel sanguine and peaceful about the future.

I work a little at Jane Austen, but find I'm working at half my usual speed. A page a day feels like progress. But I rather like the idea of being surrounded by source materials and going about the work in a serious way. I'm trying to fuse my own impressions of the novels with the historical spine of her life, and sometimes feel I'm taking liberties.

Cheers and love,
Carol

❧ There was good news about some of Carol's tests, and I wrote to express my happiness.

Date: May 3, 1999
Subject: Re: Wonderful!

Dear Blanche,

Many, many thanks for your good wishes. Now we can PLAN. And we are.

Are you thriving? You didn't say. I'm working on Jane Austen today. There is such frustration working with a writer who lived before the age of photography, recordings, etc.—in the unreachable past. And all her relatives closed the information circle on her so quickly—dear Aunt Jane.

Much love,
Carol

Date: May 10, 1999
Subject: Jane Austen

Dear Blanche,

I'm at the university today working on Jane Austen and feeling better than I've felt in some time. Despite the rain and cold winds, I'm feeling buoyant. Anne spent the weekend with us, a leg of a business trip, and it was heavenly. Sara's baby is due this week; hard to think of anything else when the phone rings.

Love,
Carol

May 10, 1999

Dear Carol,

You ask if I am thriving, and, yes, thank you, I seem to have been a great deal better than before since my rotten flu. I wonder why that is; it's almost as though there is some sort of rhythm to ailments, that the body stores up in negatives and then it all breaks loose in the ignominy of illness, and then we start again. I dare say this is fanciful (aren't all theories?) but for some reason I do feel as though a plate got wiped clean. Perhaps an adjustment to Bruce and the breakdown of his health took me a long interior time, the way people do when adjusting to the death of a dear one; in a way deep-seated changes such as we have gone through are somewhat like mini-deaths. The old order changing more radically than we are prepared for.

Today the sun at least shone and I met a friend and we went walking on the West Van seawall, then lunch at Capers where they serve strange mixtures of organic plants and manage to make them delicious. For some reason the walk and the sparkling day and the gentle sea and the bursting rhododendrons made me full of some *joie de vivre*, as though the ability to notice and enjoy had just returned after a long absence. Daughters have showered me with Mother's Day food of late, and this weekend Stephen and his eldest, Peggy, are coming down here as Peggy (age 12) just won the [award for] public speaking in French for the northern zone and will compete here against other French immersion students. All the grandchildren are thriving wonderfully and getting on honour rolls and winning sports and piano competitions, to the point where I am ashamed to brag about them. At some point we must have done something right while raising their parents.

I am reading *Captain Corelli's Mandolin* (Louis de Bernières) at the moment and finding it quite delightful. Funny and poignant at the same time, also an education on the situation in Greece after the war. Have you read it?

Much love,
Blanche

May 18, 1999

Dear Blanche,

Your May 10th letter just arrived and I want to get off a word or two on this stunning spring day.

Among our various chores is the clearing of our two offices. I can take my time, and I intend to. Almost every day I work on the Jane Austen project. I've discovered biography does not have nearly the truth of fiction, but does have other rewards. I feel as though I'm sitting here sewing together the various pieces of her life. And tossing in the odd heretical theory too. She is oddly positioned in the just barely unreachable past.

I will get to *Captain Corelli's Mandolin* soon; so many people have recommended it to me. I've just finished Pat Barker's latest [*Another World*], and it doesn't quite stick together at the end, but is full of writerly bites that stir my envy. She's very brave about writing ugly physical stuff, which I back off from. There is no joy in this book, though, not one moment, and we do have joyful moments, don't we? Like your walk on the seawall and the return of response.

Much love,
Carol

May 18, 1999

Dear Carol,

Had Jan Drabek and Joan over for lunch today. We hadn't seen them since they returned here to retire, after more glamorous pursuits like being ambassador to Kenya and then Albania, and head of protocol for the Czech Republic. Interesting tales to tell! They have retired in Yaletown.

Re *Captain Corelli's Mandolin*: Much of it was wonderful reading, but much of it wasn't, in that it was overwritten (for my taste) re Greek history. No question though that he is a terrific writer. I was interested in what you had to say about Pat Barker. I haven't read her latest, but did read the trilogy starting with *Regeneration* (which I thought brilliant) and you are right, she certainly doesn't shield us from the nastier aspects of being human. Yes, yes, there are wonderful, redemptive aspects!

I am now reading Alice Munro's *The Love of a Good Woman*, although I've already read most of the stories elsewhere. God she's good, isn't she? I finished a short story recently that I was priding myself on as being in the style of an Alice Munro story, and as soon as I read the first story of the collection I felt like a megalomaniacal upstart to even imagine such a thing.

Many, many congratulations on struggling through the last six months with courage and humour. Will you keep the Winnipeg apartment while in Europe?

Much love,
Blanche

Date: June 1, 1999
Subject: Happy Birthday!

Dear Carol,

I hope you have a wonderful birthday tomorrow, that you are now able to drink wine again, and that you imbibe same with a delicious dinner. What more can anyone ask? Thank heaven that awful year is behind you and sunny foreign skies ahead.

Much love,
Blanche

Date: June 2, 1999
Subject: Re: Happy Birthday!

Dear Blanche,

Thank you for your birthday wishes. So far it has been a splendid day—am just back from lunch with two cronies. Had breakfast with Don who presented me with lovely earrings (we'd picked them out together a few days ago), will be going out to dinner with another couple, then back here to dip into a cake another friend has baked—I do feel I've had more than my share of earthly happiness and friendship. And I feel so much better, stronger. Thank you for your advice to live it up. You can see I am doing so. I did tell you—didn't I?—that Sara had a baby daughter, Hazel, on the 21st. All is well.

Love to you both,
Carol

June 2, 1999

Dear Carol,

I'm enclosing an article which struck me because of the different take Stan Persky had on John Bayley writing about Iris Murdoch while she was still alive. An act of startling, irrational bravery, he calls it. Interesting, isn't it, the differing eye of the beholder.

Delighted to hear of your new granddaughter. Hazel, what a pretty name. Old-fashioned, I suspect coming back into new fashion as so many names are. What fun, to see and hold a new little life!

I'm plodding along with the things I do, much volunteer time for the arts commission* which I enjoy. Bruce hasn't been quite so well lately, but continues content and like his old self. He can't do many things, but we manage the odd show and play, and I have people for lunch reasonably often. I don't have as much time to write as I would like, but when does one ever?

Allison and Dave are in Montreal right now, and on the plane down there she was leafing through a *People* magazine and found and purloined and sent me the little blurb about *A Celibate Season*. I liked the word "poignant."

Love,
Blanche

June 18, 1999

Dear Blanche,

Just a short note to enclose with this letter from a dental hygienist/journalist who wrote me a few years ago about all the teeth references in my books. I was astonished, had no idea I was so dentally obsessed. But this letter, as you can see, refers to your own references.

---

*North Shore Arts Commission.

Many thanks for the article re Iris and John. I seem to be the only one in the world who has doubts about this undertaking, but then I've not read the whole book yet.

Love to you both,

C

❧In the enclosure Carol sent from Lois Hirt of Beverly Hills, she flagged all the references to teeth in *A Celibate Season* and to the character who had decided to be a dental hygienist. The references were legion, and left Carol and me astonished. I replied for both of us, saying:

I, too, am astonished. It has set me to wondering about teeth and the fact that there are so many everyday expressions that involve teeth. We say things like "flying in the teeth of convention," "he bared his teeth," "he gritted his teeth," "he fought tooth and nail," using teeth as metaphors for something courageous or fearsome. I wonder if by chance it relates back to some subconscious primitive animal time, when teeth were the only weapons at hand? (What we fear from animals is being bitten.) Or does it tell us that in assessing our fellow humans, one characteristic of the face that impresses is the mouthful of gleaming and potentially dangerous teeth.

Thank you very much for taking the time to write such an amusing letter. I'm sure Carol and I will both be much more conscious of the place of teeth in metaphor in our future writings, and very good luck with your dental column.

Date: June 17, 1999
Subject: Pen's Way

Hi Carol,

You will be glad to know that Coteau has made an offer on *Pen's Way*. Needless to say I'm thrilled.

Much love,
Blanche

∿ Carol phoned to congratulate me, and also gave me the news that *C.S.* would soon be reviewed in *The New York Times.*

Date: June 22, 1999
Subject: Yippee!

Dear Blanche,

We weren't able to get a *New York Times* at the airport the day you phoned, but my subscription copy came the next day. Oh my, how lovely it was [the excellent review of *A Celibate Season*]. I'm thrilled and don't think we could have asked for anything better, this being a paperback.

Don's retirement weekend was superb. Meg gave a most wonderful, funny and touching speech—there were many excellent speeches. I do believe he was enormously pleased. And ready for THE NEW ERA.

Love,
C

June 27, 1999

Dear Carol,

I agree with you that *The N.Y. Times* review was wonderful. I particularly liked the ending, about closing the window on the lives of those interesting people. Also, he had one insight that no one had brought up before, in spite of its obviousness: that while Jock was off learning about the struggles of women in poverty, Chas was busy dealing with the women in need who had sought refuge with him. At one of the book clubs I went to not long ago, one of the women brought a new insight that hadn't come up before: she said she wasn't surprised about the threesome sex (which remains uppermost in everyone's mind) but she was disappointed in Sue for going along with it. It just didn't jibe with the kind of person Sue had shown herself to be up to that point. I must say I had never thought of that and had no answer, other than too much wine.

Beverley is busy negotiating with Coteau. It appears that they have now agreed to publish *Pen's Way* in the spring of 2000, which is much more than I'd hoped for.

By the way, I had a lovely note from [editor] Marjorie Anderson saying that you both liked my essay ["The Anger of Young Men"]. This was a great relief to me as I found the subject pretty slippery when I started to deal with it, and was anxious not to sound like a raging feminist (I am one, but not raging at the moment).

All is pretty well here. Bruce has had some problems of late, but not too serious. For some reason I am suffering from a recurrence of something that has plagued me most of my life, namely anxiety. Seems odd that it would upgrade itself right now when so many good things are happening, doesn't it? The old consciousness of age, which I can't shed, and fear about not living to enjoy whatever success there is. It first began to manifest itself by prolonged heart palpitations when Bruce first started to have real problems, and while I am assured the palpitations are not harmful, in the last week they have expanded to occasionally involve a speeding heart, which can be harmful. I wish I knew something about meditation techniques or self-hypnosis or any of those other reputed soothers, but I've never taken the time to figure them out. I keep thinking of those yogis who are reputed to be able to control their heartbeat. Like you I'm good at concentrating and blocking things out during the day, but the white nights are another thing, as you no doubt know all too well and for much more reason than I. I feel somewhat foolish even talking about it, but oddly enough also better, as, like you, I've never discussed these things much with anyone. Did you, during the course of your illness and cure, get involved with any of these techniques, and if so, were they at all helpful?

Much love,
Blanche

Date: July 1, 1999
Subject: Heart

Dear Blanche,

Many thanks for your last letter, which, I confess, both Don and I felt we should reply to at once. The question about heart rate, etc. I had had the problem of racing heart for a couple of years, but took it rather metaphorically, and found with a little quiet and with breathing exercises I could control it. I have been told that this heart rate problem is quite a common ailment and not really serious as long as it is attended to. But I—Don too—we both think you must get yourself on some medication for it right away. I do think that you will be much more at peace if this is controlled.

My dear friend, you have been through far too many emotional arcs in recent years. I hope you don't underestimate the stress you've supported during this time, and I don't suppose for a minute that attending to this one medical problem of your heartbeat will relieve all that troubles you, but it will, I can't help think, remove one area of concern.

We are surrounded by family, here for Sara's wedding, all our daughters. Do you know that John and Audrey now have a little adopted daughter, Grace, a great and wonderful surprise. We will see them and her on Saturday morning when they arrive for the ceremony.

I'm doing well. I feel stronger every day. And I'm thrilled with the success of *C.S.*

Much love,
Carol
Don is now officially retired!

Date: July 1, 1999
Subject: Thank you

Dear Carol,

Thank you so much for your encouraging and concerned letter. I haven't had any more problems—other than minor palpitations—

but was at a dinner party the other night at old friends', Monica and Michael Angus. We got on the subject of palpitations (during the organ recital) and Thelma Finlayson, who is 85 and still goes out to SFU twice a week to supervise graduate students, gave me a pointer of a place in the brow to press. I was skeptical, of course, although Thelma is nothing if not scientifically minded. However, it has seemed to work, and Monica (psychology PhD) insists I try her relaxing tape, which I will pick up today. Michael—a retired doctor—had few comments. They live quite near John and Audrey. (Delighted about the new baby!)

I think everyone believes it is stress and I think they are right, but am not going to take any chances, and will be going in to see my doctor next week and will discuss the medication you mentioned. Thank you so much for telling me this—and no, I hadn't known about that problem. I guess when we get together there are so many things to discuss, we don't get to health.

Oh, I'm glad your energy is starting to return. Aren't bodies treacherous things sometimes? Sources of delight and sources of despair.

Much love,
Blanche

Date: July 5, 1999
Subject: Retirement, etc.

Hi Blanche and Bruce,

Thank you for your best wishes on my retirement. Today is really the first day that I realize that I am retired, in the sense that it is my first day at home, alone with Carol. I left my office on Wednesday noon, June 30, for the last time. From that moment on until last evening we were surrounded by children and grandchildren. I made the mistake of telephoning my old office number on Friday, July 2, only to receive a voice-mail message in the name of the new dean. That was a telling moment.

We had a super time with our family and the commitment ceremony. Everything went off without a hitch. Even the weather cooperated—barely. The reception was great, with excellent food and wine and beer. And a five-piece band. Carol danced most tunes, as did the 3- and 4-year-old granddaughters. We also got to see Sara's Hazel, six weeks old, and John's Grace, three weeks old. Both beautiful. Carol sat with the lactating crowd on Friday evening. There were up to four babies sucking away at one time.

Thank you again for your thoughts. We both wish you well. Carol will fill in the details soon, I am sure.

Love,
Don

Date: July 6, 1999
Subject: Re: Retirement, etc.

Dear Carol and Don,

Don, thank you so much for the lovely note re the retirement festivities. I particularly liked the bit about all the slurping babies. What fun! And now that you are officially retired, I can guarantee that it won't take more than two weeks before you voice the old retirement complaint, "How did I ever find time to work?"

And, Carol, weren't those lovely reviews Penguin sent us? Is the U.S. a little more sanguine than Canada?

Anyway, good to hear. And I saw the doctor Monday, apparently the ECG was perfectly normal and as everyone suspected the heart problems are symptoms of stress and anxiety. However, she did take the racing-heart session seriously and when I mentioned to her that a friend had been given beta-blockers for it, she said that would be a good idea, that she would give me a very low dosage to be taken only when the racing occurred. This reassurance and the little bottle on my bathroom counter has returned everything to normal without even being opened so far. (I know, these are early days, I'm not complacent.)

Aren't the ways of the brain mysterious? It's a bit like hypnotism with true deep-down belief being the factor.

Anyway, for now I am well again, and I was delighted to hear that you were up dancing at the party. There should be more dancing on the earth—as Canadians we don't do enough of it.

Keep well, dear friends, and enjoy your retirement.

Much love,
Blanche

Date: July 14, 1999
Subject: Your story

Dear Carol,

The new copy of *Saturday Night* arrived with the paper this morning and I shoved everything aside to read your story. What a good story! Loved the sly allusions and the unsaid things as much as the said, and admired greatly the ingenuity of the subject. Congratulations!

Much love,
Blanche

Date: July 25, 1999
Subject: Celibate Season

Hi Carol,

Have just had a miserable bout of bronchitis, but also a GOOD happening. Two of the women I went to high school with (60 years ago) live here on the Lower Mainland, so one of them [June Belsom] invited us to her place in Comox for the weekend. The other woman lives in Victoria, so was able to pick me up in Nanaimo, and we had a great weekend. At first I thought I couldn't go because of Bruce, but Leslie (bless her heart) offered to have him, and I can't tell you how much my morale improved by being a non-caregiver for 48 hours.

Next week we are going on a seven-day cruise to Alaska, up and back, no airports. I have mixed feelings but think it will work all right. We'll see.

Beverley still negotiating with Coteau. Oh dear, this is hard on the nerves.

Much love,
Blanche

Date: July 27, 1999
Subject: Re: Celibate Season

Dear Blanche,

Don is packing up the computer tomorrow, so this will be my last e-mail for a while. We leave on Friday, first for Iceland, then for France.

Our rounds of farewell and bouts of packing have kept me from writing, so I'm anxious to get my writing schedule back once again.

Much love for the moment,

C

Date: September 6, 1999
Subject: Glad to hear from you!

Dear Carol,

What a bonus to turn on my computer this a.m. and find your e-mail address! I've felt quite out of touch the last month or so, although Anne let me know that Harbourfront* is toasting you this year.

All is fairly well with us. Bruce has not been as agile this summer, but we did manage the seven-day Alaska cruise and it was good for my morale to leave the apartment and see lots of ice, etc. Ate too much, naturally.

---

*International Festival of Authors, hosted by Harbourfront Centre in Toronto.

Coteau Books has taken *Pen's Way* and will publish next fall. Right after signing the contract, Beverley got a strong expression of U.S. interest from Simon & Schuster who are going to consider a bid in a couple of weeks.

Love to you both,
Blanche
P.S. Read *Barney's Version** and have to say I enjoyed it—witty and current and, in the end, moving.

Date: September 10, 1999 [England]
Subject: Glad to hear from you!

Dear Blanche,

It was simply wonderful to hear from you—on the screen. We both felt a sense of relief at being connected, once again, to this marvellous e-mail network. What did we do before its inception?—lunged at the postman, of course. Now we lunge at a machine.

We're settling in, getting to know this beautiful neighbourhood, working out some sort of routine, feeling our way. Next weekend we're off to a Jane Austen conference in the small town of Wye. (The organizer just phoned to inquire, with some embarrassment, whether we'd like double or single beds. Double, we said.) We'll enjoy this outing, which includes talks and field trips to Austen sites. Oh, I am so deeply into her psyche—or rather what I imagine that psyche to be. Her oddities and eccentricities become more and more apparent.

I'm truly pleased about the Coteau publication in the fall. We know they'll do a good job. And what you wanted really was for it to be OUT there. Otherwise you might wait forever.

Much love,
C

---

*By Mordecai Richler.

October 3, 1999

Dear Carol,

What a long time since I've written to you! Anyway, here I am and there you are way over in England. I hope you are well and happy, and the last time I talked to you, you were off to a conference of the Jane Austen Society.

I saw in a clipping sent to me from the Calgary paper where you were a guest curator in Calgary for the Glenbow Museum, and passed this on to Merna who intends to get down to see the exhibit when it opens. She says she is well and thoroughly enjoying life these days. I sent off an oldish story of mine called "The Sex Life of the Elderly" to the Burnaby Writers' Society—an old and well-established group, I'm told—and it won a prize and I'm to read it this month. Hoping people don't expect too much from the subject matter.

I know I told you that Coteau has accepted *Pen's Way*, and I still haven't heard about Simon & Schuster. Snail's pace in this business. I am still trotting around to book clubs promoting *A Celibate Season*—can't believe how many book clubs there are just here on the North Shore.

I was dashed to find that *Story* has folded. They quite liked a story of mine and I revised it and sent it back, only to get a sad little letter saying that after about 27 years they had been bought out and the last issue of *Story* was in the newsstands. Not many markets left.

My life has improved greatly. I don't know if I told you by e-mail about my employing granddaughter Jacqueline (21) who is studying at Capilano College, to come when she is free and stay with Bruce when I'm out and do things with him, but it has really made my life much more livable. Today she took him to the symphony—I like the symphony, but I liked even better staying home by myself and getting a bit of writing done. And I was able to go to the all-day Writers' Union and Word On The Street stuff last Sunday with Fraidie and had a great time.

While we were looking Inglewood Lodge over, we bumped into Christie Harris* wandering around the halls with her walker. She is 95 now and although her memory is slipping, she is still quite remarkably with it, remembered me and talked about things quite brightly.

Allison and Dave went on the run for breast cancer today, and everyone wore cards saying who they were running for. Allison said to tell you her card had three names of friends, one of them yours.

All best to Don and much love,

Blanche

Date: October 28, 1999
Subject: Cabbages and kings

Dear Carol,

I have been following your adventures in Canada with immense pride. The quoted tributes to you in *The Globe* were marvellous and made me want to yell, Me too! with each accolade. And I think you were tremendously courageous to go before the Canadian Breast Cancer Foundation survivors. I know you would have been an inspiration and have given hope to the women there.

What you said about being able to live in the moment sat so familiarly with me. I too have been trying to master that diffi-cult art (sounds so easy) in not mulling over the bleakness of having to think of Bruce going into a lodge, no matter how nice it is (and it is nice). His name is in and when it comes up—probably six months down the road—I don't think we have the leeway to refuse again, as a sudden worsening would leave him nowhere to go.

Nice that Keith Maillard [*Gloria*] is up for a GG, isn't it? I had thought Lilian Nattel's *The River Midnight* would be nominated—

---

*An award winning children's author.

beautifully written, very vivid characterizations. I liked it greatly, but quite a few to whom I recommended it didn't.

Much love to you and Don,
Blanche

Date: November 21, 1999 [England]
Subject: London

Blanche!
It has been a long time since I've written. I talked to Anne the other day and she said she'd been in touch with you and that you were doing fine.

We're enjoying London. Yesterday we joined a walking tour through Pimlico, and had a marvellous guide who knew all sorts of interesting places you might not find in your guide book. We're also getting to some theatre and evening events, mostly literary. There is so much happening here. It makes it rather hard to keep nose to grindstone, Jane Austen that is, but I'm slowly making headway and should be done—with a big sigh—by the end of January. Biography is hard work, I've decided, and less rewarding than fiction.

Our love to you both,
Carol

November 21, 1999

Dear Carol,
Your lovely e-mail arrived today and I was so happy to hear from you, as you have been much on my mind of late.

I think you are right that putting in a pacemaker is not a big deal. Marilyn has one. Poor Marilyn, she has had something go wrong with almost everything. However she took me out on my birthday and stays remarkably cheerful and with it through it all.

Last night was the municipal election night, and Barbara [Perrault] ran for a fourth term. I was her bagman (bag lady doesn't work too well here) and she did extremely well, so there was a party which I was able to go to because Jacqueline came and stayed with Bruce. Alas! Jacqueline leaves for Tasmania on the 14th of December. Her course practicum will be there (she is taking administration in the tourist industry).

Stephen and family are in Vietnam for a month. Their girls— 10 and 12—hated the idea of leaving the centre of the universe, Smithers, but were finally persuaded that it would be important to see how other people in less affluent cultures live. An e-mail today from Stephen indicated that while the sentiment was noble, what the girls have really found is that shopping is terrific in such a country. Both girls are in French immersion so are doing quite well there, and they seem to be having an interesting time.

Walked over to the market with Bruce today and there was a little group of musicians playing outside on the deck facing the water, and two girls with long hair were dancing beautifully to the music. Obviously they were trained dancers, although they wore jackets and jeans like everyone else, but they were so lithe and airy as they circled and twirled around one another that I had one of those magical moments of living completely in the present (that we were talking about). Every day should have a moment of transcendence, a time to observe with the unblinkered delight of something newly discovered. I'll keep working on it.

Am reading *Pilgrim,** which I find intellectually quite engaging but emotionally cold. This week Fraidie and I are going to go and see *Felicia's Journey*, which is apparently a very good movie.

I'm so glad you are having such a good year in England.

Love,
Blanche

---

*By Timothy Findley.

13

Dark Night of the Soul

2000–2001

In *A Celibate Season* the character Chas asks rhetorically, "Is this a dark night of the soul?"At the time Carol and I toyed with the well-worn phrase, using it lightly and with a certain sense of irony. But now in our letters we returned to it with belated respect, our situations infinitely more deserving of it than was Chas's dark night.

Yet it was another phrase, this one from the Old Testament and memorized during my childhood when the road to virtue was paved with Bible readings, that kept haunting me. In the beautiful poetry of the King James Version the teacher cautions, "Remember now thy Creator in the days of thy youth, while the evil days come not."[*] Now, with the days of our youth long fled, the evil days did touch down for both of us.

I think we were rescued by that redemption peculiar to writers: the publication of books. Carol's biography of Jane Austen came out to great acclaim and my novel, *Penelope's Way*, got soul-enhancing reviews. In spite of her illness Carol completed her next novel, *Unless*,

---

[*]From *Ecclesiastes* 12:1.

and the anthology *Dropped Threads*, edited by Carol and Marjorie Anderson, went on to sell an astonishing 100,000 copies in Canada.

The evil days receded for both of us. New treatments gave Carol more than a temporary reprieve; they gave her times of joy and the return of vigour and strength. And I, after the agony of putting my husband into a care facility, began to regain the health that caregiving had eroded.

Carol and Don visited on a fine day in April and, with rhododendrons bursting from their fat buds and sun coaxing the tulips to open their hidden hearts, it felt like a sort of resurrection, or rebirth.

The following year on a sparkling June day with pink and yellow roses blooming outside the windows of their sunroom, I was able to visit Carol. She knew her options were dwindling. I asked her if she was afraid. "Afraid?" she answered, seemingly genuinely puzzled. "No," and then quietly, as though setting me straight, "There is nothing to be afraid of."

Date: January 13, 2000
Subject: Re: Happy New Year!

Dear Blanche,

Hello and greetings in the new year and the new millennium. I love the odd stray letter that drifts in about *C.S.* And I'm so grateful to you for answering. I hope—and I'm sure—you're keeping a file of them. Oh, if only Oprah would discover us! Oh my!

Your remarks about Marilyn, keeping cheerful as her body betrays her, interested me. I had coffee with a neighbour this morning (who has had cancer) who thinks that our health should be considered as a housekeeping detail to get briskly out of the way so that we can get on with our day . . . . You must know that wonderful scene in the movies when a doctor says to a patient, "You can win this battle." Not one doctor has said this to me, and I do wonder about the viability of such optimism. Or whether or not it would help. Also, I distrust this war imagery: battle, struggle, etc.

All your letters speak about Bruce's improvement, and I am full of admiration for your courage and, yes, optimism. Optimism was the subject of discussion at our Christmas dinner this year—in

France, at the house of neighbours. Where does it come from? We learn it from our parents, we decided, and they from theirs. Can you create it anew, breaking the chain?—that was another question we asked. (All this was in French, so I am a trifle vague about what we ended up with.) I have decided to live with the invented (?) hope of life going on and offering something more all the time.

Much love, and abundant thanks for keeping in touch—I have not been a good correspondent, but hope to do better.

Love,
Carol

Date: January 13, 2000
Subject: Lovely to hear from you!

Dear Carol,

What a treat to get up on this particularly dreary and raw January morning and find a nice long e-mail from you! You have been much on my mind recently, much of it happily, as I heard from Merna [Summers], who had heard from Joan Clark that she had seen you and could hardly believe how well you looked, and spoke glowingly about the return of your energy. An enormous relief to all of us. I'm not at all sure about optimism and its effects, partly because I don't think optimism is a creature of the will. No, I think it is a little bit a creature of the will, that we can take measures to banish gloom and get out of ruts, but the deep, vibrant optimism which used to blanket me sometimes, especially when young on a summer's day, comes from some other source perhaps.

Nevertheless I do think stress and depression are illness-inducing, scarcely a unique thought, and to some extent their opposite is optimism. Also as far as doctors ever giving one a clean bill of health, I don't think they do on principle. Another friend of mine complains about this, that they never say, "You are in remission," for instance.

I feel as though I've been through my own private "dark night of the soul," to quote our friend Chas. Last spring I suffered from severe anxiety, that awful state where one expects life to end in the next moment. (Read a good Updike thing about his bouts of anxiety in a recent *New Yorker.*) I phoned the daughters and made them sit down and listen to me, and I unburdened myself—poor dears, as if any of it were their fault. They did small things that helped, including the business of getting Jacqueline in to give me breaks, and funnily enough the occasion was like an enormous pressure relief, as though steam had been building and building inside me until it blew. In retrospect I think I had not come to terms with the fact that the man I married was no longer there; on good days I would think he was coming back, and I suppose I went through the characteristic stages of grief, such as anger and pain and depression and so on. After that, even though things are not good, I got better from my psychosomatic illnesses—heart palpitations, etc.—and can distance myself from this poor confused man who I must look after, but who I now feel is pretty completely disentangled from my psyche.

Nevertheless my natural optimism has returned and I seem to have found some strength outside myself, or from a source I wasn't aware I had. It will be at least a year before he can get into a facility, so the road ahead may be bumpy, but now I do think I can survive.

Sorry to go on so much about myself. Would love to explore your questions further re optimism. I have just finished *The Reader* [Bernhard Schlink]—wonderful—and *Jakob the Liar* [Jurek Becker]— wonderful too—and am up to the final story—yours—in the Desire anthology. I have that to look forward to as a treat this evening. (I do indulge in little treats now, the glass of wine at five, etc. They help.) I have loved the other stories and been astonished at the frankness of some of the younger women.

Much love. I'm so glad you are better, stronger and more positive.

Blanche

P.S. I was reading an interview with Michael Ignatieff in *Queen's Quarterly*, and thought of you as it is a question we have discussed. He said, ". . . it's a recurring conflict in my life. If you're a father you feel tremendous conflicts between what you owe yourself and what you owe your children. A lot of the cant about family values misses that. What we owe ourselves, what we owe our spouses, and what we owe our children are three separate moral duties, and they're all pulling in different directions. And you don't begin to understand what that conflict is about if you think it's just a conflict between selfishness and altruism. What we owe ourselves is a lot. We have a duty to ourselves to live a certain life and to live it well."

Date: February 4, 2000
Subject: Re: Wonderful to hear from you!

Dear Blanche,

I am slow in replying to your lovely letter, which touched me deeply. Yes, I knew you had been through a difficult time last spring, and that the life you are leading now is far, far from easy. This whole business of accepting interventions and interruptions in our ongoing lives—I suppose we must, but what a struggle, and is it fair? The fair word! What does it mean? Are you sure you are getting enough help, enough time off? Are there other places you can turn to for relief, so you can get out for a few hours on a regular basis?

We are in Vancouver the 7 and 8 of April, and I am hoping we can see you.

You probably know by now that *C.S.* is coming out in England in paperback late in the summer. It is being presented as an "old" book, but I nevertheless think it will find a readership.

Much love,
Carol

Date: February 4, 2000
Subject: I'll be here!

Dear Carol,

I am continuing to do well, and have hired a university student for Fridays and am going over to Capilano College today (Friday) for my first class at the ElderCollege in "Writing Your Memoirs."

Not that I want or intend to, but the class is taught by a friend
from the Unitarian Church Book Club, Jim Wilson (used to teach
at SFU) and is reputed to be stimulating and fun, both of which
I can use. I have persuaded Barbara to take it with me.

Congratulations on your new short story collection! As soon as
it hits the bookstores I'll get it. Have done most of the edit with
Ursell on *Pen's Way*—a friend suggested *Penny for Your Thoughts* as
a title, but Fraidie thinks it is too flippant. Got any thoughts? I
don't mind *Penelope's Way*, but Beverley thinks it too non-sexy.

I am so glad your health is creeping back.

Much love,
Blanche

Date: February 4, 2000 [England]
Subject: Re: I'll be here!

Blanche!

I am so pleased we'll be able to get together. These are hard
days for you and hard decisions. Oh, I do wish I could offer some
comfort. The course is a very good idea, and why not do some
memoir writing? You could pick a chunk from your many life
chapters and concentrate on that.

We're off to a play tonight, in a few minutes in fact. Did I tell
you we have freedom passes on the tube, for "elderly persons." We're
grateful.

A Penny for Your Thoughts? Resist this with all your might.

Much love,
C

Date: February 25, 2000 [England]
Subject: Re: I know how you feel

Dear Blanche,

When I write, glibly, that I know how you feel, I really do know
how you feel. How odd that we should have the same ailment

[racing heart]—though perhaps not so odd, since it seems to be widely shared.

This is such a difficult time for you. Everyone who knows and loves you will believe that you will find life easier once Bruce has found a good home where he will receive constant care, excellent care—but also know what this represents for you. I hardly know how to tell you my thoughts. I want to see you released from what has become a very difficult situation, and at the same time I know how grievous you will find this parting. Let me just say that you have been extraordinarily brave and constant through this period of time, which has now become a very extended period of time.

We will be able to talk soon.

Love,
C

Date: February 27, 2000
Subject: Thank you, dear Carol

Dear Carol,

Sorry to go on about health when you have suffered so much more than I have. I loved your interview in *The Globe* yesterday, and was bemused by that interviewer and her take on "niceness." Of course you are wonderfully nice, but in the minds of the young women of today niceness seems to equate with knitting, rather than a belief in treating everyone with dignity. We do live in a remarkably uncivil society, don't we?

Much love,
Blanche

Date: March 10, 2000
Subject: Bad news and good news

Dear Carol,

I'm so glad your book is being so wonderfully reviewed. My copy still sits at the bookstore nearby, but because of an unfortunate occurrence on Monday I haven't been able to pick it up. Fraidie phoned to say she loved it.

Monday I had a very slight stroke (they call it a T.I.A., transient ischemic something-or-other) and was wheeled out in an ambulance feeling very conspicuous, as one does, especially in an apartment like this where everyone gets to know everyone. After I waited three hours for an emergency bed, they did a lot of tests and decided that there had been no damage. Now, however, I am on blood thinner and beta-blockers and anxiety pills, so am feeling terribly slowed down.

Irony—as Allison supported my tottering bod back into the house after the day in Emerg, there was a letter for me from the Canada Council awarding me a grant to rewrite that novel I wrote some years ago about the girl who was a computer engineer. Instead of dancing in the streets I could only think cheerless thoughts like, Can I do it? My doctor, who is a great fan of yours, assured me that not only will I do it but I will go on to write more.

Merna sent me a wonderful British review about you and in it you speak of your health. I am taking courage from your courage.

I was lucky this week in that they were able to give Bruce a two-week stay in the lodge starting next week. I think this will be very important for me. And I've had steady home help this week—in spite of the moaning, I've certainly had a lot from the medical system.

I do hope you will still be coming through in April and will have a chance to see me.

Much love,
Blanche

Date: March 13, 2000 [England]
Subject: Re: Bad news and good news

My dear friend Blanche,

We're just home from France, one week, and found your very disturbing news on our e-mail. I do know such "events" are not always serious and that they are common, but we are very concerned.

I thought I'd try to reach you late tonight to get a report. Of course I want to know how you are doing PSYCHOLOGICALLY. How upsetting is this? Do you think you'll be able to swing around to "real" life fairly quickly? The grant is such marvellous news, and should be greatly encouraging, but if you aren't feeling well, it may just be a bother.

Take all the help that's offered. I can't wait to see you in April.

Much love from the two of us,
C

Date: April 2, 2000
Subject: See you?

Dear Carol,

All is improving here. After my troubles, they got Bruce a respite bed in the lodge into which he'll be going, and he will be there until the end of April. Today the daughters and family have rented one of their little rooms and are throwing a luncheon party for our 55th wedding anniversary.

My heart is still being somewhat erratic but no one seems too worried. Next week I get more tests and then the following week see a cardiologist—I'll be glad when all that is over. However, I seem to have been very lucky not to sustain any damage from the little stroke, and I notice a gradual relaxation having Bruce away like this. I go up every other day to see him, so am finding a bit of time for writing, which always cheers me.

I'm lapping up *Dressing Up for the Carnival* [Carol's third short story collection]. Absolutely loved the story "Scarf." My favourite so far.

All the best to Don,
Blanche

∾Carol and Don came to see me on a lovely April day. We had lunch and then I suggested that they might like to go a few blocks to 32 Books, a small independent bookstore run by a hard-working, innovative young woman named Mary Trentadue. Mary had been extremely dedicated in pushing *A Celibate Season*, and it was through her that so many book clubs had contacted me.

It didn't occur to me that Mary would perhaps have liked to be warned that a writer of Carol's fame would be dropping by, and for the only time that I have known her, she was nonplussed. She gasped as the three of us walked into the store, retreated a few steps and, running her hands over her jeans, blurted something like, "If I'd known I would have—have dressed up!"

Date: May 31, 2000
Subject: Welcome to Seniorhood!

Dearest Carol,

The Day looms close and with it all my most fervent wishes for happiness and good things to you on that day. Sixty-five still seems young to me, well before any noticeable deterioration. And I hope you have a birthday party the like of which will go down in the annals of great bashes!

All reasonably well with me, although still having trouble with fibrillations. Yesterday and the day before I had a bunch of tests and am probably still radioactive. Hopefully, though, these scans will let us know what if anything is the matter—I see the specialist Tuesday. Oh, the fun of aging!

On the positive side, *Penelope's Way* will be out in September and I must say that Coteau Books is so enthusiastic that it is very rewarding working with them. My bookseller that you met is planning to have a launch for it—wouldn't it be a treat if you could come over for it?

I got through the editing of *Pen's Way* without too much trouble, but do find my energy severely drained. Patience, I advise myself, but have never been wildly patient. Bruce is doing well at home now and I have help every morning for his bath and breakfast, which gives me a lot more free time.

Much love and the most enthusiastic of birthday greetings! Do let me know when things quiet down and you are through with moving into your new palatial digs [in Victoria].*

Love,
Blanche

Date: June 1, 2000 [England]
Subject: Re: Welcome to Seniorhood!

Hello dear Blanche,
Sixty-five—and yet, I didn't think a year ago that I'd make it. I celebrated yesterday by having a smart lunch with my editor's partner, Peter Parker, whose birthday is also June 2. This is rather nice. We had a wonderful good gossip, and I sailed home renewed.

About your heart. As you know, I had a small "procedure" in November, a cardiac ablation, which has helped so much. I do know there aren't many people in Vancouver who do it, but there must be someone. It requires only one night in hospital. It has raised my energy considerably, though it was judged only a 70% success. No general anaesthetic, just a local. You really might ask about it.

We will actually be [in Winnipeg] late tomorrow afternoon. I will be kissing the ground, not that we haven't had a perfectly marvellous time here. But home is best, especially when one is dependent on health services.

Is Bruce home temporarily or permanently? It wasn't clear. I would love to come to Vancouver for your launch in September. I have an idea that this book will do very well. We will also have a

---

*Carol and Don moved to Victoria, into a large traditional French-villa-style home, with a huge entry hall, wide spacious oak stairs and lovely sunny rooms. A glassed-in patio was set in spacious grounds with banks of rhododendrons bordering the gardens.

launch, October, for our anthology—and so we may meet at that. But I announced at Hay-on-Wye [in Wales] Monday, at the end of my reading, that this was my last public event—no talks, no signings, a sort of partial retirement in order to spend more time writing. I feel happy about this decision, and the 65th birthday seemed to make it legitimate.

Now to pack up another box.

Much, much love,
C

Date: June 15, 2000
Subject: Glad you're back

Dear Carol,

It is wonderful that Canada stacks up better than Britain in speed of delivery. Actually my recent troubles have given me a lot of respect for the system, flawed though it may be, as both Bruce and I find ourselves at the appropriate specialists very quickly and even Emergency wasn't too bad, very thorough, they won't let you leave until every possibility is explored. I am doing quite well now and just waiting for energy to creep back. (I did tell you I had a second small T.I.A.; they let my blood get too thick again.) I'm a bit disappointed—like Penelope—that advanced age is not giving me serenity. I had hoped for a devil-may-care attitude, as of one having had a long and relatively healthy life, but instead go around like a wound-up toy with resultant rising blood pressure. But it is slipping away now, amazing the capacity of the mind to adjust.

Coteau seems extremely positive about *Pen's Way*; they have moved publication forward to September 1st and given it a lead position in the catalogue.

All the very best, and hi to Don,
Blanche

Date: July 24, 2000
Subject: Radio play

Hi Carol,

I listened last night to your play, *Sisters Under the Skin*, and I thought it very witty and entertaining. I particularly admired the way you used the conference on synchronicity as a venue. That was such a good idea, making the unusual confluence of coincidences fit in with a wider philosophical theme and thereby bypassing any of the criticisms that straight coincidence often brings.

I was so happy the other day when I phoned, to know that you and Don are thrilled with your new house and having fun fixing it up. The meaning of life is having something to look forward to— there, I said I'd let you in on the secret once I found it.

Take care of yourself! Wonderful that everything is going well for you now. It is my theory of probability that bad luck and good luck go in streaks, and you've had the bad luck spell. On to golden days ahead!

Much love to you both,
Blanche
P.S. Great *New Yorker* cartoon a while ago, an old guy sitting on his porch and an aging gussied-up doll walking by, and he's saying, "Be still, my atrial fibrillations!"

Date: July 25, 2000
Subject: Re: Radio play

Dear Blanche,

Yes, the secret is something to look forward to. I have arrived at the same place. This is what keeps me going: the thought that something interesting is about to happen, and I want to know about it. I have thought about our conversation, about never coming to terms with death, never understanding, really, what it is, until we are right up close to it.

We (I really) have made the decision not to go to France this summer. It is just too much. Don is grieving a little, but I've promised to go in the spring. I haven't regretted this decision for one minute. Now I can relax and become a Victorian.

Much love,

C

Date: August 6, 2000
Subject: Joan Clark's new book

Hi Carol,

I know that Joan Clark is an old friend of yours, so I thought you might want to pass on to her that I thoroughly enjoyed *Latitudes of Melt*. It traces the goings-on of a Newfoundland family, somewhat in the manner of Bonnie Burnard's book, and there is an absolutely riveting scene of the sinking of the *Titanic*. An amazing amount of background research into many things that go on in Newfoundland as well.

Today I'm reading Margaret Drabble's *The Witch of Exmoor*. I was quite bemused to find a long discussion about an invitation to one of the (black male) intellectuals to attend a conference in Calgary on appropriation of voice. Did you know that in England they regard Canada as at the forefront—leading the charge, so to speak—of such ethnic conundrums? And then there ensues quite a vigorous, albeit cynical, debate about whether academics are jumping on a bandwagon that takes them to conferences all about the globe. Preferably, one of the characters says, Bermuda rather than Calgary. Early impression is that it is somewhat pretentious with its long and convoluted philosophical debates, but so far it is holding my interest and I think it may get fairly captivating.

Must run. Let me know how you are getting along, and best to Don.

Blanche

Date: August 19, 2000
Subject: U.K. Celibate Season

Dear Carol,

I am surprised that I didn't know the book [the British version of *C.S.*] was coming out then, but in the world of publishing perhaps I shouldn't be. I just heard this morning that the launch for *Penelope's Way* will be on November 2nd in Vancouver. Mary, of 32 Books, is going to host it.

All reasonably well here. Bruce isn't doing too well lately but I have just had a little break of four days and I was amazed at how tired I was—I'm sure my hosts were a bit startled when I kept falling asleep every few hours and retiring at 9:00. I got good help in for Bruce, but he was pretty freaked out over my going. However, I am feeling better and the new drug seems to be working. (Fingers crossed.)

Much love,
Blanche

Date: August 20, 2000
Subject: Re: U.K. Celibate Season

Dear Blanche,

Have been a bit swamped with—everything! Mainly visits from children and grandchildren. I do confess I find grandchildren exhausting. I am accustomed to an orderly house and people (Don) who eat what's on the menu. Anyway, next week I start a relaxation class for cancer folk, so perhaps that will help. The cancer centre here is spectacularly well run, and I am delighted with my oncologist and GP (she lives in the house behind us, which might be very useful).

I was shocked and saddened to hear about Marilyn in a lodge. It doesn't seem possible, someone of her vitality, but I know she has suffered from a range of ailments. Does she mind terribly being in a lodge? Oh, this getting older is getting worse and worse! I'm pleased you had a break, but you really need much more time.

Jim Munro and his wonderful wife Carole had a neighbourhood dessert party and we met everyone—everyone is lovely and friendly, and we are getting our house and garden well set up. We'll have all September here, and two little trips in October. Look after yourself.

Much love,
C

Date: August 24, 2000
Subject: Review

Dear Carol,

It was lovely to hear from you the other day and know that the most you are suffering from is grandchildren frazzle. (Been there, done that.) That is one of the negatives of having a big house—many guests, especially in such a holiday-desirable place as Victoria.

I, too, was shocked that Marilyn is in a lodge, and I haven't been to see her because of my own situation.

Am now reading rather a strange book by Lawrence Durrell which I'm not sure I like, called *Monsieur.** It doesn't inspire me to go on to the rest of the quintet as it is too dense. Not like his Alexandria Quartet, which I loved.

I'm so glad you are getting settled in and liking your new place so much. The daughters are adamant that we must get Bruce in somewhere before much more time goes by.

Much love,
Blanche

September 8, 2000

Hi Carol,

Funny about *A Celibate Season.* I still have people phone me to say how much they loved it, and yet I don't think we took it that seriously at the time. I think we underestimated.

---

*The Avignon Quintet, Book 1.

Penelope's Way will be out mid-October, and already had quite a positive (though not rave) review in *Quill and Quire*. Also they featured you in an article about famous writers who edit books, starting with the anthology and admitting that your involvement in *Pen's Way* was there but not a hands-on editing role. I tried not to make too much of it as I don't want to feel I'm exploiting our friendship, and the publishers have been equally low-key. Nevertheless I'm deeply grateful and will send you a copy of the book when I get one.

Coteau has arranged for me to go to Winnipeg and Toronto in the first week of November. At first I hesitated and tried to suggest just Winnipeg, but they have apparently had a coup in getting me and two other authors in to Chapters' main store in Toronto, so I may reconsider. I'm still a bit nervous about the continuing fibrillations, although they are greatly reduced and I will ask the specialist if it is okay when I see him this coming Tuesday. The big problem is getting someone to look after Bruce for five days. His dementia is increasing very much of late. At the moment he is in an excellent place, but just for a two-week respite for me, which I have thoroughly enjoyed. The luxury of getting up slowly and not having to be prepared for the morning onslaught of caregivers! And of turning the light on in the night and reading if I can't sleep!

I do hope your health continues good, Carol.

All the best,
Blanche
P.S. Went over to see Marilyn Wednesday and was shocked by her sudden deterioration. God, old age!

Date: September 17, 2000
Subject: Party

Dear Blanche,
Thank you so much for writing. I can't wait to see the actual book and hold it in my hand. It sounds as though Coteau is nicely

behind this, and if you're not able to do a lot of touring, you can do phone interviews from home—I think they work perfectly, better than flesh-to-flesh. Even better is the e-mail Q-and-A. You never blurt.

I wanted you to know that we're coming to Vancouver October 13 (Friday) and on Saturday night Anne is giving herself a 41st birthday party, loads of friends. She's allowed us to ask a few: I've invited my friends the Dymondses, Bill Richardson, and want to ask you too. I don't know how you feel about big noisy gatherings these days or how you might arrange care for Bruce. But do think about it.

Much love,
C
P.S. I thought *The Blind Assassin** was a long, dull read, alas.

Date: September 17, 2000
Subject: Re: Review

Dear Carol,
    That sounds wonderful. As for how I feel about big noisy parties, it has been so long since I was at one that it sounds like the idea of the century.
    Coteau's catalogue is lovely, and they have made *Pen's Way* the lead-off item.
    Have you read Reynolds Price? Merna put me on to him and I'm astonished that I wouldn't have known about anyone so good.

All best,
Blanche
P.S. Yes, Fraidie told me her friend said the same thing about *The Blind Assassin*. It seems that only *The New York Times* had the nerve to say the empress has no clothes. Too bad, as I thought *Alias Grace* a masterpiece.

---

*By Margaret Atwood.

Date: September 18, 2000
Subject: Re: Review

Dear Blanche,

I'm thrilled you'll consider coming. This is wonderful.

I do hope you succeed in getting Bruce into the temporary respite. This is far too much for you. What I mean is that you've already given so much care and now you must think a little of your own health. The thought keeps running through my head: so this is how we end up.

Yes, I do know Reynolds Price's work and think highly of it. I go to the doctor today, which always gets me into a rattle. But all is well.

Love,
C

Date: September 28, 2000
Subject: Good news and bad news

Dear Carol,

I just heard from Anne that your checkup was great. Wonderful! On with the writing.

The bad news—just had a call from Marilyn's daughter and she died in the night. She had been in hospital for about two weeks following an episode where she fell and never really recovered. They don't know for sure what caused that, but in the end pneumonia took her. I will miss her. She was my friend for 45 years.

Looking forward to seeing you.

Love,
Blanche

Date: September 28, 2000
Subject: Re: Good news and bad news

Oh, Blanche, this is so sad. Lovely, buoyant, intelligent Marilyn. It is so hard to believe, and accept.

Carol

Date: October 7, 2000
Subject: Bad news

Dear Blanche,

I am in for another round of treatment. But I still plan to come
to Vancouver for Anne's party. A thousand thoughts are in my head,
but mainly I'm fairly composed, some of the time. We will have
time to chat, won't we. The meaning of life? Have you found out
anything new?

Much love, see you soon,
C

Date: October 7, 2000
Subject: Meaning of life

Dearest Carol,

Oh, Carol, I'm so sorry you are having to face more things.

As for meaning of life, not much on that front. [I was reminded
of] that long epic poem about Job, by Archibald MacLeish, very
avant garde in the fifties, in which the protagonist ends up, as Job
did, by saying Yes to life.

All very well, but the hardest thing I found during my recent
tribulations was coping with the anxiety it produced. In the
last while, the anxiety has retreated bit by bit, like the tentacles
of a giant squid slowly releasing their stranglehold, until now I
think my mind has settled down. I'm so glad that you are
handling it so well, although I know there will be *nuits blanches**
yet to come.

Oh, I wish I had something profound to say! All I know is that
I still believe that there are dimensions out there that we cannot
access, and that it isn't all for naught.

---

*Nuits blanches is a French expression—literally "white nights," but meaning
sleepless nights.

Carol, I'm so looking forward to seeing you on Saturday night. Anne says she has a balcony area reserved "for those over 65 only," so perhaps we will be able to visit over the din.

Much love, and courage in the month ahead, dear Carol.

Love,
Blanche

∾The party at Anne's was a stimulating evening, and Carol was able to circulate among the guests and enjoy herself. We did manage to visit, although as usual the noise level was high. After my long periods of semi-isolation I found the evening brought back a sense of belonging to the world.

Date: October 18, 2000
Subject: Thank you

Dear Carol,

A note to thank you for inviting me to the party on Saturday night. I had a great time and enjoyed the opportunity to talk to you (and Don, of course, although you can tell him I didn't believe ALL the stories he told). Also was wonderful to see you looking so lovely, and hateful to think of you starting all that again. Dear Carol, I wish there was some wonderful thing I could offer other than my prayers (I do pray). If love helps, and I know it does, you are surrounded by loving family and loving friends.

Also thank you for introducing me to Bill Richardson. I hope he will have me on his talk show; certainly I'll do my best to remind him.

Friday Bruce goes into a respite bed, and I wouldn't be surprised if this is it, as the place he has his name in should come up before the month is up. I feel terribly sorry for him, but I know there is no alternative.

I'm so glad you are writing. I once read an analysis by Hannah Arendt of some of Aristotle's thinking, in which he talked about the speculative (and writing) facet of his mind being like a timeless country, separate and distinct from the everyday self which can be lonely and trapped in time; a place to which he could withdraw for respite from the world. Arendt was discussing duality, I think, but I often think of this nameless country into which one can retreat and which is such a comfort.

Much love, and don't despair. There is so much out there in the medical world and many tales of remissions. I think of you both every day.

Blanche

❧ In November 2000, Allison accompanied me to Winnipeg for the promotion of *Penelope's Way*, and on a cold blowy night, Elisabeth Harvor and I read from our novels at McNally Robinson Booksellers. I went on to Toronto for further readings.

Date: November 21, 2000
Subject: book, etc.

Dear Blanche,

I'm doing much better after a few rotten days. Now I understand how the cycle goes and can plan for the future. I've been slow replying to mail, but was very interested in your tour and your meeting up with Elisabeth Harvor.

The sun continues to shine. I am hoping Bruce gets to keep his respite bed, since you have been caregiver for too long a time. This is easy enough for me to say, isn't it, but harder when your ties are long and strong. The meaning of life: valuing love and work and deriving pleasure from both???

Much love,
C

Date: November 21, 2000
Subject: Re: book, etc.

Dear Carol,

I was delighted to get your note today as I have been worrying about you and wondering how it is going. I'm so sorry you've had some rotten days but, as you say, now you can plan your life around the rotten days. Oh, I wish I could wave a magic wand, but then there would be no meaning of life.

About the meeting with Elisabeth Harvor, I don't know if you saw the vicious, and I mean vicious, review in the *National Post*, by Noah Richler. When I met her I wondered if she'd seen it, but she brought up the matter herself and said she wondered what he had against her, but that she wasn't going to let it get her down. She feels confident about the work, and I bought a copy so will let you know what I think.

Today I got the news that Bruce is to get a permanent bed. I have to tell him tomorrow and am dreading it, as everyone has to start in multiple bedrooms and wait for a single to become vacant and he definitely doesn't want that. It is the same in all the facilities, so I'm going to grab this one as he quite likes the place otherwise. It has to happen but it is a bit heart-wrenching. (A lot, I should say.) None of the kids will let me change my mind and I don't want to, of course, but at least their determination makes me feel somewhat better.

And, yes, I liked your meaning of life. Valuing love and work and deriving pleasure from both.

Much love,
Blanche

Date: November 22, 2000
Subject: Re: book, etc.

Dear Blanche,

Just to wish you steadiness of nerve in telling Bruce about the shared room. I can understand his reluctance, and understand how hard it is for you to break the news. A tiny thought: might he, in fact, get some pleasure from company? Depends on the company, but it would be wonderful if he found it congenial, knowing it is only temporary.

Yes, I saw the Noah Richler review and thought it cruel— the headline, which he wouldn't be responsible for, doubly cruel. I suspect this is a male refusal to take women seriously.

Love,
C

Date: *November 22, 2000*
Subject: *Re: book, etc.*

Dear Carol,

Thank you, thank you for taking the time in your own tough life to send these greetings. I told Bruce yesterday and today Leslie and I are going up to move him. He was very downcast. But he really likes this care centre, old and somewhat shabby, but wonderful hands-on care and small enough that he already knows everyone and is very popular.

Had a wonderful visit the other day with Barbara Lambert, whose *A Message for Mr. Lazarus* impressed me greatly. It turns out that I knew her in Penticton where she was Barbara Schwenk [maiden name].

It seems as though we go through wonderful years and then terrible years, perhaps like those fractals that came out of chaos theory. I'm praying that you two will soon be able to shed the rotten years and go back to enjoyment of your retirement.

Much love,
Blanche

Date: *November 27, 2000*
Subject: *Re: book, etc.*

Dear Blanche,

First: I think a few days of adjustment will make an enormous difference to Bruce. This is terribly hard on both of you, and I can't think of many changes that demand more. If only you can get through this first little while. Thank goodness your kids are supporting this decision.

Next: I got your news of the review too late yesterday to find a copy. Please e-mail me the review [in *The Vancouver Sun*] if you have a minute. I think your sales in Vancouver will be great, and that that will spread. Word of mouth in the book industry is a reality.

Much love,
C

Date: December 7, 2000
Subject: Things

Hi Carol,

Just a note to say I hope all is going well. I went to a launch of a documentary that Ross Howard [Bruce's second cousin] has been working on for a couple of years, and while there met again Anne's delightful friend Maureen, as she has been working as editor on the project for the last few months. She told me all about the wonderful book club meeting they had *chez toi*, and said you seemed quite well.

All well here. I am getting used to Bruce's changed status, although the first week or so was very hard, for both of us. However, I think he is settling in nicely and Allison and Dave fixed his half [of the] room up with pictures and his own dresser, and yesterday I got the phone installed. All of these things improved his morale, and I try to get him home about once a week so he won't feel that he no longer has a home.

Pen's Way has been flying off the shelves here in North Van, but unfortunately now is running into distribution problems. However *The* [*Vancouver*] *Sun* article did a tremendous amount of good and I'm amazed at how many people read it.

Bill Richardson did phone me and was going to phone again to set something up.

Much love to you, and to Don,
Blanche

Date: December 13, 2000
Subject: Re: Things

Dear Blanche,

I'm slow responding. Had a couple of rotten days, then a good
day, then some more low ones. Now I feel my gusto returning.
The sun is shining on our winter pansies and we have our tree up,
an eleven-footer, the largest we've ever had or ever will. I am feeling
rather at peace these days. I do understand that I am being given a
life extension through this ghastly medication, and I have accepted
that. But I'm awkward as a teenager in knowing how to spend it.

I know these last weeks have been horribly hard for you and for
Bruce, and I did feel a spasm of comfort that you wrote he was
adjusting with each small improvement. A room of his own—how
long will that take? What about Christmas itself?

Must go get dressed.

Love,
C

Date: December 15, 2000
Subject: More things

Dear Carol,

I was so pleased to hear from you but terribly sorry to hear of
your rotten days. Hard to keep up the morale, I'm sure.

I do hope you were able to enjoy your Christmas party at the
Empress Hotel. Yes, a very Victorian thing to do—what a wonderful
old institution it is! Years ago Bruce used to go over there in his role in
the Citizenship Court, and I used to tag along for the pleasure of
staying at the Empress and just bumming around downtown.

I actually had a call from Bill Richardson's producer yesterday
and they are going to interview me [for *Richardson's Roundup*] after
all, first or second week of January. What an enormous break, as
although I've had good publicity here, it hasn't gone beyond
Vancouver's borders. The feedback I've been getting has been very
encouraging and I am enjoying my 15 minutes of fame.

Bruce is adjusting well, and I no longer am suffering over the decision. I hadn't realized the enormity of the task when I was coping day by day, but now am amazed at the way my energy is coming back. And he is sufficiently confused now that he doesn't really take in the finality of where he is. I get him home as often as I can and I think he feels that this is his home and he's there just to give me a break. The other day I took him over town for a lunch with his former Immigration Board cronies. He loved that.

I must go. I think about you so often and wish I could offer you the meaning of life.

Much love, and to Don,
Blanche

Date: December 22, 2000
Subject: Merry Christmas

Dear Carol and Don,

I hope you have a wonderful Christmas with your family all about you. I will bring Bruce home Christmas Eve and then we will go to Leslie's for dinner. The Christmas season feels a bit vacant this year, but life rolls on.

I do hope you are well over the holidays, Carol. I think of you both often and hope that 2001 will beat out 2000 in happiness.

Much love,
Blanche

Date: January 1, 2001
Subject: Happy New Year

Dear Carol and Don,

All went well over Christmas. Bruce was home Christmas Eve and on Christmas we went to Leslie's for dinner. On Friday Allison had a nice party because Gregory (now 24 and a commercial pilot) was home with his new partner and her two sweet children, 9 and 10.

Bruce had a wonderful time at this and in fact could hardly be persuaded to leave. In spite of all this I did feel stressed over Christmas; I'm afraid it is a holiday with too much emotional baggage. I tried to distance myself but don't think I succeeded.

I read *Anil's Ghost*** and was impressed with the beautiful prose and tight structure, but still it didn't grab me. Anil is quite well drawn but other characters remain mysterious and unexplored.

Much love to you both,
Blanche

Date: January 1, 2001
Subject: Re: Happy New Year

Happy New Year, Blanche!

And thank you so much for your good wishes. The sun is shining, and Don is out, starting the year with a hike, along with a walking group he's joined. So right now he's on a mountain (hill), and I've just untrimmed the tree, that odd, necessary and strangely satisfying task. Back to reality. Humbug, etc. I must agree with you about Christmas, the over-muchness of it, and its ability to drill straight back to other strong feelings. I remember driving around Ottawa in a panic, trying to get the right gifts for the children, the right brand names, the fear of possible disappointment they might experience, and probably did.

Anne loves *Pen's Way*, as you by now know, and she is sure the others in the club will. Your being there, of course, will be perfectly wonderful. You do know, Blanche, what an accomplishment this is! We'll be in touch.

Love,
C

---

*By Michael Ondaatje.

Date: January 9, 2001
Subject: Re: Anne's column

Dear Blanche,

Yes, I was thrilled with Anne's piece and knew you would be. [Anne wrote a wonderful column on aging and featured Penelope, with excerpts from the novel.] I love the quotes she's chosen. You really are a wonderful writer. Good luck with Bill [Richardson] and please give him my love. He is a wise man, I think.

Much love,
C

Date: January 24, 2001
Subject: Your anthology

Dear Carol,

I got my copy of the anthology [*Dropped Threads*] yesterday and want to congratulate you and Marjorie on a major piece of work very well done. Such a lot of interesting viewpoints!

Sandra Martin's interview with you in *The Globe* was very beautifully done. She is a thoughtful and perceptive person, isn't she?

Love,
Blanche

Date: January 25, 2000
Subject: Your anthology

Dear Blanche,

I am afraid that the *National Post* got the title of your book wrong. It was a phone interview, one of those "What's on your bedside table?" things—but I was sure they would get that straight.

I'm looking forward to seeing you at the anthology launch. Don and I have just eaten lunch outside. In January.

Much love,

C

To the *National Post*
Erratum

They say there is no such thing as bad publicity as long as your name is spelled correctly, and you did spell my name correctly in the Jan. 20 interview with Carol Shields. However, my novel that she said is on her bedside table is *Penelope's Way*, not Pen's Way. Penelope would be very indignant if anyone called her Pen.

Blanche Howard
North Vancouver

Date: January 26, 2001
Subject: Re: Your anthology

Blanche,

About the reading in Vancouver, I'm going to do a brief intro-duction, introduce you one by one, then call for a discussion on the subjects raised or the general subject of what we're not told. Do you think we need to plant the first question? Are your daughters coming?—and might they be willing to do this?

Much luv,
Carol

Date: January 26, 2001
Subject: Your anthology

Dear Carol,

I hadn't known whether I was to be among the readers—although I gather from you that I am—but had already decided that if I was asked I would read only the wraparound story about

Rosalind Franklin.* I think the rest doesn't lend itself well to oral presentation (sounds vaguely salacious).

Yes, the daughters are going and I'll ask if one of them would get the questioning started.

Much much love,
Blanche

Date: January 26, 2001
Subject: Your anthology

The Rosalind Franklin story would be perfect. I've just reread it— last night—and found it heartbreaking. I read *The Double Helix* when it came out, and NEVER EVEN NOTICED. I can't imagine where my head was in those days.

Much love,
C

Date: January 28, 2001
Subject: Thanks again

Hi Carol,

I tracked down the mention you gave me in the *National Post* and want to say thank you again for giving me the publicity.

Sorry *Dropped Threads* got such an iffy review in *The Globe*, but I think anthologies are notoriously hard to review.

I think I told you I read David Adams Richards' winning book and thought it wonderful. I wasn't nearly as taken with Ondaatje's [*Anil's Ghost*], although the language was brilliant. I'm reading Beth Harvor's novel [*Excessive Joy Injures the Heart*] and it is nowhere as

---

*Franklin was a 31-year-old crystallographer when she began to work on taking X-ray diffraction pictures of the patterns made by the molecules in DNA. These pictures were instrumental in unravelling the structure of DNA, for which James Watson, Francis Crick and Maurice Wilkins received the Nobel Prize. In his book James Watson suggests that he used unethical methods in obtaining her pictures. Her story was in the article I wrote for *Dropped Threads*.

bad as Noah Richler made out. The writing is excellent and the main problem with it is that the protagonist is so goofy you keep wanting to shake her and tell her to get a life. There isn't quite enough to hang a novel on, unfortunately.

I hope and pray that you are doing well.

All the best and love,
Blanche

Date: February 1, 2001
Subject: Great interview!

Dear Carol,

Fortunately a friend alerted me to your publicity for *Dropped Threads* this morning, and I thought it was wonderful.

This morning I got a copy of *A Celibate Season* in Mandarin. It is very amusing to see the set-up in a language so foreign. Front cover has a dimly seen copy of the marriage photos on the original, and a very Chinesey-looking house below.

Congratulations on *Dropped Threads.* All in all a great accomplishment. All is well here, I'm reading and trotting around to book clubs on a fairly regular basis. Must run (figuratively). Continue to heal, dear Carol, and looking forward to the 13th. Love to Don too.

Blanche

Date: February 1, 2001
Subject: Great interview!

Dear Blanche,

I'm looking forward to the 13th and feel I must get a new outfit. I'm a little thinner, so everything hangs on me; there was a time I would have rejoiced. Still, I'm getting along quite well. I'm off now to my cancer relaxation class, which does me a great lot of good.

Much love,
C

Date: February 1, 2001
Subject: Great interview!

Dear Carol,

I'm going to have to wear the [outfit] I bought for my book launch until I've amortized the cost over the life expectancy (accountant talk).

All best,
Blanche

❧The launch of the anthology *Dropped Threads* exceeded everyone's wildest expectations. A large church hall in downtown Vancouver had been rented, but extra rooms had to be opened up with loudspeakers to accommodate the overflow crowd of over two hundred. Many were turned away.

Carol sat next to me at the table where we, the readers, Anne Giardini, Claudia Casper, Sandy Frances Duncan and I were lined up. Carol whispered to me that she was being held together by strong pills, but when the time came for questions no one would have guessed. She handled the question-and-answer period with her usual grace and precision, until Don called a halt and whisked her away.

Somehow Carol found the energy to sign books for Allison and me as follows: "For Allison, my almost daughter," and "For Blanche, who has helped me toward the ultimate mystery."

It was a memorable, triumphant night. The love of the crowd for Carol was palpable. I shall never forget it.

Madeleine Nelson, the person who introduced me to Carol, remarked that Carol's ability to listen to others was never more evident than "on the occasion at Trinity Anglican Church in Kitsilano when the first *Dropped Threads* was launched. I came in out of a rainy, wintry night to all this buzz. And finally, there she was. Cancer challenged, surrounded by media, booksellers, adoring fans, family and friends. She began and there was, for me, an unusual mix of her calm and audience excitement."

Dropped Threads went on to become a huge best-seller, bestowing unexpected earnings on each of us who were contributors. Marjorie

Anderson, Carol's co-editor, in her foreword to the book, gives us an insight into its evolution:

> The focus for this anthology floated out one day amid soup and salad at one of those gatherings where Carol and I take the emotional pulse of our worlds—or The World, it seems to us.
>
> [A discussion about the surprises of menopause] quickly led us to wider, more lively musings on what else had caught us unprepared. . . . We were surprised by the number of topics and by the ease with which they came to mind. The image of dropped threads from the fabric of women's talk occurred to us, and the familiar satisfying assumption that women could talk about anything unravelled as we spoke.
>
> In the afterword Carol Shields writes a characteristically wise, gentle unfolding of the central theme as it relates to her personally. She tells of meeting the "surprises of self-discovery" with "gratitude" and then nudges the reader into embracing the unexpected: "Who isn't renewed by startling scenery or refreshed by undreamed-of freedoms? Surprise keeps us alive, liberates our senses."
>
> We hope readers of all ages and backgrounds . . . will be drawn to examine their own crevices of surprise and silence.
>
> —Marjorie Anderson

Date: February 13, 2001
Subject: You were (are) wonderful!

Dearest Carol,

I can't begin to imagine what that performance last night must have cost you. You handled it all superbly and I doubt that anyone would have detected that you had been ill that day. I wouldn't if you hadn't told me.

It was so courageous and kind of you to do all that—you are bringing a whole lot of women writers to a new sense of worth, plus giving them needed publicity.

On top of that it was wonderful to see Sandy again—she said to me as she was leaving that we mustn't wait twenty years for another get-together. I pointed out that that might be a good idea, since in twenty years I would be 97.

On the way home my carful of people were exclaiming over how well you handled the question-and-answer period, how your answers were always thoughtful and profound, yet without ever making anyone feel stupid or put-down for asking.

Oh, Carol, I take heart that you are still able to do so much, and I hope the news is positive. You mentioned that you would be back in two weeks, and even though you may not feel like any get-together, do phone if you feel up to it.

Much love, and admiration (enhanced, if possible),
Blanche
P.S. I thought Don looked very well last night, although I thought he was worried about the strain on you. Anne looked lovely and sounded lovely, and isn't Claudia Casper a delight? I'm going to buy her book, which somehow I missed.

Date: February 20, 2001
Subject: Anne's book club

Hi Carol,

I had a fun evening last night at Anne's book club, but oh the high energy that group generates! I worried that I wouldn't be able to keep up, but managed to hang in. They are a bright, thoughtful, thoroughly engaging group of young women. Were we like that, I often wonder? When I saw Madeleine Nelson (Basford) at the reading the other night, I tried to think back to some vague recollection of what we talked about at the book club years ago, at your house, when we met, and all I draw is a blank except for you and me talking briefly about publishing.

Anne says you will be here this Saturday, so call if you get a chance. I'm so glad *Dropped Threads* was so successful, most of which can be attributed to your excellent promotion. Anne says that things are looking more hopeful, and I am so thankful. Take care.

Love,
Blanche

Date: February 22, 2001
Subject: Re: Anne's book club

Anne couldn't stop raving about your impression on the book club.
Intelligence, grace, everything. And they were tremendously taken with the way you defend your positions. Ah, Blanche, I basked (reflectively) hearing all this.

Love,
C

Date: February 26, 2001
Subject: (TWUC) Guardian: column on gender & writing novels

Carol,
Loved seeing you and Don on Saturday. As you say, you have been spared little, and I wish I was sure there is a sparer to blame.

Much love,
Blanche

Date: March 5, 2001
Subject: Re: Translation of A Celibate Season by Pierre DesRuisseaux

Dear Blanche,
Good luck at the reading and thank you for finding out about the French sale. I realize now that operating without an agent has its problems.

I've just had lunch out with Rachel Wyatt, who is a marvellous woman, a writer, playwright, etc. Don't know whether you know her. Now I'm about to tackle a short intro to *Mansfield Park* for the new Everyman's Library series. Should I object on the grounds of gender? Probably.

Much love,
Carol

Date: March 7, 2001
Subject: Tests

Dear Carol,

You say your spirits are reasonable and I do think Nature gives us some sort of mechanism to deal with blows like this, something that is triggered by shock. I remember a couple of times in my life when that seemed to kick in, such as on my father's death. (I hadn't known how much I loved him until afterwards.)

I'm sorry you've had to cancel accepting your honorary degrees, as I know these things are interesting and stimulating. I presume this will mean you won't go to France, which might have put quite an added strain on you. It's a truism that home is where you want to be when ill.

Oddly enough I've had a good feeling about you lately, for whatever that's worth, but I do tend on occasion to be somewhat psychic, or perhaps, as Penelope would demur, it has seemed so after the fact. But I don't think so.

Am just reading Jack Hodgins' *Broken Ground* and I do like his writing. Not the kind I usually read, but interesting and humorous and touching so far.

Much love,
Blanche

Date: March 18, 2001
Subject: Caring

Dearest Carol,

Anne has just answered my e-mail asking about you and she says it may mean more awful chemo. There is no point in my uttering platitudes, except to say that love is being beamed to you from every corner of the earth, I know that. Surely it will make a difference.

Adrian [Lang] Macdonald phoned me yesterday (loves *Pen's Way*) and told me when I wrote you to pass on her concern.

Call on me for anything that I can do that would possibly give you comfort.

All love,
Blanche

Date: March 19, 2001
Subject: New treatment

Oh Carol, I'm so glad there is further treatment they can do, extension of time is critical in this fast-moving world of cures. At the same time my heart goes out to you for having more procedures and all the pain and discomfort involved.

Last night I read at West Van Library, and Audrey came along, which was very sweet of her.

We're all rooting for you in this ongoing fight against the dragon.

Much love,
Blanche

Date: March 19, 2001
Subject: Encouraging story

Dear Carol,

Sorry to e-mail you twice in one morning, but I just talked to Leslie who told me some encouraging news. A friend of hers has been battling breast cancer and its after-effects for seven years and has been through the whole spectrum of chemo, and not long ago they decided to give her this embolization treatment that you are going for. It has apparently been very successful with her and one of the best things about it is that she is not nearly as sick after the treatments as she was with the regular chemo. She says she starts to feel better in three days instead of struggling on for several days as she did before.

Anyway, I thought anything positive was worth sharing.

Love,
Blanche

Date: March 20, 2001
Subject: Encouraging story

Blanche,

This is simply wonderful news. There are so few cases of this procedure done for breast cancer patients. There are no real stats as a result, only anecdotal backup. And you have given me such a good, hopeful story. Of course I feel that, having been given this extra time, I must use it well—this is, working on the novel. We will be in touch in Vancouver.

Much love,
C

Date: March 27, 2001
Subject: Thinking of you

Dear Carol,

You will be heading for Vancouver soon for your new treatment, and I just wanted to say that I hope it will work well and not be too unpleasant.

Looking forward to seeing you on TV tonight on *Life and Times.* Also pleased with the coverage in *Quill and Quire* of the Jane Austen bio, although I thought the reviewer a tad too academic.

I'm a bit wiped from having Bruce home Sunday and overnight and most of Monday. I think I may have to give up the overnights, especially as he asked me if I minded if he started dating! You've got to keep an eye on these care facilities.

Much love,
Blanche

❧ These are excerpts of an e-mail from the translator:

Date: April 8, 2001
Subject: A Celibate Season, translation by Pierre DesRuisseaux

Could you please explain certain passages from your novel, *A Celibate Season.*

Page 60. A short silence followed, also some embarrassed harrumphing on my part. What does harrumphing mean?

Page 82. By the time we finished breakfast Mia was telling us a string of knock, knock jokes. ?

Page 95. Ceremoniously took her hand, and kissed it right beside the Hope diamond she wears on her ring finger. ?

Date: April 9, 2001
Subject: Re: A Celibate Season, translation by Pierre DesRuisseaux

Dear Blanche,

I am so grateful to you for dealing with these queries. Cultural puzzles are so close to being inexplicable. Untangling the language from the social moment. Suddenly nothing makes sense. My respect for translators is enormous.

Cath has been visiting, and she does lift my heart. Nobody makes me laugh the way she does, but while she does her comedy performance she is also cooking and freezing meals for us. She never stops.

I wouldn't be surprised if *Penelope* lands on a prize list. It's wonderful knowing that readership is there!

Much love,
Carol

Date: April 11, 2001
Subject: Maledictions

Dear Carol,

I have been sending off waves of mental maledictions on the B.C. Book Prizes judges who, in their unenlightened lack of discernment, failed to put *Pen's Way* on the short list. Among those on it are Anita Bau Radami, Eden Robinson, and Barbara Lambert—none of these a surprise to me, I must admit. In fact Barbara Lambert's *A Message for Mr. Lazarus* impressed me tremendously.

I am so glad you are able to enjoy the sunshine and lovely spring and able to keep your optimism in place.

Must run, all love,
Blanche

Date: April 22, 2001
Subject: Re: Visit

Blanche,
    David Watmough and partner were here yesterday and took us for lunch in the un-gentle breezes, much good talk. I ate an enormous hamburger and cleared my plate of fries (am now worried about gaining weight for the first time in my life, such a luxury).
    We'll meet somehow this week and have a good talk.

Much love,
C

Date: April 29, 2001
Subject: Re: A Celibate Season

Dear Carol,
    I'm glad you were able to go home. To much better food, which I hope you feel like eating.
    It is a good thing I had the wonderful review [in *The Globe and Mail*] to float around with yesterday, because all of three people turned up at Chapters for the reading, one of whom was staff. They blamed the nice day, but the location of the readings at the remotest corner of the third floor under the Stephen King paperbacks is probably not the best venue. Oh well, you have to roll with the punches, and my uniform needed cleaning anyway. (Fully amortized now I think. Bought a new one for the judge's welcoming ceremony and reception on the 8th.) [Austin, my son-in-law, had been appointed to the bench.]
    Many, many more hopeful vibes from me and all those who know you.

Love,
Blanche

❧Allison had returned to university in her forties and was to receive her degree in social work at the University of Victoria in June. I wrote to Carol and Don, hoping to be able to see Carol while I was over there. Carol was slated to receive an honorary degree at the same time.

Date: May 15, 2001
Subject: Re: Visit

Dear Carol and Don,

I'll give you a ring and perhaps we can work in a brief visit around Allison's activities. I will have been to the Writers' Union AGM by then and can give Carol any news or hopefully gossip I pick up.

Take care, and love to you both,
Blanche
P.S. We are delighted that Bruce finally has a room to himself at the care centre. It has boosted his morale immensely and makes me feel a great deal better. Aging is the pits, isn't it?

Love,
Blanche

Date: May 16, 2001
Subject: Re: Visit

Blanche,

I had so looked forward to having you HERE. My strength does seem to dip during the day. But I am absolutely sure there will be plenty of time for all of us to get together. What a bore all this health business is. But I'm anxious to see you so we can talk of INTERESTING things.

Much love,
C

Date: May 16, 2001
Subject: Re: Visit

Dear Carol,

Yes, health is certainly a pain, literally and figuratively! I'm so sorry to hear that you've been having pain from the procedure, and sincerely hope all settles down before too long.

The novel is progressing—about page 80. Some days I'm astonished at my brilliance and others I feel lower than Danielle Steele.

I will phone before I come. We might manage a cup of tea or *quelque chose.* Much love and look after yourself.

Blanche

Date: May 30, 2001
Subject: All is well

Dear Blanche,

Bless you—I really mean this—for remembering my birthday (how did I get so old?) and with this delicious-looking Penelope Fitzgerald book, *The Golden Child*, which I will sink into this very evening.

All is well. I'm where I always am, waiting for a scan or waiting for the results of a scan. Up and down, but feeling pretty good today.

Much, much love,
Carol

Date: June 3, 2001
Subject: See you!

Dear Carol,

I'm so glad you like the book, and hope you had a wonderful birthday. I have just come back from the Writers' Union conference and had a great time. Everyone sends their regards, especially Merna and Sandy, and on the first night an actress named Nan Gregory gave a wonderful performance of "Mrs. Turner Cutting the Grass." I say performance because she had the whole thing memorized and her delivery was great.

I'm looking forward greatly to seeing you. Allison and Dave hope to find time to pick me up before the reception and say hello. Allison made the Dean's List and is pretty thrilled about it.

I just had an e-mail from Beverley Slopen in which she described a *National Post* reviewer [of *Penelope's Way*] as humourless, pretentious, pedantic, hectoring and inarticulate, which leads me to believe they gave me a bad review. Unless someone sends it to me I won't read it. Beverley says if she ever meets her she'll say it to her face.

Bill Deverell gave a good talk which he started by saying that it was daunting to fill Carol Shields' shoes, which had the Chair making a point of looking at Bill's feet and [prompted] general laughter from everyone. He was quite funny throughout and self-deprecating.

Much love,
Blanche

Date: June 4, 2001
Subject: Re: See you!

Blanche, yes! On Wednesday. I will have to make up an agenda so we make sure we talk about everything we need to talk about. Will we get to the meaning of life?

Hurray for Allison making the Dean's List. Women are amazing. Imagine someone as busy as Allison still making top marks.

The *National Post* review is one of the silliest I've ever seen. You need not read it. Don and I both thought she was proposing another book which she would have liked you to have written. Her airy notions of fiction theory were self-contradictory, and any reader would see through them. She calls herself a novelist, but I must say that I haven't heard of her.

It'll be so good to see you. I hope the sun is shining.

Much love,
C

∾As it turned out, we were able to see Carol that day in June. Dave and I took Mom to Carol's home and stayed briefly. Carol looked remarkably well and took us on a tour of the main floor of the house and around the beautiful garden. We chatted a little and Carol confided that she felt somewhat overwhelmed with the size of their grand home and that she had always pictured herself spending her last years in a small ivy-covered cottage.

We took pictures in front of the fireplace and then Dave and I departed so that Carol and Mom could have a good visit. [Allison Howard]

Date: June 8, 2001
Subject: Jane Austen

Dear Carol,

Just a note to tell you how much I'm enjoying the Jane Austen bio. I love the way you've handled the historical settings of the time as well as the way in which you've paid attention to and yet distanced yourself from reading too much of her into her novels. I think only another novelist could have done this, and you have done it superbly.

I do hope the day yesterday of the convocations wasn't too wearing. Allison's was lovely and went very smoothly. She was so excited by it all and is throwing a big party tomorrow night for friends to celebrate. Actually it's a potluck, but I just stopped by and she is cooking up a storm, so no one should go hungry. Now she's talking master's degree, perhaps in another discipline if possible.

We were lucky on the way home to go through a pod of whales. I've never had such a good look at them, and never before from a ferry.

Much love,
Blanche

Date: June 9, 2001
Subject: Re: Jane Austen

Dear Blanche,

Thank you first for the warm words about Jane Austen. It was the perfect task for me at the time; I see that now; a puzzle to fit together rather than a narrative to construct. One of the reviews said it took me 3 months—not true, it was eight or nine months.

It was so good to see you. And Allison. And no wonder she's celebrating and thinking of a master's. Her mother's daughter, I would say.

My Honorary day went well, a long day for me, and then last night's dinner. But today is the fifth day in a row that I have felt better, stronger. I think it is the embolization kicking in at last. It just took time to get over the procedure itself. Anne, Catherine and Sara were at the ceremony, passing Ezra back and forth between them. All three of them were rocking back and forth in that familiar baby-comforting gesture—I could see all this from the stage.

I can't tell you what a lot of good it did me to see you. Thank you for your prayer waves. I'm sure they're reaching Victoria.

Much love,
Carol

Date: June 24, 2001
Subject: Happy!

Dear Carol,

Last night Audrey and John very kindly asked me over to a small family dinner—a lovely break and fun. But while there I heard the wonderful news that you have been feeling really well for the last couple of weeks, and I can't tell you how happy I am. Oh, such good news! I hope all scans and so on will show nothing but good things from now on. And that you will be able to take your trip to France in the fall.

Tomorrow I am actually going on a little five-day holiday to the Okanagan for friends' fiftieth anniversary and other visiting. Can't tell you how I'm looking forward to it! I haven't told Bruce yet as I know he will be very upset, but I'm hardening my heart.

All love,
Blanche

Date: June 26, 2001
Subject: Re: Happy!

Dear Blanche,

I expect this will arrive too late to wish you a good and guilt-free few days away. You NEED these days, and you'll have a lovely time relaxing and seeing old friends. So glad you were able to go to John's— they both admire you so much. I'm doing well and writing like mad.

Love,
C

Date: July 4, 2001
Subject: Good holiday

Dear Carol,

I had a wonderful time on my five-day holiday—stayed two days in Vernon with the Buchanans, then in a Penticton hotel for three days and used it as a base to run around having lunches and dinners with friends. The anniversary party [at the home of Carol and Roy Meiklejohn, old and dear friends] was terrific and I saw people I hadn't seen in years—came back refreshed and anxious to write again.

I'm so terribly glad that you are having this wonderful respite from all the lousy stuff.

Sad about Mordecai Richler, wasn't it? I had no idea he was so ill. Take care and finish that novel!

Much love,
Blanche

Date: July 9, 2001
Subject: Re: Good holiday

Dear Blanche,

We are just home from Winnipeg and know how wonderful it feels to renew bonds with old friends. Oh my, we had a wonderful time, and my strength held. I was so proud of my two grandsons, 5 and 10, at the Government House ceremony and dinner; I thought I'd die of pride!

I'm reading four novels at once, not a good idea. I'll settle down to something today. Having a good summer after a rotten spring feels like rebirth.

It is perfectly fine to tell people I'm doing better, though I'm still in treatment.

Much love,
C

Date: July 20, 2001
Subject: Happy anniversary!

Dear Carol,

Aren't I clever to know this? The truth is that Audrey was just here for a cup of tea and told me, and she also tells me that you are doing really fabulously, Carol. How terrific to hear this. I hear you are now able to count on your wonderful trip to France.

Just finished Anne Tyler's *Back When We Were Grownups*, and I note that they quoted from your review of *A Patchwork Planet* on the cover. It was such a treat to bury myself in a really lovely novel.

I understand your novel is going great guns. Why am I so much slower than you? But I am, and have just passed the 100-page mark. Mind you, I'm doing it slowly *à la* your formula of trying to write finished work instead of a draft, and I'm so happy with the procedure as I feel it will end up much more polished.

All the best to you and hope you love France as much as always.

Love,
Blanche

Date: July 22, 2001
Subject: Re: Happy anniversary!

Hello dear Blanche,

Thank you so much for your anniversary greetings—44 years— Don gave me a goat cheese from Salt Spring Island, beautifully presented, and we had dinner at a "smart" bistro.

I have just e-mailed off the seven-eighths of the novel now completed, and this is such a satisfaction that only another writer could possibly appreciate it. I know where the rest of the novel is going; this is a great relief. I did pick up a good deal of speed in the last two months, so don't be discouraged by your progress. I think 100 pages is more than respectable to have produced in the same year you've had a novel published—people don't quite understand that it takes up a lot of energy to put that novel out there; there's so much "stuff" that goes with it.

I have many good days, and this seems a gift. Don has booked us for France in September, and I do hope we can make it. I'm rereading *A Room of One's Own* [Virginia Woolf] and marvelling at its structure. If only people had listened to her we wouldn't have had to have the women's movement.

Much love,
C

Date: July 22, 2001
Subject: Your novel

Dear Carol,
    Life is much better for me these days. I have gradually moved back into a circle of friends that had to be abandoned during Bruce's time at home. Onwards and upwards!

Love,
Blanche

Date: July 22, 2001
Subject: Re: New Yorker

Dear Blanche,
    I was so glad to hear from you. I'm feeling fine today after a not-so-fine week, but my novel is done. DONE. And sent away. Can you send me Allison's address and let me know if she's still interested in doing something for *Dropped Threads 2*.

I've been catching up on *New Yorkers* lately and thought Alice Munro's new story was extraordinary and intricate, one of her best.

Much love,
C

Date: *August 5, 2001*
Subject: *Congratulations and Wow!*

Dear Carol,

I am so thrilled for you that the novel is DONE! That wonderful feeling, and at the same time that lost feeling as you stop living in the life of a very significant other.

Allison is very interested in doing a piece for *Dropped Threads*— now that her degree is finished I think she wants to tackle something else that is challenging. (I wonder where she gets that characteristic?) She and Dave will be home this Saturday after a month in England and I can hardly wait to hear all their news.

Delighted to hear that you are coming this way and would love to see you. Am also sorry that you had a rough week. Looking forward greatly to seeing you.

Much love,
Blanche

Date: *August 13, 2001*
Subject: *Feeling content*

Dear Blanche,

Have you read *Electricity* by Victoria Glendenning? I loved it. I am now reading the history of the screwdriver, recommended by Don. Actually, it is lovely. I am feeling very content these summer days and hope you are too.

Love,
C

Date: August 13, 2001
Subject: Smithers

Dear Carol,

I go to Smithers on August 22nd for five days, Stephen's 50th birthday. Looking forward to it, except that my absence upsets Bruce. He is much more alert these days, which is surprising but more interesting.

Allison and Dave got back from England Saturday and had a wonderful time. Allison was pleased and excited when I told her you had asked if she was still interested [in having her write a piece for *Dropped Threads 2*].* Would you believe I'm reading *Moby Dick*? There are always so many references to it that I decided to find out what it is all about. Am enjoying it thoroughly, love the old-fashioned 19th-century writing. Next on my list is Alistair MacLeod's *No Great Mischief.*

Oh, I hope that France is a great success!

Love,
Blanche

Date: August 29, 2001
Subject: Bruce's letter

Dear Carol,

I can't tell you how thrilled Bruce was to get a letter just to him from you! I took it up to him today and read it aloud, and then he wanted me to leave it so he could peruse it at his leisure. It is enormously kind of you to take the time out of your busy and stressful life.

I am just back from my five days in Smithers for Stephen's 50th birthday. They rented a small community hall and celebrated several other occasions at the same time, and it was a memorable party. A band that didn't blare but that got everyone

---

*Allison did write a piece for a second edition of *Dropped Threads*, but the co-editor decided they would take stories only from previously published authors.

up dancing, from little children to grandmas (yes, I danced a little bit). Leslie and her two children and Allison and Dave also came along, and we had a great time with the Fall Fair in full swing, and Irene in several trotting events (with a buggy) and their 12-year-old, Stephanie, in riding events. They roped me into helping to judge the parade the first night, something that has never loomed large on my list of talents. And there were trail rides and fly fishing and all sorts of bucolic activities.

Love to you both,
Blanche

Date: August 30, 2001
Subject: Re: Bruce's letter

Dear Blanche,
This is a quick note before we go off to France on Tuesday. I feel rather imprisoned in that old cliché about living one day at a time. On the other hand, the new novel has been sold, contracts signed, and I am going to try to get you a hard copy soon. You know how much I always value your comments.

Don is thrilled about the journey. We plan to take loads of books. My latest favourite is Pat Barker's *Border Crossing*, a literary thriller, quite wonderful.

Much love,
Carol

Date: September 28, 2001
Subject: How was France?

Dear Carol,
By my reckoning you must be home now, and I do hope your time in France was wonderful and warm and entertaining and not too tiring. The awful events of Sept. 11th have certainly cast a pall over our lives, haven't they?

I have an interesting book to recommend: *The Archivist*, by Martha Cooley. It begs a certain knowledge of T.S. Eliot's life (not so much of his poems, but that would help), but even without too much knowledge of these things it is well worth reading, especially the diary entries she has included of a manic-depressive woman.

I just reread *The Turn of the Screw* [Henry James], and the intro about all the various interpretations that have been put on it over the years. A strange, strange story.

Thank you so much for the second little letter to Bruce. He is pleased to be remembered.

Love,
Blanche

Date: *September 29, 2001*
Subject: *How was France?*

Dear Blanche,

We are happy to be home, about to go off for a pub lunch with my old prof from U of O. I am mailing you a hard copy of the novel, which is full of critical comments by several hands, and it will be in galleys within weeks. As always, I am grateful for your point of view. (I hope you have a red pen or pencil.) I can still make a few changes.

France was good. Don is glowing, though he mostly did *bricolage*. We saw many friends, and I was mostly well. I hope you saw the [September 11 terrorist] crisis issue of *The New Yorker*, a black cover, no cartoons, and some wise words from Susan Sontag. "Let's all grieve together but let's not be stupid together." I thought it would return to the stirring of a peace movement in the States, but have heard no whispers yet.

Much love, dear friend,
C

Date: *October 4, 2001*
Subject: *Your book*

Dear Carol,

Your ms arrived this morning and I wasn't able to wait. Carol, I love it! I'm only at page 15 but have to remind myself to get on with what I must do (see Bruce, shop for small Thanksgiving dinner with Allison and Dave). Oh, Carol, your first-person narrative is exactly right! I do have a red pen but so far am not using it for quibbling but for words like *Wonderful.*

Do keep writing. It is the one thing a person can do to move into another room where past and present can be put on hold.

Much love,
Blanche

Date: October 4, 2001
Subject: Your book

Dear Blanche,

As I write this, Sara is sitting in an immense room with 339 other women, and they're all breast-feeding their babies at once—this is to be a Guinness record apparently. I keep wondering what the atmosphere is like, and the smell of flowing milk.

Blanche, my dear friend, thank you so much for such encouraging words. I am dancing (in my head).

Much love,
C

Date: October 8, 2001
Subject: Your book

Hi Carol,

I have finished reading your novel and I am ecstatic over it. To me it is "true," in the sense that nothing seems artificial or fictional. You've done a marvellous job of bringing in the worry over Norah at the same time as carrying on with your narrator's life, so it is like a mournful melody running through the entire work. Also you've put into perspective how little the day-to-day irritations matter in the face of major pain.

The first-person narrative is exactly right—this isn't a novel where we need to get into anyone else's head, their pains are all obvious. I have to say, I love this novel more than any of your others. I find the structure perfect.

All love and I hope you are feeling reasonably well.

Blanche

Date: October 9, 2001

Hello my dear Blanche,

Thank you, thank you for your warm words. I opened your letter with trepidation. Lordy, how we need propping up. Do you suppose writers ever get to the point of complete faith in their blatherings? I don't know if this is a question or an exclamation.

Much love,
C

Date: October 16, 2001
Subject: Your visit

Dear Carol,

I am greatly disappointed that I can't be at John and Audrey's on Saturday night, I would love to see you. But it is a law of nature that if one interesting thing is going to happen on a given night, another even more attractive thing will come up. The North Shore Arts Commission has an annual arts gala (food and theatre) and I was instrumental in setting the thing up, so I support it every year.

Audrey tells me you are looking wonderful, and this is great news to hear. I hope everything is still in remission.

I had a request from Pearson Education (used to be Prentice Hall) to use "The Anger of Young Men" in a textbook. However, they wanted electronic rights as well and offered no money, so I consulted the Writers' Union chat line and got six indignant responses saying a major textbook publisher shouldn't expect to get our work for nothing. So I've written to ask them what their standard fee is.

Love,
Blanche

Date: October 23, 2001
Subject: This and that

Hi Carol,

Something I forgot to mention to you about your ms was how much I liked the places where you talked about the invisibility of women. This has been in my mind a lot lately with the world in the grip of terrorists and bombing, all male. Not that I don't think there are plenty of very peaceful men, there are, it's just that at the extreme of warlikeness it is pretty well exclusively a male domain (to which they are welcome, except that we have to be partakers).

Next week is my birthday, oh horrid plight! Seventy-eight, I can't believe it. Anyway, I'm beavering away at my novel and making progress.

Love,
Blanche

Date: October 25, 2001
Subject: Re: This and that

Dear Blanche,

Yes, this whole war is a testosterone effort. There is a way in which one can view it as a war between men and women; certainly it is about men and women. I'm not being very clear, still working it out.

Much love,
C

Date: November 25, 2001
Subject: Everything

Dear Carol,

Thank you so much for the nice birthday card. I had as nice a birthday as possible considering the years—Allison and Leslie took me to lunch (a custom) and Stephen sent flowers, and there were also nice gifts.

I was so glad to read that you had attended the Giller Prize dinner but was terribly sorry (and, I must admit, appalled) that [Carol's] *Jane Austen* wasn't entered. Sometimes I wonder how publishers manage to screw up on so many things, especially with all that you've done for them, but to screw up is human, as Heather Mallick points out in Saturday's *Globe*.

I am most anxious to hear about your health. Is everything stabilized?

I am making arrangements to have a holiday in Florida with a very old friend [Ruth Beatty] who owns a terrific condo on San Marcos Island on the ocean (Gulf side). Bruce and I visited there a few years ago and now her husband is dead and she wants me to drive down with her from Toronto in early January. She is the friend who, at age 75, has just cut a wonderful CD—her beautiful singing voice has not eroded over the years.

Much love to both of you.
Blanche

Date: December 3, 2001
Subject: Your party, etc.

Dear Carol,

Thank you so much for your invitation [to their Christmas party] and also for offering to put me up so I can be there. Needless to say I am very sorry to hear the bad news [that the cancer was spreading], but the drugs are potent and I have heard that sometimes a new drug will be more effective after a change.

Much love,
Blanche

14

A Differently Ordered Universe

2001–2003

ᔌPerhaps it was the darkness looming on the periphery that has left me with a recollection of a weekend of theatre-like lightness and intensity, as though the actions and words and laughter and talk were lit by an incandescence that turned even the evening shadows luminous. And in the morning, enthusiastic talk of books and authors with Carol and Anne and Sara and the other house guests: Maggie Dwyer, who had been Carol's friend in Winnipeg and who now lived farther up on Vancouver Island, and Freydis Welland, a distant relative of Jane Austen's whose mother, a great-great-grandniece of Austen's, had been one of Carol's resources for Austen family folklore.

The Shields family had acquired many friends in the short time they lived in Victoria and I renewed acquaintance with writers I knew. Carol circulated among the guests, chatting and laughing as though the hovering ghoul had been banished, excluded from the party and shut out—but later, in the night, there was a howling and thrashing outside as though something were venting its wrath. The storm brought down trees and cancelled ferry sailings, but I slept through it all, as if in Carol's house I was safe, protected the way I once was when the invincibility of my parents kept the storms of my childhood at bay.

Date: December 20, 2001
Subject: Wonderful party!

Dear Carol and Don,

Thank you so much for your hospitality and for the great party.

It is wonderful that *Maclean's* is making you one of its acclaimed persons of the year. Much love to you both, and have the best possible Christmas.

Blanche

Date: January 26, 2002
Subject: Thank you

Dear Blanche,

Thank you, belatedly, for this wonderful book, *Stet.* I devoured it. I love her, Diana Athill, her fairness and wit. Don't you just sense what a wonderful conversation we could have with her? She is open and tactful and cordial and polite. And smart.

Much love and good spirits in the new year.
Carol

Date: January 26, 2002
Subject: Back from Florida

Hi Carol,

It was lovely to get a nice letter from you when I got back from my travels, which went very well.

Unfortunately I got back to a bit of a crisis re Bruce. He had fallen and broken his arm right through, and they had to have surgery and pins put in. They made the mistake of discharging him too soon, and when I got in Tuesday night Leslie took me directly to the care centre. They sent him to hospital the next day and stabilized him with a transfusion and so on. Allison and Leslie were exhausted from staying with him, but they had been determined not to tell me until I got home. Fortunately Stephen arrived for a convention and decided to forget the convention to help us. Bruce was in Emergency until this morning when they got him a bed.

Hi to Don, and much love,
Blanche

Date: January 30, 2002
Subject: Re: Back from Florida

Blanche,

I've just now read your note with all this bad news. What a misery! I'll phone you tonight to see how you're doing. Welcome home, but I am so sorry about Bruce.

Love,
C

Date: February 22, 2002
Subject: Celibate Season

Dear Don and Carol,

I do hope you had a relaxed time in Palm Springs. I like the dry desert air around there, don't you? I hope it did you some good, Carol. My thoughts are with you both.

Bruce was in hospital three weeks but is now back at the care centre. Physically he is improving but this took quite an added toll on his mind.

Love to you both,
Blanche

Date: February 22, 2002
Subject: Re: Celibate Season

A quick note, Blanche. We cut our trip to Palm Springs a day short, and I have not been doing well since then, more sofa days than I would like. I'm reading a little science, *Mother Nature* by Sarah Blaffer Hrdy (odd spelling). Every page has something of interest. She's a primatologist, anthropologist, humanist, wonderful. I'm trying to get Eleanor [Wachtel] to interview her.

Does it sound New-Agey to say that people should be allowed to have their pain? I read this recently. Hmmmmm.

Love,
C
Onward with the book!

Date: February 25, 2002
Subject: Glad to hear from you

Dear Carol,

Thank God for reading! What would we ever do without it? At the moment I'm reading *An Equal Music* by Vikram Seth. Finished *The Passion* by Jeanette Winterson—our book club discussed it and I seemed to be the only one with reservations. It is beautifully written and has an interesting historical background, the characters speaking in their own voices from their various stops. Still, it seemed to me that something was lacking, but I'm less sure of myself than I used to be when it comes to judging novels.

I'm so sorry you are having more couch days, and that you had to cut your little holiday short. How I wish I could say the perfect words of consolation, but other than reminding you that we all love you, there isn't much else.

Bruce is pretty frail but improving.

My love to you and Don,
Blanche

Date: February 27, 2002
Subject: Re: Glad to hear from you

Blanche,

You must hie yourself off to the bookstore and buy *Mother Nature*, by Sarah Hrdy (odd spelling). I don't read much science, as you know, but she makes it a joy, and I love being in this book. I think you should read this book, then pass it to your daughters. By the way, this brilliant woman hails from Texas; so much for stereotypes. I'm finally figuring out what a mother is.

Love,
C

Date: February 27, 2002
Subject: Book recommendation

Dear Carol,

Thank you for pointing me to *Mother Nature*. Also thank you (from the bottom of my heart—I don't go in for clichés) for wanting to read my ms, *So Long Judas*. I wouldn't have suggested it and I certainly don't expect any editing input, but it will give me a great lift to know that you've seen it.

Much love as always,
Blanche

Date: March 21, 2002
Subject: How are you?

Dear Carol,

I wonder how you are bearing up through this gruelling time, and especially hope you are not too fatigued to do a bit of writing.

Monday we had Bruce moved to the facility near me. It is way more modern and bright than the place he was in, but I feared he might find the uprooting hard. He seems to be making the adjustment quite well, but he is failing more mentally (as well as physically). I've been trying to get over every day during this time of transition, which leads to a lot of frustration in not getting on with the novel. I know I shouldn't complain, he's the poor soul with the awful things happening, but where would we be without complaints? I've been especially irked lately by people who refuse to complain about the weather. To my cheery remark, "Lousy day, isn't it?" all sorts of determinedly cheerful responses, "Oh, but it's not snowing," or "Last week was good." What will be the fate of good Canadian conversational openers without weather complaints?

You must be getting excited about the new book's [*Unless*] debut. Alma Lee has asked me to be one of the readers at the tribute to you on April 17th. I do hope you will be well enough to be there. Didn't I read that you won a Writers' Trust of Canada Award for *Jane Austen*? Richly deserved—I thought it a masterpiece.

Much love to you both,
Blanche

Date: March 21, 2002
Subject: How are you?

Dear Blanche,
Re: Complaining

Yesterday I complained to Don that I was feeling a bit blue, and he immediately relayed this information to Sara, who has now alerted the whole family that I am depressed. And, of course, I woke up feeling quite bright this morning. No more complaining, I've decided.

Love and to Bruce too,
Carol

Date: April 1, 2002
Subject: Wonderful second time around

Dear Carol,

I've read *Unless* again and am even more excited about it than when I read it the first time. Even though I knew how it was going to end I found myself holding my breath over the outcome.

We had a great visit from Stephen and family on their way home from kayaking in Mexico—*chacun à son goût*. Bruce loves to see Stephen and he spent all day with him, while the ladies, young and old, went shopping. Well, old got tired and left them on their own, I must admit.

I do hope that last scan that you were waiting for when I phoned had something good to say. Perhaps you are back on chemo, and if so, hope you aren't feeling too lousy.

Much love to you and Don,
Blanche

Date: April 10, 2002
Subject: Reviews

Oh Carol,

What wonderful reviews! And more than well deserved. I loved the *Globe* one, also thought *The Vancouver Sun* one worthy. Good for you! I hope it is giving you a lift, and am delighted to learn that you are writing fiction again.

Basking in the thrill of your success!

Much love,
Blanche

Date: April 17, 2002
Subject: Sun article

Dear Carol,

That was an excellent article about you in *The Vancouver Sun* today and I loved the picture.

Tonight is the tribute here in Vancouver and I'm looking forward to it. When we had a rehearsal last week I saw Keith Maillard for the first time since the days of the eighties Writers' Union meetings. We both stared at one another, searching, I suppose, for the person we knew beneath the ravages of years. He is the same gentle, self-deprecating man he always was, immensely likeable, although now middle-aged and slightly plump and with all that bush of wonderful curly hair now tamed and thinning. He read—with Joy Coghill— that hilarious dialogue when the supercilious editor comes to visit her [the protagonist] and he was quite wonderful. It will be a great note to end the evening on.

No need to say how much I pray that you aren't having too much pain.

Much love,
Blanche

Date: April 17, 2001
Subject: Sun article

Blanche,
Yes, the concern of others does help. I suppose it is all part of the connections that make our lives worth living, that series of conversations tipping one way and then the other. I would dearly love to hear you read tonight, and you know, I believe, how grateful I am that you were willing to do this. Break a leg, but gently.

Much love,
C

Date: April 18, 2002
Subject: Last night

Dear Carol,
I'm sure John and Anne have told you how successful the tribute was last night—a very bittersweet triumph. The place was full, must have been about 300 there.

I wonder if all these tributes are easy or hard for you. On the one hand, it is nice to be celebrated while you can enjoy it, but on the other, it does bring a note of finality—something I'm not willing to concede yet.

Oh, and thank you for the lovely tributes you gave me in the *National Post.* I am becoming famous for being your friend.

Oh, I hope things aren't too uncomfortable for you, that there are days when you can still feel the joy of spring and blossoms. I think of you every day.

Love,
Blanche

Date: April 18, 2002
Subject: Re: Last night

Blanche,

Everyone has been telling me how marvellous you were, every word, every syllable, articulated. I can't thank you enough for doing this. Meg and her Rebecca are here at the moment, and Anne and family are coming over tomorrow. I do feel ringed with love.

Much love,
C

                                                            May 4, 2002

Dear Blanche,

Carol has asked me to write thanking you for participating in the launch of *Unless.* She has been overwhelmed with happiness by such strong support from the writing community, and your own kindness in taking part.

Our whole family sends thanks and good wishes.

Warmly,
Audrey [Shields]
[From Carol, handwritten]
P.S. My dearest Blanche, you were magnificent! Love, C

Date: May 7, 2002
Subject: Everything

Dear Carol,

I talked to Audrey the other day and she said you were still fairly strong. I hope and pray that you aren't suffering any pain and that there are lots of rewards still in your life.

I've been reading Shaena Lambert's collected stories [*The Falling Woman*] and some of them are excellent. She is Barbara Lambert's daughter, and they had a wonderful launch, she and Timothy Taylor, at a lounge with music, dim lights, a total bar scene. Seemed to work well with the youngish crowd there. It was quite fun and the first time I've been on the night club scene for a lot of years.

Carol, all the best on your lonely road. I think of you every day.

Love,
Blanche

Date: May 10, 2002
Subject: Re: Everything

Dear Blanche,

Just a quick note to wish you well at the Writers' Union AGM. I know I can count on you to bring back your acute perceptions and glances of irony. I will positively count on a letter.

We're doing well day by day.
Much love, and to Bruce,
C

Date: May 28, 2002
Subject: Meaning of life

Blanche,

What about this as the meaning of life. Life constitutes the spreading centre of order in an otherwise increasingly less ordered universe.

Or this: Life constitutes a centre of known order spreading to a differently ordered universe???

Much love,

C

Date: Mary 28, 2002
Subject: Meaning of life

Dearest Carol,

I think both your definitions are brilliant and are making me think, which I seldom do on serious subjects any more, although at one time they occupied my mind greatly. Another of the aspects of aging, resignation. Your first definition, life constituting a spreading centre of order in an increasingly less ordered universe—this implies that the universe undergoes a transformation from a prior form of order before life emerges, and that life in effect steals order gradually from the prior order and leaves it increasingly in a state of chaos. What an interesting idea! In my mind's eye I picture the order that exists before life as a large blob of yellow that is gradually being eaten away by the rest of life. It is as though life is imposing a new form of order on the universe, and the old order is becoming more and more obsolete.

When you think of those millions of whirling galaxies obeying laws that should be immutable, and then stealthy life eating away at the laws with new ones, it is an immense thought.

I think I like the second one better, since the words "known order" (for life) and "differently ordered" seem to me to be closer to the mark. This way we are allowing the laws that govern galaxies their own form of order rather than eating away at it, while noting that life imposes a new order that seems not to be subject to the physical laws of galaxies. It underlines the fact that life is a kind of order that is distinct from the laws of physics, and once again we are up against consciousness. Consciousness is the order that we can know, even though it is capricious and unpredictable—which

I believe. I believe that trying to reduce life to the sum of known physical laws is a conceit like those of the men of the 19th century, who believed they would soon solve all the riddles of the universe.

I am writing this off the top of my head, but you have given me much to mull over, and indeed that erosion of one type of order by another may indeed be the meaning of life.

On more mundane subjects—the AGM was interesting and distracting. One of the things that was brought home to me more forcibly than ever was the difference in the way men and women talk. It happened that I lunched one day with a group of men, Bill Schermbrucker, Brian Burtch, and two other nice men I hadn't met before. The talk was about books and movies, ones we had loved and why, and it was an ordered conversation, taking turns, no interruptions, no discussion of their ex-spouses or children. That night I sat in a room with a group of women, mostly children's authors, Norma Charles and others I had just met. Again the conversation was interesting, but fast with constant interruptions and references to personal experiences and the cupidity of their exes. Both were fun, but the women were closer to the marrow while the men tended to stand back with more impersonal observations.

Not that any of this is new, of course, but it did strike me more forcibly than usual. On the night of the final banquet and the tribute to Penny Dickens, the literati was out in force. I saw Atwood there, and Eugene Benson gave a wonderful speech. There were tears and gifts and shaking of hands and good fellowship all over the place. Aided and abetted by much wine. Dorris Heffron was there. The last time I saw her was at the Winnipeg convention—remember, when we did a final edit on *A Celibate Season* for Random House! Dorris was denouncing [John] Bayley for his exploitation of Iris Murdoch.

Another subject—be sure, if you can, to see *The Fast Runner* (*Atanarjuat*), the Inuit picture that has received great reviews. It really is remarkable.

I will think more about what you've said. Maybe between us we'll get this thing figured out yet.

My love, as always,
Blanche

Date: June 2, 2002
Subject: Carol's birthday

Dear Carol,

I hope you have a wonderful day. Leslie and family are coming here for dinner tonight and I'm looking forward to entertaining for a change; the time has come when they have the dinners and I sit. Not as soul-enhancing as I used to imagine—I think we all long to be givers before being getters.

I'm quite sure Anne has told you that she's invited me to go with her next Sunday for the day to see you. If you aren't feeling well enough, don't hesitate to let me know, even at the last minute. I am hoping to bring my ms—but remember, don't read it if it's too tiring and also don't worry about doing any editing, I just want you to see it.

Much love,
Blanche

Date: July 10, 2002
Subject: Fiddling

Blanche!

A warm hello on a Wednesday in beautiful July. How odd to be ill in the midst of such sumptuous summer. Cath is here for a few weeks, having rented a house nearby, and she'll meet with the doctor this afternoon—decisions to be made, and one thinks how lucky to be able to make decisions. Well, if we live to 90—or 100, would there be enough time for the kind of fiddling we love?

Much love,
C

Date: July 11, 2002
Subject: Summer

Dear Carol,

It was lovely to have a note from you, but it seems somewhat unbearable that you should be coping with illness, as you say, during these hot July days. Unbearable—a ridiculous word, because nobody asks if it's worse than one can bear. Oh, I do hope you are reasonably comfortable and not having pain. I think of you every day and hope and pray that there will be a respite.

I have been in Comox for a couple of days, the annual reunion with two of the "girls" I went to high school with, all of us 78 and counting. Much reading of diaries and sighing to think it was such an innocent-seeming world, along with the usual changeless heartaches of adolescence. Also laughed that we used the word "swell" in those days, I'd forgotten there was such a word. And "coozy-bumping," as in X and Y were coozy-bumping in the back seat.

I am reading Philip Roth, *American Pastoral*, and am enormously impressed. And it is such a treat to get back to fiction of this calibre. Roth amazes me with his ability to slip between past and present in a seamless way.

Bruce is not doing well, there has been quite a falling-off lately, not only mentally but physically. For some reason I feel much worse about it when I go away even for a couple days, as though I were magically the thing that keeps it all under control.

As always, my love to you,
Blanche

❧I went with Anne to Victoria as planned and we had a wonderful day. Carol as usual rose above her illness and we sat in the lovely sunroom of their house and talked as furiously as we always did, anxious to finally get everything said—which of course we never could.

Date: July 16, 2002
Subject: Wonderful to see you!

Thank you so much for the lovely visit on Sunday. It was such a treat to see you both, and I was heartened by how well you look, Carol, and how much you maintain your interest in the goings-on around us. And books, of course. Anne was so kind to pick me up and take me.

Much love,
Blanche

Date: July 17, 2002
Subject: The review

Dear Carol,
Thank you so much for sending that piece about Rosalind Franklin. Ever since I wrote the piece for *Dropped Threads* I've wondered why no one seemed to be protesting the injustice done her. This is good news.

I understand your decision to forgo more rotten chemo and steroids. It is vital, I think, to feel comfortable with your "self," as you say, and I know from others that steroids do have a distorting effect on the psyche. As always my love and concern and hope that this respite from chemicals will restore whatever it is you have missed.

I am going to Smithers tomorrow to visit Stephen and family for a few days.

Much love,
Blanche

Date: July 23, 2002
Subject: Back from Smithers

Dear Carol,
I've been thinking about you a great deal, especially during the recent hot spell, although I expect your large house stays cool in its arbour of trees.

I had a lovely time in Smithers visiting Stephen and Irene and the two daughters. I won't bore you with a list of their accomplishments, suffice it to say that they are certainly terrific kids. Leslie's daughter Katherine starts McGill in the fall and has also aced her exams. *Quel* brilliant family!

I have just begun reading *Mother Nature* and am finding it fascinating. Also on my trip I read Audrey Thomas' *Isobel Gunn* and was very, very impressed. I wrote to her about it, and am amazed that it won no prizes or acclaim. The outrage of a woman pretending to be a man!

If you feel up to it, let me know how things are going. I pray that you aren't in too much discomfort, hope the cessation of chemo is making you feel better.

All love,
Blanche

Date: August 1, 2002
Subject: Re: Back from Smithers

Dear Blanche,

So glad your trip to Smithers was a success. It is a place I can't picture. The summer here has been so astonishingly abundant, flowers everywhere, such growth. I was delighted with the photos you sent. Don and his son-in-law are building a cupola for the garage, a folly and [he] is so pleased with it. Men and their projects! Haven't managed to come to much understanding about gender other than an appreciation of serious differences.

I did read *Isobel Gunn,* speaking of gender, and thought it wandered off a bit thinly at the end, but was otherwise an amazing story. We send love to you and were sorry to hear that Bruce is not doing well. This is so grossly unfair.

C

Date: August 5, 2002
Subject: How are you?

Dear Carol,

Last weekend I went with Leslie and Austin to their fairly primitive cabin on Nelson Island—no electricity, running water from a little gravity fed lake above them. It was great to see it, except for the two bats which made their appearance, flying enthusiastically around my cowering head, after I settled down in the loft. Naturally I freaked out and Austin tried to get them but without avail. Then the bats quieted down and he assured me that they had settled for the night, so I snuggled down with something over my head and they didn't put in another appearance—I believe.

Next week I am going to the Sechelt writers' festival. Remember the time years ago when we went? I think longingly about it—it was, I believe, about 15 years ago. How *tempus fugits*.

All my love and hope for you. And to Don.

Love,
Blanche

Date: August 13, 2002
Subject: Writers' festival

Dear Carol,

I am back from the Sechelt writers' festival and thought you might like to hear some of my impressions. But first of all, I must correct my erroneous statement that we were there 15 years ago, it was actually 10.

Writers have become good stand-up comedians by and large, and all the sessions were wonderful. Bill Richardson was, as usual, funny and warm, and read from one of his poems, which sounded better spoken than merely read. He greeted me like a long-lost friend and inquired about you. Richard Wright's repartee during question period was very funny. An Inuit named Michael Kusugak was wonderfully funny, could make his living as a comedy act. Also Bob McDonald of *Quirks & Quarks* fame; as a matter of fact I think he stole the show. Barbara Gowdy has a lovely stage presence. Barbara

Nichol, who wrote *Beethoven Lives Upstairs* and a funny book which she read, *Dippers*, also showed slides and wove her talk in with funny home anecdotes. Timothy Taylor needs to read more slowly but is attractive and very friendly. Lorna Crozier and Patrick Lane read well together, but I must say Lorna is the one who stole the show. She is still so attractive—remember she read the year we were there?

For my money the hit of it all was Rex Murphy who gave the Bruce Hutchison lecture. His talk was lively and erudite and thought provoking. He spoke passionately about the written word and pointed out that it is often words that show a nation who they are, and went on to cite *Moby Dick* and Martin Luther King as having defined U.S. words, and Churchill as a defining English example. During the question period a simple question would elicit a five-minute answer through related ideas, all fascinating.

The thing ran like clockwork thanks to the 200 volunteers who ushered, cooked, supervised, etc. etc. What a marvellous community effort!

I hope you are enjoying the beautiful weather as much as you are able, and that you aren't suffering. I think of you often and trust that the presence of so many loving family members makes your life more bearable.

My regards to Don as always.

Much love,
Blanche

Date: August 13, 2002
Subject: Re: Writers' festival

Dear Blanche,

I do admire Rex Murphy, though I was too intimidated by him to go on *Cross Country Checkup* some years ago. He sounds like a self-educated man, yet I was told he was Rhodes Scholar. A couple of his long book essays have impressed me tremendously, and he can be tough. Oddly, he was terribly benign about the Pope and Pope Week in Canada, more than I was feeling. Oh, I do think it is time that old man stayed home. He's so expensive a guest. Grumble, grumble.

We're doing fine in our day-by-day rhythm. I'm so glad you have liked *Mother Nature*. I am mailing off my copy to a friend in the States. I kept thinking it was full of facts that I should have known when I was feeding—bottle-feeding—my children, but I might not have believed any of it then.

Much love,
C

Date: August 22, 2002
Subject: Article

Dearest Carol,

Freydis tells me that she had lunch with you and that she was pleasantly surprised that you looked so well and seemed to enjoy yourself. I'm sure your energy is low, but as long as you can take pleasure in the small joys life has to offer, that is the main thing.

Somebody gave me a copy of *Canadian Living*. I can't tell you how moved I was, and was so interested to know that you were able to live one day at a time, a thing I still haven't mastered although I would love to. I was particularly interested in your description of the various phases of grief and acceptance, and of the embarrassment you felt at having previously given a talk when you didn't know what it would really be like.* You always are able to articulate so well, even thoughts and feelings that must be painful. And I was gratified to read your apt musings on what it must be like to be poor or alone with such an illness. I am so glad you recommended *Mother Nature*. A bit chilling,

---

*In the *Canadian Living* article, Carol wrote, "In early November 1998, less than one year ago, I came to Toronto to give a talk at a fund-raising lunch for the Healing Journeys programs . . .

Less than three weeks later I was diagnosed with third-stage breast cancer . . . I remembered the terrible ease with which I'd spilled forth my so-called ideas about how to cope, endure, how to go on living. *I had no idea.*" [Italics hers.] The article goes on and details her treatments and the impact on her family. She also wrote, "It was the kindness of other people that carried me through the transition from disbelief to acceptance."

isn't it, the way the evolutionary process has reached into our supposedly human and altruistic natures and selected for the ones that bring a net benefit, even when that benefit involves infanticide.

My love to Don as well as to you,
B

Date: August 25, 2002
Subject: Re: Article

Dear Blanche,
Your letter was so welcome and your warm words. I am feeling better moving away from the chemo sessions, though I know this feeling is temporary. I hate the phrase "quality of life," but can't find a better.

I'm doing a little writing on good days, about a 67-year-old woman who writes sonnets. It meanders endlessly, no plot, just scattered thoughts.

I have lost all respect for our Prime Minister and his boyish tactics.

Love,
C

Date: August 27, 2002
Subject: Time

Blanche!
We are as well as you can imagine we are, under our circumstances. The days go by quickly, and we both feel in tune with the weather, the climate, the whole rhythm of (what we call, I suppose) life. Now, who exactly sets that rhythm? Don is just finishing a good book on TIME, and it brings up the question: why is there anything? Have you ever tried to explain this to a child? I suppose I am grateful to be left with this unsolved problem, which can't help but give one a boost into the other-world that is undefined and unquantifiable.

Much love,
C

Date: August 31, 2002
Subject: Mother Nature

Dear Carol,

I finished *Mother Nature*, and I agree with you that it was quite mind-boggling. And thought-provoking. I haven't read any non-fiction for a long while and it was good brain-stretching exercise. The only carp I have is with the last couple of chapters, since the hypotheses in them didn't seem to follow as rigorous a path of scientific evidence as the others. Her guess that lack of sufficient commitment between mother and child might account for something as awful as psychopathology struck me as speculation. She seems to avoid the prevalence of child abuse and its undoubted pathological results, and it would have been interesting to have her discuss its prevalence and why evolution would have allowed selectivity to proceed in that direction.

On the whole, I learned a great deal about women's possibly greater role in setting the direction of evolution. Just starting on *The Jade Peony,** and finished Timothy Taylor's book of short stories, *Silent Cruise*, which I thought beautifully written and much more polished than *Stanley Park*.

Much love to you,
Blanche

Date: August 31, 2002
Subject: Re: Mother Nature

Dear Blanche,

I am so glad you found *Mother Nature* as extraordinary as I did. I had a strong sense of how mammal-like and how ape-like we really are, and how this (instincts and manifestations) doesn't just go away because we happen to live with electricity and plumbing. Lordy,

---

*By Wayson Choy.

there is so much to think about, for which I'm grateful. Big ideas and very small ones.

Much love,
C

~On September 11, Bruce, my husband of fifty-seven years, died. His death was not unexpected; neither was it expected, in the sense that no amount of forewarning can ever translate into the experience, nor lessen the confusion of loss. He lay in a coma for the better part of two days. Stephen and Leslie sat with me while we waited. Allison was in Ottawa and was unable to get an immediate flight back.

Of course I talked to Carol and Don during this time, Carol insisting, in spite of her advanced illness, that they would come for the memorial service. And also, in spite of her weakness, she had reviewed my manuscript and returned it to me.

Date: September 14, 2002
Subject: ms received

Dear Carol

Stephen just left for the airport and Leslie has gone home, so for the first time since Bruce's death I am alone. The kids were wonderful— the whole thing was complicated by the fact that when he first took ill I had arranged to have new carpets installed in the apartment, so everything was in turmoil, and they helped me straighten all that out as well as deal with obits, memorial services, etc. Allison wanted to fly home early from her two-week holiday visiting Dave's parents and children, but we persuaded her to wait until next Friday when she was due to return.

Your wonderful thoughtful and encouraging letter arrived today [re my manuscript]—I am overwhelmed at your managing all this when I know your energy is low. It has given me a tremendous boost, which is something I can really use right now. And your ideas are so good!

I have just received a contract from *Prairie Fire* re printing my
old foreword in the upcoming publication dedicated to your writings. Needless to say I am honoured to be included. And on the
subject of writing, *Dropped Threads* never ceases to amaze—
78 weeks [on the best-seller list].

Much love, and thank you and Don for your kind thoughts
when you phoned.

Love,
Blanche

> *Carol Shields*
> *900 Terrace Avenue, Victoria, B.C*

September 17, 2002

Our dear Blanche,

Here we are—with no words, faced with our conventional
phrases, thinking of you, grieving for you.

I do believe Bruce had a happy life, and that you, and your love for
each other, was the base for that happiness. It is really quite incredible,
all the two of you have done, all you've achieved. It must have seemed
a great risk going off to Ottawa, but you were both in such good heart
and made such a success of it. His gentleness—that's what I'll remember most. His willingness. The ability he had to take an interest—in
art, travel, language, society, all of this enterprise we call life.

Your loving friend,
Carol

Date: September 19, 2002
Subject: Atonement

Dear Carol,

Just a note to tell you that I finished *Atonement** last night
and found it wonderful and gripping. He built the suspense so

---

*By Ian McEwan.

well that I did something I never do—sneaked peaks at the ending. His war scenarios were on a par with *Birdsong** or *Regeneration,*** and all his characters so well drawn I felt I knew them perfectly. He made me wonder why I bother.

I must admit, however, to a definite letdown when I learned that that wasn't the way it happened, that there was no happy ending. Of course I realize that the happy ending he had led us up to was perhaps too good to be true, but to do that switch at the end left me grieving for what might have been. I also realize that the happy ending would perhaps have been too pat, and in the imagined scenes the writing was less detailed, as though what didn't happen was somehow obscure. I'm sure this is quibbling about a marvellous book, so much detail, so much suspense.

There are a lot of little details to be attended to [following Bruce's death], bureaucratic mostly. I wonder why we can't have one-stop shopping, but they do keep me occupied. Also many phone calls and so on, which makes me glad that Bruce was so well respected. He would have been gratified.

I hope you are continuing to do well, and much love,

Blanche

Date: September 25, 2002
Subject: The Booker!

Dear Carol,

I am so excited to hear of your making the short list [with *Unless*]. Wow!

Thank you and Don for those warm letters you sent. I didn't realize how much people cared for Bruce, all of them characterizing

---

*By Sebastian Faulks.
**By Pat Barker.

him as a warm and gentle man, which he was. (Well, most of the time—he was, after all, only human.) How Bruce would have laughed at Don's description of the famous wall-chinking in the Jura. And the Ikea shopping trip.

It looks as though there will be quite a few at the service. I do hope you will feel up to it that day, although I know you have to take it one day at a time. If only you can get to England for the Booker Prize ceremony! Even if you don't win (although I think you will) there will be lots of parties and interviews and so on.

All love, and we are all immensely proud,
Blanche

❧ Carol and Don did come to Bruce's memorial service on October 2nd. By then, I had come down with a painful bout of shingles across my back, and so at the reception Carol and I sat together on a couch in the corner. At one point, we both tried to get up and circulate, but Don steered her back to her seat and I flagged before I had made it halfway across the floor.

In a day whose details remain a jumble, one tiny beacon stands out: as Carol and I sat together we took each other's hands in a silent tribute to loss. The comfort of that small intimacy found its way into memory.

Date: October 14, 2002
Subject: Thank you

Dear Carol,

Again I want to thank you and Don and Anne and Audrey for coming. It meant a great deal to me.

I came across three novellas by Flannery O'Connor. I am dazzled by her powers of description and her ability to keep you fascinated by the doings of quite unpleasant people. *Wise Blood* is the one I'm reading at the moment.

Take care and reserve your strength for all the honours coming your way.

Much love,
Blanche

Date: October 25, 2002
Subject: Congratulations

Dear Carol,
    It is wonderful that you are being honoured again in the Order of Canada awards.*
    I absolutely loved Ian McEwan's *Black Dogs*. Wish I had read it before I suggested *Atonement* for the next book club, but too late I'm afraid.

Much love,
Blanche

Date: October 27, 2002
Subject: Re: Congratulations

Dear Blanche,
    It was a wonderful day yesterday at Government House in Victoria, Iona [Campagnolo, lieutenant governor of B.C.] at her most charming.** Three of our children were there, and there were a few other children as well, making a nice buzz in the background. About sixty friends came, and I do believe half of them were Winnipeggers. A warm occasion in every way. The ceremony, tea and cookies, and the sun shining. Oh my, life is good.

Much love,
C

---

*Carol had earlier been recognized as an Officer of the Order of Canada. This time she was made a Companion of the Order of Canada.
**The ceremony had been moved from Ottawa to Victoria.

Date: October 27, 2002
Subject: Re: Congratulations

Dear Carol,

Thank you so much for the pictures—you look lovely. And the medal looks so impressive, not your common or garden variety of costume jewellery.

Much love to you both,
Blanche

❧ Under a picture of Carol listening to the governor general read from *Unless,* Carol wrote, "I love the bit she read. It was such a nice event. And I think that even with the other photographers buzzing around like mosquitoes, I did OK."

Date: December 27, 2002
Subject: Shopping

Dear Carol and Don,

I hope you had a good Christmas. I had a very nice time, went to Leslie's Christmas Eve and we went to the light display at VanDusen Botanical Garden (overwhelming).

And, Carol, this will bring back memories. Desperate for a good-looking suit I made the trek to Chapman's annual sale today, and came back with not exactly what I had in mind but nice anyway. Wish you had been there to nod or shake your head.

I read *Clara Callan** and am partway through *The Stone Carvers.*** I liked *Clara Callan,* thought it worked very well. The jury is still out on the *Stone Carvers.*

Oh, I do hope you are not feeling too tired, Carol.

Much love,
Blanche

---

*By Richard B. Wright.
**By Jane Urquhart.

Date: December 29, 2002
Subject: Re: Shopping

Blanche,

I'm delighted you went shopping and spent money on yourself. We have a rather Chapman-like store called Wilson's, where everything they sell is both wearable and beautiful—and I've had a recent spending spree there, never mind waiting for the sales.

I'm able to read and am in the middle of *A History of Celibacy* by Elizabeth Abbott. Perhaps too much detail, but just the sort of stuff we love. Celibacy has certainly wrought much damage and distress. It seems notions of impurity go way back in the gene pool.

Christmas was lovely. We have been having just one family at a time, but we still have too much food around. Oh dear.

Love,
C

Date: January 9, 2003
Subject: History of Celibacy

Dear Carol,

Just thought I'd let you know that I got *History of Celibacy* out of the library and am finding it fascinating, as well as being extremely readable.

I got Margaret Visser's *Beyond Fate* for Christmas and it propounds some interesting ideas, well thought-out and well written also. I strongly recommend it.

Love as always to you both,
Blanche

Date: February 8, 2003
Subject: Celibate Season

Dear Blanche,

On March 22, at the Sorbonne, a professor called Manina Jones from the University of Western Ontario will give a paper called

"Scenes from a Marriage: The Prosaics of Collaboration and Correspondence in *A Celibate Season*." I will send you the paper when I get it—I'm sure we'll find it illuminating. (I picture her looking like Sarah Maloney.) All the papers will eventually be published by McGill–Queen's University Press.

I seem to be spending a lot of time sleeping, which is such a miserable waste of time. Eleanor Wachtel is here for the weekend. She's just finishing interviewing Nicholson Baker—you must read him.

Love,
C

Date: February 8, 2003
Subject: General greetings

Dear Carol,

Imagine, *A Celibate Season* at the Sorbonne! Thank you for letting me know and I'll look forward to reading it.

I just finished Margaret Drabble's *The Peppered Moth* and found it very enjoyable. Relaxed reading which is pleasant. This morning in my Shakespeare class we worked over the highlights of *Antony and Cleopatra* and I must say I found it fascinating, especially since I hadn't read it before and needed prodding to get at least some of the undercurrents and nuances, of which there are plenty.

How nice for you to have a chance at a visit with Eleanor W.

Much love as always,
Blanche

꙳In what was to be Carol's last e-mail to me, she returned once more to the enigma which we, half-jokingly, half-seriously, had been circling around these many years: the meaning of life.

Date: March 12, 2003
Subject: The Meaning of Life

Blanche,

What is the meaning of life? It is known to "everything except language" and the "ignorant freedom of my talking mind" (Les Murray). That is, I think we all know and recognize it, but have no words for it.

Looking forward to seeing you.
Carol

Date: March 12, 2003
Subject: General greetings

Carol,

I love both those, especially "the ignorant freedom of my talking mind." How wonderful! In my new novel I have Penelope deciding to abandon her search after a visiting Unitarian minister said that there is no meaning of life, but that every life has meaning. Penelope isn't about to waste her time on semantics. Looking forward greatly to Saturday.

Love,
Blanche

15

Flightless Birds
2003

❧Allison and Dave took me to Victoria, and I had a visit with Carol that I feared would be my last. Don met us at the door with an admonishment that I stay only an hour, as Carol was quite weak. He asked Allison and Dave to go upstairs with me to Carol's lovely large bedroom for a moment as she wished to say hello.

In the end I stayed for an hour and a half. Carol was propped up on pillows in an attempt to ease her aching back. We talked more or less as we always had, except that now the heavy knowledge lay between us and made our words fall about us like flightless birds.

She was very tired when I left, and we said goodbye as though we would meet again. We never did.

Date: March 17, 2003
Subject: Lovely to see you

Dear Carol,

Prairie Fire has just sent me the lovely anthology [*Carol Shields: The Arts of a Writing Life*] and I think it is beautifully done and look forward immensely to reading it.

It was such a treat to see you Saturday. As always, and in spite of the curves Fate has thrown, we seem still to be able to talk as though speech had only lately been invented. I do hope it didn't tire you too much. I know that being up for conversation is more wearing than one could have ever imagined in the full bloom of health.

I agree with you about the banality of Timothy Findley's diary in the *The G and M*, although I couldn't help feeling just a tad sorry for him because I think he himself would have cringed to have had that youthful twaddle published. I think it was rather a breach of his privacy. I wish I had ever felt even a fraction of his belief in his own shining destiny, especially at that young age.

Much love to you both. My thoughts and hopes are always with you on your very rough journey.

Love,
Blanche

Date: April 10, 2003
Subject: Your novel

Dear Carol,
Your first instalments of the novel* just arrived and I am looking forward immensely to reading them. I'll give you my first take on it very shortly and return the ms with suggestions. If any.

Much love,
Blanche

Date: April 11, 2003
Subject: Your manuscript

Dear Carol,
Your novel is wonderful—as always. I read straight through first, pretending it wasn't by you, hoping to eliminate that bias that is always difficult to overcome when reading the work of family or good

---

*Carol did not finish this novel, but excerpts have been published since.

friends. And I was caught up in it immediately. And of course your use of language can only make the rest of us drool.

In answer to your questions, yes, the protagonist is very likeable. And I like the tension that is becoming evident about the strains in their marriage. She is smart and not too cheery, since her underlying malaise is coming through beautifully and so we see a woman who is cheery on the outside but hesitant underneath. I am very much reminded of Mrs. Ramsay in *To The Lighthouse*,* and also of the portrait of Mr. Ramsay as seen through her eyes.

I've nearly finished *The Arts of a Writing Life* and find most of the essays revealing and thoughtful. My lack of formal English education shows in that I was only able to understand about every third word of Marta Dvorak's essay (*topological? extradiegetic?*) and some essays I found more compelling than others, but by and large they've done a great job.

You've got to finish this one! I need to know how it turns out.

Love,
Blanche

Date: April 12, 2003
Subject: Your novel

Dear Carol,

When I was reading *To the Lighthouse* I was struck by the similarity of the way you and Woolf unfold the mind of your central woman, and the ambivalence tempered with love about the husband. I have always tried to think of who your writing reminds me of—I'm pretty good usually at seeing the links between writers, their influences, etc.—but I never have before with you. But there is more than a hint of concurrence between you and V.W. in your writing and on your take on the role of a woman, whether wished for or not. By the way, I hadn't read it since the fifties but I remembered the marvellous

---

*By Virginia Woolf.

description of a house returning to the earth and I wanted it for my novel, and lo and behold!, I remembered correctly where it was—although finding my glasses is a whole other thing.

Much love. I'm dying to know where this one goes.

Blanche

June 8, 2003

Anne Collins of Random House Canada phoned today (Sunday) to say that Carol had won the Canadian Booksellers Association Author of the Year Award. Carol was thrilled. And I was too.

Love to you all,
Don

Date: June 9, 2003
Subject: Re: Carol

Wonderful news! Congratulations Carol! *Unless* is a wonderful book and deserves all the accolades it collects. And thank you, Don, for letting us know.

Love,
Blanche

Carol died at home on July 16, 2003, surrounded by her loved ones. I had been keeping in frequent phone communication with them, aware of what it is like to wait for the final breath. The next morning every major newspaper in Canada carried front-page pictures of her, and I'm told that papers around the world gave her great acclaim.

On a hot cloudless day in August, Alma Lee drove Allison, Dave and me to a private memorial at the Shields home in Victoria. Carol and Don's children and grandchildren were there, along with a number of close friends. The day was cheerful and handled with exactly the kind of hospitality that Carol herself would have applauded. A small formal ceremony was held outdoors on the lawn, and family and friends paid tribute to an extraordinary life.

August 5, 2003

Dear Sara,

Just a note to tell you how beautifully organized yesterday's reception was. I think we all came away thinking that Carol would have liked that. And thank you again for letting me speak, I wanted to tell people that Carol had lived her life with humour and gladness. All of you spoke movingly and lovingly.

Love,
Blanche

August 5, 2003

Dear Blanche,

I'm so happy that you spoke, your stories were just right about Mom. I've thought today about your wonderful comment that perhaps it is possible, that people can get it right the first time. Very glad you made it, we all did all right. Today I got the overwhelming feeling, as I pulled my dear, hilarious children along the sidewalk in their wagon, late on a summer afternoon, of the unfairness—to her—of not being here, while we all get to be. She was one of the most appreciative people this earth could ask for. Luckily she taught a lot of us to appreciate as well. I hope your trip home was smooth.

Love,
Sara

August 21, 2003

Dear Blanche,

Thank you for your bright and cheerful sympathy card—and for your supportive words on the passing of your friend and my wife Carol.

Thank you, as well, for your warm, humorous, and heartfelt message which you delivered personally in Victoria and which was read for you in Winnipeg. Both times, you were a hit—as always.

I sit here in Burgundy with memories of that dance not so far from here—and with tears.

Much love to you,
Don

Acknowledgments

~We wish to thank our contributors: Marjorie Anderson, Wayson Choy, Maggie Dwyer, Sandy Francis Duncan, Anne Giardini, Leslie Howard, Fraidie Martz, Madeleine Nelson, and Barbara Perrault, all of whom complied willingly and eagerly with our request for a submission, or permission to include a previously published article or excerpt.

Special thanks to Meghan Corbeil, our first reader who provided enthusiastic encouragement and the viewpoint of a younger generation; and to Fran Moore for her thoughtful analysis and pithy comments.

We would also like to extend our thanks to the ever-helpful George Brandak and his staff at The University of British Columbia, Special Collections and Archives Division, and to Catherine Hobbs, archivist, and her staff at the Literary Archives, Library and Archives Canada, in Ottawa—both of whom were extremely obliging in the thankless task of locating, photocopying and mailing material. And thanks to Annie Pope, the reference supervisor at the Kelowna Library, for her diligent attempts to locate archival photographs.

Thanks to Don Shields, who as literary executor of Carol's estate provided legal permission for publication of Carol's letters or excerpts of letters.

The editorial staff at Penguin Group (Canada): Andrea Crozier, editorial director, and Sandra Tooze, senior production editor, have both been helpful, enthusiastic and accommodating. Particular appreciation goes to Allyson Latta, our copy editor, for her respectful, articulate and efficient editing expertise. She has made the process fun and stimulating.

We wish to express our gratitude to typists Debbie Leslie and Elaine Tkaczuk, who responded ever-willingly to the challenge of typing over one thousand pages of original manuscript, and to

Brian Funt for so obligingly transporting sections of manuscript back and forth.

Enduring thanks to Blanche's agent Beverley Slopen for her faith in this project.

Finally, Allison wishes to thank Blanche for the opportunity to co-edit this fascinating journey into her personal life, and for her unfailing faith in my judgment.

And Blanche wishes to thank Allison, without whom this project would not have been possible.